The
Handbook
of
Magazine
Production

by
Jeffery Parnau

Edited by Deborah Schwab

Folio Publishing Corporation
1985

TO MY FATHER: Richard Parnau, who gave me
a very early start in this business

TABLE OF CONTENTS

SECTION V: COMPLEX COLOR STRIPPING

SECTION VI: LITHOGRAPHIC PRINTING

SECTION VII: IMPOSITIONS AND FOLDERS

SECTION VIII: PAPER AND THE BINDERY

SECTION IX: IN PURSUIT OF QUALITY: PROBLEMS AND SOLUTIONS

PREFACE

If you've been around for any length of graphic arts time, you know that there are dozens, maybe hundreds, of books on the topic of printing. Unfortunately, there are few books on the topic of *purchasing* printing. There are even fewer on the topic of purchasing *magazine* printing. This book's purpose is to describe the problems confronted by the magazine print purchaser, and to discuss intelligent solutions.

Throughout this book, heavy emphasis is placed on information that is important to the magazine production buyer: We won't teach you how to strip; we'll explain what stripping is and how to purchase it sensibly. We won't teach you how to run a press, but we'll point out how your money is spent on presswork.

Therefore, no attempt has been made to make this a comprehensive graphic arts manual. The reader is advised that pure graphic arts knowledge, in general, is easy to come by. You can select from the wide variety of books that describe presses, paper or even the chemical activity that makes lithography possible. If you need highly technical knowledge of printing, other books will be supportive and informative. But if you want the solutions to the production problems faced by every magazine staff, then this book is for you.

This book concentrates on offset lithography for magazines. By implication, that means we will not be addressing gravure or letterpress printing. The reason is that *most* magazines are printed via offset lithography, few are printed gravure (only those with multimillion circulations), and even fewer by letterpress.

So, we'll stick to offset lithographic reproduction for magazines. Those magazines that print via gravure or letterpress might better form a club than look for a reference manual. They are in the minority in 1985, and in the United States.

INTRODUCTION

What is production management?

Magazine production management. Just what is it? This book will address production management from the standpoint of the buyer—that person employed by the publishing operation who is responsible for purchasing. Obviously, production managers employed by magazines have different responsibilities than do production managers employed by printers.

It is no secret that magazines—as we know them today—spend a good deal of money on the reproduction processes. In some operations, half the publication's gross revenue is devoted to printing. Other operations might see that figure go as low as 35 percent. But in any case, outside purchases of printing and related services are normally the most costly single expense for any publisher.

Yet for all its economic importance, magazine production management has been largely ignored. To prove this, walk into any job service office and try to look up "Production Manager—Magazine." You will find that there is no such job classification. The closest you may get is "Managing Editor," a job that is certainly more than a leap away from the production manager's slot.

Why then is the professional magazine production manager ignored?

First, few publishers believe that such a person even exists. There is no school of production for the buyer, while there are many schools for the seller.

Second, up until the early 1970s, even those magazines that were poorly managed on a production level didn't suffer too badly. Paper was inexpensive, labor was cheap and competition among printers was healthy enough to keep prices in line.

Third, the early seventies had not yet seen the invasion of electronic pre-press technology.

Then came waves of change. Paper began routinely to double in price. Inflation pushed labor rates to unseen highs, with no breathers between increases. Postage costs started to climb consistently. The economy tightened, insertion orders from advertisers became sporadic and—all the while—dramatic changes in the technology of producing a magazine were occurring.

So where does that leave today's production manager? According to some, there has been no change. Many publishers continue to think of the production manager as an internal, service-oriented individual whose duties are somehow to keep the entire staff happy, while keeping the magazine on a schedule.

In other operations, the production manager is recognized as a person keenly aware of the purchasing triangle (speed, quality and cost) as it relates to magazine reproduction. The three factors interplay to achieve a predetermined result: a magazine produced with adequate quality at the right time, and at a cost that allows for a healthy company.

In order to monitor the purchasing triangle, the production manager must have a working knowledge of just how magazines are produced. In general, that covers four major areas: preparation, printing, paper and bindery.

Sounds simple enough. And 50 years ago, it was. In the letterpress days, preparation and printing were virtually one and the same. The type that was set was the type that actually came into contact with the paper. Paper was cheap and so was the labor required to ink the press.

Today, the scene is far different. Preparation starts with typesetting, a field that has moved from the factory into the office. The entire prep field, including the creation of the printing plate, has proven capable of going totally "soft," or fully electronic, with no usage of film or chemicals until the plate is created.

Presses have become tuned to the paper problems of the past decade, and—for the sharp buyer—offer a wealth of data on the most basic raw material of conventional publishing and printing: paper.

The bindery has felt the effects of the electronic revolution, too. The technology exists that will allow magazines to be fully tailored to the individual reader—more or less a physical version of the electronic magazine, which is also available.

Who then is the production manager? This book will assume that such a person is responsible for directing the entire *physical* transmission of information from the publisher to the reader. Such a person would first need to have a thorough working knowledge of typesetting, paste-up, camera procedures, stripping and platemaking. Then, an understanding of printing equipment—types of presses, their strengths and weaknesses and their ability to produce quality materials. And finally, a knowledge of options in the bindery, including speed, cost and versatility of equipment and techniques.

But not one of the above areas of expertise will be of any use to the production manager who doesn't know people. In order to be an effective interface between editor and ad director, publisher and printer, the production manager must handle all the technical areas, and their associated pressures, with a genuine concern for the feelings of others. More than one publisher has paid for a bad attitude, and no employee has more power to generate bad feelings with the printer than the production manager. These bad feelings can be reflected by unrealistic increases in the printing invoice or estimate.

The production manager, then, is a magazine technician, an economist and a social worker. So, given 1) the technical complexity of magazine printing, 2) the often curious personalities of publishers, and 3) the need to get along well with "the enemy" (the firm with the huge invoices), production management is not an easy job.

I hope that this book will give you the basic technical knowledge that you need. And I hope that you can maintain a pleasant, rewarding social position in the high-pressured world of magazine publishing. Clearly, if you have a handle on mechanical technique and know how to deal with people, there will be no stopping you.☐

SECTION I:
TYPESETTING

A BRIEF REVIEW OF TYPESETTING

You don't have to be very old to be an "old-timer" in the field of of typesetting. But to recall the state of the art in the late fifties and early sixties, you might need to be the kind of person who enjoys remembering nightmares.

Of all aspects of magazine production, typesetting has made the most dramatic and rapid changes in the past two decades. Take a stroll back in time, if you will, to the typesetting shop of 1955.

Hot metal

You walk in the door and see rows and rows of machines. The room is very hot, too, because of the amount of molten lead and tin in the shop. Operators sit at their stations, furiously punching keys, which form lines, which suddenly trigger the mechanics of setting type: Hot lead pours into a slot, is quickly cooled and then ejected into a carrier.

Today, one cannot tell the difference between a computer and a typesetter. Today, the professional sits in an air conditioned office and breezes through a complex job that could not even have been created a few years ago.

We won't dwell on hot-metal typesetting. It is no longer "on the way out" for magazine production. Rather, it is totally dead and buried. But for purposes of terminology—and to give the newcomer an idea of where today's equipment came from—we will cover the topic of hot metal at least briefly.

As you have probably determined, hot-metal typesetting is so named because the procedure involved melting metal to produce a line of typeset copy. The operator would key a character of type and the machine would drop the appropriate matrix (or mold) of the letter into position. When enough characters were keyed to fill a line, strips of spacers would automatically be inserted (to justify the margins or make them even), and the mixture of lead and tin would be injected. The line was then ejected, the matrices returned to their ready positions, and a new line would be keyed.

To control the amount of space between each line, the operator would call for "leading" (pronounced *led-ding*). A line was said to have additional leading whenever more space was used between lines than physically needed.

Already, some of the limitations of hot-metal typesetting can be deduced: Each character of type had a physical base, called the matrix. Similarly, each line of copy could be placed only so close to the preceding line—otherwise it would physically bump into it. Phototypesetting, as you will see, is inherently free of these limitations.

Hot-metal composition served several purposes during its long career. With "modern" hot-metal machines, the type would be "locked up," or organized into page form. Then, the actual type produced by the machine would be placed on the printing press.

Thus, the material coming from the typesetter would actually become the material used to print the job itself.

As lithography changed the way ink was put on paper, this fundamental aspect of hot-metal machinery was violated. Lithography needed a flat, positive image—not the three-dimensional negative that was produced by the hot-metal machine.

There were several transitional steps before phototypesetting was more or less "invented" by lithography. The most common conversion method (before the ultimate death of hot metal) was to print a proof, or galley, of the typeset material. This proof would later be pasted into position on a board (thick paper or thin cardboard), and the final product placed on a camera and converted into a lithographic negative.

Today, the paste-up method is still one of the most common ways to produce a magazine page, although there are many electronic alternatives.

But regardless of how deeply into history the hot-metal machines are thrown, one thing remains: terminology. When we call, today, for additional leading, do we really mean we want lead? No. Is a single line of type truly a "slug"? Of course not. But much of the terminology used to describe hot-metal type remains with us.

Strike-on

Before we jump to the modern days of phototypesetting, accuracy demands a brief mention of strike-on typesetting.

Strike-on systems are little more than fancy typewriter devices. Unlike a typewriter, though, the strike-on machines had changeable fonts (alphabets) and gave appropriate widths to each character. For example, the lower case "i" would be given less space than the letter "M".

Varityper manufactured a machine under its name that dominated the low-cost strike-on market for years. Then IBM entered the field with its Composer, which featured a wide selection of changeable type balls similar to those used on a Selectric typewriter.

Publishers seriously began to consider doing typesetting inhouse with the introduction of the IBM MTST unit, which stored the typed information on magnetic tape, allowed for editing and ran the output automatically. In the 1960s, an in-house strike-on system could be installed for as little as $20,000, which was cheap compared to hot-metal systems.

By today's standards, the nonmemory Varityper and magtape memory IBM Composer are almost useless for moderate-volume typesetting. And IBM's magnetic tape unit is no longer manufactured. Its vast number of moving parts, slow speed, and limited ability to set larger-sized fonts generated sure-fire obsolescence when the market moved toward phototypesetting.

Phototypesetting

Both strike-on and hot-metal machinery were highly complicated mechanically and subject to breakdown. A specialist was needed for repairs and had to be available for emergencies. So, in a sense, the publishing industry was ready for the phototypesetting machine (which would also prove to be subject to frequent breakdown and would require a specialist for repair).

The first phototypesetting units, which were introduced many decades ago, have little significance today. Generally, they were little more than metal-less versions of then-current technology. They were awkward, not versatile, and presented little competition to the hot-metal machines.

However, this "first generation" line of equipment did set the stage for the important "second generation" equipment. For practical purposes, consider first-generation machinery a mechanical pile of good ideas. The next generation would see the development of low-cost, reliable typesetters that would find their way into publishing operations.

To be precise, the term "second generation" designates a piece of typesetting equipment that uses a photographic negative to expose an image onto light-sensitive paper.

There are too many brands of equipment on the market to allow detailed comparisons of their mechanical differences. For that matter, constant product improvement has made it difficult to select from even a single manufacturer's line, such as the AM Compset/CompEdit series. But there are some basic parameters that can be discussed.

First, the second-generation typesetters have three different methods of storing the photographic negative of the character. One that gained quick popularity was the strip method of storing a font (full alphabet) of type.

Typically, four fonts would be on one filmstrip. And typically, two film strips would reside in the typesetter at a given time, allowing for eight fonts "on-line" (or active).

The second most common method of handling type was the film disc, which was somewhat similar. In this case, four fonts would be on the circular disc loaded into the typesetting device.

Third was the quadrant method, which broke the disc into four segments. The advantage of this system was that it allowed infinite mixing of fonts—something not possible with either the strip or disc method.

The advantages of each system of handling fonts really depend on the needs of the user and will be discussed later in this chapter. For now, we'll concentrate on the basics of how the equipment generates typesetting.

All second-generation equipment has a common mechanical method of exposing the image to the paper. The fonts are either spun

4

on a drum (filmstrips), or rotated on their axes (disc and quadrant).

The speed at which the font moves can give the novice an appreciation of just how fast the exposure must be made. For example, on a unit with an eight-inch diameter type disc and a rotational speed of 1,800 revolutions per minute, each character of type is traveling in a circle at more than 40 miles per hour.

For that image to be exposed to the typesetting paper, a strobe light is fired with such intensity—and brevity—that the photographic image that hits the paper appears to be a perfectly formed character (see Illustration 1).

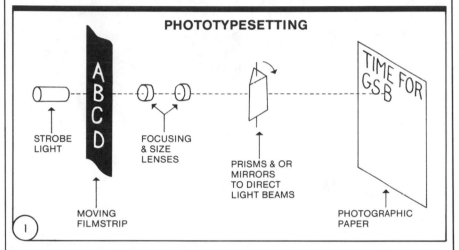

The problems with second-generation phototypesetting, then, should already be obvious. Although unquestionably superior to hot-metal equipment (in magazine production), it is a highly mechanical way to produce a character, a line, a page. For each revolution of the film carrier (or disc), the unit must use photocells to accurately find its position on the font, then fire a strobe—timed to millionths of a second—to expose and to properly position the character.

More mechanical features are involved in changing the size of the type itself. Some systems use a zoom lens method of enlarging the tiny photographic image to something usable. Other machines use a turret of lenses and rotate them into position by operator command.

The ultimate result is hundreds of moving parts, the likelihood of frequent breakdown and a built-in limitation: The font can be spun only so fast before the laws of nature take over. Either there will be insufficient time to make an exposure or the machine will fly apart.

It was these limitations that set the stage for the third generation of phototypesetting equipment: digital type.

To conceive of how digital typesetting works, imagine placing a sheet of light-sensitive film in front of your home television. If you held it there for the appropriate amount of time, you would, upon developing the film, get a rough image of what was on the TV screen.

That, to be simplistic, is the fundamental technique used in

CHAPTER 1

A conventional phototypesetter is little more than a high-speed automated camera. The computer senses the positions of characters on the moving filmstrip (or film disk). When the appropriate letter is in position, the strobe light fires. A series of lenses, mirrors or prisms directs the image to its proper position on the photographic paper. The computer then looks for the next character to expose, the prisms change positions, and the cycle continues.

5

A BRIEF REVIEW OF TYPESETTING

In digital typesetting, the characters of type aren't any more real than a talk-show host on your television. The computer creates the shapes from information stored in the system (usually on a floppy or rigid disc). Shapes are usually stored in the system's RAM (random access memory). Thus the higher the RAM storage in a system, the more fonts will be "on line" (available for setting without accessing the disc for shapes). To expose a character, the digital typesetter brings it up on its CRT (cathode ray tube, or picture tube), passes it through lenses and/or prisms, and onto the paper.

creating a digital image of typeset characters. Unlike hot-metal and second-generation phototypesetting, the character does not physically exist. Rather, it is stored in an electronic format. When the operator asks for the letter "A", the computer in the typesetter uses the electronic information in its file to "create" the letter on a small cathode ray tube (abbreviated CRT, and identical in nature to your TV screen). This image passes through the lens system and onto the typesetting paper (see Illustrations 2 and 3).

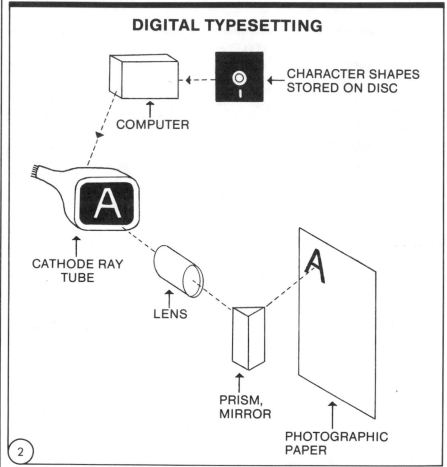

DIGITAL TYPESETTING

CHARACTER SHAPES STORED ON DISC

COMPUTER

CATHODE RAY TUBE

LENS

PRISM, MIRROR

PHOTOGRAPHIC PAPER

②

And unlike second-generation equipment, there is no real common ground in terms of how a CRT unit exposes its characters. The size of the exposing unit may be as small as one inch in diameter, or it may be one inch by nine inches, or it could be quite large, depending on the manufacturer and the technique.

One aspect is common, though: By their very nature, digital typesetters have very few moving parts. Aside from their storage systems (floppy disk, hard disk, tape or other magnetic storage mediums), it is not unheard of for a digital typesetter to have less than six moving pieces inside. As a matter of fact, the only piece of equipment that truly needs to move is the paper transporter.

There are a few obvious reasons why this third-generation

6

wave of equipment will soon totally dominate the market. First, it has no built-in limitations on speed. There are some units that can already set thousands of characters of type in a second. Next, the lack of moving parts makes for better reliability. Third, digital type has no limitations in terms of increments of size, so a virtually infinite range of output sizes are available.

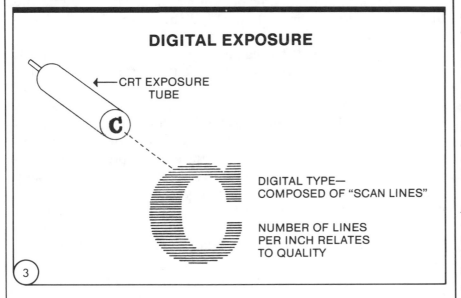

DIGITAL EXPOSURE

←—CRT EXPOSURE TUBE

DIGITAL TYPE—COMPOSED OF "SCAN LINES"

NUMBER OF LINES PER INCH RELATES TO QUALITY

3

Then there are the radical aspects. Because the typeset character does not actually exist in physical form, it can be electronically modified to a great extent. Although the designer may have wanted the letter "H" to look a certain way, a digital version of that same character could be increased to several times its original width—without modifying its height. The aesthetics of such modifications are always a topic for debate.

Page composition

If you look into the preceding minihistory of typesetting, you may notice something very strange. At the hot-metal stage, either galley proofs or full-page composition was available to the buyer. True, the printer's employees would literally have to place the typeset copy into position. But the point is, 30 years ago, page composition was part of the typesetting business.

With second-generation equipment, page composition moved out of the hot-metal room and into the art department. This was reflected by the large number of art departments in operation at printing plants less than a decade ago. The second-generation machines, although capable of producing a full page of text (all elements in their proper place, including areas in which photos would later print), just weren't very good at it. So as typesetting moved from the foundry into the office, it was followed closely by the assembly function, or paste-up.

Like your television set, the image on a digital typesetter is composed of scan lines, normally measured by the number of such lines in an inch. The more scan lines per inch, the better the quality of the formed character. While a television picture generally has 520 scan lines (horizontal rows) in its entire screen, digital typesetters have up to 2,400 scan lines in an inch.

A BRIEF REVIEW OF TYPESETTING

Naturally, during this stage many printers found themselves going out of the "art" business. Assembly of a page, although not truly a typesetting function, tended to be done wherever the equipment was located. When publishers began installing their own typesetting equipment, they soon began to do paste-up, or manual page composition, in-house.

The third-generation revolution may well change the picture once again. Large publishers have already begun to take full advantage of electronics. Magazines can be designed, electronically "pasted-up," corrected, revised and finalized—all on the operator's VDT (visual display terminal). The paste-up function, in other words, is being threatened.

In fact, typesetting equipment has been easily integrated into the other sophisticated graphic arts tools: Color scanners, color modifiers (previewers) and text have all been melded—computer-to-computer—to provide a TV-like picture of the ultimate product. That image has been successfully transmitted to electronic platemaking machinery. In summary, there is no apparent end to the amount of physical labor that could be replaced by the computer terminal operator. The technology does exist to publish a completely electronic magazine and send it to the reader either on paper or via a computer link.

But to return for a moment to page composition, bear in mind that 1) it was available in the hot-metal typesetting era, 2) it was available, although quite clumsy, during the second-generation revolution, and 3) it is again becoming feasible with the advent of the more powerful third-generation typesetting equipment. The key to successful page composition appears to be the previewer. While most second-generation operators lived in a world of mnemonics, codes and other obscure machine-like messages from computers, the previewer displays a close approximation of what the commands will produce.

The second-generation system might show the operator this:

[H/72][L/72][HD1.5]Hello[C]

The previewer, coupled to its high-technology typesetting computer, would merely show the operator the word "Hello," set at one inch in height, displayed at 150 percent of its normal width and centered on the screen. Similarly, each column of type, or even a rule that would later print around a photo, would be shown in the proper position.

The real future of full-page makeup rests on two rather unpredictable variables: First, when will the ever-falling prices of computers and related programs stabilize and will the stabilization point reflect a nominal investment by publishers? Second, how much operator involvement will be required?

For practical purposes, electronic page makeup will have to be a faster, less time-consuming endeavor than required by any person with a pair of scissors and a can of glue.

Summary

In a sense, the early half of the 1980s—the time during which this book was being written—could be considered as exciting, transitional years of dramatic change. But in reality, the magazine professionals of today have already learned how quickly, dramatically and thoroughly this business changes. Typesetting will offer few surprises to the production manager who has been watching the electronic evolution unfold. It will not be a shock to see a machine that will recognize the spoken word and accept verbal typesetting commands. Rather, the shock is that we have become so accustomed to radical changes that we impatiently await the next impossibility, knowing full well that the better machine, the better system, is just around the corner.□

CHAPTER 1

TYPESETTING: HOW A TYPICAL JOB IS PRODUCED

Whether you purchase typesetting from a vendor or produce it in-house, most jobs follow a standard routine through their production life. (Captured keystrokes, interfaced typesetting and other alternatives that don't fit this typical mold are discussed elsewhere in this chapter.) Basically, the production flow (and terminology) is as follows:

1. *Origination of material:* The material, whatever it is, is typed. Then it is edited, possibly retyped and given the final okay by the editor to be set in type. Although it is possible to work with handwritten copy, few typesetters will tolerate it and, if they do, only at a premium.

2. *Markup:* At this stage, the manuscript (the material to be set in type) is "marked up." This means the instructions to the typesetter are written onto the copy. The basic information needed falls into four general parameters:

•Size: This is expressed in points, such as nine point. A point is about 1/72nd of an inch. The point size of the typeface is measured from the top of the tallest character to the bottom of the lowest character (such as the letters "l" and "y").

•Leading: This specifies the distance between the typeset lines. For example, if a job were set on 10-point leading, there would be 10 points from one baseline to the next. The baseline is the bottom of a nondescending lowercase letter (such as the bottom of the letter "m").

•Pica width: This simply indicates how wide the lines of typeset copy will be. A pica is about one-sixth of an inch. Thus, copy set at 21 picas wide would be set in columns about three-and-one-half inches wide.

•Font: This is the "family" of typeface that will be used. Examples would be Helvetica, Century Schoolbook, Futura and so forth.

In addition to the above parameters, many other specifications might be given to the typesetter. (See the section on copy markup for more details.)

3. *Typesetting:* At this stage, the typesetter keys the material into the TV screen-like entry terminal, which is called either a VDT (video display terminal) or a CRT (cathode ray tube).

4. *First proof:* After entry into the typesetting system, the material is "set" in type for the first time. This might be called a first proof—and there might be a few errors in it. Or, the material might not be "set" in type at all, but rather printed by a typewriter-like unit called a line printer. The line-printer copy could be edited or marked up for errors, but it would not show what the characters will actually look like. A true first proof is actual typeset copy.

5. *Approval:* At this time, the editor or the typesetter (or both) read the first proof (or line-printer copy) and mark it up for two purposes: First, to find any mistakes made by the typesetter. Second, to allow the editor to make changes, a common (though not sound) practice at this stage.

Arbitrary changes by the editor are called alterations and are considered chargeable extras. Mistakes made by the typesetter are called typos, typographical errors or corrections, and are usually corrected without charge.

6. *Correction/alteration procedure:* There are several different ways to make the corrections and alterations marked on the first proof. One is to look at the typeset job on the typesetting terminal's screen, make the changes and rerun the entire job. Another is simply to set the correction lines, and either paste them onto the first proof or splice them in with tape.

7. *Delivery:* In theory, the corrected material is now finalized. There should be no more corrections or alterations. In practice, this is often not the case. When the material is finally placed on the paste-up (a sheet later to be shot on camera), editors often read the material and make a few more changes. This cycle is sometimes short, or sometimes seemingly endless. The endless versions are always costly.□

CHAPTER 2

HOW TO SPEC TYPE

④

Is 36-point type really 36 points tall? Almost never. The basic point size is the distance between the top of the tallest letter and the bottom of the lowest (such as the g or y). A better feel for the "size" of type is x-height, which is the height of a lower-case letter (typically the x). When it is said a typeface has a large x-height, the implication is that the lower-case letters use a relatively large percentage of the total point size. Thus, two faces set in 36 point could look like entirely different sizes to the reader.

Specifying type is often considered an esoteric technical skill, the thought of which can tempt the beginner to consistently say, "Set to fit."

The fact is, it truly can be difficult to properly spec a complex job. And by missing a beat here and there, the exercise can be expensive: Rerunning a job at today's hourly rates can mean a bad dent in both your wallet and schedule. But before the newcomer attempts to spec a tough job, he or she must have at least a grasp of the fundamentals. This section won't load you down with high level theory or aesthetics, and it won't make you an expert typographer. But it will enable you to examine simple typewritten magazine copy and estimate its final typeset length—using different sizes, leadings, widths and fonts.

Terminology

Although the days of hot-metal type appear to be behind us forever, the terminology—as mentioned earlier—lingers on. The terms we use today have no relation to modern equipment, so don't be disturbed if some of the words don't relate to the problem.

•*Point*: This term is used to indicate the size of type, the thickness of rules, and the space from one typeset line to the next. A point is .0138 inch, or about 1/72 of an inch.

You might notice that one typeface set at a size of 36 point looks larger or smaller than another face set at the same size. The reason is that the point size indicates the letter height as measured from the top of the tallest letter to the bottom of the shortest. The reason one might look larger has to do with "x- height" (see Illustration 4).

X-height can best be described as the height of the lowercase "x". While one face might have an x-height of 50 percent of the point size, another might have an x-height of 60 percent. Optically, this will make one 10-point character look larger or smaller than another, even though both are technically the same size.

The point is also used to indicate the thickness of a rule or line. If a line is 1/16-inch thick, it is about four-and-one-half points in height. A two-point rule is about 1/32 of an inch.

Finally, the point is used to state leading as described below.

•*Leading:* This term indicates the amount of space between lines of typeset material. It is derived from the original practice of placing thin strips of lead between lines of typeset copy to give them some visual breathing room. Leading may also be called "body leading," or "line space," depending on individual preference.

All typesetting must be set with leading. In the hot-metal days, the minimum amount of leading between lines was the size of the typeface itself. This is obvious when you remember that the face (in hot metal) was a physical entity: One line could get only so close to the next.

12

Phototypesetting doesn't have that built-in limitation. Therefore, a little confusion has drifted into the picture. While a hot-metal enthusiast might want type set with one-point of additional leading, a phototypesetting machine could literally set 10-point type on one-point spacing. The result would be garbage.

To simplify the matter, most people prefer to call for the total leading. Therefore, if you ask for 10-point type on 11-point leading, you will have one additional point between lines—not 11.

•*Pica:* This term describes the width of typeset copy. There are 12 points in a pica, and six picas in an inch. It is best to buy and use a true pica ruler to measure widths (rather than use a ruler and multiply the picas from inches). The pica ruler is more accurate and reduces the chance for error.

To make matters more visual, the following samples use points and picas:

Sample 1: 9-point type, 10-point leading, 20-picas wide:
NOW IS THE TIME FOR ALL GOOD MEN TO COME TO THE AID OF THEIR PARTY.
Now is the time for all good men to come to the aid of their party.

Sample 2: 9-point type, 11-point leading, 13-picas wide:
NOW IS THE TIME FOR ALL GOOD MEN TO COME TO THE AID OF THEIR PARTY.
Now is the time for all good men to come to the aid of their party.

Sample 3: 11-point type, 11-point leading, 18-picas wide:
NOW IS THE TIME FOR ALL GOOD MEN TO COME TO THE AID OF THEIR PARTY.
Now is the time for all good men to come to the aid of their party.

Sample 4: 11-point type, 14-point leading, 20-picas wide:
NOW IS THE TIME FOR ALL GOOD MEN TO COME TO THE AID OF THEIR PAR-TY.
Now is the time for all good men to come to the aid of their party.

Obviously, the size, leading and pica width all interplay to affect readability and appearances. Only you can decide for yourself what is good or bad copy for you.

When you decide how much space should be between lines, remember that all typefaces are different. Some look great when set "solid" (leading equal to point size), while others will look loose or tight at the same leading. This is the effect that x-height has on general appearance.

•*Characters per pica:* Finally, we get to the nitty-gritty of specifying type. Characters per pica (CPP) is the number of characters of a given typeface at a given size in one pica. This isn't usually a whole number. For example, 10-point Century Schoolbook might average 2.55 CPP.

There are different ways to determine the CPP for any point size or typeface. The easiest is to look into a decent typeface catalog, usually supplied either by your typesetter or the machine's manufacturer.

The other—and universal—method is to figure out the CPP yourself. To do it you need only know what the point size of a sample printed piece is, and then count. For example, if you knew that this type was set in 10-point, and your pica ruler told you the text was 20-picas wide, you could count the characters in several lines. If 10 lines of copy had an average count of 55 characters, you would divide 55 by 20 to come up with the average CPP, 2.75.

In some respects, determining your own CPP figure is a good idea. You might make excessive use of capital letters in your copy, which would affect the character count. Or you might use very narrow columns of type, which would ultimately translate into fewer average characters in a pica than the published figure for that typeface.

The above covers the basic terminology needed to do rudimentary type specification. Certainly, there are many more terms used in the field, but for now, forget about kerning, negative leading and other buzzwords. They could be considered more important to the art director than to the production manager.

The primary maneuvers

With command of these basics—point, leading, pica and characters per pica—you have the basic tools of type specification, or "copyfitting." The procedure involves simple, logical mathematics: If you know how many average characters fit into a pica, you can determine how long (in inches or picas) any normal magazine text will run.

We will use two common problems to demonstrate the point. The first: How long will this copy be if set with "x" parameters? And second: What must this copy be specified at to fit in "x" area? For both samples we will use the text in Illustration 5 (next page).

In the sample text, the numbers in brackets following each paragraph are not material to be set. They represent the total characters in each block of copy.

Why do you count paragraphs individually rather than the total of all the characters in the text? The reason is that a typeset paragraph will rarely fill out its last line. Normally there is "dead" space in the last line. To account for this, you will need to determine how many lines—and partial lines—each paragraph will use. Of course, a partial line takes up as much vertical space as a full one.

i The specification of copy to be set in type involves using the following: average characters per pica, pica width of the copy, leading or line space, and total characters per paragraph. (181)

ii Characters per pica can be determined in two ways. First, a published reference source can be utilized. When unavailable, a sample of typeset material can be referred to. (167)

iii Even the newcomer can do fairly accurate specification by knowing the relationship of these variables to one another. (115)

iv But unfortunately, too many novices are frightened away, falling prey to their own misconceptions about the difficulty of the procedure. They routinely hand over the copy and mark it "set to fit." That's not acceptable! (214)

(5)

Problem 1: Estimating length

To tackle the first problem, let's determine how long the text will be if we have it set in Helvetica, in 9-point type, using 11-point leading, set at 16-picas wide. Using either a published chart or our own estimate (from a printed sample), let's say that 9-point Helvetica has an average of 3.3 characters per pica (CPP).

The first step is division. We know from our character count that Paragraph 1 in Illustration 5 has a total of 181 characters (including spaces between words and punctuation). How many picas long would that paragraph be if 3.3 characters fit into one pica? Divide 181 by 3.3 for the answer. It would be 54.8 total picas long. Round it off to 55 picas.

Next: If there are 16 picas in each line of typeset copy, how many lines of copy will equate to a 55-pica-long paragraph? The number 55 divided by 16 results in 3.4 lines of typesetting. And since a partial line takes as much vertical space as a full line, Paragraph 1 will be exactly four lines deep when set in the type mentioned above.

If you perform this same trick on the subsequent paragraphs, you should come up with the following:

Paragraph	Characters	Lines
1	181	4.0
2	167	4.0
3	115	3.0
4	214	5.0
All lines rounded up, total: 16.0		

Paragraph 4 is the tricky one if you want to be accurate. Your figures should show that this copy will 4.05 lines long, or almost exactly four lines. Which way should you round it off? Most often, you will be correct to round the number to the next highest typeset line— even when you fall a shade under. And the narrower your column measure (pica width), the more rounding you will do, because words that cannot be hyphenated will stretch your copy out a bit. So, let's say that Paragraph 4 will have five lines of typeset copy.

How long the column?

So far we know that we will have 16 lines of typeset copy in our sample. How long, or deep, will the column be? We picked a leading of 11 points. We know that each of the 16 lines will consume 11 points, so the copy will be 176 points deep when set in type (11 multiplied by 16).

Going back to the basics, there are 72 points to an inch. The typeset copy must then be 2.4 inches deep (176 divided by 72). Or to use picas, the column will be 14.7 picas deep (176 divided by 12, the number of points in a pica).

Problem 2: Making it fit

Now, what if the art director stated that the copy had to be three inches deep, rather than 2.4 as we have estimated? To spec the sample copy to fit that depth, we have to change one or more of the parameters. If we change point size alone, the copy will be deeper. Or, we could change only the leading. Both of these changes could possibly have a negative effect on appearance, though. Changing only the point size will make the piece look tighter. Changing only the leading will make it look looser.

So let's use a hit-and-miss approach. Let's do a quick check to see how 10-point copy on 12-point leading will come out. We'll say that 10-point Helvetica averages 2.9 characters per pica. A quick calculation gives us the following number of lines per paragraph in 10-point type:

Paragraph	Characters	Lines
1	181	4.0
2	167	4.0
3	115	3.0
4	214	5.0
All lines rounded up, total: 16.0		

Already, we can see that none of the line counts have increased. The increased size has been absorbed by the dead space in the previously-estimated paragraphs.

But to continue the exercise, using the same estimating technique as described in the first example, 16 lines of 12-point leading each should come out to 2.7 inches long.

That, of course, is not long enough. So, run though the test on 11-point copy using 13-point leading and a CPP of 2.7.

Paragraph	Characters	Lines
1	181	5.0
2	167	4.0
3	115	3.0
4	214	5.0
All lines rounded up, total: 17.0		

Those 17 lines, at 13 points each, give us a total depth of 221 points, or 3.06 inches. Close enough. And 11-point type on 13-point leading is conventional to look at, so the job should be attractive, rather than squeezed or stretched.

Tricks

That is the basis of estimating copy length. There are also a few simple tricks that will make it easier still.

The only time-consuming and boring activity is the character count. One way to speed up the process is to make (or purchase) a plastic or acetate grid that has vertical lines every five (or 10) typewritten characters apart.

Better yet, if you can talk your editors into it, have them type their final drafts with line lengths that equal your average character count per typeset line. (If your copy normally runs 55 characters per column, have the editors type 55 characters to the line.) The truly lazy person (such as the author) takes it one step further. If your editors are using word processors, have them give you the computer's character count at the end of each story or section.

The first draft of this material was typed using a 45-character column. As this material is being entered, the readout shows 15,158 characters of text, and 638 double-spaced line advances. From those numbers, a rough copy length could be determined very quickly.□

BUYING TYPE OUTSIDE

Although many publishing operations have installed typesetting equipment, there are no clear-cut guidelines to use to judge whether or not this is a good idea. Therefore, it is logical to assume that, for the foreseeable future, many publishers will purchase their typesetting from specialty shops, printers or other publishers.

There are many areas to be aware of and many variables to consider when purchasing typesetting. Before we get into the actual mechanics (equipment, fonts, quality, speed), let's start with the area that could give the average publisher the worst headaches: storage (or loss) of time-sensitive material.

Nonstorage equipment

Many newcomers would be shocked to know even the recent history of typesetting equipment. For years, it was common for a small print shop or publisher to operate typesetting equipment that could not store a job: not on floppy disk, or on paper tape or on any other media. This meant that once a job was set, it could not be rerun with corrections. If a typesetting processor were to make lunch of a two-hour job, it had to be completely redone.

Fortunately, the nonstorage period in typesetting was relatively short. Today, it is almost unheard of to find a vendor who doesn't use some temporary (or permanent) method of storing the keystrokes that go into your work.

Magazine typesetting doesn't belong on any equipment that does not store typesetting material. And, a type shop that doesn't automatically keep your keyboarded material on file for 30 to 60 days should not be considered a magazine typesetter.

Storage is essential

For magazine work, then, it is logical to assume that all your material must be produced on machinery that has the ability to retain the material for rerunning. The reruns might be for corrections, alterations or even later reprints of the same material for another product (such as a book).

There are many advantages to having your material electronically stored. Two of the more important ones follow.

•*Maintenance of schedule:* Material that is routinely stored electronically (and backed up as described below) is always available for rerunning. Even in the event of a total system breakdown at the typesetting house, stored material could possibly be run by another vendor.

•*In-house backup of material:* If your typesetting firm agrees (and there is no reason not to), you could purchase electronic duplicates of your typeset copy. This might be handy for several purposes. First, maybe that vendor will lose your original files (which you were planning to rerun for a book or reprint). Second, maybe you'll want to change vendors at some point. Having the material stored in some readable electronic format could save you the cost of rekeyboarding it for later use.

Storage is also critically important for items such as annual directories or product guides, which may retain most of the prior issue's text. Here too, having your own electronic copy can be a blessing. There are several firms that specialize in converting material from one machine to run on another, so that you could change vendors without incurring the expense of starting from scratch.

Storage media

Let's start with a now-primitive storage medium to begin our description of keeping material "on file."

Paper tape was the rage for many years. Briefly, paper-tape storage involved the high-speed punching of holes into long spools of narrow (one-inch) paper. The distinct advantages of paper-tape storage are these:

1. It is the only purely mechanical method of storing keystrokes for high-speed computer re-creation at a later date. All other mediums use magnetic storage, which is always susceptible to failure.

2. The punching of the codes on the tape is universal. Virtually any machine can read another machine's tape, which is definitely not the case with a magnetic tape or disk.

However, there also are severe limitations to paper tape. While a floppy disk can be randomly accessed (meaning that any portion of the disk can be read or written to), paper tape must more or less be read from start to finish.

Still, even if paper tape is attractive to you, it is becoming rather rare in the industry. Although there are many shops still using it, most (if not all) new equipment installations use some form of magnetic storage. They are described below.

Floppy disk

The most popular medium in use in the early 1980s—not only for typesetters, but for all small computer users—is the floppy disk. Its odd name comes from the fact that these circular, thin sheets of Mylar are rather flexible.

Briefly, here is how an eight-inch floppy is manufactured and used:

The disk itself looks like an extremely thin 45-rpm record with a large hole in the center. The Mylar from which the disk is made is coated with a thin layer of metal oxide. This is functionally very similar to the recording tape on a cassette.

The disk is not ever used "loose." Rather, it always comes in

19

a plastic carrier that is square, and has holes punched in it to accommodate the machine's spindle and recording/playback head. (The carrier also protects the disk from human hands and handling.) When inserted into the machine, the disk is rotated. The recording head runs on a track and can access any point on the disk quickly.

So, in use, material that is generated on the typesetting screen passes through the typesetting computer. The computer sends impulses to the disk head, which records material in the same fashion as a tape recorder records voices. Later, the head reverses its role, and instead of passing information to the disk, it reads from it.

Disk problems

Despite the advantages (including easy, random access of material and quick updating) some people believe that it's a sad thing that floppy disks ever became popular. The reason is they also create some distinct problems. The most notorious is the "crash." This term is not technically quite accurate, but it does roughly state what can happen to a floppy.

Either because of consistent wear or a mechanical problem, the recording head of the computer can scrape away enough metal oxide to make the disk unreadable by the machine. And unfortunately, the particular track that tends to wear out first usually happens to be the "directory" or instruction track, which keeps a record of where everything is located on the disk. Thus, it is not uncommon for a typesetter to lose a disk now and then.

This is most critical when a job is originally being entered. A typesetter may spend three hours on a job, only to find that the disk went bad and the job was lost.

But common sense tells most typesetters not to put themselves into such situations. So, it has become routine for a conscientious typesetter to duplicate all important files every hour or two, providing backup in the event of a mechanical catastrophe. As a buyer of typesetting, you may want to know what the practice is at your local shop.

There are several types of floppies. A common one is the eight-inch, which, as of this writing, holds up to several million characters.

The five-and-one-quarter-inch disks are also popular. Currently, they hold up to a million characters per side. Other than convenient size (both of the disk reader and the disk itself), there is no distinct advantage common to either disk.

Three-inch disks are now beginning to emerge on the market. They are not likely to gain in popularity for typesetting purposes simply because there is no obvious advantage to their small size.

In order to compare floppy disks fairly to paper tape, one must consider universality. While paper punching uses a common code to generate a stored letter, all manufacturers of floppy disk readers seem to have gone in different directions. It is uncommon for one machine to be able to read material stored on a competitor's machine. Actually, this was not done to harass the buyer. Rather, floppy disks exploded onto the small computer market quickly—so everyone invented the wheel at the same time.

Even though there is massive incompatibility in the floppy disk arena, there are escape routes. First, many small firms specialize in "media conversion." This is a trick whereby a device will read the codes intended for one machine, and translate them into codes that can be read, or accepted, by another.

A second bailout is electronic transmission of the material. Virtually all typesetting systems and small computers have the ability to talk in a common computer language over normal telephone lines. While the actual typesetting commands (size and leading, etc.) might not be salvaged, it is rather simple to save at least the words themselves. This could be a significant advantage on a long, complicated project. (These transmissions will be discussed in detail later in the "interfaced" typesetting section.)

Magnetic tape

Although popular on low-cost typesetting systems a few years ago, magnetic-tape storage of material isn't too popular any more. The exception is its use on extremely large typesetting systems coupled to mainframe (big) computers. The most common mag-tape devices used standard recording cassettes, nearly identical to those used in small tape recorders.

Like paper tape, the main limitation of the low-cost mag-tape devices was their inability to randomly access material. In addition, they were not noted for their reliability. It is unlikely that the contemporary type buyer will run across a mag-tape machine.

Hard disk

Closely related to floppy disk storage is the hard-disk system. It is what its name implies: hard, rather than flexible disks used for storage of magnetic information.

There are three clear advantages to hard-disk storage for the typesetter. First, hard disks are faster (finding files and doing searches for material). Second, they store much more information per disk. Third, they are more reliable. Their reliability is based on mechanical facts. Hard disks are hermetically sealed and less prone to dust, wear and other kinds of physical abuse that send files to the morgue.

The disadvantage to hard-disk storage is largely to the typesetting customer. You cannot ask for a duplicate hard-disk file: The disks themselves are permanently installed in the typesetting machine.

21

BUYING TYPE OUTSIDE

The same precautions must be taken with hard disks as with floppies: The material must somehow be backed up. With a hard-disk system, this means the typesetting firm must have at least two disk units: one active and one for backup in case the first goes to pieces. There are, though, relatively inexpensive methods of copying vast amounts of hard-disk data onto magnetic tape for backup purposes.

In the event you find yourself on a hard-disk system, there are two possibilities for getting a backup file into your own office. First, it is possible that the system uses both hard disk (for permanent) and floppy disk (for jobs in progress) storage. If this is the case, the firm might sell you a floppy version of your file.

Second, the unit almost certainly can transmit information to another typesetter, computer or even small word processor in your office. It would be a rather simple matter to have your file transmitted over the phone, thus providing you with a backup copy in the event of a failure at the typesetter.

It deserves mention that there is more than one type of failure possible at the typesetting plant. Yes, the equipment could fail, but so could the firm itself. It is not uncommon to find hundreds of thousands of dollars of typesetting equipment being peddled after repossession by a leasing company or a bank. It is not comforting to know that your files probably will *not* be salvaged during the sale.□

VARIETIES OF TYPESETTING PAPER

As the foregoing discussion implies, the first priority you might have in shopping for typesetting is storage. But even short-term storage can be a problem. Your material must remain in decent shape in the interval between the time you place it into position and the time the printer converts it to a printing plate.

Which brings us to the question of the type of paper used by the typesetting firm.

There are two common papers on the market, stabilization paper and rapid access paper. Both supposedly perform the same function: keeping the image on the paper.

Stabilization paper derives its name from the chemical process. The paper itself carries its own developer on its surface. After being exposed in the typesetting machine, it is placed in a processor containing two chemicals. The first chemical it passes through is the activator, which gets the developer (already on the paper) to do its job. Almost immediately thereafter, it goes into the stabilizer, which stops development and "freezes" the image.

The other common paper is called rapid access, so named because it uses conventional processing techniques rather quickly.

This paper has only a photosensitive carrier on its surface. After being exposed, it is placed in the processor—which performs the following: Development, which brings the image out; Stop Bath, which halts development (this bath is optional on some processors); Fixer, which clears the unwanted silver halide crystals from the paper (these crystals are responsible for any image that appears on the paper), Wash, which is the rinsing of the paper once or twice with water; and Dryer, which is exactly what it sounds like.

In my opinion, the only reasons a firm would use stabilization paper would be 1) they have no need for quality, 2) they have no need for permanence, or 3) they have no money for a good processor.

A stabilization processor could be purchased for less than 20 percent of the cost of a rapid access unit. In 1982, a stabilization unit cost $600 and a rapid access unit $4,000 (including plumbing).

The following quality comparison chart speaks for itself:

Factor	Poor/Low	Fair	Good/High
Permanence	■		●
Definition	■		●
Stability	■		●
D-Max		■	●
Relative Cost	■		●
Repeatability	■		●
Translucency	■		●

Stabilization ■   Rapid access ●

For the magazine publisher, the above factors are important for these reasons:

•*Permanence:* Will the material be usable in a month or two? A year?

•*Definition:* How crisp are the letters? The quality of a letter depends somewhat on how quickly the paper can change its image from black to white.

•*Stability*: Will the sheet stretch? Lie flat? A poor rating here can mean that nine-point type will actually be 9.25 or 9.4 points because the sheet expands during processing.

•*D-Max:* How black are the exposed characters? For some purposes (such as contacting directly to film), stabilization paper is impossible to work with.

•*Relative Cost:* The chart discusses only the cost of the processor and the paper, but this cost should also include any possible losses (for instance, when poor quality material has to be redone). It seems that stabilization paper should be less expensive to the typesetter and customer, but that may not be the case in real life.

•*Repeatability:* If a correction must occasionally be placed over some already-set material, will the exposures and developments be similar enough so that the correction will not be noticed? Or will some typesetting look light and other parts look dark?

•*Translucency:* When assembling a page many persons work on a light-table (with light coming through the paste-up board and the typeset copy itself). The more transluscent the paper, the easier it is to work with.

Although it may seem to the novice that the quality comparison is stacked in the favor of rapid access paper and chemistry, it is quite factual. One paper *is* that much better than another for certain purposes.

While the author believes that magazines should not be produced on stabilization typesetting paper, the reader is free to make another decision based on his or her own needs. There are many situations where cost must be favored over quality, and others where quality simply doesn't matter to either the publisher or the reader. In those cases, stabilization paper is a viable alternative.□

CHAPTER 5

EQUIPMENT CAPABILITY

Before the typesetting purchaser begins to solicit prices for typesetting, an important question must first be answered: What are the capabilities of different equipment?

On the surface, this question might seem routine. It is not. All typesetting equipment was not created equal. The buyer of type must find a situation that balances the equipment's capabilities with a particular job's demands.

For example, in the early years of low-cost phototypesetting, virtually anyone with guts and $4,000 could start a typesetting service. But there were limitations. Just imagine the problems you would face with the following limitations: Only two fonts (alphabets) available on the machine at one time (such as Roman and Italic *Century*); no size-changing ability while setting a job (meaning everything will be nine-point or whatever single size is selected); each line is set immediately after keyboarding; no electronic storage of a given job or file, and stabilization paper in use (meaning little, if any, permanence to the finished piece).

Sound ludicrous? To cite a true example, I witnessed a small shop—with the above limitations—take on the typesetting of a book. About 200 typeset pages long, it was to be keyboarded during slow periods over a six-month span. Because the equipment could not store the material for a later update, the author was shocked to find out that she could not make alterations without having the entire job done over. But it didn't matter. By the time four months had elapsed, the first month's work was already unusable because the stabilization paper had deteriorated. The project was scrapped.

Fortunately, most of the low-end equipment used on that job is no longer on the market, and most typesetters would not make the mistake of working without some kind of storage. But the point of the example is clear: The equipment itself is a major consideration for the typesetting purchaser.

Major mechanical considerations

Let's look at the seven major mechanical areas of typesetting equipment and their importance to the customer.

1. *Number of fonts on-line*: By font, we mean a single, full alphabet, such as Helvetica light italic. By on line, we mean loaded into the machine and available for access (by the operator).

As of this writing some machines on the market have as few as four fonts on line. Example: Helvetica medium, italic, bold and bold italic. The obvious limitation here is this: What if the job needed the above four fonts, plus a Century bold for headlines? Although the equipment might have some clumsy method of stopping the job for this "fifth wheel," the net effect would be trying to make a single-engine plane compete with a jumbo jet.

A typical minimum number of fonts on-line would be eight.

Some of the more powerful machines carry more than 100.

In addition to knowing how many fonts are on-line, one must ask whether these fonts can be randomly mixed. Some phototypesetting equipment has four fonts on a strip or wheel. If the machine has an eight-font limit, the customer cannot mix fonts at random. Rather, the only logical mixes would be "families," such as four fonts of Helvetica and four fonts of Century.

Finally, the font question should be expanded to the full library of the given type house—if, that is, you need a wide selection of typefaces. While one shop might have a total of 50 typefaces available, another might have 1,000. Bear in mind that there could be a relationship between total fonts available and the overhead of the shop: 1,000 fonts could cost $120,000, which would eventually have to be recovered in charges to the customers.

2. *Sizes:* For most purposes, all of the contemporary equipment in the typesetting arena will offer an adequate selection of point sizes. However, your particular needs could dictate exceptions. If you need 96-point type routinely, or four-point type, you would have to look for a vendor who offered that range.

Then, too, there is the question of "steps." A machine might set from five to 72 points in steps of one point. Another might set the same range in steps of a tenth of a point. Still another might set in half-point steps from five to 12 points, and then in one-point steps to 36 points. Some phototypesetting equipment manufactured a few years ago could not set 15-point type no matter what: It had only predetermined sizes, such as 14, 16, 18 and 22.

3. *Modification/distortion:* Digital typesetting equipment normally has the ability to alter any typeface. A unit might be able to set a face anywhere from 30 percent of its normal width to 200 percent of its regular width. Other abilities include artificial italics (*i.e.,* slanting a typeface for which no italic was designed), setting type in reverse, or outlining it.

Modification of faces is normally not important to the magazine-type customer, but can have useful applications in setting advertising, or work that involves the forcing of copy into specific areas.

4. *Storage, quality, type of paper:* These factors are covered in the general discussion of phototypesetting. Refer to that section for background.

5. *Aesthetics:* There are four basic areas of aesthetics that are directly affected by the machine being used.

•True font: A type font is designed by an expert who produces a master. But once the font is on the market, chances are that it will

EQUIPMENT CAPABILITY

be pirated by another firm and later show up as a slightly inferior font. To be legal, a few minor details (and the name of the font) are often changed. The purist would want all the aesthetic perfection that the designer has built into the original design. Such a design is called a licensed font.

•Adequate escapement: Escapement is best described by watching a ball-element typewriter in action. After each character is typed, the typing ball moves one space forward and is ready to type the next character. In other words, the ball has escaped its prior position. Typesetting equipment must have the electronic knowledge of how far to move forward after typing each character. Because this information consumes computer memory, the more electronically crude the equipment, the less room there will be for storing this information. Therefore, some equipment has better escapement values than others. This translates into more attractive typesetting.

The best way to find out if the equipment meets your escapement requirements is simply to compare Helvetica set by one machine to Helvetica set by another. If you can't tell the difference (or don't care), then forget about escapement.

•Kerning: This is the ability of a unit to "tuck" part of one letter under another. One example would be tucking a lower case "y" under part of a cap "T". Some machines have automatic kerning features; others will accept operator commands as they are entered.

At this writing, one might say there is a "great kerning debate" in progress. As machines have become more powerful, manufacturers are claiming hundreds and even thousands of "kerning pairs" being active at all times. This means the machine examines each two adjacent letters, then scans its kerning file. If it finds the letters, the machine uses the appropriate space for tucking the pair.

Is all this necessary? You must decide for yourself.

•Ligatures: A ligature is a special character that takes the place of two or more other characters that—when set in regular type—tend to look clumsy. The "fi" ligature is the most common: The upper right of the "f" becomes the dot on the "i".

Again, it is as common to set type without ligatures as with them. Some machines have ligatures available for all fonts, some need a special "pi" font on-line with the normal font, and some perform all ligature insertions automatically. You must decide whether these aesthetic refinements are important to you.

6. *Communication ability:* You may want to question whether your equipment and your typesetter have the ability to communicate with other equipment, such as computers and word processors. Data communication gives you many options: You can have a price list transmitted by an advertiser at the last minute directly from his or her

28

computer. Also, at some point you may wish to do your own basic keyboarding and then transmit the files to your typesetter for the actual typesetting.

7. *Hyphenation:* Finally, all computer typesetters must approach the subject of hyphenation. There are four different ways to do so:

•Operator hyphenation: The simplest way to make a typesetting machine hyphenate is to make it ask the operator. In practice, the unit will automatically stop whenever a line cannot be properly spaced because of a long word at its end. The operator must specify where a given word can be broken. The advantage (if you call it so) is that a real person will make each hyphenation decision. The disadvantages are the slower speed and the liklihood of operator error.

•Logical hyphenation: In this mode, a machine will use roughly 11 rules of hyphenation in our language. The advantage: speed. The problem: At best, our logical rules of hyphenation work only most of the time. Therefore, a conscientious operator will have to check all logical hyphenations for accuracy.

•Exception word/logical: Moving up the scale, a machine might have both logical hyphenation and an exception word dictionary. In use, all logical rules will be followed, and a small electronic dictionary (programmed by the operator) will be scanned for certain words that either break the logical rules or are unique to the customer or typesetting company.

•Dictionary hyphenation: On the more expensive installations, the typesetting unit might be coupled to a large computer that can access the unabridged dictionary of the English language. Some of these might include full medical or technical dictionaries. Better yet, the system might have a spelling verification program and automatically check for spelling errors. One can hardly argue with such a procedure, but because of the expense involved and hardware required, most typesetting shops do not offer this ultimate luxury.

Other considerations

In addition to the above "basics," you might also want to consider such frills as full-page makeup, vertical/horizontal ruling ability and automatic pagination. For most magazines, these are not absolute requirements, although it appears that the industry will eventually move along these lines. Briefly, these additional abilities work as follows:

•*Full-page makeup:* Allows the operator to view a page as it will eventually be set in type. The headline will look like a headline, and an area for a photo will have a rule indicating same. In other words, the entire page can be viewed on the terminal as it will later be set in type. This feature is quite handy for 1) creating advertisements and 2) staying on schedule with a weekly or daily publication. As equipment costs fall, we might expect full-page makeup eventually to become a standard practice in typesetting.

•*Vertical/horizontal ruling:* Allows the operator to place all rules on the screen (or embedded in nongraphic command codes), rather than have an artist draw the rules in after the type is set. Most equipment can generate rules, but the function is most useful when coupled with a full-page makeup system.

•*Pagination:* Allows a machine to automatically set long text in page formats, including page numbers, datelines, headers and footers (as used in books), and footnotes. For book publishers, it is almost a necessity. For magazines, the procedure is more complicated because of fixed page counts and frequent shuffling of material by ad directors, art directors and publishers. Once again, as equipment prices fall, in the future pagination will likely become more popular.□

SOLICITING PRICES & SELECTING A VENDOR

Selecting a firm to set magazine type is as difficult as picking a spouse. Not only must the firm have the physical attributes you admire, but you also have to get along with—even *like*— the other party.

So before outlining a method of picking a typesetter, it pays to repeat something brought up in the introduction: Magazine production is a game of personalities. With all your vendors, you will be demanding—because of the nature of the work—the utmost in speed and accuracy, while in all likelihood returning little more than new demands and a few dollars. To "pull off" such a scenario requires that you get along with your vendors. For those of you who do not set type in-house, your first vendor is the typesetter.

Equipment

It is difficult to say where the search for a good typesetter properly begins. Which is more important: equipment capability, a qualified staff or timeliness?

Although you may logically disagree, I'll say equipment capability. The reason is that without the proper equipment, not even a qualified staff can maintain professional output (timely, high-quality work). Therefore, purchasing type starts with a review of all the factors brought up earlier in this chapter, including machine speed, fonts on-line, type of paper, and so on. But there are a few additions.

Is there backup at the typesetter?

Just like the pilot who won't fly a single-engine plane, many production managers won't deal with a "one-horse" vendor. The backup question has been answered by all serious magazine typesetters. One large firm signed a contract with a competitor agreeing to back up each other in the event of a catastrophic breakdown. Another firm, with no such option, increased its investment by nearly a million dollars, just to be able to stay "up and running."

Depending on the size of the operation, the term "backup" can be extended further. It is not unheard of for a small company to have only one person trained to run a machine. (This is even more common with small publishers than the average commercial typesetter.) But the point is: People have to be backed up, too.

Once you've answered the questions of equipment and backup to your satisfaction, you can start the qualification procedure discussed below.

Who are the customers?

One shortcut to finding the firms that will be capable of doing your work is to see who's doing what for whom. Some shops specialize in setting type for ad agencies; others sell commercial work to anyone who walks in off the street.

32

Chances are that you will eventually have to work with a firm that specializes (at least in part) in magazine typesetting. An ad-agency type shop, for example, might well be accustomed to taking several days to set a single page, after which many revisions will follow. The magazine shop specializes in fast turnaround and as few reruns as possible. To do otherwise would be to compromise the publication schedule itself.

So, look first for a firm that already has publication customers. Although you could argue that you would then be just another fish in the sea (rather than "the important" customer), you will save the headaches of teaching that firm how to set magazine type on a magazine schedule.

A firm that already has publication customers also tells you something about the shop's experience. If they are successfully setting magazine text for other vendors, they *do* have experience. Assuming that they have more attractions than just a low price, you can logically assume that they are professional magazine typesetters.

Checking references

All companies have references. Some companies have reputations, too.

A company with nothing to fear will often supply a potential client with a complete list of customers. If you get such a list, go ahead and randomly check these references. And, without sounding too basic, if a company refuses to give you references or a list of customers, something is dramatically wrong. Then go back to "start," and roll the dice again.

Why is the firm selling type?

Bear in mind that many publishers that have installed in-house typesetting have found that their volume doesn't warrant the investment. This is also true of other small firms that wanted to meet their schedules at any price. So another question is, just why does this firm sell type?

I don't want to condemn those publishers who offer commercial typesetting services any more than I would want to condemn a typesetter who published a magazine, yet the distinctions are important. Although there are exceptions, you might agree with this statement: A publisher's first responsibility is to his or her own magazine. A typesetter's only responsibility is to his or her customers. In the event of an oversold schedule or equipment malfunction, you—the customer—want to be in a priority position.

To be fair, though, you must also relate this statement to equipment: If a publishing operation is fully backed up, both with people and machinery, one could also assume that there will rarely—if ever—be a day when you, the customer, suffer a late issue because of the typesetter.

If backup and priorities are not problems, you can look at the benefits of working with the publisher-typesetter. After all, who could be in a better position to understand the problems of setting magazine text on a timely, accurate basis, and who could be better qualified in the type of work itself?

Schedules

Any typesetter under your consideration will, in all probability, have other magazines to set. Another qualifying question: When do those magazines get worked on?

Scheduling conflicts in magazine production circles are more common than not. It is no secret that "all magazines should be created on the same day," regardless of their status as weeklies, bimonthlies or annuals.

To check out scheduling, use the reference list supplied by the typesetter. Call the customers and ask them for a rough idea of their typesetting schedules. If you detect a conflict, don't just drop the matter: Bring it up with the salesperson. It is possible that the typesetter will have already anticipated the matter. But maybe they need one more job at that time. Maybe they are adding a second or third shift. Maybe they are lying through their teeth. Find out which it is.

This leads to the final qualification: Is the firm willing to sign on the dotted line?

That dotted line can either be a commercial order for work or an actual contract for your typesetting needs (say, for a year or two). Although contracted typesetting isn't as popular as contracted printing services, there is no reason to let a vendor 'off the hook' with only verbal promises.

Would your typesetter agree to the following?

It is agreed that XGY Typos, Inc. (vendor) shall set in type from original manuscripts, similar to attached sample A, approximately 150 manuscript pages. Proofreading will be done by May Publishing, Inc. (customer). Errors made by the typesetter will be corrected at no charge; alterations made by customer will be charged at $1 per line. Manuscripts will be given to vendor over a period of five working days starting January 20, 19--. At least 20 percent of all manuscript pages will be given to vendor on each of those working days. All typesetting will be completed, including a second set of galleys within seven working days. Vendor agrees to reduce original estimate by 10 percent per each working day that exceeds the above agreed schedule.

Pretty rough stuff, isn't it? But it may well be that each working day you are late costs you hundreds—even thousands—of dollars at the printer. If so, you would need some sort of guarantee that a slip in another company's schedule won't put you out of business.

Please bear in mind that the above sample agreement is not an absolute. If you do choose to make such statements in writing—either for a first-time order or in a formal contract—you need either a great deal of experience in purchase orders and contracts, or an attorney. Maybe both.

After you've answered all the above questions—from equipment through people through schedules—you can proceed to what many newcomers think of as the top priority: prices. I do not place prices at the end of this list by accident. Your own experience has shown you—or soon will show you—that money is what you consider after you have met your needs. If you need to stay on a schedule, need backup, need high-speed equipment, you don't start by looking for the lowest price. Only after you have more than one vendor who can fill your needs do you do comparison shopping.

Getting prices

Unfortunately, there is no universal method of estimating magazine typesetting. There probably never will be, either. First, no two magazines are alike. One might differ radically from another in terms of complexity of style alone—indented initials and type running around photos. Second, there is no universal method of running a typesetting operation. While one vendor might insist on estimating by the hour, another might use a computer and do all estimating on a per-character basis.

This brings up one of the routine tasks of the production manager: Just how does one compare apples to oranges? It is possible. But first we must look at the fruit.

There are three general methods of type estimation: hourly, per character and averaging. Some of these have several different sub-methods, too, and all have advantages and disadvantages—to both the customer and the vendor. Let's take a look at each one.

•*Hourly estimates:* An hourly estimate isn't really an estimate at all. Rather, it is the result of someone answering "yes" to the question, 'Would you buy a used car from this typesetter?'' And be advised that I am not frowning upon this method. It can work.

In practice, a firm tells you they will charge "x" dollars per hour to set your work. Then, regardless of the complexity or length of the material, they are ready to roll.

The distinct advantage to the typesetter is that regardless of how the material comes into the shop —in Greek, handwritten, or spoken—they will be remunerated properly for their efforts. The advantage to the customer is that he or she needs to meet no prescribed formula for supplying the type to the vendor. It needn't be double-spaced or error free, and it needn't match the simplicity of the prior job.

But there are disadvantages. The first and worst is that the customer—at least during the first few production cycles—may not have any idea of how much the job is going to cost. In addition, paying by the hour necessitates that you trust all of the typesetting company's employees working on your job. Kathy, the keyboarder, might rather put 2.5 hours on your time sheet—rather than 1.7 hours typesetting and 0.8 hours talking to her boyfriend Jimmy. She'll look like a better employee and the company will make more money: your money.

If you remember some of my comments about typesetting equipment, you may be wondering something about an hourly rate: Aren't some machines faster than others? Won't that affect the total number of hours spent on your job? Not only does the equipment itself affect the total time, but some operators are faster and much more accurate than others.

Look at this: Shop A has a 25-line-per-minute typesetting system that requires the operator to make all hyphenation decisions. The operator has an error rate of .003 (three mistakes per every 1,000 characters), and can input complex coded material at 6,000 characters per hour.

Shop B has a 150-line-per-minute machine with logical and discretionary hyphenation and on-line spelling checking. The operator has an error rate of .0007 (less than one error per 1,000 characters), and can input complex coded material at 7,000 characters per hour.

It is safe to say that Shop A will produce less attractive copy in possibly twice as much time as Shop B.

The smart shopper, then, must almost ignore the hourly rate. To determine true costs, it would be far better to have each shop set the same test job for you (text, an ad or whatever), and bill you the normal hourly rate. Then compare the figures and the quality.

It is not our job here, though, to say that hourly billing is inappropriate. If you own a type shop, you may well feel it is the only way to stay in business. And, if you are honest about the billings, nobody would be getting less than what they were paying for.

•*Per-character methods:* Another common way to estimate type is per character, or—for practical purposes—per thousand characters.

The obvious advantage of this method is that both the customer and the vendor will know ahead of time how much money 10,000 characters will cost. No question about it. And either the customer or the vendor could, at least approximately, verify the character count. If you take into account that typesetters must count command strokes as characters (switching to italic and back, for example), you could get quite accurate.

But the per-character method falls short in other areas. What if you decide to have a lengthy manuscript set to run around an illustration? True, the character count remains the same. But it might take three times as long to set the job.

What if you hand-wrote an article? A realistic penalty of two-fold could be expected, but the per-character method would not account for it.

These problems are better answered by the hourly method.

Of course, the publisher who has routine, formatted, typographically boring text to set issue after issue could probably use the per-character method exclusively.

•*Averaging techniques:* Now, to the method that is actually a cornucopia of estimating methods: averaging. All of the following are valid.

Average per manuscript page: If all your manuscripts have the same complexity, the same cleanliness and the same language, the typesetter may wish to estimate at "x" dollars per original double-spaced manuscript page. Double that price for the single-spaced submission. Certain publications—such as those with page after page of full text and no advertising—are good candidates for this method.

Average per inch: This is a reasonably accurate method to estimate straight text set at predetermined parameters. Most shops should be able to tell you what they'd charge per running inch of Helvetica, nine point on 10-point leading, 20-picas wide. Of course, any changes in those parameters would invalidate the estimate.

Per line: Estimating per typeset line is the same as estimating per inch. It is just expressed differently. Still, all of the type parameters must be uniform (as described above) for the method to be accurate.

Average per job: This is a rather loose method of estimating. In effect, the typesetter says "We'll do your magazine for 'x' dollars per issue." The leeway here is obviously frightening. What if you add eight pages to the publication? Or subtract eight?

There is a common problem with all of these averaging methods: They require uniformity of the input or manuscript copy. If virtually all the copy is not the same from issue to issue—in length, accuracy, punctuation, complexity and so on—then these methods are not going to be too accurate.

Again, there are situations where such uniformity is the norm. In those cases, all of these averaging methods might be suitable and functional.

Comparing the bids

To compare any of these methods, use any common denominator. For an example, we will use one magazine page, completely saturated with type.

Our parameters: 9-point type; 9-point leading; 13-picas wide; 2.92 characters per pica; three columns on the page; 38 average characters per line; 70 lines to the column.

If you absorbed the material in the section on how to spec simple typesetting jobs, you should already know what we're doing here. Let's say one firm gave you a price per manuscript page. By doing a type-fitting job in reverse, you can determine exactly how many manuscript pages would be needed to fill the above sample page.

The vendor bid per inch? A quick calculation using the above parameters tells you that there are 8.75 inches per column on our sample page, 26.25 total.

The bid per issue? This one is rather tricky. To accurately convert it, you would need to determine how many full magazine pages of nine-point type, nine-leading, etc., would be in the issue. To do this you may have to use the approximate total characters in the issue, or some other technique. When you have determined how many of our dense pages (as we're using in the sample) will result from all the copy in the average magazine, you can come up with a comparative cost.

Common sense and a little math will allow you to convert any of the typesetter's estimates into an apple, orange or peach. You must do this if you are doing comparison shopping.

Who does the proofreading?

We have not included proofreading in the above comparisons for two reasons. First, the quality of proofreading by typesetters is difficult to measure. Second, some type firms proofread everything they set, while others do no proofreading at all.

Given the fact that proofreading (checking for typos, spelling, punctuation) is as much an editorial skill as a typographical function, and given the fact that it is a qualitative procedure, it is almost impossible to compare the service provided by one firm to that of another.

To resolve this, bear in mind that typographical trade customs put the responsibility for accuracy in the eyes of the customer. You must, like it or not, give the "okay" to a typeset job.

In plain English: *You* must proofread the job anyhow. So, it makes sense to ask for minimal proofreading, or none at all.

As you buy more and more typesetting, you will probably find that any major errors (such as an indent command being missed and the entire job then being set at the wrong measure) will be corrected by the typesetter before you see the first galley. Simple pride is the reason: The typesetter most likely will not want to show you anything that belongs in the garbage can.

But the minor errors—style, spelling, punctuation—are probably not so easy to detect—and, in fact, could be impossible to detect by someone unfamiliar with the idiosyncrasies of your editorial style.

You must catch those. Consequently, the best and most realistic typesetting prices usually result when it is understood that the customer will do all the proofreading.

The best method for you

In summary, there is no single "best" method of getting typesetting prices. Your magazine will have one "best" way, while another's "best" method will be completely different.

Just as likely, you will have need—during your relationship with a typesetter—to have different manuscripts priced using different estimating techniques. The per-character method is fine for English, but you'd expect to pay more (an hourly rate, say) if you needed a few thousand words set in German.

So feel free to ask for the hourly rate up front, even though you may be using another method for most jobs.

Just remember: What one person does in one hour, another person can do in 45 minutes.□

INTERFACED TYPESETTING

Most people know that modern phototypesetting equipment—be it digital or photographic—is driven from internal computers. The computer in a typesetter is no different from any other contemporary computer. For example, it may well be that the actual computer chip—the heart of a home terminal—is the same chip that drives a typesetter. It is logical, then, that phototypesetting machines can communicate with other typesetters and other computers. This is the concept behind interfaced typesetting.

Just what is interfaced type? As the term is used today, it is the practice of inputting (keystroking) material on one computer (or word processor or any other computer-driven unit), and then transmitting it electronically to a typesetting device. As practiced in the magazine publishing industry, an interfaced typesetting arrangement allows either an editor or a typist to work with a word processing terminal—that is, a computer with a software program that allows for easy inputting and revising of material.

The overriding concept behind an interfaced system is this: The publishing operation takes responsibility for producing clean, correct copy before releasing it for typesetting. The type company, then, produces the material without rekeyboarding it, thereby reducing both their labor, and any of the potential errors likely to occur during the retyping stage. The result should be better typeset copy at a lower cost then would be available in a conventional typesetting situation.

A typical job

Here's how a job might typically run through an interfaced system. Let's assume that the publishing operation has a small computer terminal that is used by an editor for both original material and for retyping material from other contributors—material which then must be typeset.

1. *Input:* This can be as simple as typing, or as complex as true typesetting. The options will be discussed later, but for now, assume that the editor is comfortable enough with the terminal to get the information into the machine. The information itself is stored on the computer's memory, either a floppy or a hard-disk system.

2. *Proof:* It is practical to assume that the editor will want to review a hard copy (printed copy) of the material before transmitting it. The copy could then be shown to the publisher, another editor, a proofreader, etc. But the proofing stage is not required: The editor might just as easily review the copy on his screen. When it is required, the proof can be done on a line printer, which is nothing more than a fancy, computer-driven typewriter.

3. *Corrections:* Original material is rarely perfect in the editor's eyes. Word processing on a computer allows for easy

changes, alterations or updates to a file. The editor might then rerun the line-printer proof. Again, this is optional.

It should be noted that the line printer does not produce a facsimile of typeset copy. It will not show a true typeface. Its purpose is merely to show that the words, punctuation and so forth are what the editor wants.

4. *Transmission:* When the file on the screen is exactly what the editor wants to see in print, the file is then transmitted to the typesetter. There are several different ways to transmit the copy:

•Modem: A telephone modem (abbreviation for modulator/demodulator) can use ordinary phone lines to transmit information from one computer to another.

•Direct line: Another variation of the modem, with one additional aspect: The computers would be connected directly via a special line leased from the phone company.

•Direct disk: Although one computer normally can't read a disk written by another, that situation is rapidly changing. Manufacturers are standardizing both the way a disk is written and the way ''utility'' programs can read a foreign language (meaning another computer's codes).

•Direct: In the truly direct transmission, a cable connects one computer to another. This is feasible only when the typesetting machine and the input terminal are not more than about a mile apart.

There are no standards

There is no way to fully describe the interfaced system that your firm might become involved in. Why? Running an interfaced typesetting firm is like publishing a magazine. It offers an unlimited opportunity for creativity because there are no rules about how the system should work.

One firm might run a highly automated system where there is no human involvement. Example: Your computer calls their computer; their computer sets the type. One person doesn't ask another person any questions; nobody even sees your job until it is placed in the delivery envelope.

Another firm might use extensive people involvement. You pick up the phone and ask if someone is ready for a transmission. When that person is ready, you both turn on your computers and let the information fly.

Similarly, one firm may demand that you put in all the typesetting commands. These would include the fundamentals of font, leading, width and size—and perhaps tabulation, indents and

INTERFACED TYPESETTING

special "pi" characters.

Another firm might suggest that you just put in the keystrokes you want to see in print, and then send them a marked up manuscript (as you would have done with a conventional job).

Advantages

There are some obvious advantages to an interfaced system.

1. *Accuracy*: The editor keystrokes the job and that's that. Nobody types it over—meaning nobody creates errors.

2. *Cost:* In theory, interfaced typesetting should reduce costs substantially. (Of course, you might find a firm that figures out how to turn this into an additional expense. The field, being relatively new, is prone to such activity. Shopping around is your best insurance.) Why should costs go down significantly? While the editor *must* type as a part of his creative function, the typesetting professional is not paid for mere speed with the keyboard. On the contrary, anybody can type. The typesetting pro is paid for his/her knowledge of aesthetics, and for the full abilities of the typesetting system.

In other words, the typographer is overpaid for much of what he or she does. It is work like coding, markup and hyphenation checks, that needs skill and experience. The typing function is merely the burden that gets in the way of producing a typeset product.

This, then, is the real beauty of an interfaced system. The editor does what he's supposed to: Type a nice story. The typesetting pro does his job: He makes sure the work meets the specifications (and has the proper command structure) to produce perfect galleys of type.

3. *Speed:* An interfaced job should be produced much faster than a conventional one. The reason is that the burden of retyping it is gone. The typesetting pro simply reviews the material on the screen and then runs it.

4. *Overhead:* For the publisher, the alternative to interfaced typesetting is either conventional purchasing or setting type in-house. When compared to the latter, an interfaced system shines. Compared to a phototypesetting system, a word processing system is extremely low cost.

5. *Training:* To take that comparision further, in-house typesetting managers must be aware of the problems that exist in training and turnover. These problems are greatly reduced by the editor learning to use a word processor.

Word processors are designed for virtually anyone to use with ease. Typesetting machines, it seems, are often so complex they make you wonder if anybody—including the manufacturer—can be productive with them.

6. *Productivity:* When interfaced type is examined in a publishing operation, it is often discovered that the editors are more productive working on word processing terminals than on typewriters.

Disadvantages

If that all sounds like a dream, it's because it overlooks the downside. To determine the disadvantages of interfaced type, we must compare it to the alternatives. First, let's compare it to conventional purchasing of type from an outside vendor.

First, the transmitted material must be accurate. Although a *computer* doesn't always know the editor's intent, a good typographer often makes routine correction of errors when he's doing a job from scratch.

Second, coding can be a problem. If the type company insists that the customers learn to use—and then routinely insert—all the coding that will eventually produce the job, one must ask a very serious question: Does the editor want to be a typesetter?

If, in fact, all the codes must be in the text, then that is exactly what the editor will become. It is reasonable to assume that if this route is followed, there will be no need for the professional typographer at all.

It would be naive to assume that typesetting companies don't need professionals who know all of the ins and outs of type. To transfer this burden to the editor strikes me as ridiculous, but given certain simple, straight, uncomplicated text, it *is* a possibility.

On the other hand, some firms will prefer to do all the coding, or at least the complicated aspects of it.

Now, let's compare interfaced to in-house typesetting.

1. *Speed/control:* Obviously, if you consider setting type in-house, you are looking for turnaround time and possibly more control over aesthetics and schedules. Any time you work with a vendor, you lose some of this control.

2. *Equipment:* It is not likely that you would be able to dictate the kind of equipment used by the type firm. Maybe it is too slow. Maybe it can't produce the kind of quality you need. True, these problems can be overcome by sheer competition among interfaced typesetters. As I write this, relatively few firms are highly adept at the procedure.

3. *Backup:* This variable has two edges: Is there adequate equipment and adequate personnel backup at the typsetting shop? Although you could control those backup questions with an in-house arrangement, you cannot fully control them with a vendor.

Summary: Interfaced type and the editor

It would be nice if we could wrap up this discussion with some advice, but that wouldn't be realistic. There are too many variables, and anyway, each company must find its own niche.

However, there is one general view that you should keep in mind. While the question of conventional versus interfaced versus in-house will never be answered, the editor and the terminal seem to be here to stay.

Word processors for editors appear to be highly advantageous. If this trend is permanent, then you will eventually become involved in interfaced typesetting at some level.

If you are setting type in-house, your editors will use either terminals supplied by the typesetting equipment manager, or off-line, independent computer/processors. (Off-line means there is no physical connection between units.)

If you do not set type in-house, but still see a trend toward computer terminals for your editors, you would be foolish to have someone retype your material. In the end, it will be transmitted to a typesetting firm anyway.

Even if most of your material comes from outside contributors—and the trend toward computer terminals is as strong as it appears—you might be foolish not to have your field editors dump their copy to you via computer. Why retype it when it is already in an electronic format?□

SETTING TYPE IN-HOUSE

During the past decade, a strong trend toward in-house typesetting built up, then slowed down, and even seemed to reverse. Why?

Two reasons. First, the cost of equipment fell dramatically. Second, the typesetting manufacturers started an advertising campaign that basically said, "Anybody can set type."

Now that 1) publishers have learned how much baloney was in that statement, 2) typesetting systems have become more sophisticated and expensive, and 3) the interfaced option has become a reality, the logic of in-house typesetting is being examined all over again.

Let's say up front that some publishers should set type in-house, no questions about it. But, how do you determine if you're in that type of operation? I suggest you start by answering this question:

In terms of quality and schedule can an outside firm meet your needs?

Again, you'll notice that I do not bring up the question of price. There are two schools of thought on this: The ads placed by the typesetting companies state that in-house typesetting saves money. The literature distributed by the typesetting associations states that this is generally a fallacy. Somewhere between these extremes is the truth—and this book cannot point it out for your individual operation.

So, if you can meet your needs of quality, price and delivery by using an outside firm, you should buy your type outside. If you can't, then answer this question:

Do you want to establish, capitalize and manage a typesetting business?

And if that answer is "no," then the final question is, Do you want to establish, manage, and lose money on a typesetting business?

I hope you've noticed the key word in the above: "business." If you consider setting type in-house, the best advice you can get is also the most simple: Approach the concept with the idea that typesetting is a business—not a hobby, and not a very logical thing for a publisher to do. It is a separate activity from publishing, even though the compatibility with word processors and typesetters seem to build a natural bridge between the two.

For example, publishing and printing are related very closely. Without publishers, there would be nothing to print. A more symbiotic situation would be hard to find. Yet few publishers have any financial interest in printing firms and vice versa. Why?

Because they are distinctly different businesses. Publishing is, fundamentally, the business of thinking up things that other people will want to read or see. Printing is the business of mechanically reproducing those words and pictures. Typesetting is the business of transforming information into aesthetically pleasing shapes.

Countless publishers have lost money on in-house typesetting because they have not approached it as a separate business, one that should account for its own profit or loss. Yet many publishers have invested in printing, then divested themselves of it because it was not profitable.

CHAPTER 9

Finally, many publishers are running extremely profitable, lucrative in-house typesetting operations, and they don't even know it. Why? Again, because they do not approach it as a separate business.

The answer

If you set a small volume of type — say a bimonthly magazine -- it is likely that an interface or outside-vendor arrangement is your best bet. Simple enough.

If you have a high volume with weekly deadlines, similarly, it is probable that you could meet your own needs better than a vendor.

If you are in the gray zone, you might want to do a careful cost analysis. Solicit prices and investigate equipment, and keep in mind that in-house type is just like in-house printing.

Will you be able to afford equipment backup? Will you have enough trained, full-time typesetters to ride out someone's bout with the flu? What will it cost to retrain a key employee? How quickly will your investment depreciate? Will your operation lose money, but by keeping you on a schedule keep your advertising dollars healthy? If your operation appears to be lucrative, will you respond as a "regular" owner would and expand it, solicit more work, and try to make more money with it?

Nobody can answer these questions for you. Neither the equipment manufacturers nor the professional associations are speaking from an unbiased stance. You must approach the questions keeping in mind your own specific needs, likes, dislikes and the financial risk involved.

Three general options

This chart briefly compares the three typesetting options: vendor supplied, vendor/interface and in-house. For in-house type, we assume that the installation is technologically current and fully backed up—both in personnel and in equipment.□

	Vendor	Vendor/Interface	In-House
Turnaround time	Varies	Varies	Fast
Investment in equipment	None	Moderate	High
Personnel training	None	Moderate	Extensive
Space requirements	None	None	Yes
Technical quality	Varies	Varies	Controlled
Accuracy of typesetting	Varies	Excellent	Varies

47

SECTION II: PASTE-UP

FUNDAMENTALS OF CONVENTIONAL MAGAZINE PASTE-UP

Paste-up is the term used to describe any material that has been assembled for printing. Depending on your needs and the quality you desire, that material can be anything from a piece of art on a white sheet of paper to a complex mechanical drawing. However, despite the varying levels of complexity, the paste-up must meet one basic requirement: It must be able to be "shot" on a lithographic camera.

In order for material to be "shot," the material to be reproduced should be black, if possible. However, other colors can also be easily photographed by the lithographic camera: Red and orange, for example, do not provide many camera problems.

But, as you may already know, certain colors will not be easily recognized by the printing process. Blue is basically invisible to the camera. Although a very dark blue can be photographed, a light blue is almost impossible to reproduce. Yellows can occasionally be shot, but the results vary: A successful reproduction will depend on whether the yellow is more "gold" or more "sunshiny."

The material must be crisp

That's not to say that simply because something is "black" it will look good. The art or type that you shoot must also be very crisp.

The problem of "crispness" often pops up when a buyer asks to have an old piece of material reprinted. If the original is missing, a previously printed sample is frequently substituted. The result is an unavoidable shift in the quality of the work: All printed pieces are slightly less crisp than their originals, and reprinting a printed piece degrades the quality even further.

In summary, in printing, as in computer programming, the GIGO theory holds true: Garbage In, Garbage Out. The final piece will look no better than the originals you started with.

Everything prints

If you are familiar with the "rules" of printing, keep in mind that the camera "sees" all kinds of things: A fingerprint, if dark enough, is the same to the camera as a headline.

Thus, paste-ups must be kept exceptionally clean, or better yet, perfect. Two easy ways to do this are 1) to make sure that everyone handling material you intend to reproduce is aware that everything appearing on the original art will print, and 2) to protect your paste-up with a sheet of artists' tissue (often called parchment), which can be purchased at most office supply stores and at all art supply stores.

Glue, spray, wax, or tape?

The term "paste-up" implies that you are literally "pasting"

50

something into position—and that was certainly true in the past. But over the years, many different adhesives have been developed for the graphic arts.

Glue comes in a variety of configurations. The most widely used professional glues are rubber cement and spray adhesive. The former, which is a bit tricky to work with, provides the most durability. The latter can be hard on the lungs. In any case, the point is that if you use glue, you must be sure to leave no glue "unattended." If a spot of glue finds its way to the camera, it might pick up dust, hair, or lint. These imperfections will photograph as clearly as if they were part of the job.

Wax has become a very popular adhesive with those who do a great deal of paste-up. Waxing machines can be a hand-application type (about $50 for a unit) or an elaborate desk-top device ($400+). When using wax, the paste-up person applies a coating to the piece to be affixed, places it in position, and then "burnishes" it. This is done by placing an intermediate sheet of slippery paper over the paste-up and then rubbing it with a burnisher (a smooth plastic bone) to make the material underneath adhere.

The main disadvantage in using wax is that, with age, it mellows and loses its tackiness (though it may take several years for this to happen). Another disadvantage is that the equipment can be expensive.

Finally, for a "quickie" paste-up, many people use simple tape, the kind purchased in a drugstore. There is nothing wrong with this for the unprofessional, commercial user, but for magazine production, it would be unheard of. The same applies to glue sticks, which also are for amateurs.

Steps to the paste-up

The paste-up artist may or may not be a layout artist. What's the difference?

Some people feel that doing paste-up is a mechanical, tedious task, a skill rather than a creative art. Others demand that the paste-up person be creative—able to conceive of a design and then execute it on the paste-up table.

There is no "correct" definition of these jobs. But to set the record straight, the design aspects are considered "layout," while the actual mechanical assembly is called "paste-up."

All printed products have something in common: They start with an idea and end up as a product reproduced hundreds or thousands of times. Naturally, there are some intermediate steps that take place between the idea and the finished product.

Let's follow a job from the time the idea has been conceived to the time when it is ready for the camera (and subsequent printing activities). Of course, we're not discussing a creative jam session, just the steps that directly relate to the paste-up itself.

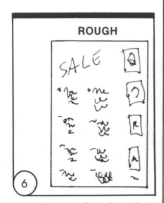

A rough scketch is just what the name implies—a very loose drawing of what the piece should look like. Here you can see that the page will have a big headline on the left, a vertical row of photos on the right, and copy on the lower left.

The rough sketch

The first step in transforming an idea into a printed product is the "rough sketch." This is also called a "thumbnail" in some shops, but the basics of the activity are the same: An artist (or editor or anybody with an idea) simply scratches out a very loose drawing of what the printed piece should look like. The rough sketch is named appropriately: Depending on the artist, you might not even be able to read the headlines on the page. Certainly, you wouldn't see any actual copy. But in our example (Illustration 6), the rough shows the idea quite well: This page will have a big headline on the left, a vertical row of photos on the right, and copy in the lower left.

The comprehensive

After the staff has its standard disagreement over the "rough," the next step in getting the idea across could be the comprehensive sketch, or "comp." According to the unwritten handbook of design and layout, a "comp" should show the product in a manner that resembles the finished piece as closely as possible (Illustration 7, next page). This can be done in several ways.

Years ago, creating a comp was an elaborate, lengthy task that required an artist to letter each character meticulously by hand, to show the illustrations (or photos) in reasonable detail, and to add color to show how the piece would look in print.

But time has become expensive, so now the comp might be lettered in one of the transfer letterings on the market, and the photos might be represented by actual photostats of the prints. But even this type of presentation is expensive. It is used most often by ad agencies that must present a "finished" idea to a customer.

Today it is more common either to do a "tight" sketch (a more detailed rough) or to skip the comp stage entirely and go right to the paste-up.

The dummy

After the type has been specified and set, the person in charge might decide to do an actual "dummy." The meaning of the word dummy, like the meaning of the word comp, has changed over the years. Originally, the dummy was a very sloppy paste-up from hot-metal proofs. The customer would cut and tape, rearrange and paste, and eventually get the typeset copy into a final position. The object was to work with a close facsimile of the actual typeset copy before the reproduction proofs were pasted into position. This would give the paste-up person an accurate, line-for-line guide to follow when preparing camera-ready paste-ups.

But today, the term dummy is used in several ways. For instance, many multipage products (magazines, catalogs) are planned by a pagination-type dummy. This is simply a series of sketches showing how the pages will be used, such as story "A" on pages one through five, or advertisements on pages 11, 14, and 19.

Regardless, we'll assume that you're using the term "dummy" in the classic sense. In that case, you'd be talking about a taped-together version of type, photos positions, and so on.

This kind of dummying is quite important if you do not perform paste-up functions in-house. There are always little problem areas of fit, position, or odd-copy breaks that will show up at this stage, and it's much better to work them out before a printer assembles the product.

If, on the other hand, you have in-house control, you might do as many others have done: skip the comp and skip the dummy. This decision depends on the complexity of your work and the aesthetic eyes of your paste-up personnel.□

CHAPTER 10

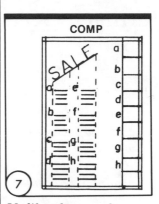

Unlike the rough sketch, the comprehensive sketch (or comp) shows the page more nearly as it will be when finished. Because of the time (which means money) involved, however, a comp is more likely to be a detailed "rough" or a stage skipped altogether.

GENERAL PASTE-UP TERMINOLOGY

*T*he term "paste-up" hangs on. It has given only a little ground to "mechanical" (which sounds like an adjective, but is used as a synonym for paste-up) and to "board."

When describing either a paste-up or a printed magazine page, he above terminology applies. The bleed area will, of course, be absent on the printed piece. (It will have been trimmed off.)

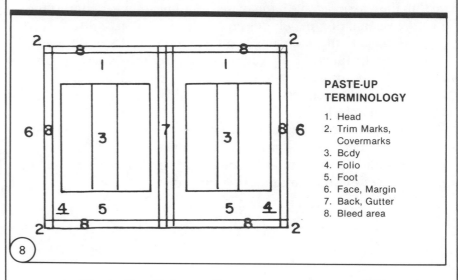

PASTE-UP TERMINOLOGY

1. Head
2. Trim Marks, Covermarks
3. Body
4. Folio
5. Foot
6. Face, Margin
7. Back, Gutter
8. Bleed area

As Illustration 8 shows, there are several areas of the paste-up that have names. Without getting overly esoteric, let's discuss each.

•*Head:* This is simply the top or upper area of the page. The term is used most often when someone says, "We jog this book to the head," which means that when the book or product is assembled during the bindery operation, a mechanical device raps each printed section at the tops of the pages to align them.

In the real world of paste-ups, the term "head" is used only to give someone a sense of geography, as in "Put this photo at the head." And, by the way, it is also an abbreviation for headline.

•*Trim marks or cornermarks:* Trim marks show the final size of the piece. They are a necessity for most paste-ups and can be used by the printer in two ways: First, when the paste-up is converted into a negative, the "stripper" will use them to position the page. Without trim marks (or some other more sophisticated form of indication), there is no way to tell exactly where the page should print. The stripper might position it too high or too low, and the final piece would show that error.

Second, in some operations, trim marks are actually printed on the paper and removed (trimmed, of course) during bindery by the cutter.

If it's not already obvious, we'll make it so: Trim marks should always be used. They should be as precise as possible (within one-sixty-fourth-inch isn't asking too much) and as thin as practical in order to provide an accurate line for others to follow in positioning and cutting.

How important can cornermarks be? Consider this situation:

Company X spent a lot of time and money to develop a very specific, graphic image for their corporation. They used "white space" (simply, open areas of white paper) generously. The objective, the concept—for which they dearly paid an advertising agency—was to impart a feeling of isolation, independence, and uniqueness.

The company followed most of the printing rules to the letter. But when they prepared the artwork for thousands of business cards, they simply pasted up their company name, logotype, and the names of their division managers on a board. Somehow somebody forgot to include any cornermarks. When the printer received the job, no mention had been made of the fact that the information on the business cards was to appear well below the middle point on the card—that is to say, that the top half of the card was to be blank.

The result? Thousands of cards in the trash bin. The president of the company, who signed the check paying the art studio that designed the cards, was furious. And all because of a lack of cornermarks.

The point is, if you have a specific idea of exactly where an image is to appear on a printed product, you must transmit that information to the printer.

•*Body:* This is the "live" area of the page. It is the area that can be used effectively, without risk of something printing in the fold or getting chopped off. Although this seems almost self-explanatory, there are a few critical subtleties. The body of a page has maximums that vary from printer to printer. The purpose of the maximums is to ensure that the body does not get dangerously close to the trim or bleed, or too close to the fold or backbone area (sometimes called the "gutter").

•*Folio:* This is the term used to denote information at the bottom of the page. That's usually the name of the product, the page number, and, sometimes, the date. It's a handy term. "No Folios" is easier to write than "No page number or date."

•*Foot:* Opposite of head. Some magazines and catalogs do "jog" to the foot, and this can be very important when you're considering partial-page inserts.

•*Face:* This is also called the "margin." It is the outer edge (the one not near the fold).

•*Back:* The term "back" is derived from the book-type product. But in saddle-bound material, it is often called the "gutter." In either case, it is an important "dead" area. And aesthetically, material can get too close to the gutter to be readable.

•*Bleed area:* A "bleed" is ink that is printed beyond the trim marks (usually one-eighth of an inch) and later trimmed off. As we said before, material can bleed off the face (margin), and it can also bleed off the head or foot.

Those are, basically, the idea-through-paste-up terms used in the magazine publishing business. However, the list is by no means definitive.

Windows and overlays

If you've ever seen professionally assembled magazine paste-ups, you are probably aware of a few more items that pop up on them. Two of them are windows and overlays. Illustration 9 shows their respective proper use. Not shown is the all-important tissue, which protects the overlay and the paste-up from dirt and damage.

This is a typical magazine paste-up with an overlay for a second color. Putting the items that will print in color on the overlay saves time later in the production cycle (at the stripping stage). If the printer requests windows for photos (red, orange, or black paper on the paste-up), use them: When the paste-up is converted to a film negative, the window becomes clear, and the photograph is stripped (taped) into it. If the printer states that he doesn't use windows, you would use a keyline (thin black line) to indicate the photo position.

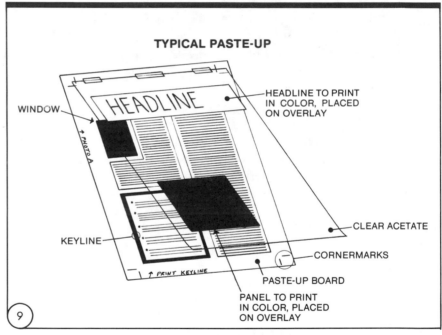

TYPICAL PASTE-UP

WINDOW

HEADLINE

HEADLINE TO PRINT IN COLOR, PLACED ON OVERLAY

↑ PHOTO A

CLEAR ACETATE

KEYLINE

CORNERMARKS

↑ PRINT KEYLINE

PASTE-UP BOARD

PANEL TO PRINT IN COLOR, PLACED ON OVERLAY

9

• *Window:* A piece of transluscent red paper, waxed or glued into position and trimmed to the exact printing size of the photo area. As mentioned before, any black or red item on the paste-up is identified by the camera as black. Photos are not normally put in place on the paste-up. Rather, a "window" is put down where the photo will eventually print.

The reason is this: The window will photograph as a black image. But the page will be shot as a negative piece of film. Thus, the area where the photo will print will appear as a "clear" area, or a window. Later, the photo will be shot as a halftone and can be taped directly behind this window.

Windows, however, are not universally used. Some printers use windows and will strip halftones into them at the prep stage. But others treat photos separately and prefer that no window be on the

56

board, or paste-up. Rather, they require that only a position-indication be put on the paste-up. The indication is normally a thin black line (a keyline, as it is called), forming a square or rectangle in the shape of the photo to be printed. There is no "best" way, and whichever your printer prefers should be suitable to you.

•*Keyline:* The keyline is marked "print keyline." It means that the black line will print. The alternative is to write "drop keyline," in which case the printer knows that the keyline is only to indicate position, and will not print.

•*Overlay:* The overlay, another paste-up technique, is used to break out portions of the page. Overlays have several purposes. Say you want a square tint of ink to print over a block of copy. So, you take a piece of acetate, tape it to the paste-up board, and put a "window" on the acetate. Later, the acetate is shot separately. Then, the printer can put the tint on the window and "double burn" the type and tint together.

Another use of the overlay is for colored elements. Let's say you want to print all headlines and subheads in one color and the rest of the text in another color. It is standard practice to put all the material that will be printed in color on the overlay and all the black-printed material on the paste-up.

Some printers prefer overlays; others do not. There is no universal procedure; whichever your printer recommends should be fine.

Both windows and overlays are preparation activities and will be discussed in detail in that section.□

CHAPTER 11

PASTE-UP TOOLS AND GENERAL PROCEDURES

There are many acceptable tools and techniques available to paste-up people. The more popular are those listed here:

•Wax: Major manufacturers of automatic waxing machines include Schaefer, Goodkin, and Artwaxer. In addition, LectroStik produces a hand-operated waxing device.

Although wax is suited to virtually all magazine production, there are a few special cases where it is a problem. If, for example, a paste-up is to be subjected to significant heat, the wax will melt and ruin it. Or, if a person has to work with very thin, porous paper, the wax—which is applied in a melted state—could pass through the paper, damaging it beyond use.

•Burnisher: This is little more than a smooth plastic "bone" used to rub down waxed material. When it is rubbed hard, the wax distends and is forced into contact with the pores in the paper.

The garden variety burnishers are white plastic, with one end tapered more than the other. The laws of physics dictate that the narrower end tends to apply much more pressure (and thereby adhesion) than the wider end.

•Slip sheet: For practical purposes, the paste-up professional would never burnish directly on any piece of type or any other paste-up element. Rather, the professional would use a slippery sheet of paper. In the author's opinion, nothing is better suited for this than the blue sheets found in a package of Letraset, the transfer-lettering available in most art stores. It is smooth and will not give you any trouble (the way a sheet of normal tissue will).

•Exacto knife: The venerable Number 11 Exacto is, by far, the most common knife in use on the paste-up table. Its main drawback is that when the tip breaks off, the blade is nearly useless. Some people solve this problem by buying a lot of blades. Others use a $25 honing stone to sharpen dull blades. Still others purchase surgical steel blades (made for the medical profession), which just happen to fit into an Exacto holder.

•Ruler: Ideally, the ruler is metal and reads in both picas and inches. The benefit of pica measurement will be discussed under the section on scaling photos.

•Scale: See the chapter "How to Scale Photos", discussed later in this section.

•Tissue: This is used for covering paste-ups. Most people use cellophane tape to keep the tissue in place. The paste-up tissue is another place on which to write specific instructions to the printer.

•Technical pens: There are a variety of these on the market.

Over the past few decades, they have almost totally replaced "quill" type pens, which were metallic renditions of bird feathers. It should go without saying, but won't: The difference between a technical pen and a ballpoint pen is night and day. Ballpoints do not have the density, consistency, or quality necessary for lithographic reproduction.

•*Heat:* When you need to remove a well-burnished piece of waxed copy from a paste-up, place the sheet or board on a warm portion of a waxing machine or other hot surface. Even holding it beneath a light bulb will do the trick. If you use this trick, the "stuck" piece will easily be removed, but so will all other pieces. So, once you've gotten the culprit off the paste-up, allow the sheet to cool; otherwise, everything else will fall off, too.

•*T-square:* The T-square, the basic tool of the paste-up person, comes in many varieties, with the following qualities:

Aluminum units tend to oxidize and occasionally leave residue on the paste-up, but they are inexpensive.

Plastic devices usually have a clear edge, which some people like because it allows them to see what they are working over. However, plastics tend to become sliced up when used near razors or Exactos.

Stainless steel T-squares are the Cadillacs of the drawing board. Although they can't be seen through, they are durable and leave no residue on the work.

Units such as the "Glide-Liner" are also available. Basically, these are T-squares that are attached to the drawing board and easily manipulated with one hand. Although some people consider them less accurate than a conventional T-square, others swear by them (or at them).

•*Triangle:* Like T-squares, these come in plastic, aluminum, and stainless steel. The same qualities mentioned above apply to them.

•*Kneaded eraser:* Commonly called the "needed eraser" because people keep losing them. This is a blue, pliable eraser with one endearing quality: It leaves little or no residue on the paste-up. In comparison, a pencil-type eraser does its job by wearing itself down.

•*Spray glue:* A popular version is Scotch Spray Mount, but there are others on the market. Some shops use spray glue exclusively, while others don't use it at all. Generally, it is not considered an "equal" to a waxing machine. But there are cases, such as when you need to temporarily glue a very thin sheet of paper, where spray glue will outperform any other adhesive.

•*Tint sheets:* Many art departments carry a library of "tints"

CHAPTER 12

59

that can be applied directly to a paste-up.

This discussion cannot be extensive enough to include the full pro-con debate of whether this is logical or of high quality, and so on. Suffice to say that a tint applied with conventional stripping methods is far superior to any tint that is applied directly to the paste-up. Any tint, halftone or other element applied to the paste-up must pass through the lens of a camera. On the other hand, conventional stripping of tints and halftones is a direct, non-lens method of duplicating the desired effect.

Once again, the paste-up/prep connection surfaces. Refer to the prep section for more detail on the subject.

•*Spray fix:* This is the generic term for a protective finish that can be sprayed onto artwork, drawings, or other items that might otherwise smear. (Tip: There are those who swear that hairspray is the same stuff, and cheaper, too!)

•*French curve:* Just to make sure your vocabulary is competitive, let's mention the french curve. This is nothing more than a piece of plastic with a lot of curves used to draw arbitrary curves. It is a difficult tool to describe, but when you need one, you will know exactly what it should look like.

Cutting corrections into paste-ups

As we mentioned in the typesetting section, some buyers (and in-house typesetters) choose to rerun all of their copy, rather than "cut and paste" a few correction lines into the final copy. But there are very valid reasons to use the techniques of cutting corrections into paste-ups.

The most obvious reason is this: If only a line or two of copy is bad, why go through the time and expense of a rerun? And, just as important, if the job is already pasted up before the error is found, cutting in a few corrections also saves the task of redoing the entire paste-up.

Naturally, there are good and bad ways to cut in these corrections. A bit of history:

Years ago, virtually all type was set "hot." That meant that each line was cast in metal, inked, and "pulled" on high-quality stock called "repro," or reproduction paper. Thus, the term "repro proof." That material was hard to handle. It smeared, tore at the slightest tug, and couldn't easily be cleaned of glue or wax (if the paste-up artist got a bit sloppy).

Today, the problems associated with hot-metal type are confined to the few shops that still use it and to those firms using strike-on typesetting. Most type is now set on photographic film, which doesn't smear and can easily be cleaned of stray wax when pasting up. That makes cutting a correction into a paste-up a simple task.

Here's the method that many professionals feel works best:

When ordering a few random lines to be typeset, have additional space inserted between them. For instance, if you have a two-liner to insert, have both lines set at the same leading as the original and then have an extra line (or two) of space inserted before the next correction is typed. To make it easier still, have an "identification" line set above each correction. Example: "Page four, top right." This will make the correction easier to identify when you are mechanically inserting it.

To cut the correct copy in, put the paste-up on a light table. If you're using a relatively thin paste-up board (as you should be), you'll have no trouble seeing through the type when you place the correction directly over the old type. And that's the trick: With a T-square, and relying on the transparent quality of photographic paper, position the waxed correction directly on the paste-up and align it. Now, with the T-square as a guide, use a blade to slice through the correction paper—and the original copy—above the correction, below it, and at both sides.

You can now lift the correction galley from the paste-up. The corrected lines themselves, if you waxed them as usual, will remain on the copy. You could call it quits at this point and burnish the correction down, but there's a better way.

If you leave the correction pasted over the original copy, you create three potential problems: 1) The correction may slide around a little when you burnish it; 2) it may cast a shadow when the page is shot and thus create more work for the opaquer; and 3) the adhesive may collect dirt or dust that will later photograph (Illustration 10).

So, at this point, pull the correction off the paste-up. Because you also sliced through the original, you can also remove that piece from the paste-up and then reinsert the correction. The original copy will have a precise "hole" to accept the correction. It can't slide around, and it's not "stacked up," so chances are you haven't increased your opaquing time.

Because phototype doesn't smear, you can now clean up the excess wax (which may have transferred to some of the uncorrected original copy) with a soft cloth wetted with a little bit of rubber cement thinner, if needed.

There you have it: If you make your cuts accurately and use sharp blades, you won't be able to tell just where the correction was inserted.□

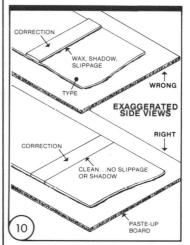

There are right and wrong ways of placing corrections on paste-ups. The wrong way will cost you money or information: Dirt creates work for the printer, while slippage means your correction may cover up the wrong line or fall off.

HOW TO
SCALE PHOTOS

Of all the simple skills in graphic arts, you would hope that scaling a photo would be one of them. But over the years, this author has come to believe that no other "simple" skill is as difficult for the newcomer to master.

Yet scaling a photo involves nothing more than elementary math. If the original photo is four-inches tall and you want it to be two-inches tall, what should it be "shot at" on camera? Fifty percent? Obviously!

Unfortunately, it isn't so obvious. In this section, we'll start from scratch and describe both of the proper methods of scaling (or, as some say, "sizing") a photo, a piece of art, or a headline. In addition, we'll discuss some of the common mistakes that are made all too frequently.

The tools

Although "simple math" can obviously be done on a pocket calculator, most professional graphic-type people still use the inexpensive, mechanical plastic "reduction wheel." The name is deceiving in that a reduction wheel (Illustration 11) is also used for enlargements.

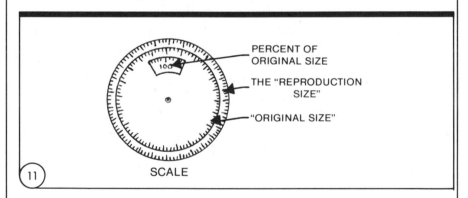

PERCENT OF ORIGINAL SIZE

THE "REPRODUCTION SIZE"

"ORIGINAL SIZE"

11 SCALE

What does the wheel do? Basically, it is a stripped-down version of a conventional slide rule. Fortunately, you need no knowledge of calculus or high math to use it.

The wheel has three reference points: 1) The outer wheel, a series of numbers that represent the "reproduction size" of the item being scaled; 2) the inner wheel, a set of numbers that reflects the current size of the item being scaled; and 3) the window, a hole in the inner wheel that will show the percentage of reduction or enlargement that the cameraperson will use when shooting the item in question.

Other common tools used in photo scaling:

•*Ruler:* Most people prefer one that measures in both inches and picas. The reason people like pica-measurement ability has nothing to do with typesetting. Rather, picas can be a handy measurement increment. You will learn this on the job when you try to scale something to a reproduction size of one-sixth of an inch.

•*Tissue:* The same tissue used on a paste-up is handy for use in protecting photos and for writing instructions.

•*Marker or grease pencil:* For writing on the edge of a photo, a marker or a grease pencil is handy. However, some people write all pertinent information on the tissue itself. But beware: Never write on a tissue that is over a photo, and never write using "hard" pressure on the back of a photo. Both can damage the photo's smooth finish and both of these imperfections will photograph later on.

Now, rather than attempt to "tell" you how to scale a photo, let's go through the process on a hypothetical job, step by step. In our example, we will use an "oddball" photo, one that wasn't even shot properly in the first place. If you don't fully understand the procedure the first time through, just read it over again and practice with a reduction wheel. By the time you fully understand what goes on here, you should know almost all you need to know about scaling a photo.

Step one: Aesthetic judgment

The first step is easy. Look at the photo. How do you like it? Our example (Illustration 12) shows a photo that was, in all probability, handled poorly by the photographer. Unless this person was standing on an angle, someone tilted the camera. Although cameras supposedly don't lie, the lithographic process does. If you think this photo was shot improperly, now is the time to correct it.

How? This brings up one of the fundamentals of photo scaling: You need to use only what you want to use. Just because this photo happens to be cocked to the right doesn't mean you have to print it that way. Thus, you may want to "crop" the photo differently. Cropping means using less of the photo than is available and translating those wishes into commands for the litho cameraperson.

In looking at the example, you may agree that we will want to use the center portion of the photo and crop off the outside edges. If we use a small enough portion of the center, we will also be able to rotate that portion of the photo prior to printing it, thereby creating a more pleasing aesthetic appearance.

Step two: Will it fit?

Next, look at the area into which the photo is supposed to be printed. The question is, can it be done?

This is an eyeball-method of determining whether you're barking up the right tree. Let's say the layout artist indicated that our photo must fit into a very horizontal area. Illustration 13 shows how it might appear. Although there is nothing mechanically wrong with printing a photo as it is shown here, is it okay with you, and your publisher, and your art director?

Probably not. The determination to make here is whether you can aesthetically fit a square into a rectangle (or vice versa). If the photo in Illustration 13 looks abominable to you, then you cannot

12

13

scale it. Rather, you must redo the layout of the page and come up with a more-vertical space in which to print the photo.

Step three: Measure it

So, let's assume that we aren't going to try to fit a square peg into a rectangular hole. If anything, our sample photo is more suitable to a vertically shaped reproduction area than to a horizontally shaped one.

To take the measurements, just use your pica ruler. Although a ruler that measures in inches is suitable for most purposes, things get tough when you try to measure something smaller than an inch. Because picas are much smaller than inches, they are handier to work with.

(And don't be misled by the proportion wheel itself. Although it probably has everything marked in inches, the wheel is mathematically independent of this base-12 unit of measure. It works just as well in picas, meters, or miles.)

For a simple photo, we merely would measure the vertical and horizontal dimensions. But the photo we have here isn't so simple. If we have already determined that using the full height or width would make the photo appear just as cocked as it already is, then we must determine what the usable live area of the photo will be if we want to straighten it out.

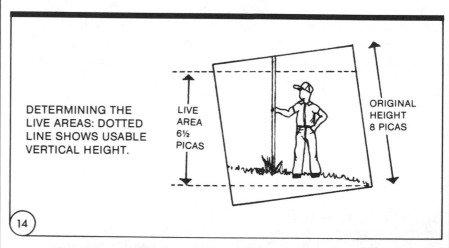

DETERMINING THE
LIVE AREAS: DOTTED
LINE SHOWS USABLE
VERTICAL HEIGHT.

LIVE
AREA
6½
PICAS

ORIGINAL
HEIGHT
8 PICAS

14

Illustration 14 shows that we are starting to straighten out this photo. Keep in mind that the dotted lines in this illustration are not drawn on the photo. That is a no-no. Rather, they are drawn on the tissue that is protecting the photo.

And keep in mind something mentioned earlier: that one never draws on or puts pressure on a photo. Although the tissue has these lines drawn on it (and the lines can be solid, of course), the tissue must not be on the photo when they are being drawn.

To write on the tissue, you simply put small tick marks at its edges, flip the photo away, lay the tissue down on a flat surface, and draw the lines. If you have taped the tissue to the back of the photo, everything will be in order when you flip it back down. Then you will have something that resembles Illustration 14.

Now, what do we have? Instead of the original height of the photo (eight picas), we have established a new usable height (six-and-one-half picas). The lines on the tissue are parallel to the visual effects of the photo itself. Obviously, the live area of what we consider the usable photo is less than the height of the original, which cannot be used without the cocking effect.

In summary, if this photo hadn't been badly handled by the photographer, we would have needed to measure only the true dimensions of the photo's image. Instead, we have literally had to create a different live area. This can be done to straighten out a photo or to use a small segment of a photo when the background or whole image is not wanted.

To continue with our measurements, we will now consider the photo as horizontally shaped (rather than vertically or squarely shaped). But Illustration 15 indicates that this photo is to be printed in a vertical format. How does a horizontal photo fit into a vertical shape? More cropping, that's how.

In the above procedure, we established the usable, or live, vertical area of the photo. We must now determine which dimension relates to which. Knowing which dimension to scale first is instinctive to the seasoned photo scaler. But you aren't seasoned, so how do you know what to do?

Try this exercise: What if the live area of Illustration 14 were as tall as the reproduction area in Illustration 15? To put it another

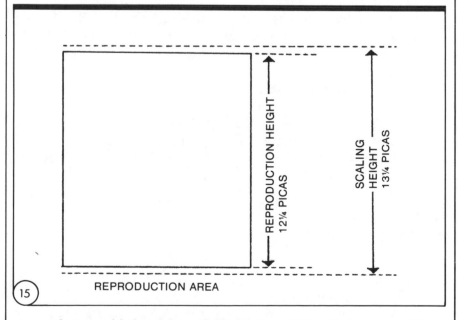

REPRODUCTION HEIGHT 12¼ PICAS

SCALING HEIGHT 13¼ PICAS

15   REPRODUCTION AREA

way, what would the shape of Illustration 14 be if we enlarged it to the vertical height of Illustration 15?

The vertical live areas of both would be the same, but Illustration 14 would be wider than Illustration 15, right? Right. Small rectangles have the same relative shape when you make them bigger.

What this means is that we can't measure the horizontal shape of Illustration 14 and scale it to the horizontal shape of Illustration 15. If we did, our photo would still be a rectangularly shaped element floating in the middle of Illustration 15, which then would have unused space above and below the reproduction area.

It all boils down to determining *which* measurement to scale. In our case, we want to enlarge the height of the live area of the photo to the height of the reproduction area. This will mean a lot of the horizontal image in Illustration 14 will not fit. It will be cropped off, and that's what this whole exercise is all about.

Step 4: Determine a scaling height

If you're still with me, you now know that we want to scale the live height of the original to the reproduction height. What is the reproduction height? It is simply the intended dimension that the photo will eventually fill.

But it is not what we will scale to. In this business, you must always allow a little breathing room. If we scaled the photo to the exact dimension it will be printed at, we'd soon find out that 1) cameras aren't always that accurate, 2) scales aren't either, 3) neither are we, and 4) stripping techniques require a bit of overlap on these kinds of dimensions.

Therefore, we will try to determine a *scaling* height rather than a reproduction height.

The scaling height is a wing-it figure. In most cases, assume that the stripper will need about one-sixteenth of an inch in all dimensions to ensure a proper fit. If you are using a pica ruler, call it a half-pica on all sides.

So, finally, we've determined that our live area—six-and-a-half picas on our original—will be scaled not to the reproduction height of 12-1/4 picas, but to the scaling height of 13-1/4 picas (Illustration 15). Remember, this is a wing-it determination. If all things went well all the time, we could scale it to 12-1/2 picas and still have it fit.

Scale the photo

At last we can scale the photo. On the inner scale, locate 16½ picas. Align that figure with 13-1/4 picas on the outer scale and look in the window. There it is: 204 percent (or 203.846, if you want to check it with a calculator).

What if it looks like 203.4 percent? Always use the larger figure. It will still be 204 percent when you write it down. Round up, not down. Rounding down reduces your chance of having it fit.

The readback

Assuming that all things are going well, we can now do the readback—that is, we can determine how much useful live *width* we will get out of the original photo if it must fit into the shape of Illustration 15.

The wheel is still set on 204 percent. The question now is, at that setting, if the reproduction width (Illustration 16) is 10-1/2 picas, what width should we draw on the tissue to indicate the live width of the cropped photo?

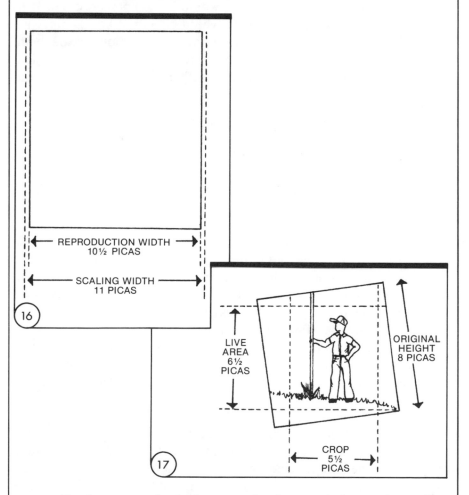

On the outer wheel (the reproduction area), locate the scaling width. As before, we will make the scaling width reflect a figure somewhat larger than the actual reproduction width.

Let's use 11 picas this time. Locate the number 11 on the outer wheel and read the number that it aligns with. You should see a figure just shy of five-and-a-half picas. That will be our live width area for the original photo, and the measurement that we will put on the tissue.

Illustration 17 shows that measurement drawn on the tissue. Now, that's it. If you've done everything right, this particular photo, scaled this particular way and cropped as we have cropped it, should fit nicely into our intended reproduction area if shot at 204 percent.

Stats and other line shots

Scaling a photo is slightly different from scaling nonphoto material, such as a headline or a piece of line artwork. While the photo must slightly overfill its intended area (window, keyline, and so on), a headline should be scaled to its actual dimensions. In other words, if you have a piece of art that is five picas wide and you want to print it 10 picas wide, the scaling would be 200 percent even. If it happened to be a photo, the scaling would be more like 204 percent.

The bottom line: When scaling photos, you should scale them to a size slightly larger than the space that you want to fill. When scaling non-photo material (anything other than a halftone), you should scale to their exact sizes.

Common photo scaling errors

An improperly scaled photo is trouble, and that usually means money and time. Although it may not be part of your job to check the scalings of each halftone, you are probably involved in proof-checks and alteration costs.

But because of the often-muddy quality of BPs (brownprints, bluelines, and so on), a poorly fitting halftone (for example, one that is supposed to butt a rule but doesn't quite make it) might not be apparent until the job is running on the press. Fix a few bad halftones on the press some time, and you're sure to become a nasty person to work with. The cost of a single press plate, holding time, and stripping could easily be $100, $300 or a lot more.

It's better to prevent the problem in the first place. You can do that by showing your staff where they're likely to make common mistakes. Here are the most frequently made errors, and why they're made:

1. *Too small:* The photo just doesn't completely fill the window or keyline as it should. This mistake has the highest occurrence rate of all. One simple rule applies here—and I've said it before: Never scale a photo to exactly fill a hole. The reason for this is that the halftone film must be stripped into the intended area, and even a fraction of a percent in variation will make the fit impossible. Also, don't make the mistake of rounding off to a lower percentage. If your reading is between two percentages, use the higher one.

A properly scaled photo normally allows for a shy one-sixth-of-an-inch (or a shy half-pica) on all sides, to give the stripper a bit of necessary leeway.

2. *Too big:* This mistake is attributable either to carelessness or to a lack of basic photo scaling knowledge. To prevent it and most

68

other mistakes, devise a "scaling test" for your staff. Give them several photos to scale to several different sizes, check their results, and then spend training time with the people who score less than perfect.

3. *One-dimensional fit:* Here again is a simple mistake that occurs when a photo is scaled to the wrong dimension. For example, a tall, narrow photo can be scaled to fit a square window, but the width of the original and the window are what determine the final percentage. The height of the window will dictate where the original is to be cropped.

Again, give your people tests, and you'll know who needs retraining.

4. *Just right:* After scaling a few hundred photos to overfill their intended areas, an artist may assume that he or she should do the same with line material, such as a headline. But that makes no more sense than shooting a same-size stat at 103 percent. Line shots are made at their exact percentage requirements.

5. *Flopped:* This is the easiest of all the scaling problems to prevent. Just be sure to write the instructions and percentages as close as practical to a reproduction area of the photo. To do this, you may need to tape a piece of paper over a nonimage area, but it's worth the effort. Later, when the stripper gets the film, he'll have your handwriting in front of him. When instructions aren't close enough to a reproduction area, they're often omitted from the final film or sliced off before stripping.

Another way to ensure that a photo will be easily identified by the printer and not flopped is to use photo tags (discussed later in this section). Then, be sure to advise your printer that the tags should be shot along with the photo.□

USING TAGS TO CONTROL PHOTOS AND ART

As your probably know, a lot can go wrong at the printing plant. Because you're not the only customer, it's possible that your material will become mixed with that of another. And nobody's perfect—so you run the constant risk of either being misunderstood (in your technical communications with the printer) or of forgetting to pass along some important information to him.

One way to help avoid these problems is to make sure that all your material—each photo, loose headline, or piece of artwork—is "tagged" before you release it to the printer. The tag needn't be an elaborate device. In fact, a two-and-a-half by five-inch sheet of bond paper, imprinted with key pieces of information, will do the trick just fine.

Feel free to copy this photo tag. Have a batch printed and use them to identify your photos. It will keep your instructions clear and your photos your photos. (It is mighty easy to mix up a group of my shots in a print plant).

Publisher: _____

Publication: _____

Issue: _____

Page and Key No.'s: _____

☐ Halftone   ☐ Duotone

☐ Line Neg   ☐ Paper Pos

☐ Process Sep ☐ _____

PERCENTAGE: _____ **%**

Notes/Special Instructions:

_____

_____

_____

_____

_____

_____

_____

By: _____

⑱

How tags are used

In practice, you can make it policy to tape the tag to each piece of material that you release. Photos, for example, can have a

70

slip of paper taped to the bottom margin or taped to the back so that most of the tag appears when the photo is viewed from the front. That way, all the information will be shot on camera along with the photo. The printer will then have a negative that includes your name, the page number, and any other instructions (cropping, position) that you include.

The photo/art tag shown here (Illustration 18) represents one suggested format. Copy it if you want, insert your company name (logo, address, and so on), and have a suitable quantity printed. Pads are even more handy.

In practice, you need only check the appropriate boxes, fill in the percentage (100 percent if the material is being shot same-size), and jot down any special instructions. Cropping information is best given directly on the photo tissue (or in the margins of the photo if your don't use the tissue). And, if you don't want to mark up the original, you can simply write, "Crop from top only" (or from top and right).

Also note the word, "By..." On the bottom right of the tag. If you're having trouble identifying the person who constantly scales photos poorly, this little addendum will quickly reveal the culprit.

How and why to use transmittal sheets

One of the routine aspects of dealing with any printer is getting the material into his or her hands. For small, simple jobs, that can be as easy as picking up the phone and saying the work is ready. But for complex work composed of many or hundreds of parts, you'll often find plenty of room for error.

Typical problems

There are countless ways for the transmission of material to give you trouble. They include, but aren't limited to, the following:

1.*Material accidently not shipped:* The person who organizes material for the actual delivery to the printer has quite a task on his hands. So, it's not uncommon for that person to inadvertently forget to include a photo, headline, or a piece of artwork. (After all, people are human.)

The result is that when the printer's crew dips into the package, it will spend time looking for something that isn't there. Worse yet, it's common for the offending party to deny the mistake until he's proven dead wrong. This confusion slows the job and often builds ill will between the buyer and the seller.

2. *Material misplaced at printer:* But even when all the material is included, who's to say the printer won't lose it? And when he does, his first reaction will be to ask you where the piece is. (Printers are human, too.) You will insist that the piece in question

was shipped, and he will gently suggest that you don't know what you're talking about, and you'll both build some more ill will until the missing component mysteriously reappears.

3. *Material not returned:* Even if you're lucky enough to have kept track of everything while the job was being produced, your downfall may come when your work is returned. Whether it's art, negatives, positives, or separations, it can be lost.

This can be a particularly sticky situation: Do you (or your staff) actually check to see that each insignificant or useless piece of art is in the package that the printer returns? Or does this sound familiar:

A job that you produced six months ago included an advertisement, which suddenly must be returned to the advertiser. You check the (still-unopened?) package, and the piece isn't in there, although everything else seems to be in order. When you call the printer, however, he says that the entire job was returned. His "records" can even prove it. So then you call the advertiser and explain that at this late date you can't be liable, etc. All this can be avoided with some paperwork.

Add some paperwork; reduce the errors

These problems can all be reduced or even eliminated entirely with the use of transmittal sheets. These forms do take time to fill out, but they can help both you and your printer to spot trouble quickly and resolve minor problems immediately.

The sample transmittal sheet in this chapter (Illustration 19) will do the job for you. You're welcome to duplicate it and to try it out. Here's how it works:

Note that this sheet states that all material listed must be returned to the publisher after the job is produced. If you don't already have that understanding with your printer, now is a good time to get things straightened out. There just aren't many good reasons for you to let the printer keep your material.

In addition to that information, the form includes space for some self-explanatory notes: who you are, who they are, and what you are producing. There is also a small box for someone in your plant to check when the material is returned. (More on that later.)

To use this form, you need only a little bit of time. Sure, the job is late and there's not a second to spare, but that's the kind of pressure that causes those unexplainable disappearances. You can spend the extra time now with the transmittal sheet or later while you search for a lost negative, but the fact is you *will* spend the time.

In filling out the form, remember that unless each piece of material is noted, you will have no record of its existence.

The column titled "Form" should be simple enough to complete. Some publishers use letters to designate the forms, while others

In addition to keeping everyone informed as to who was sent what, a transmittal record of each item sent to the printer comes in handy later on. It can help you verify that everything you sent to the printer has come back.

Transmittal Record_____

PUBLICATION:_____ COMPANY:_____

ISSUE:_____ DATE:_____

SHIPPED TO:_____ SHIPPED VIA:_____

FORM	PAGE	NO. PIECES OF:			PHOTO IDENT	DESCRIPTION	INSTRUCTIONS	√
		Negs	Art	Pix				

call them "Cover," "Body-1," "Signature 4A," and so forth. But rather than invent your own labeling, why not use your printer's terms? That way, you'll both be talking the same language, and the transmittal forms will be that much more useful.

The next column, "Page No.," needs no explanation, but we'll throw in a hint: In both this column and the form column, use ditto marks to cut your workload. For example, if there are five items for page three, just put ditto (quote) marks beneath the first "three." Then, in order to mark the place where you begin talking about the next page or form, skip a complete line or two and toss in a few asterisks to clearly indicate the break.

The remaining columns should be filled out with as much detail as necessary. You must always put a number in one of the "Photo/Neg/Art" columns, and it's a good idea to always include at least a brief description of the component. If you use identification numbers for photos, also include them on the sheet (even though you've already used them on the photo tags). The easiest "Photo Ident" is to use "page" (such as 55) followed by "position" (such as B), which is abbreviated, 55-B—page 55, photo position B.

As a final photo note, you might also record the percentage, cropping instructions, and duotone or halftone notes in the "Instruction" column.

Your own experience should tell you just how much information to include on the sheet. If you want to go all the way, your sheet might include all the details entered in Illustration 20.

You can use your personal shorthand to fill out a transmittal sheet, as long as the printer understands what you mean.

FORM	PAGE	Negs	Art	Pix	PHOTO IDENT	DESCRIPTION	INSTRUCTIONS
B	85	1				BASIC PG. NEG	(EDITORIAL STRIP)
"	"		1			"HOELER" ADV.	SHOOT + STRIP
"	"			2	85-1 85-2	"HOELER" PIX	" " " (#T's)
"	"		1			"HOELER" KEY NO.	STRIP # 352-M
"	"			1	85-3	PIX OF M. GARDNER	SHOOT + STRIP (H.T.)
					*	*	*
B	86	1				BASIC PG. NEG	(EDITORIAL STRIP)

(20)

How the printer can use the sheet

After you have filled out this form, what happens? Well, if your printer is sharp, he'll use a copy of it to review your material before he begins working. That way, if he notices that you mention a piece of art that he doesn't have, he can call you right away. Naturally, the transmittal sheet won't prove that the art didn't fall out of the package in the restroom, but it will quickly identify that it isn't now where it should be.

The printer can also use a copy of the sheet to assist him in compiling your material later on. And, when the job is completed, he can use your original transmittals as his final checklist. Then, if he returns everything that you say you've given him, he's in the clear.

How the publisher can use the sheet

But that's not all. You, too, will have retained several copies of the sheet. When the material re-enters your plant, take the time to have someone go through it piece by piece, recording the return of each piece. Note the "check-mark" column on the form. This activity should take place the instant the material arrives. If you can put it off for a minute, then you will put if off for a month.

Now, if anything is missing, you can call the printer immediately and have him search for the lost piece. If he's ever going to find it, it will be now—not six months from now when he's forgotten that the piece ever existed. Also, if he can't find the missing component, now is the time to settle the matter, with replacement, credit, or cash.

Paperwork: Is it worth it?

As stated earlier, this type of activity does add to the time you put into each job. But when all is said and done, it can save you a lot of scrambling and disputes later on. It adds one more element of control to your system, and it is usually appreciated by your printer.

Some paste-up time savers

Trick 1: A loose-corner sticker. Many times while you're inspecting a paste-up, you will notice that a corner of copy is loose. You know that that piece of copy is pretty well attached, but you might not have an easy answer for fixing the loose corner. Here's a quick remedy that takes no special equipment and will prevent you from pulling off a large piece of copy when fixing a small area.

You make the "tool" by running a small piece of paper several times through your waxer. If you allow the paper to cool between passes through the machine, you can quickly build up a thick coat of wax on one side. Then, next time you notice a loose corner, slide the waxed piece under the trouble spot, lay a sheet of tissue paper (or any clean sheet that's available) over the loose spot, and press down firmly. Now, slide the waxed sheet out. Some of the adhesive will have transferred to the loose corner. Burnish as usual, and it's stuck.

Trick 2: Rulers as dividers: This one's as old as the hills, but it works, and some of your new people might not have seen it.

Take any ruler and line it up between two parallel vertical lines. To divide into three, you could use the "one" and "12" as references. Make a mark at the "four" and "eight," and there you have it: division.□

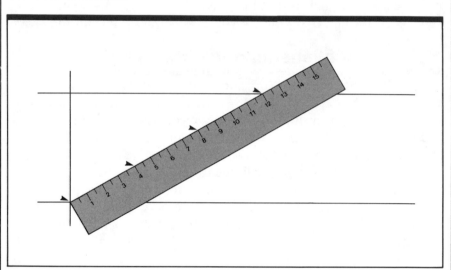

POSITIVE PASTE-UP: WHAT IT ACHIEVES

A fairly recent development in the preparation stage that significantly reduces costs and increases efficiency is "assembly in contact positives." The object of this system is to eliminate the camera stage in shooting paste-ups while reducing the time required to "strip" (or assemble) a job.

Conventional paste-ups

Before I explain contact paste-ups, let's review the process of reproducing a standard, board-type mechanical.

Type, artwork, and, in some cases, screened halftone photographs are commonly pasted, glued, or waxed into position on all types of material. Some firms use thin preprinted "blueline" boards, which have trim marks, gutters, and column positions indicated in blue nonphotographic ink. Others use one-eighth-inch thick illustration board for their paste-ups. But most shops that have any kind of volume will go for a thin, preprinted sheet.

Type can be pasted directly over old copy—and dirt can lie beneath elements of type or art. In short, the paste-up can be a pretty messy creature and still perform adequately during later production stages.

The actual assembly of the material varies, too. While one department might rely on standard drawing boards, another will use light tables. These allow the indication lines to show through, facilitating a quicker, more accurate placement of copy.

The paste-up is then sent to the camera department, where it is shot and converted into a film negative. The negative, in turn, is stripped into the "form," or "sides" or "flats." The task of stripping each page involves the visual registration of the cornermarks, which were drawn (or printed) on the original and now appear on the film negative.

What the positive paste-up achieves

As I said at the beginning of this chapter, two time-consuming activities that are part of the "normal" paste-up are circumvented in the positive-contact paste-up: the camera operation, which is replaced by direct off-camera contact exposures, and the visual aspect of stripping, which is replaced by mechanical alignment. Because this significantly reduces the amount of time needed to do a job, it also reduces cost.

Before explaining how positive paste-up works, however, I must explain some of the equipment needed to do the job.

Requirements of the positive paste-up

Contact-type paste-ups aren't necessarily difficult to create, but they do have some restrictions and some minor equipment requirements. First, let's discuss equipment.

•*Light table:* As previously mentioned, many studios already rely on light tables for paste-up. It's nice for normal paste-ups, but it's an absolute requirement for positive-type mechanicals.

•*Punch:* The punched holes used in positives are one key to reducing stripping costs. For a firm to get started in positives, a highly accurate multiholed punch is required to prepare film and acetate (better yet, Mylar) for use.

•*Mylar or acetate:* Sheets of this material entirely replace the "boards" or sheets used in standard paste-ups. Although acetate isn't cheap, keep in mind that it needn't be preprinted with corner-marks or column indications.

•*Registration pins:* These are not expensive, and each drawing station, contact frame, and so on, must be equipped with them.

•*Master grid:* Again, each drawing or paste-up station needs to be equipped with an accurate master grid of the typical page. A master would include gutter indications, folio positions, live area, and possibly standard layout positions for often-used elements.

•*Other equipment:* If you wanted to contact your paste-ups to the negative stage, the operation would require a suitable contact frame for converting positives into film-negative form. Above the contact frame would be a transformer-controlled "point light source," which is the graphic arts exposure lamp. Because most publishers and studios will forever leave that job in the printer's hands, we won't discuss such equipment requirements in great detail.

The equipment listed above is only what most operations would have to acquire to do positives. We have assumed that the firm interested in converting to positives would already have access to high-quality, resin-coated typesetting paper.

This paper is a bit more expensive than the inexpensive stabilization sheets—and the processing equipment it requires can cost between $3,000 and $11,000. However, it is the only paper suitable for contact paste-ups.

As you may have guessed (and will soon read), this entire process is based on passing light through the paste-up itself. Stabilization sheets, which are relatively thick, hamper light transmission. Furthermore, they are not as consistent or as dense as resin-coated paper, and they do not give as clear an image.

Positive paste-ups: How they work

The best way to see how a positive paste-up works is to follow one from start to finish. As we move from one production step to the next, those aspects that the paste-up person should look for will

POSITIVE PASTE-UP: WHAT IT ACHIEVES

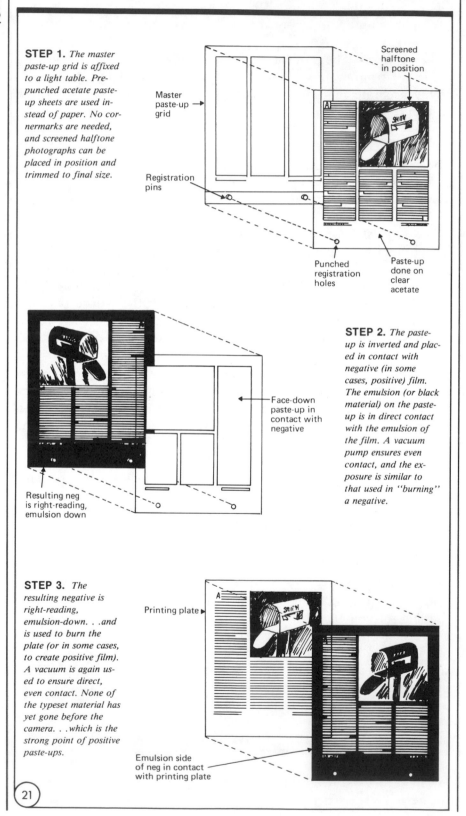

STEP 1. *The master paste-up grid is affixed to a light table. Pre-punched acetate paste-up sheets are used instead of paper. No cornermarks are needed, and screened halftone photographs can be placed in position and trimmed to final size.*

Screened halftone in position

Master paste-up grid

Registration pins

Punched registration holes

Paste-up done on clear acetate

STEP 2. *The paste-up is inverted and placed in contact with negative (in some cases, positive) film. The emulsion (or black material) on the paste-up is in direct contact with the emulsion of the film. A vacuum pump ensures even contact, and the exposure is similar to that used in "burning" a negative.*

Face-down paste-up in contact with negative

Resulting neg is right-reading, emulsion down

STEP 3. *The resulting negative is right-reading, emulsion-down. . .and is used to burn the plate (or in some cases, to create positive film). A vacuum is again used to ensure direct, even contact. None of the typeset material has yet gone before the camera. . .which is the strong point of positive paste-ups.*

Printing plate ▶

Emulsion side of neg in contact with printing plate

(21)

First, examine the typeset material closely. Ideally, the density of the typesetting itself is read with a densitometer (another investment of about $1,000 for those firms currently without one). If the densitometer reading is out of range (in other words, if the copy was set too light), the typesetter must find out what caused the problem, correct it, and rerun the galleys. The problem might be chemical, mechanical, or a combination of both.

Now, with good quality material in hand, sit down at the light table and prepare to work. The master grid, which shows where all typeset columns are, where the folio lines go, and so on, is taped in place. It also has two permanently attached pins.

The punched acetate or Mylar is placed over the master's pins. Now comes assembly. You first wax a test strip of typesetting paper and check the thickness of the application. Wax applied too thickly will interfere with the contacting procedure, and wax applied too thinly won't keep the material affixed.

After trimming the columns of type, place each one into position on the acetate sheet. But, before putting any element down, carefully check the backside for dirt, dust, loose bits of paper, or any other unwanted particles that would later interfere with the transmission of light through the sheet. (Those of you addicted to nicotine may have a problem here: Ashes are disasters when they fall near a positive paste-up. The paste-up person must also be very careful not to overlap any material. All elements should be trimmed tightly and butted to one another whenever possible, but never overlapped. Overlapping will also cut down on the amount of light passing through the paper, which could result in large lines on the final film.

Corrections

The paste-up now goes to the proofreading department. Then, when they're done, they send it back to typesetting, and finally it returns to the light table.

Corrections are cut into the paste-up in much the same fashion as described previously in the short section "How to cut corrections." There is no other way to put them in. As stated above, a correction cannot be laid on top of existing copy because it would then interfere with the transmission of light through the paste-up.

When corrections at this stage are excessive, it can be more economical simply to rerun the copy. Why? The fact is, it is tedious, meticulous work to properly cut a correction into material that is going to be contacted.

Inserting photos

The paste-up person now finishes the page by inserting any photos directly onto the acetate. The photo, in this case, is a V-lox (made by first exposing a film negative and then printing a thin-paper positive). The thickness of the paper print is just as critical as the

CHAPTER 15

thickness of the typeset galley material. Any publisher who attempts to work with positive paste-ups would probably be wise to send out its halftones for conversion to the thin-paper variety. Why? Density control is critical on many levels: There is the density of the emulsion itself and of the highlight, the shadow and the middletones. Suffice to say that a professional litho camera operator is an absolute necessity.

The paste-up is now ready for contacting to the negative. This is normally done at a printing plant geared up for the operation. (You couldn't suddenly ask your printer to convert to positive paste-ups: It's a unique operation, and a great deal of experience and preparation is necessary before any shop develops the proper techniques.)

Finally, the paste-up is placed into the contact frame over the negative, and the exposure is made. This contacting stage saves a lot of time, thanks to the pin registration system. The stripper no longer has to eyeball each cornermark, gently nudge the film into position, and then tape it. Rather, the pins are used to precisely align each page until it is stripped.

The resulting negative is a one-piece sheet, including both the halftone and the line copy. For many printers, a one-piece negative is a requirement, and the positive paste-up can save the cost of the intermediate stages—which, using conventional techniques, ultimately result in wasted film.

Net result: Economy and quality?

At this point, it's business as usual. The result of the entire procedure is 1) the elimination of the camera operation in shooting paste-ups and 2) the reduction in stripping time to assemble the flats.

Money is obviously the goal here, and money is certainly saved. But what about quality?

Experience shows that it is no problem for single- or two-color work. If you already put halftones into position on your boards, you should expect even better results because you are skipping the camera stage—which isn't as accurate as contacting directly to film. But the final quality will be directly related to the cleanliness of your paste-ups, the density of the material you use, and the printer's experience in working with this technique.

I don't recommend that you dive into positives immediately. That step takes considerable planning and communication between you and your printer. But, as a few publications and print buyers have already found, the technique demands little more effort than that needed to produce a crisp paste-up in the first place.□

82

IN-HOUSE PRODUCTIVITY

Before we leave this section on paste-ups, we need to discuss two related questions: How productive should a paste-up person be? And should you or should you not do paste-up in-house.

Just how productive is a paste-up person supposed to be? For that matter, how productive is the entire in-house magazine staff, all of whom must work in concert to meet a production deadline?

When I was the publisher of *Print Buyer* (a monthly newsletter for magazine production professionals), I tried to answer what seemed a simple question: How many people does it take to put together a typical publication (catalog or magazine)? Some operations that I had visited had large production departments, while others had none.

I did an informal study and came to this conclusion: Some publishing houses have extensive art/type/camera operations, while others have skeleton crews, if any. How do you compare? The following is reprinted from the magazine's late 1970s report. Read the case studies, and see where you fit in.

Shop 1: Weekly periodical. The first example is a publisher of weekly educational periodicals. Circulation at the time of our survey was 400,000. Pages of production per month totaled 256.

•*Art/layout:* One full-time art director/paste-up person. Layout work shared by the managing editor. Also, one part-time person. All 256 pages per month designed and assembled in-house by the above personnel.

•*Typesetting:* None in-house. All body copy farmed out to local suppliers. Headlines created with rub-down lettering.

•*Camera:* None in-house. Stats, negatives, and so on, all farmed out to local suppliers.

•*Proofreading:* In-house, with a two-person editorial staff.

•*Conclusion:* This strikes us as a fairly efficient operation. The paste-up crew is one-and-a-half people thick and averages 7.87 pages of paste-up per person per working day (based on five-day week). Paste-ups were not complicated, though. Offhand, the weekly schedule and volume might warrant in-house type, but the publisher has chosen not to make that move.

Shop 2: Trade journal publisher. This publisher produced five magazines of varying frequency at the time of our association, for an average of 140 pages per month.

•*Art/layout:* Layout and design work shared by the managing editor and art director, who also performed all in-house paste-up.

•*Typesetting:* Strike-on, mag-tape system in use. All type set by the art director and circulation manager. Headlines done on a Varityper machine.

•*Camera:* None. All work farmed out to local printers.

•*Proofreading:* Performed by the art director, managing editor, and circulation manager.

•*Conclusion:* We think this trio is overworked. For a group this small to perform all editing, design, paste-up, typesetting, and proofreading work would tax even the most talented and ambitious. Not to mention that the circulation manager has other duties as well, and that the managing editor rewrites most of the copy.

Productivity per person per day based on two-and-a-half employees (the circulation person cannot spend even one day away from recordkeeping) is 2.58 pages. We tag this as excessive productivity because it includes everything from writing copy to handing the complete pages to the printer. In other words, we don't think you can get a quality product when you push that hard.

Shop 3: Consumer magazine. Averages 100 pages per month, excluding heavy catalog work, books, and promotional materials.

•*Art/layout:* All in-house. Staff of nine, including an art director and a chief illustrator.

•*Typesetting:* All in-house, with a staff of three.

•*Camera:* All B/W work and same-color transparency work in-house, with a staff of two.

•*Proofreading:* All in-house, combined with an editorial staff. Also, three proofreading specialists.

•*Conclusion:* Based on the publication alone, on the surface the operation doesn't seem very productive, averaging only one-quarter of a page per person per day.

Shop 4: Specialty magazine. Approximately 52 pages per month in tabloid format.

•*Art/layout:* None in-house. Farmed out to freelancers.

•*Typesetting:* None in-house. Farmed out to local suppliers.

•*Camera:* None. Done by printer.

•*Proofreading:* None in-house. Done by typesetter.

•*Conclusion:* Wow! This is a one-person publishing house that produces a decent-looking, hefty tabloid read by over 50,000 people. We can't evaluate this efficiency anymore than we can the consumer magazine. But in this case, we can't evaluate it because the product seems to put itself together without any staff whatsoever.

Should you do paste-up in-house?

If you are already doing paste-up in-house, this is a question you don't need to answer. If you are not, read on.

Even before publishers started becoming involved with in-house typesetting, many were already doing their own paste-up. As a matter of fact, as soon as letterpress printing became passe, the paste-up function (which replaced the heavy-iron method of putting a page together) was routinely considered an office function, rather than a printer's job.

Today, some publishers perform their own paste-up functions, while others do not. What criteria can a production manager use to decide whether or not to do paste-up in house?

The answer to the inside/outside question is based on the standard variables: cost, speed, and quality. But, in addition, there are the considerations of aesthetics, peak workload periods, training, and the relationship to the stripping process.

Unfortunately, many production managers are not in a position to make an intelligent decision on the paste-up question. Why?

By sheer force of habit, it seems that most publishing companies that do perform paste-up in-house do it to stretch the deadline. Rather than have an issue go "late" because of a missed deadline with a freelancer or studio, the typical publishing staff makes one scheduling error after another—which means all the deadline panic falls on the paste-up department. Such a publishing operation will never be able to deal with an outside paste-up house, which is exactly why there is no decision to be made.

Start from scratch

Let's assume, though, that you either work for a rational publisher or are in a position to clearly rethink the way your company gets things done. Then, let's compare inside and outside paste-up.

1. *Cost:* This is certainly the most deceptive figure to get a handle on. While outside costs will be estimated with flat figures, the temptation is to eliminate a lot of your own internal figures in the comparison. To realistically compare costs, use whichever of the following will be applicable to your operation:

•Equipment: You or your accountant should consider the amortized cost of decent paste-up equipment, which would include light tables, chairs, T-squares, a waxer, and all the other necessities.

•Floor space: Unless you truly have extra space that is currently being wasted, it is also fair to include a portion of your rent, utilities, and so on.

•Wages: Naturally, you would include all of the costs of an employee: unemployment contributions, FICA figures, and so forth.

•Training and turnover: The publishing industry is notorious for turnover. If you anticipate losing 25 percent of your paste-up staff each year, then you need to add a significant amount for both slow trainees and slowed-down employees-turned-teachers.

To compare your cost figures to those of outside firms, you need only look at both sets of numbers rationally. Let's say, for example, that based on your sample magazine, a firm bids $9 per page on the average and is willing to stick to that price. If you then estimate your total annual pages, say 1,200, and then divide by your total in-house expenses, you'll have a comparison.

Suppose you have two part-time employees who cost you $35,000 annually for paste-up and another $5,000 in overhead, space, materials, and so forth. Your cost per page would be over $33 in-house. Comparing that to an outside estimate should make your decision easy.

2. *Speed:* As mentioned earlier, publishers often let delays accumulate to the paste-up stage. But once the paste-up staff has met the deadline, the added cost of doing so always seems worth it.

But if we're trying to be open-minded about this, let's go back to the outside estimate. What if the studio or freelance group can offer more concentrated speed than your firm? For example, you might barely be able to afford two employees whose primary duties are to bail you out at deadline time. But what would happen if you stuck to a schedule with an outside firm?

Even though you may still want to go down to the wire, if you contract your work and become a decent customer, you may find that a shop will put a half-dozen people on your job during the last week of the month. Thus, it is feasible that you could pick up speed with a small outside firm, rather than lose time at the deadline.

Similarly, the opposite might be true. If you deal with a single freelancer who just happens to be overbooked during your deadline, someone's going to suffer. In either case, you should make a realistic comparison.

3. *Quality:* This is a heavy question, and one that is difficult to answer. First of all, quality is relative. What's "good" to one person can be garbage to the next. However, your own concept of quality is the one that's important. How straight must a rule be? How perfectly must your columns of typesetting align?

Naturally, meeting your standards with an outside shop is a matter of finding the right organization. But the inside shop must set its own standards and then train the personnel to meet them.

This brings up a point: If you do paste-up in-house, do you meet professional standards? Can you meet them if you have to train people from scratch? In your geographic area, are competent personnel available, or will all of your paste-up people start as trainees?

The skills of the paste-up personnel directly affect both the aesthetic appearance of the paste-up and the subsequent stripping efforts required to produce the magazine.

And that might complicate things a bit: If you hire paste-up people who make oversights when preparing the mechanicals (which then translate into increased stripping costs), shouldn't these potential increases be added to the cost of in-house paste-up?

The answer is yes, and let's illustrate it with an example.

Suppose your paste-up people use black lines to indicate where photos should print (keylines), but the printer actually needs windows (red or black paper). Then the printer must create the win-

CHAPTER 16

dow himself, and charge for it.

By the same token, your employee might simply indicate, "tint this area 10 percent black." If your printer wants a window cut to the size of that area, will he then charge you for cutting it himself? Probably.

What's the answer? It's this: If you do paste-up in-house, have at your disposal knowledgeable professionals who have the technical wherewithal to do a job that meets the printer's expectations.

4. *Aesthetics:* Like quality, the area of aesthetics is also relative. Here are two possibilities:

When things go well, an outside shop will put the magazine together exactly the way you would.

When things don't go well, you will constantly disagree with the position of a rule, a widow at the end of a column, the space being added to fill out a page, and so forth.

Again, a relationship to cost exists: If you make arbitrary decisions, will an outside shop charge you for them as alterations? Probably.

Making the choice

So what's the bottom line?

Only you can tell. Paste-up can be done inside or outside. If you can isolate a single, all-important variable (cost, speed, or quality), your decision should be an easy one. But if you are free to go either way, you can either flip a coin or use this guideline: If it doesn't really matter whether you do paste-up in-house, you might as well have it done outside. Common business sense will tell you that it is more comfortable to work with a smaller staff—thereby avoiding the costs of additional employees, of training, of general overhead, and of the high cost of another manager (should your department become large enough).

Training

If you do decide to work in-house, how can you upgrade the skills of your paste-up staff and where can you find trained people? There are several good options.

Most technical schools offer courses in printing, including paste-up. Better yet, some art schools offer training in the graphic arts. An artist who's accustomed to working cleanly and possesses paste-up skills, is a good bet.

Also, anyone with the ability to work with detail could be trained in proper paste-up techniques. Trade schools offer night courses, and there are several seminars in paste-up techniques that travel throughout the country.

Don't overlook another possibility: your printer. Most

printers don't want to do paste-up, but just as many of them know good paste-up when they see it. It could be extremely productive to have your printer give a miniseminar to your group, and for him to bring a variety of samples submitted by other customers. Or you could take your crew to the printing plant and review good paste-up methods. A general (informational) tour of the plant would also be another fringe benefit.□

CHAPTER 16

ELECTRONIC PASTE-UP

What's all this talk about electronic paste-up, computer-assisted design, and other such wonders?

Although it is not the purpose of this manual to blow you away with a full technical description of electronic paste-up, I will describe it and discuss its potential. Then, if you are so inclined, you can do the (endless) legwork and research needed to install a system.

The basic concept

As most of us already know, computers have come a long way in a short time. In the typesetting field, there are systems available that can imitate most of the functions performed by the paste-up person. And that, in a nutshell, is what electronic paste-up is: a computer emulation of a once-mechanical task.

Let's pretend for a moment that I am currently sitting in front of a machine with the ability to perform electronic paste-up—or, calling it by its real name, electronic page makeup. What do I do?

I turn on my computer and give it a few commands. It then digs into its memory and retrieves the article that I want to lay out.

I give the computer more commands, including the pica width of the copy to be set, the size, leading, and font. And then I tell it the depth of each column, the number of columns on the page, and the amount of space between columns.

A few more pokes at the keyboard, and my screen lights up. What do I see?

Basically, I see the very same image that will print on the page. The typeface size is nine-point. The columns are the proper width. Everything looks normal, except that I am seeing it on a TV-like screen. My screen also has a message area that informs me that there are five inches of copy left over.

So, now I call back up onto the screen the article on which I previously worked, kill a five-inch filler item, and run the balance of my copy on the page. And so it goes. I do my paste-up work right on my terminal screen.

Electronic page composition is obviously closely related to typesetting. The terminal is capable of showing a facsimile of the face, the size, and the widths of each character. But it is also related to paste-up. In fact, it supposedly combines both fields into one integrated system.

How does it output the copy? A sophisticated system is capable of either printing its images onto photosensitive paper (typesetting paper) or transmitting full pages over phone lines, via satellites or computer disk.

Integrated systems

That's not all. Let's hook up my imaginary system to a digital scanner. Such a unit is capable of breaking photos, line shots, logos, or any other simple image into computer information that can be fed into the terminal and typesetter. Net result? Let's say I'm working on page five. I have a photo, some text, and a company logo, all of which must appear on the page.

CHAPTER 17

I run the text through the composition system as usual. Then I digitize the photo and add it to my electronic paste-up. Similarly, I add the company logo. If it doesn't all fill the page the way I like, I can make the photo bigger, change the point size of the text, or enlarge the logo — all electronically — and all without actually setting copy or going ahead with a conventional-type paste-up.

When I finally get what I want, I command the machine to output the page as a one-piece positive image, including the halftone and the artwork.

Color scanner unit

Now let's add color photos to the layout.

This time I work on a color monitor that is coupled to a full-color, digital color scanner (which also scans black-and-white images). All works, in concert with my phototypesetting device to produce the final film for my magazine.

Now I can really cut loose. Fancy color layouts, image manipulation and distortion, right on down the line. It all sounds too good to be true.

And, as of this writing, it pretty much *is* too good to be true. Although a complete system as described above could be installed today, it would cost you well in excess of a million dollars (possibly closer to several million) to do so.

The negative aspects

In other words, as I write this, technology has not crossed paths with economy. Although a few very large publishers are installing rudimentary systems, the state of the art will not filter down into the other 10,000 magazines until the following problems are solved:

1. *Cost:* Obviously, a company doing a million-a-year can't afford a $2 million device to replace a $25,000 employee.

2. *Memory:* One of the reasons the cost is so high is that full-color photo requires millions of bits of informatin to be stored in the computer. Memory costs money and must be manipulated—and the larger the memory, the more powerful and expensive the computer needed to manipulate it.

3. *Incompatibility:* Here we speak of "material" incompatibility. It will be of limited use to totally digitize a magazine if all the ads come in as plate-ready negatives. Imagine the waste involved if someone has to mechanically insert all the black-and-white and color ads on a page that is otherwise totally complete.

4. *Training:* Although computers are becoming easier to operate every day, they still are not that simple. While a paste-up person can be trained in a month or so, and a typesetter in a year or so,

what about the computer operator who needs both those skills, plus a magnificent programming ability? This will change as computers get "smarter" and easier to operate.

5. *Schedules and memories:* Let's couple a magazine schedule with a computer memory. What if you've solved the first four problems (which will be easy to do in a short while) and now have your magazine on a computer—and right before press time, your computer goes on the blink? What if you have a severe "head" crash, and the computer loses the whole program?

If your answer is that you would have hard-copy backup anyhow, your answer implies that, in order to guarantee the success of your electronic version, you will need to duplicate all the mechanical aspects in some manner. This kind of waste on top of an already expensive system just might become totally intolerable.

The positive aspects

But I don't mean to imply that electronic composition won't eventually become the ultimate tool in producing magazines.

Imagine the comfort, when you are right down to the deadline wire, of repaginating the entire book, shifting the editorial, cutting and adding stories, dropping an ad and inserting another in its place, and then coming up with the final version—all in 20 minutes!

Then, instead of driving, flying or worrying the paste-ups to the printer, you simply push the "transmit" button—and your entire magazine is fed into the printer's computer via satellite. Plates are automatically burned. It goes on press, and it always looks fantastic because you've fully corrected the color right in your own office.

How did you do the color corrections? Even though you may be one of many publishers who will never go into color separation, your computers might well be hooked up to computers at a color separation house.

And, of course, all of your editors, contributors, and proofreaders would be connected to the same system. And so would be the savings in materials: no paste-ups, no typesetting output, no film and, no handwork. You just sit at the computer and punch buttons.

As of this writing, a moderately priced, powerful system like this is not available. But the field is changing rapidly, and within a few short years, an encyclopedic volume of information will be available for the potential buyer.□

THE IN-HOUSE CAMERA

Before we move from in-house paste-up concepts to standard preparation functions (camerawork, stripping, proofs, and so on), let's look at an area where there is often overlapping: simple litho-camera operations.

The litho camera

Depending on their abilities and size, litho cameras fall into several general classifications. On the low end, there are simple, bare-bones cameras that can produce photostats, halftones, and negatives. On the upper end, there are large color-separation cameras that can produce all of the above, plus separate primary colors from original photos or artwork.

Color separations and related equipment will be discussed later. For now, let me say that a small photostat-type camera is a realistic consideration for the publisher who performs in-house paste-up.

Let's look at an example. Suppose you decide to do your own paste-up. You want a headline to be a bit narrower, and you want to reduce a line drawing to fit the page.

If you don't have an in-house camera, you simply scale the artwork, scale the headline, and send the material to the printer. He, in turn, looks at your paste-up and where you have indicated (probably in blue pen or pencil) where you want the elements to fall.

The printer can do one of two things. First, he can shoot a photostat of the material and paste it in position. Or, second, he can shoot a negative of the material and later, at the preparation stage, strip it into position.

There are four possible disadvantages to these procedures.

1. The printer is forced to perform and charge you for functions that could have been performed at the paste-up stage. In other words, you are not doing all of your paste-up in-house: You are farming some of it out.

2. The printer may not be using economical materials. There are several different ways to shoot a photostat. The photo-mechanical transfer method is the least expensive. But it is so closely related to the paste-up function that, unless a printer performs paste-up, he may not bother to have these materials (and the related equipment) in stock. Some printers shoot all material on film and later strip it into position.

3. The printer may substitute a more expensive procedure for a paste-up function. This is the other effect of the preceding point. If the printer uses the more expensive method to shoot material, in all likelihood he will use the more expensive activities to insert it. If the material is shot as film, it creates the need for more complicated

stripping, more complicated proofs, and more complicated plate burning.

4. Given the above limitations and costs, the economy-minded artist may well decide to sacrifice aesthetics rather than have all the material photostated as desired. If the artist knows that each headline reduction will create a $10 (or more) charge at the printer, he may simply say "what the heck," and put it into position a little over- or undersized.

It is these problems that convince many publishers to install a simple, inexpensive stat camera. And this type of camera has more abilities than we have discussed so far.

What the camera can do

Suppose you do purchase a small, functional camera. What abilities will you have? What kind of training will you need?

First, the equipment. For a very minimal operation, you would need the basic camera, plus a stabilization processor. This processor develops material with a single chemical via a contact-type transfer process.

In addition, the camera will probably (but not necessarily) require a small darkroom. (There are several "daylight" cameras on the market. but because their costs are generally higher, you might decide that a cheaper camera in a dark closet is a better bet.)

Now, simply install a few standard safelights, and you're up and running.

What can this camera do? With simple available materials, you can start shooting your own photostats of artwork, headlines, and so on. Add a $100 film screen, and you can also shoot halftones and paste them into position on a paste-up (the quality here would not compare to a conventional film-negative halftone). Reverses will also not be a problem if you use the automatically reversing films that several manufacturers offer.

For the ambitious publisher, there are also color materials on the market that allow you to make full-color enlargements and reductions of photos and art. These can either be sent to the printer for separation and stripping or used for special presentations of paste-ups or comprehensive layouts.

Is training necessary?

So, assuming you bought the camera, how much training is involved?

For simple photostats, the average training time is almost nil. The actual operation is not complex: set the percentage scale on two wheels (or the camera bed), set the percentage on the lens, insert the material, and make the exposure. Then, remove the negative paper.

Sandwich it with the positive receiver and pass it through the processor. Wait 30 seconds, peel them apart, and you've got your photostat.

For most publishers, that is all the training desired. True, once you have the camera, you can consider shooting halftones, and there's no special trick to reverses. But the simple photostats are what those with in-house operations crave the most.

Cost are reasonable

A small camera isn't too expensive. In 1983, there were several on the market for under $3,000. If you need only stats, you need no plumbing, and the entire operation could be installed for about $3,000.

The automated daylight cameras are more expensive and possibly, easier to use. They start at about $8,000 but eliminate the need for a separate darkroom. It would be easy enough (and logical, too) to compare the cost of remodeling with the additional expense for a daylight camera.

Materials are also another cost consideration. Materials and the chemicals needed to produce a single 10″ x 12″ stat cost less than a dollar. The time required, including the walk to the darkroom, is about two minutes. Now, with an approximate total cost for an in-house shot, you can easily compare your total per year cost for stats and make an intelligent decision.

Should you get a camera?

You can take any approach in deciding whether you need a camera. The old ''I want one'' is good enough for many.

For those whose primary concern is the bottom line though, a brief study would be in order. How many stats do you send out to be made? How are they shot? What is the total cost? How many would you send out if they were less expensive?

By doing a simple evaluation, you will come to the right conclusion. After all, no in-house function is best for *all* publishing operations. Your special needs, your costs, and your preferences will dictate the proper direction.

Who sells cameras?

There are several manufacturers of either low-cost or daylight (easy-to-operate) cameras.

On the high end, Itek Graphic Products sells an automated daylight unit that includes a rapid-access processor. This is a virtually self-contained darkroom and cost about $14,000 in 1983.

On the low end, NuArc sells a small, conventional camera for less than $3,000. It includes no processor at all, but a photostat-type processor can be purchased for between $300 and $600.

The prices and abilities of most other potential in-house cameras fall somewhere in between this range. If you want to investigate this, contact any printing equipment sales firm in your nearest metropolitan area.

In larger cities, you will often see litho cameras (and other printing equipment) advertised in daily newspapers. These can be a good buy ($500 and up) but may not be a good choice for a "first-timer." If you do look at a used camera, have someone demonstrate that the bellows are sound, the lens has not deteriorated or been scratched, and—toughest of all—that the camera is either aligned or *can* be aligned. As a camera wears out, it becomes impossible to make it shoot with accuracy and detail.

One final caution: There are still a number of used cameras on the market that use conventional incandescent lighting. In my opinion, these cameras are not worth installing. Their light sources are impure, unstable, and incapable of performing all the functions that we've covered in this section.

The in-house camera as a safety tool

Many production directors fear the ultimate catastrophe: losing paste-ups. You may know the feeling. After weeks of work with an in-house art department, you pack up your efforts and trust them to a delivery service. The computer generation has similar fears: a bad transmission of data or a major crash right before transmission.

For comparative purposes, let's say that paste-ups are also a form of data, subject to loss. How can one protect them?

Take the average magazine. Many are typeset and pasted up in-house. The process begins with information that originates either from an outside contributor or from an in-house writer, but, in either case, the information is quickly transformed into digital information at the phototypesetter's shop. This is a form of data backup: the hard-copy original (paper manuscript) and its electronic counterpart (tape or disk file) are intact.

But what happens next? Initially, the electronic output is used to create typesetting galleys. No problem, because they can be run again. But then the galleys are the object of intense manual labor. They are organized into the actual paste-ups.

Photographs are the next concern. While a few publishers shoot halftones in-house, most do not. And when the photos are to be run in full color, virtually no publisher has the facilities to separate them.

What happens when these materials are lost?

Starting with paste-ups, a loss during shipment could be overcome if the publisher had the time and manpower to simply rerun the material and reassemble it. But time, particularly in magazine publishing, *is* money.

And the photos?

THE IN-HOUSE CAMERA

Replacing the "perfect" color slide can be an impossible task.

So what protection can you give yourself if you cannot afford to lose material that simply cannot be replaced—either because of its original nature or because of the time needed to duplicate it?

A few years ago, the answer would have been to invest in a prep shop complete with color duplication facilities (try $15,000), a good film processor ($5,000), a lot of planning and wiring (maybe $2,500), and a few skilled employees (each at $20,000 annually.) For all that, you would get a product that cost quite a bit to produce and back up—a product that, if you were lucky, you would probably never ever need.

Hardly a bargain, but you might sleep better.

Well, if losing paste-ups and original photos is a concern, you can take heart in knowing that technologies have changed in the past years. Let's discuss some equipment and backup techniques that not only will prevent the ultimate catastrophe (losing the magazine) but will also save you money.

The first step is an in-house camera.

Any stat camera can also produce film negatives. One of the problems in shooting your own page negatives is that you need a processor—any common rapid-access processor. But if you have a camera and you happen to have an RC (resin-coated) or RA (rapid access) processor, you can shoot your own negatives. The films and papers use common chemistry.

How then do you protect your halftones? That same camera will produce halftones, but it can be a bit tricky. So you could either 1) train a person to shoot a good-quality, rapid-access halftone or 2) merely shoot backup halftones—my term for a continuous-tone (no-dot) version of a photo. Actually, it is a duplicate photo, so to speak, shot from the original and held as backup.

There is one more option: shooting screened PMT (Photo Mechanical Transfer) halftones. Although they do not offer much in the way of quality when pasted directly onto a paste-up, they are a viable, inexpensive alternative.

What about those irreplaceable color prints and slides? If you have already taken the above advice, you are only about $200 away from total protection against the potential "lost magazine." Both Kodak and Agfa-Gavert have introduced color duplication materials that work in the average, poorly controlled darkroom—meaning, little temperature control, untrained operators, and minimal equipment budgets.

With these simple systems, you can use a standard-process camera to make a duplicate color print, either at the same size as the original or scaled to its appropriate printing size.

For color slides, a simple enlarger will allow you to make prints from slides or small transparencies. Contact-printing is also available for larger transparencies.

It won't take you long to figure out that if you can duplicate your color material, you might as well dupe it to size and mount it into its eventual printing position. The dollar savings in both separation and stripping costs will pay for the setup in as little as half an issue. However, if you're quality-conscious, you might not want to put your backup material into the production cycle.

What's the bottom line? In effect, for very little investment, you can do the following:

1. Ensure that your paste-ups will neither be lost nor fall apart during transit.

2. Ensure that you will never lose a color slide that cannot be replaced.

3. Provide either a backup photo or the actual printable photo for halftones.

4. Save money on separations and stripping.

On the other hand, you must also examine the extent of your own potential financial damage should you ever lose a major shipment to the printer. If you find that you could suffer through such a loss with relative ease, it might be just as logical for you to let the printer do all of the prep work while you stick to the business of publishing.◻

SECTION III: PREPARATION WORK FUNDAMENTALS

THE MYSTERIES OF PREP

Preparation, like many terms in the graphic arts, means different things to different people. Why? Because its meaning has been constantly changing. Let's go back a few years to the days of hot-metal typesetting and letterpress printing.

In those days, preparation encompassed all the activity that occurred before the job was placed on the pressbed. So, typesetting was prep. Getting "cuts" made was part of prep. (A cut is a raised impression of artwork or photos used in letterpress printing to actually pick up the ink from the platen rollers; it is applied with pressure to the paper.)

Today, lithography has changed the meaning of prep. Many publishers perform their own page makeup. But years ago, it was impossible to perform page makeup unless you were a fully equipped letterpress printer. Similarly, many publishers consider typesetting an office job. But years back, it was a factory-type activity that required a full shop of technicians and laborers.

Today, and in the context of this book, we will use the term "prep" or "preparation" to describe the work performed after the paste-up is completed and before the printing plates are burned (or exposed).

With that definition in mind, prep will include line shots, halftones, stripping, color separations, and proofs. And, of course, it will include all the activities related to those respective areas. In this section, line shots, halftones and stripping will be covered; in the next section, color separations and proofs will be explained.

While prep is probably the least understood of all the graphic arts functions, there is no real reason for this lack of knowledge. For magazines, prep costs are frequently a relatively large part of production costs. The smaller the magazine, the more relatively important it is; the larger the circulation, the higher the overall costs. Therefore, it is wise for any production manager of any size publication to become as well versed as possible in preparation activities.

A general overview

Prep can be broken down into four major areas: image capture, duplication, positioning, and alteration. Virtually all the supposedly "mysterious" functions related to prep fall into one of those areas. A few examples:

Cameras, scanners, and enlargers all capture the image of the material to be reproduced. Duplication is used to duplicate film, make proofs, or convert positives to negatives. Positioning can be done by hand or with computer assistance, but functions to place elements in their intended positions. And alteration includes color corrections (performed by hand or by computer) and the handwork required for such tasks as adding a rule or removing the background from a photo.

As you may have noticed, these four areas are quite broad in scope. They have been presented that way deliberately so that, as prep continues to become highly computerized, our definitions will still hold. If we were to say that "stripping" involves the placement and the taping of a piece of film into position, we'd be knowingly ignoring computerized strippers, computer-assisted cameras, and other fairly recent developments.

CHAPTER 19

Process color and nonprocess color

For magazine preparation, there are generally two categories of work: process color and nonprocess color. Process-color preparation relates to its goal, process-color printing. If a photo is to be printed in full color, the printing process used is called process-color offset lithography.(This book does not encompass other terms of printing, such as gravure and letterpress.)

On the other hand, simple black-and-white printing and most two-color printing require other related preparation procedures. They could be called "nonprocess" activities, but for practical purposes, all nonprocess work will be referred to as either black-and-white or two-color printing and preparation.

Let's begin with the simpler forms of preparation and then proceed by degrees of complexity to the process variety.

Black-and-white preparation

As stated earlier, all preparation falls into the major areas of image capture, duplication, positioning, and alteration. These terms may sound strange to the old-timers in the business, but will make perfect sense to the novices. The "novice" is often better versed in computerized technology and finds it easier to accept both mechanical and computerized concepts.

Although the electronic varieties of prep will possibly take over completely some day, a technical concentration on them would take volumes of material—all the way from the theory of data communications to the highly customized techniques being used by today's weekly newsmagazines. So we will concentrate on the mechanical or conventional aspects of performing simple preparation.□

LINE SHOTS

In the previous section, we discussed the abilities of a simple camera, installed at a publishing site. The printer's camera is usually (but not always) more sophisticated than the publisher's, but the general procedures remain the same. The camera will shoot either "line" work or "halftone" work. Let's describe the line shot.

"Line," in the printing world, does not mean the shortest distance between two points. That would be called a rule. Rather, "line" describes any material that does not have any middletones.

What you are now reading is line material and was shot on camera as a line shot. The typesetting that you see is the result of solid ink printing where it should and not printing where it shouldn't. No attempt has been made to print any gray areas, or densities between black and white. Illustration 22 shows the same kind of line shot, except in this illustration the original material had gray tones (this type did not). Can you see the effect? Only the darkest parts of the photo printed because the film saw those areas as being dark enough to have no effect on the photographic emulsion.

The term "line" does not mean the image is literally converted to lines. Rather, it means that the material is shot as either black or white, with no gray values in between. The stark look of this photo results from shooting it as line rather than as a halftone, which would preserve the gray values.

(22)

Line shots, then, are a method of creating a high-contrast photographic image of any material. This type was shot as line, had high contrast, and therefore produced a final film image that went from black to white just as we wanted.

But the photo is no different to the camera. The original photo had very dark spots and very light spots. The film read the dark parts just as it read this typesetting. It read the very light spots just as it read the spaces between the words that you are seeing. The only difference was that the many gray areas in the original photo were not captured.

The result is that the film, which again is very high in contrast, made "breaks" between the black and the white. Because the film is specially designed for line work, it cannot accommodate gray tones. Thus, the resultant image is lacking in all middletones, and has only "pure" whites and "pure" blacks.

If you are having difficulty comprehending, consider this: What if the film you bought at the drugstore was line film? Then your picture of Grandma would have all the contrast shown in Illustration 22. There would be no gradual change from the shadows of her wrinkles to the reflection off her nose. But drugstores don't sell line film. Few people have use for it—that is, except those working in the graphic arts.

If you have followed this discussion, then it should be apparent that all cameras can handle line shots. It is the *film* that dictates the contrast. Therefore, a line shot is any camera shot, using the appropriate film, that produces a high-contrast image: black and white and nothing in between.

There are a wide variety of graphic arts films and papers, and virtually all of them are of the line variety. You will understand better as we continue this discussion later in the chapter on halftones.

Using line shots

So, keeping in mind that most lithographic films are destined for line uses, what are the typical situations that call for a line shot, and which type of base will the material have, paper or film?

The photomechanical photostats described in the section on in-house cameras happen to have a paper base. But if you were to shoot a conventional negative for subsequent use in platemaking, it would need to have a film base. The paper line shots are photostats, which in most cases will be put on the paste-up and then shot on camera again. When the line shot must later burn a plate (or be duplicated by a contacting process, which will be described later), it must allow unrestricted passage of light. In other words, the areas that are to be duplicated must be totally clear.

Thus, the types of material put into the "exposure" end of the camera (the film board) are selected based on their intended use. A quick paper stat can be made if the goal is reflective (nonfilm, non-

105

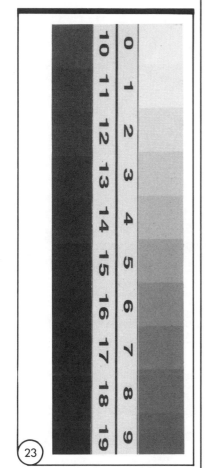

(23)

The gray scale is used as a guide in determining halftone exposures and the length of a line shot. Remember that this is merely a halftone reproduction of a gray scale. A true gray scale could not be reproduced in this book because it contains no dots. This photo is little more than a crude representation of the scale, which has fine divisions of density between one "step" of gray and another.

transparent) artwork. But a film base is used when the goal is material that needs to allow unrestricted passage of light through the exposed areas.

The magazine page: Processing and opaquing

Using these conventional methods, it makes sense that the magazine page is shot as a line negative. (Naturally, the photos are not shot with the same film, nor at the same time. That process will be described in the next chapter.)

What happens to this magazine page when it leaves the camera? It is processed and opaqued.

Processing chemicals, processing time, and eventual contrast of the film negative all vary, depending on the film used.

Rapid-access films use the same type of chemistry as do high-quality phototypesetting processors. These films are described as having wide latitude, which means that development temperatures or times are not critical.

Lith films require more critical controls over both development temperature and time. They also frequently require much more expensive processing machines.

Why, then, doesn't everybody use rapid-access film? The difference is the final contrast of the film and its ability to make the "break" between image and nonimage.

This is best described by referring to the gray scale (Illustration 23). This typical gray scale has 12 different levels, each a little lighter (or darker) than the others. When the scale is shot on camera, the rapid-access negative will show a very dark end, and a very clear end, but several steps—possibly four or five—with tone in them.

The lith negative will show an even darker dark, a clearer clear, and only two to four steps with tone. Thus, it is a better negative. Although it is a better negative, the difference may mean nothing to you. There are a few situations in which you could see the difference in your printed magazine, but only if the prep department were taking other shortcuts that lead to low quality work.

(Editor's Note: Since this original manuscript was drafted, rapid-access films have been introduced that have qualities similar to lith films. Kodak's version is called the Ultratec line, and it produces an extremely high quality line shot or halftone dot as first-generation.)

Following our typical magazine page further, what next? Now it is time for opaquing.

Because no process is perfect, the negative will in all likelihood have tiny pinholes that allow light to pass through. These should not print. Therefore, they are "opaqued," or painted out with a special fluid.

If you have ever seen a professionally prepared paste-up, you may wonder why the negative doesn't "see" the blue pencil marks, the preprinted blue guidelines, or other blue material. Only the black stuff shows up. Why?

The line shot has a few rules of its own. Red, orange, and deep gold photograph as black, and light blues do not photograph at all under normal circumstances. Thus, blue pencils are used to write instructions on paste-ups because these notes will not later be seen by the line film.

Conversely, it is possible for the negative to "see" things that should not have been there in the first place. A poorly prepared paste-up will have attracted dust, dirt, and fingerprints. A person may have written on it with a blue pencil that was too dark. Now recall the photograph described earlier: At some point of density (too much dirt), the film will suddenly "see" the image, and there it will be in black and white.

At the opaquing stage, then, someone must take pains to ensure that only what is "wanted" is actually on the film. As you might imagine, opaquing when performed by the printer is least expensive when no decisions have to be made. And that means keep paste-ups clean! No dust and no dirt equals no decisions, equals minimum opaquing time, equals low cost. Remember that formula.

Using film negatives

As we mentioned briefly, the film negative might be used to burn a printing plate, but there are other uses for it as well: The line negative is one step to a paper, reversed print.

A reverse describes the activity of switching blacks to whites and vice versa. Let's say that you have a headline on your paste-up and that you want it to be white inside a black panel, rather than black inside a white panel (Illus. 24). The printer might shoot a line negative of the headline and then make a contact-exposure print of that negative to a piece of photographic paper. The new result would be a paper negative that could be placed directly on the paste-up.

As we continue to discuss preparation throughout this section, you will notice cases in which a negative is shot solely for the purpose of making a duplicate exposure of itself. These situations involve double-burning, buildups, and other activities that need to be described in greater detail.

Summary: Line shots

Thus far we have discussed line shots in the broader terms of image capture (the camera shot) and a bit of image duplication (contact prints, reverses, and so on). Image alteration might include the "scratching" or scribing of a rule into a negative; image positioning—more commonly called stripping—will be discussed later when we assemble our sample magazine page along with some other pages and photos.□

CHAPTER 20

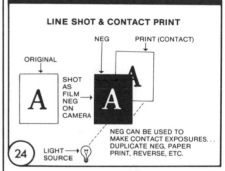

This sequence shows a simple line shot followed by a contact print. The original is placed on a camera and exposed to line-sensitive film. After processing, the film is positioned in contact with another photo-sensitive receiver— paper being one choice. Light passes through the film and exposes the print, which is then developed. A variety of films and papers can be used for both the camera shot and the contacting procedure.

107

HALFTONES

It should be apparent from our previous discussion that a photograph cannot be handled as a line shot. Yet it was also stated that most lithographic films are of the line variety. How, then, does the lithographic process simulate the printing of photos that carry blacks, many shades of grays, and whites?

It is all an illusion. Lithographically produced magazines use only the full intensity of black ink to print these supposedly gray-toned images. A bit of physiology is required to understand the reason.

The human eye, like the eyes of all other animals, has a built-in limitation as to the amount of detail it can discern. You've heard of "eyes like a hawk"? That phrase comes from a basic difference between the hawk's visual acuity and our own. The hawk can see a small moving object from a much farther distance than either you or I. Why? Because inside the hawk's eye, on the rear wall, there are many more light receptors.

Our own eyes have cones to receive light images during the day and rods to receive the fainter images at dusk. The number of cones and rods in the human eye dictates the smallest objects or the most minute detail that we will be able to detect.

Illustration 25 shows a pattern of dots. We clearly see this as a pattern of dots because the light receptors in our eyes more or less "outnumber" the dots. A small number of dots, a large number of receptors. We can also see that some of the dots are bigger than others. This is the secret to halftone production.

This greatly enlarged shot of a halftone demonstrates the true nature of the beast: It is composed solely of larger and smaller dots. The lithographic process does not print the grays, which the eye sees. Rather, by printing small, variably sized dots, the eye is fooled into seeing gray.

Illustration 26 is also very coarse, given the topic of this discussion (photos). It would hardly pass for a magazine halftone or a photo, but it is beginning to fall together and make some sense to our eyes. Although we can still see that some of the dots are larger than others, it is harder to make the distinction here than it is with the first pattern.

This halftone has 33 lines to the inch, resulting in a coarse image. 33-line halftones would never be used in normal magazine production.

The term "line screen" actually refers to the number of dots in a horizontal inch, in a halftone. These three halftones of the same photo demonstrate that the more lines per inch (or dots per inch), the better the eye is fooled into seeing a quality image rather than a collection of dots.

Illustration 27 shows the dots getting much smaller. At this density, we are finally in the range of a commercial quality photo. There are 65 dots in a one-inch length of the image, meaning that a square inch of these dots contains approximately 4,225 little dots. This is typical for a newspaper, whose rough surface limits its ability to reproduce a dot pattern much denser than this. If you have a good eye, you may be able to look at individual dots and notice, of course, that some are bigger than others.

This 65-line halftone shows more detail and quality than the 33-line halftone. It is not acceptable for magazine work, although many newspapers run their halftones at this coarseness. They do so because newsprint is not a quality stock and could not hold much smaller dots.

In Illustration 28, we've increased the number of dots in an inch to 100, meaning that a square inch of these dots involves 10,000 little specks. At 100 lines to the inch, some eyes can break the dots apart, while others are totally fooled into thinking they are seeing a gradual change from black to white. They think they see gray because their eyes are processing an image that they cannot break into its respective elements (10,000 dots). Therefore, the eye blends all the elements into a cohesive mass and tells the brain, "This is gray," instead of telling it, "These are large and small dots."

This 100-line halftone begins to approach magazine quality. However, the typical magazine uses even more density—133 lines to the inch. Because printing quality is critical in demonstrating halftone dot structure, it would be misleading to print a 133-line halftone and call it "perfect." Rather than demonstrate 133-line printing here, review printed magazines and compare the halftone quality on your own.

The 100-lines-per-inch photo in Illustration 28 is a standard in the lithographic industry for low-to-moderate quality printing. But because 100 lines in an inch (or 100 dots in a row) is still too limited for holding all the detail available in the average photo, magazines typically use a finer screen (more dots). Generally, an average quality magazine will use a minimum of 120 to 133 dots to the inch. These are called "120-line" or "133-line" screens.

It is possible to use even finer gradations, such as 150-line or even 250-line screens. The question, though, is not "how fine" we can get the photo, but rather what can be faithfully reproduced on the press we will use, with the paper we will buy, at the speeds we will run? Press limitations will be discussed in more detail in that section of this book. For now, let's continue with the halftones.

Why halftones?

You may have an obvious question: Why are halftones shot at all? Why not just print the photo, with its middletones or gray tones?

The answer is this: Lithographic magazine presses are limited to printing only full intensities of ink. As described above, the eye can be fooled into thinking that there are middletones, or "light" applications of ink. Regardless of what the eye is fooled into seeing, the lithographic press has a very major limitation. It can print and ink only at full intensity when the press is running properly. The procedures do not reliably exist whereby a photo can be printed with a little ink in the light areas and a lot of ink in the dark areas. The halftone preparation is a means by which the photo will be represented by a dot pattern, not because we like dot patterns but because 1) the press can print the dots with full-ink intensity while 2) the human eye can't tell the difference between small dots and real photos.

The halftone shot

To make this clear to you, let us now talk about photographs and halftones as two separate and different creatures. The photograph is a snapshot, a color print, or any other multitonal representation of a face, a landscape, or any image. When we use the term "halftone" we will be talking about material that carries all of its tones in dots, with the object being to *simulate* a photograph—meaning, a halftone is a lithographic representation of a photo. We shall say that we *can* print halftones, but we *cannot* print photos.

Litho-camera halftone shot

The photograph is put into the end of the camera called the copyboard. And a sheet of film or other photographic receiver is placed in the other end—the filmboard (Illustration 29).

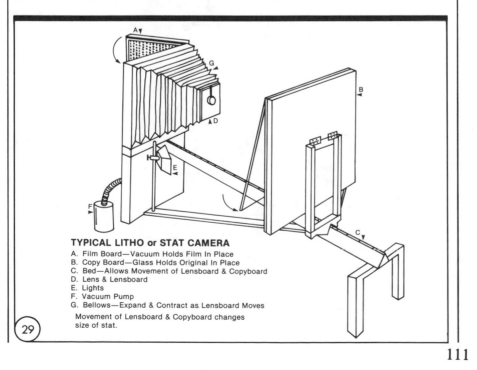

TYPICAL LITHO or STAT CAMERA
A. Film Board—Vacuum Holds Film In Place
B. Copy Board—Glass Holds Original In Place
C. Bed—Allows Movement of Lensboard & Copyboard
D. Lens & Lensboard
E. Lights
F. Vacuum Pump
G. Bellows—Expand & Contract as Lensboard Moves

Movement of Lensboard & Copyboard changes size of stat.

29

111

HALFTONES

Now, if we were to do nothing else, we'd get a line shot. So, we will add the magic tool of halftone shooting—the halftone screen itself. A halftone screen is designed to generate a specific dot pattern. For example, if we want a 120-line halftone, we have to use the appropriate 120-line halftone screen.

How does the halftone screen "decide" whether to make dots large or small? Imagine this: If you were to use a very soft pencil and draw very hard on tissue paper and then hold the paper up to a bright light, some light would pass through the areas where you pressed hard with your pencil. In the areas where you didn't draw at all, much more light would pass through.

Now suppose you started pressing very hard to draw all over the top of the tissue, but gradually pressed lighter and lighter until you reached the bottom. If you then held the paper up to the light, the bottom of the sheet would allow more light to pass through than would the top. And, if you held it up to an extremely bright light, it would allow more light to pass through your dark areas than would a dim light.

That is the secret of the halftone screen. The photo is placed on the copyboard (Illustration 30) and illuminated with a very bright light source. Light bounces off the photo, through the lens, *through the halftone screen*, and finally onto the film. The more light that is

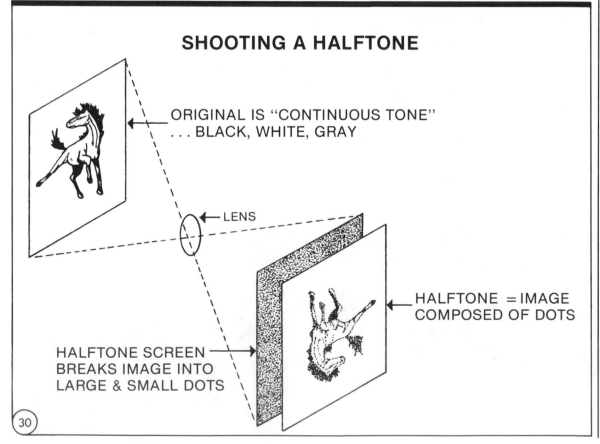

SHOOTING A HALFTONE

ORIGINAL IS "CONTINUOUS TONE" ... BLACK, WHITE, GRAY

LENS

HALFTONE = IMAGE COMPOSED OF DOTS

HALFTONE SCREEN BREAKS IMAGE INTO LARGE & SMALL DOTS

30

reflected by the photo, the more penetration through the halftone screen. So, in dark areas of the photo, only a little light is reflected (meaning there was little light penetration through the dots). And correspondingly, the brighter an area of the photo, the more penetration through the screen and the more exposure to the film.

Now to make sense of it all. The film that we are using is "line" film. Remember, it cannot see varying shades of gray. Either enough light passes through each "faded" area in the halftone screen to make an exposure or it doesn't. In a sense, there is no in between.

Yet the dots are either larger or smaller. This is because when *enough* light gets through the screen to create the image of a tiny dot, *enough* light is not present to "blast" through the slightly darker areas of the screen. So, when a part of a photo is dark, that same part of the halftone will be given less light (meaning a smaller area is given line exposure). The brighter areas of the photo literally "blast" enough light through the screen to make a larger exposure.

And that is the halftone screen: the creator of large and small dots on regular line film.

Flash, highlight exposures

Actually, it is a little more complicated than that. The exposure just described is called the "main" exposure. But because of some of the rather esoteric limitations of the halftone process, most photos need even one or two additional exposures.

The "flash" exposure is used to enhance the ability of the film to hold more of the original photo's range. The flash is done with the halftone screen in place, but the photo is not exposed at the same time. Rather, the film receives light through the screen from either a short exposure of a white piece of paper placed on the copyboard where the photo would normally be, or from a special light (usually a yellow-filtered safelight).

The flash does make a slight exposure on the film, but with even intensity. So, rather than actually placing an image on the film, the flash exposure "sensitizes" the film and allows it to gain more detail from the dark areas of the photo. If the flash exposure were long enough and bright enough, the film would receive an even exposure of a pattern of dots, but then the result would not be a halftone: It would be a screen tint.

There are cases when another exposure can be used to enhance the highlight, or brighter areas of the final halftone. Although some printers consistently use this type of exposure, others use it occasionally, or not at all.

This is called the bump exposure. It is performed without the halftone screen in place, but with the photo on the copyboard. Another way to describe it is as a short line shot. This short line shot more or less "blasts" a lot of light off the bright areas of the photo, but has only a limited effect on the dark areas. The film, in turn, receives a major effect in the highlight areas and a minor one in the shadow areas.

In practice, it is common to shoot the flash first, the main second, and the bump third.

Halftone variables

If all this doesn't make things complicated enough, each halftone also has its own intensities of light and dark areas. On one photo, the brightest portion (highlight) may be rather gray, while the darkest (shadow) may not be as dark as it should. In the snapshot world, these would be called bad photos. But in the world of halftone lithography, they are just typical problems.

If no accommodation is made for the differences between one photo and another, the results might look like the comparison between Illustrations 31 and 32. While Illustration 32 looks rather normal, Illustration 31 appears to have gray highlights and gray shadows. So one thing is clear: These two photos could not be shot at the same time (grouped or shot together on the copyboard) without one of them turning out poorly. While the artist might think, "I'll save some money here and scale both pictures to the same dimension and create only one shot," the camera operator might quickly anticipate that the results would be similar to our samples.

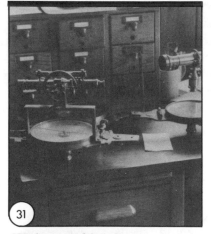

31

32

Without taking into consideration the density, or reflective quality, of an individual photograph, the litho camera operator might produce these results: grayness in the light areas, flatness in the dark areas. This is a poorly shot halftone.

A properly shot halftone has a small highlight dot to optically approach whiteness and tiny white dots (shadow dots) to maintain control over the entire printed photo.

114

Illustration 33 shows what the litho-camera operator would want to do with the original photo in Illustration 31. By adjusting the flash, main, and bump exposures, he has brought the halftone into printable quality. Manipulating these three exposures alters the size of the highlight, shadow, and middletone dots (Illustration 34).

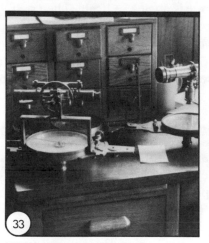

The same photograph was shot here as was shot for Illustration 31. However, the camera operator made adjustments in the exposures to control the highlight and shadow areas, which were both too gray on the original photo. Thus, even a poorly shot original photo can be forced into a better printed product than one might expect.

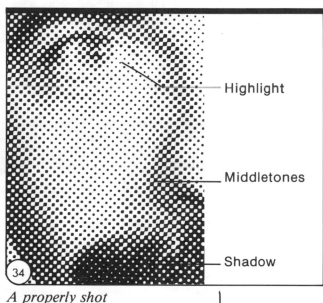

— Highlight

— Middletones

— Shadow

A properly shot halftone has small dots in the bright areas (highlights), transitioning to half-sized (50 percent) dots in the middle tones, to the better than 90 percent sized dot in the shadows (dark areas). This sample was greatly enlarged to show the three basic dot categories.

A good halftone dot

Just how big or small should the dots be? Generally, this rule is followed: The highlight dot should be between zero and seven percent in relation to its total possible size. The shadow dot should be as large as possible without eliminating all the space between dots, or 90 percent to 95 percent of its possible size. The trick is this: These goals are for the *printed* version of the halftone, *not* for the film negative.

When the halftone film is used to burn a printing plate, slight distortion takes place. More distortion occurs when the plate prints onto the rubber blanket. Certain presses automatically (and not intentionally) make all the dots larger (called "press gain"). Finally, depending on the surface of the paper, all the dots will spread to an extent. Some papers (newsprint, for example) allow the dot to spread a great deal, while others (such as enameled stock) hold the dot rather faithfully.

Obviously, shooting a halftone is a trick in itself. Then matching it to the specific press and paper to be used adds another set of problems. Top that off with each photo being a touch different (or even radically different) with highlight and shadow densities, and you can understand why some people consider halftone shooting an art.

Measuring halftone intensities

There are ways for the camera operator to measure the densities of highlights and shadows. One way is to use a Kodak Reflection Density Guide. The operator simply compares the preprinted gray paper to the photo and uses the information to adjust already-established exposures.

A more reliable method is to use an electronic densitometer, which gives a digital readout of the highlight, middletone, and shadow. This information is processed by computer to provide the halftone exposures. The computer can also keep files of modifications required for printing on uncoated stock, enamel, and so on.

Grouping halftone shots

As you know, it is possible to shoot more than one photo at a time on the litho camera. The size of the copyboard is one limitation. In practice, if you have two photos to be shot, one at 77 percent and one at 75 percent, it can be more economical to shoot them both at 76 percent (if they will still fit in the layout). The printer normally gives a price break on such group shots.

But keep in mind that it's the similarity of densities that will dictate the ultimate quality of the photos. If the printer says that the densities are too far apart, he is saying that the final quality will suffer. You then make the final choice between quality and economy.

PMT halftones

As we proceed to the stripping section, you will note that each halftone is shot as a film negative that must later be positioned.

There are shortcuts to this method. If you use a photomechanical transfer material and specially designed halftone screens, the halftone shot can be made as a paper print. This paper halftone can be cropped and placed on the paste-up. Then, when the paste-up is shot, the result is that all the photos are already screened and on the negative.

The quality ramifications of such procedures are hard to describe because some printers are better than others at the technique. For that reason, we will not attempt to illustrate the process.

Rather, bear in mind the following: A 120-line halftone is often considered minimal magazine quality in terms of the detail it can produce. That means each square inch of halftone will have 14,400 dots. These dots must pass through the camera lens, which distorts them somewhat. To compensate, when the halftone is originally shot on paper, the highlights are made larger, and the shadow areas are kept more open (flat). The paper print will look somewhat poor (again, flat), but the resulting negative will fill in and bring the dots into proper range (as described above).

Using this method, the cost to the buyer is in quality, which is sacrificed for economy. You simply get a lot less out of the photo.

If you wish to experiment with placing halftones directly on the boards, either run tests with your printer or, if you have an in-house camera, shoot a batch of halftones and then have the printer run them through the normal production procedure. Only by working with your photos, your printer, and your paper, will you ultimately determine whether the quality level suits your purposes.□

HARD AND SOFT DOTS

Now we address a technical beast: hard and soft dots. What are they, and what do they do to printing?

We must keep in mind our earlier discussion of the halftone being created on "line" film. Here is the basic theory: Although the film is line, it doesn't make a perfect, abrupt break between image and nonimage when the halftone is shot. Rather, it has a small transition zone—a halo, if you will—marking the difference between image and nonimage.

Suppose you are having a halftone shot with the rapid-access process, using one of the newly developed specialty screens. That negative halftone could be used to make a proof or print, and that print might look good.

But what about that transition area of dark to light? What if a far brighter light were used to expose the proof? Wouldn't the size of the dots be altered somewhat?

Yes. The reason is that a soft-dot halftone is a first-generation halftone that has a noticeable transition area from image to nonimage. If you vary the intensity of the light source when proofing (or plating), the dot sizes are subject to change.

This same "soft dot" problem arises when the photomechanical process is used, meaning that photos are placed directly on the paste-ups. Even though the screened photo on the paste-up is "first generation," the line film also reacts as first generation.

When soft-dot halftones are used to make printing plates, the results are, unfortunately, unpredictable. One printer will gain a great deal burning the plates, while another will gain very little. Even the freshness of chemicals at the time of negative development can alter the effects at a given printer's system.

The hard dot solution

The solution is to work only with hard dots at platemaking time. How are hard dots achieved from soft-dot originals? By contacting or duplicating with a stable exposure and light source.

Although the plate burn (with its intense light source) is unpredictable in its effects on soft dots, the contacting procedure in the darkroom is not. The "transition zone" between dot and no-dot can be "hardened" or "defined" by making a duplicate of the halftone via the contact process.

The halftone is placed in contact (emulsion to emulsion) with duplication material (as shown in Illustration 35) and a controlled exposure is made. Because of the nature of the contacting process and the films used, the receiving film simply cannot hold the transition zone itself, so it makes a clean break between the image and the nonimage. The result is called a hard dot.

This is one way to achieve a hard dot. Another way to get almost the same result is to use lith films (described earlier), high quality cameras (conventional or scanning), and controlled processing. Some firms will say that it is not possible, while others can produce very acceptable results with the first halftone negative.

More common, though, is the belief that contacting to a hard dot is the most reliable method of achieving a good, reliable negative for plate burning. Trust your printer's opinion rather than trying to prove that "it can be done another way."

Contacting to a hard dot is only one application for the contact procedure. It also has other uses, which we will address later in the chapter on stripping.

(Editor's Note: Since this original manuscript was drafted, rapid-access films have been introduced that have qualities similar to lith films. Kodak's version is called the Ultratec line, and it produces an extremely high quality line shot or halftone as a first-generation dot.)

CHAPTER 22

Soft dots are unpredictable when making printing plates. Therefore, if the original halftone film is "soft," the printer contacts it to a "hard" dot. Lith films and some of the newer rapid, access films achieve a nearly perfect dot on their first pass, but other factors often necessitate the halftone contacting procedure anyhow.

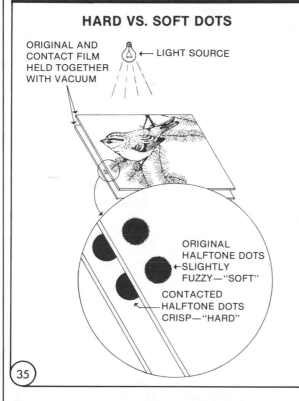

HARD VS. SOFT DOTS

ORIGINAL AND CONTACT FILM HELD TOGETHER WITH VACUUM

← LIGHT SOURCE

ORIGINAL HALFTONE DOTS ←SLIGHTLY FUZZY—"SOFT"

CONTACTED HALFTONE DOTS CRISP—"HARD"

35

Duotone and other oddities

We originally stated that this "black-and-white" section would cover the simpler aspects of halftone and prep work. Well, duotones also fall into that category.

First of all, a duotone is a halftone that prints in two colors. Frequently, this is black and one other color.

The effect achieved varies with the color of ink and the exposure technique used. For example, one might shoot a photo as a duotone to print in black and orange inks. If the black were the predominant color and the orange the subordinate color, the effect would be

HARD AND SOFT DOTS

a dark-brownish photo. This photo would appear to have somewhat more depth than a standard halftone.

However, it might be that the printer makes the orange the predominant color. Then, the result would be an orangish-brown printed image.

Why don't we illustrate all the possibilities? They are virtually unlimited. Each color in a duotone could be printed in densities relative to each other. That is 64 possibilities, using only two inks. There are hundreds of ink colors, so there are hundreds of thousands of possibilities.

The key is that duotones are a nonprocess color method of introducing tonal color variation and interest into photos. Therefore, the expense of color separation (covered in a later section) is avoided, while at least some inexpensive variety is introduced into the magazine.

Again, for an honest demonstration of the duotone combinations that you can expect from your printer, have him shoot some tests for you. Send in one photo, have it shot as a duotone using the variations that the printer has developed, get proofs made, and take it from there. If you are a novice, use the following color combinations in your request: black and yellow, black and orange, black and red, and red and blue. That last combination will give you a proof in the purple range and should point you toward understanding the almost unlimited variations available with duotones.

Again, printing samples in this book would be misleading. We would be showing you what our printer can do with our colors, not what your printer can do with yours.□

STRIPPING AND CONTACTING

The term "stripping" as it relates to preparation work is rather outdated. Some people find it odd that men and women in the lithographic industry call themselves professional strippers, but it's true. The term hangs on from years long gone.

At that time, neither the lithographic nor the photographic procedures available were very sophisticated. When an exposure was made, it was made onto a glass sheet, which carried an emulsion. As this material, which served the same purpose as today's films, continued through the production cycle, the emulsion had to be removed from the glass. Thus, "stripping" described the actual removal of the film emulsion and its reapplication onto another surface. The glass sheets themselves could not be used for burning printing plates or for any other purpose.

What stripping is today

Today, even though the term hangs on, stripping does not involve the stripping of anything, but the *positioning* of the material. This can be film negatives, film positives, halftones, color separations, or any other components that eventually will become part of the printed magazine.

Earlier, we discussed the process involved in creating a film negative or a halftone negative, and briefly described the contacting procedure. Assuming that each page of our sample magazine was shot individually, and assuming that all the halftones were shot as film negatives, everything must now be organized into some form that will allow us to burn all the photos and page negatives onto the plate and into their proper positions so that they can be printed.

Stripping, then, is an assembly procedure.

A simple strip

Illustration 36 shows a line negative that was shot from a paste-up. Because the paste-up person anticipated the subsequent in-

This represents a film negative of a paste-up that had a "window" for a photo to be inserted. Although it reproduced here as black and white, in reality it is black and clear: The white areas are clear film, the black areas are dark film.

122

sertion of a halftone, he inserted a black or red "window" to indicate where the material should fall. A simple strip, then, could be described as inserting any material into this window. Most often, such windows are used for halftones. In Illustration 37, the halftone is being taped into position into this window.

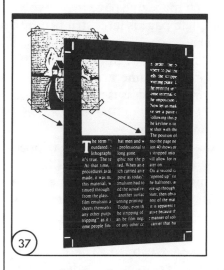

(37)

Obviously, this is not a difficult procedure. It involves the simple taping of one element onto another. Because the paste-up carried a "black spot" or "window," the resulting negative will accept the halftone without any manipulation.

For a simple magazine, it is feasible that all halftones could be taped into their respective positions. The next question would be, "What do you do with the pages?" The answer involves another aspect of preparation work: impositions.

The above procedure was a strip. It is also a strip when a page negative is taped into its proper position relative to other pages. Illustration 38 shows several pages of negatives taped onto a carrier sheet, which also may be called a "flat," a "lay-up," a "side," or a few other terms.

(38)

EIGHT NEGATIVES STRIPPED INTO A FLAT

CHAPTER 23

The same film negative shown in Illustration 36 is now shown with the halftone being taped, or stripped, into the window. The negative is shown reading backward, which is the way it would actually lie on the stripping table when the halftone is stripped to its emulsion side.

Another stripping activity entails the taping of several pages—eight in this case—to a carrier sheet, often called goldenrod. After taping the negatives in place "upside down" to the goldenrod, the entire assembly is turned over. The goldenrod is cut away to allow light to pass through the areas of the negatives that are intended to print.

STRIPPING AND CONTACTING

39

The term "print key-line" means that rather than serve as an indication of where a photo or other element will go, the line itself will print in ink.

These two negatives both carry material that will print on the same page, in the same colored ink (black). One burns the rule, or keyline, and the text; the other burns the halftone. The negs could be exposed directly to the printing plate or be used to create a final, one-piece film with all elements in place. The former is called a double-burn to plate; the latter is called one of the following: composite film, duplicate final film, single-piece final film.

The position of each of these pages is critical. If they are not in order, the book, when printed, will not be in order. Knowing where to put the pages is called *following an imposition*, a chart that tells the stripper where each page of the magazine will fall on the printing plate. Impositions themselves will be addressed more fully in the printing section, but the point is, each magazine page may involve some internal stripping, and each complete page is later stripped into the imposition of the magazine proper.

Now let us make things a bit more difficult. In Illustration 39, we see a paste-up with a notation, "Print keyline around photo." Following this paste-up through the camera process is no problem. If the keyline is to print, then obviously it will stay on the paste-up and be shot with the rest of the material on the page.

However, it is apparent that the photo could not be stripped into the page negative because there is no window available. Illustration 40 shows one manner of solving this problem: The page negative is stripped into a carrier that has holes punched into it; these holes will allow for repositioning and re-registering the page as necessary later on.

On a second carrier, the halftone is stripped. The carrier is "opened up" (in other words, the window is now cut in order to crop the halftone), and we now have two sheets of carriers with material

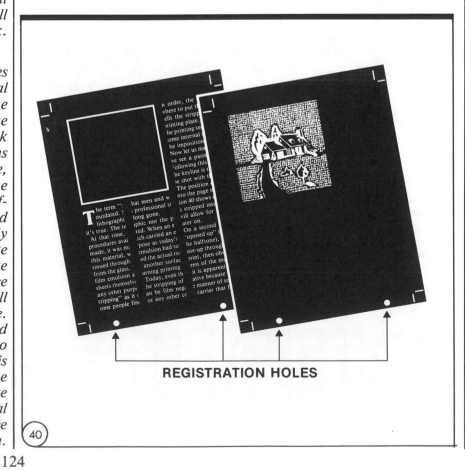

REGISTRATION HOLES

40

124

that will go on one page.

There are two distinctly different ways to handle the pair of carriers. One way would be to put them into the contact frame and expose each of them to the same piece of film. This would be called duplicating the film. Then, if negatives were desired, and both the halftone and the line shot were negatives, duplication film would be used to achieve a "single-piece negative" that would include halftone, the rule, and all of the text copy on the page.

The other way would be to use both these carriers to make an exposure onto the printing plate. This procedure is almost identical to duplicating the film, except it eliminates the expense of the duplication film itself. Rather than making a single burn (exposure) on the printing plate, the line material would be exposed, the carrier would be removed, the halftone would be registered to the plate, and a second exposure would be made.

If you recall our earlier discussion about soft-halftone dots, follow this logic: There would be no need to "harden" the halftone dot prior to stripping if it were known that final, duplication film would be made prior to burning the printing plates. On the other hand, if the halftone dots were soft, it would be risky (and possibly foolish) to attempt to burn the printing plate using the double-burn method because you could not anticipate the quality of the halftone.

We have described the double-burn and duplicate-film process for a single page. In addition, a full eight pages can be double-burned. All of the text (paste-up negatives) would be on one "flat," while all the halftones would be on a second. These eight pages could all be contacted to a single eight-page sheet via the duplication process or, if all the halftones were hard-dot, both of these sheets could be used to burn the printing plate.

Other reasons for double-stripping, double-burns

As we have said, the addition of a rule around a photo can create the requirement for double-burning, or contacting, to final-piece negatives. There are other reasons why a second stripping sheet, or a lay-up, is required.

Illustration 41 shows a side view of a halftone stripped directly onto a line negative. As you can see, the emulsion of the halftone must be in contact with whatever material it will be exposed to. Similarly, the emulsion of the page negative should be in contact when the exposure is made. The thickness of the halftone film does not go undetected through the lithographic process. The page negative simply would not maintain perfect contact during an exposure later on. Therefore, if the halftone is too close to text on the page, it can literally prevent that text from contacting properly. The result would be the type spreading or distorting when the plate was burned or the contact film made. This is another reason for stripping some material on a separate flat and other material on the "main" page flat.

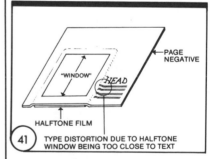

41   TYPE DISTORTION DUE TO HALFTONE WINDOW BEING TOO CLOSE TO TEXT

Liftoff can occur when a halftone is positioned close enough to text to prevent it from fully contacting the printing plate during exposure. This is one of several reasons that the double-burn or, alternatively, duplicate final film, is pursued rather than a strip into a window.

125

Printer preferences

There are different schools of thought as to how this double-burn/duplication procedure should be attacked. Some printers routinely insist on stripping all halftones into a separate flat. They may decide this for reasons of soft-dot control, for reasons of maintaining proper contact, or because they routinely duplicate all film into final, single-piece material before burning the plate.

Other firms will strip halftones into windows when they find it feasible, but more frequently a small photo embedded too close to text will make this procedure impractical.

Is stripping simple?

If stripping is merely the positioning of film relative to its final printed appearance, does it seem very difficult? Keep in mind that we are addressing extremely simple stripping procedures at this point. When we begin to discuss color stripping, we will be describing a far more complicated area. Becoming a journeyman stripper with the skills required to perform all types of complex stripping can take more than six years. It is not the intent of this book to oversimplify stripping. Although we can describe some of the more complex procedures, this is not to be taken as technical instruction in preparation. There's a lot more to it.

Proofs

Let us now return to one of our eight-page flats, as shown in Illustration 38. These eight pages represent what the printing plate will later produce on paper. Because stripping involves manipulation movement and decision-making on the part of the responsible party, "proving" what was done is virtually always the next step. If, for example, several halftones were put in the wrong places and printing plates were made, the customer would soon become an ex-customer.

There are several different types of proofs available on the market, and they are discussed in a separate part in this section. For now, let's describe the proofing procedure itself.

Since one or more flats can be used to burn a printing plate, these same flats can be exposed to proofing material. This is a contact exposure, and as with all contact exposures, the orientation of the film is important. The emulsions of the film are placed in contact with the proofing material. Then a light source passes through the open areas of the negatives onto the proofing paper. The resulting proof shows what was on one or several flats. In other words, it shows what will be burned onto the printing plate—which is, of course, what will print on the paper.

There are many types of proofing materials available. For those that are thin enough and can be proofed on two sides of a sheet, another eight-page flat would be exposed onto the backside of this proof. Later, someone would slice the proofs into four-page sections and then trim, fold, and staple them together. This would give a good approximation of what the printed magazine will later look like.

Contacting

In our discussions on halftones and of proofs, we have described the contacting procedure. To elaborate just a bit, let's refer to Illustration 42. We are looking at a side view of film. When any material is placed on camera and exposed to a conventional lithographic negative, that negative will pick up a reversed/flopped image of the original. This occurs in all photographic processes using conventional lenses, including your pocket camera.

When the negative is processed, the result will be "right-reading emulsion down." Imagine it this way: If the negative's emulsion carries a reversed/flopped image, then the only way you can get a clear picture of what it would look like is to lay it down on a light table (or other light source). The emulsion would be away from you; the film base would be toward you. All the material would be readable. This means that when the emulsion is down and you can read it, you have a "RRED" (right-reading emulsion down) negative. That is what we need when we are working with the negative-acting process in lithography.

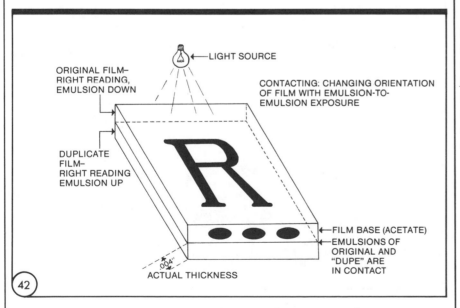

Whether the object is a duplicate negative, a contact print, or a reverse, it is important that the emulsions of both original and receiving film are in contact.

If we were to lay that negative onto a printing plate and expose it, the plate would pick up the same image that we would see if we were viewing the negative on a light table. Because printing plates for most magazines do need a right-reading image on the plate, it makes sense that the emulsions of the negatives must be down when the material is readable.

127

This can be particularly important when requesting material from advertisers. Although a simple advertisement (no halftones or tints) with straight text might not suffer damage if the emulsion were wrong, a more complex ad could present significant problems.

If you consider that each dot occupies as little as 1/17689th of a square inch, it is easy to see that a wrong orientation of emulsions could severely damage the image (Illustration 43). Therefore, whenever contacting is required in lithographic prep, it is often critical that negatives are oriented toward emulsions. If a negative is burning a plate, the negative emulsion will be down and the plate emulsion will always be up. If a duplicate piece of film must be made of a critical ad, then the original material should be emulsion up, which will produce an emulsion down (and plate-ready) negative.

For these reasons, it is important for the production director to work closely with the printer to understand and to learn both film-duplication and plate-burning procedures. Although many magazines are successfully printed without regard to proper emulsion orientation, the occasional problems of advertiser complaints always seem to get the fingers pointing everywhere except at the emulsions. The emulsions can be the culprit.

In contrast to Illustration 42, this illustration demonstrates an out-of-contact situation. The emulsions not being in contact will produce a change in dot size because of light scatter, thus changing the values of the dots—which, of course, changes the halftone itself. Depending on whether the contact was to a positive or negative, the halftone will get lighter or darker when it is finally printed.

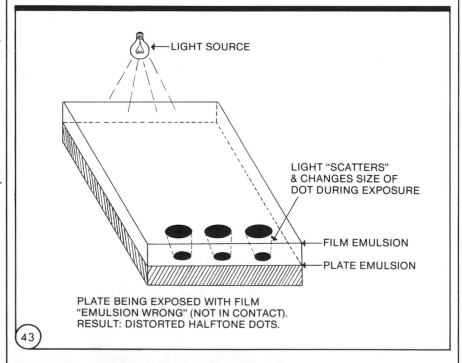

PLATE BEING EXPOSED WITH FILM "EMULSION WRONG" (NOT IN CONTACT). RESULT: DISTORTED HALFTONE DOTS.

(43)

Other contacting applications

Contacting, then, is a rather powerful tool in the preparation field. It can be used to create duplicate film, reverse an image, flop an image, reorient an emulsion, make a proof, or burn a plate. It is, in some ways, a very simple procedure but very important in controlling the overall quality of the printed product.□

SECTION IV:
COLOR SEPARATIONS AND PROOFS

THE FUNDAMENTALS OF COLOR SEPARATION

Years ago, when I started giving seminars on production management for magazines, one of my topics was (and still is) color separations. I recall doing several hours straight during one seminar and feeling rather proud as we headed for lunch. One of the attendees took me aside and quietly said, "Listen, I guess I'm ignorant, but nothing you said meant a thing to me. What the hell is a color separation?"

Live and learn. I learned: Not everybody is born with knowledge of color separations. So let's correct that before we proceed. After an introduction describing what separations are, we will relate them to magazines, money, proofs, and stripping. As you will see, a discussion of color separations can't be properly done without constant references to dollars, so we'll do that, too.

The reflective primaries

When we view a magazine page printed in "full color," we are receiving light in our eyes that is bounced off the page. Naturally, the only light we can receive comes from whatever is illuminating that page, *less* the amount of light that the page absorbs. Thus the term "subtractive color." The magazine page subtracts certain colors from the colors being bounced off it and reflects others to the eye.

A white page would bounce back what we would call the full spectrum of the light source. A page that looked magenta would subtract, or absorb, most of the light except magenta itself. A cyan page would do the same with cyan, a yellow page with yellow. In other words, when we put yellow ink on a page, we are really putting a filter on the page that absorbs all but yellow light, which it reflects.

In normal magazine color printing, there are four reflective primaries: magenta, cyan, yellow, and black. These four colors are not adequate to duplicate the entire range of color that can be detected by the human eye; however, they are quite adequate to reproduce what we interpret as a "full color" reproduction of a photo.

For example, you might have a snapshot with green grass, brown trees, and blue sky. The full color, or four-color, printing process can, via color separation, use the four subtractive primaries to give you a close reproduction of the original photo. That is what prints in "full" or "process" color in a magazine: a replication, via offset lithography and subtractive-color theory, of the original image.

How separations are made

As we discussed in the section on halftones, offset printing cannot print "tones." It can print only full applications of ink. The ink, for photos, is broken into tiny dots, which the eye blends back into tones.

Full-color printing requires what might be called four

132

halftones of the same photo. One halftone is to print in black ink, one in magenta, one in cyan, and one in yellow.

Color separation is the chore of getting the right values into these four primaries. Then, when they are all printed in register, enough light in each wavelength of the spectrum is absorbed to provide the eye with an approximation of the original photo.

Basically, color-separation shooting is quite like halftone shooting. A key difference is this: Appropriate filters are used to filter out "unwanted" colors. For example, when generating the yellow halftone negative of a photo, filters are used to prevent the magenta and cyan tones from reaching the film.

Another important factor is that each screen—halftone screen, if you will—must be at a slightly different angle. When the four primaries print in the same place (which is what will make them look like a photo), the orientation of the dots in each colored ink must not coincide.

Illustration 44 shows what happens when two halftone screens are used at angles too similar. The result is a moire effect. Illustration 45 shows the same two screens at angles 15 degrees apart.

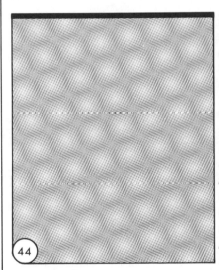

CHAPTER 24

44

45

Several different halftone screen angles are required to prevent this from occurring on press. This moire effect would occur frequently if strippers and other technicians were not constantly exercising control over screen angles used in assembling (or separating) a page. We have, of course, enlarged the dots to show what happens —but the disturbing moire effect is just as obvious when it occurs with 133-line screen in print.

The same screens as were used to create the moire in Illustration 44 are now carefully stripped 15 degrees apart, creating this typical litho-dot pattern. If the image were part of a full-color printed photo, it would offer a hardly noticeable visual effect.

Color printing, of course, does not reproduce each halftone screen in black. Rather, each prints in one of the primaries. But the moire effect is the same. Angles must be controlled or the effect will show on the printed piece.

That, then, is the basic principle of color separation: Using a photomechanical process to simulate the effect of the original photo

THE FUNDAMENTALS OF COLOR SEPARATION

in terms of its light absorption. To put it another way, color separation involves the identification of the amount of each of the four primaries in a photo, and the converting of these amounts into screened halftones. Later, in the actual printing of the photo, all four screened halftones will print in the ink color that relates to the reflective values: If there is a blue sky, then the blue negative (similar to any halftone negative) will be used to burn the blue printing plate (not the color of the plate, but the color that the plate will print), which will pick up the appropriate amounts of blue ink from the inking fountain on the press, etc.

Let's now outline the general characteristics of three common separation systems: conventional, direct, and scanned. Then let's compare the three techniques to one another in relation to quality, cost, and limitations. And finally, we'll review traditional and innovative methods that you can use to get the most from your color-separation dollars.□

CONVENTIONAL SEPARATIONS

In today's world of graphic arts, some people tend to think of "conventional" color-separations as old fashioned. In a sense, they are right: Technology has advanced the art to a great extent. But there is always room for craftsmanship, so conventional techniques will probably continue to be with us for the foreseeable future. The conventional process involves the following steps:

First, the original artwork, photo, or transparency is placed on a "process-color camera," which is simply a very accurate litho camera with color-corrected lenses and filtering ability.

Four exposures are made onto four different sheets of film. The exposures filter out the intensities of magenta, cyan, yellow, and black (the "subtractive primary colors" used in printing processes). As with all separation methods, filters are used to prevent the unwanted light waves from reaching the film. The resulting four negatives do *not* have a dot pattern, but rather, each is composed of "continuous tones."

But, as you know by now, the lithographic process cannot print continuous tones. So these continuous-tone negatives must later be converted into screened (dot pattern) negatives. Before they are converted, though, the continuous-tone negatives (often called intermediate negatives) can be handworked to correct color.

What color is corrected? Keep in mind that no lithographic separation system is perfect. A skilled artist could look at the continuous-tone negatives and say, "Given that amount of tone on this neg, the sky will not be as blue as the original photo." He could then remove some of the negative material with a chemical-etching process, thereby allowing more light to pass through when the film is used in subsequent procedures.

Color correction at this stage is the main strength of conventional separation: Hues can be modified just a bit (to match an elusive flesh tone, for example) or dramatically changed (making a blue automobile green, and so on).

Such corrections are performed by highly skilled color artists, who have the uncanny ability to look at the four pieces of film and conjure up a mental image of what the result would look like. Because of the skills involved, good correction artists are hard to find—and they command top wages.

The next step in conventional color separation is conversion into screened negatives or positives. This is achieved by using a halftone screen, similar to that described in the B/W halftone section, to break the continuous tonal changes into large and small dots for each color.

From the four screened negatives (or positives), a proof is made. (Possibly a Cromalin, a registered trademark of DuPont; Color Key, a registered trademark of the 3M Co., or a press proof, all discussed under the section on proofs.)

After the proof is viewed by the customer, the screened negatives can still be modified somewhat by "dot etching." This pro-

136

cess entails the physical alteration of dot sizes by the application of chemicals. It is a local, manual process, which means that at this stage of the game you can still slightly modify a portion of the magenta negative or bring up the blue in the "sky." In other words, if you ask for less red on the "face" portion of a photo, the color artist will alter only that area of the magenta and, possibly, yellow negatives.

The dot-etching process is not as versatile as continuous-tone alterations. At this point, you couldn't expect to do any major alteration, but you do have enough control to make minor changes.

After the final corrections, the finished negatives (or positives) are stripped into their intended positions and used to burn the images onto the printing plates or to make duplicate sets of film, and so on.□

CHAPTER 25

DIRECT SCREEN AND SCANNER SEPARATIONS

The camera color separations involve four exposures, via screens and filters, of the original photograph. It is more complicated than this schematic in that masking filters, generated for the particular subject being shot, are also required for quality purposes.

The main difference between conventional-separation techniques and direct-screening procedures is this: There are no intermediate negatives (the continuous-tone film just discussed). Instead of creating the intermediate negatives, a halftone screen is placed over each piece of film during the initial exposure (Illustration 46). Again, four exposures are made onto four different pieces of film, each the result of filtering out unwanted colors.

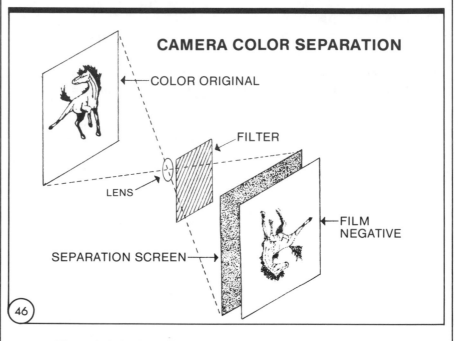

CAMERA COLOR SEPARATION

COLOR ORIGINAL

FILTER

LENS

SEPARATION SCREEN

FILM NEGATIVE

46

The result is that direct-screen separations are produced in less time than it takes to make conventional separations. But speed has a price. While conventional separations can be greatly modified by artists who work with intermediate negatives, all post-separation color corrections for direct-screen subjects must be accomplished with dot etching alone. And because dot etching is basically limited to small changes in color (a maximum of about a 20 percent change in the dot size), no major alterations are practical once the separation has been shot.

In other respects, though, direct screening resembles conventional separations: The four shots are made, the resulting negatives (composed of halftone dots) are either used to make a proof or contacted for other purposes, minor corrections are made, and the film is used to expose the printing plates.

Scanner separations

The third common separating system is the color scanner. Scanning, controversial when it was introduced several decades ago, has come of age in recent years. Here's how the scanning process, a noncamera procedure, works:

The subject to be separated is wrapped around the scanning drum. A light-sensing stylus travels the length of the drum while it is rotated and senses one or more of the primary colors. The information is fed through a computer, modified as necessary, and directed to another stylus (this one emits light, rather than sensing it), which in turn exposes a piece of film. On some scanners, the halftone screen is part of the computerized output unit, so the result is the same as the direct-screening procedure: a screened piece of film, produced without an intermediate negative.

Other scanners produce continuous-tone negatives, which must later be given a dot via the contacting process. Which is better? There are no clear answers. Each professional has his own opinion.

Scanners that produce screens, then, are also limited to dot-etched color correction with one exception: Some separation houses don't do any manual correcting. Rather, they look at a proof of the separated subject and, if alterations are required, they simply reseparate it. The scanner is programmed by the operator to increase or decrease the offending colors, and new film is produced. The logic here is that it's cheaper to run a machine than it is to hire a correction artist.

Other firms, though, have their scanners so heavily booked that they choose to have corrections done manually. Certain scanners produce a dot so hard that few corrections can be accomplished, while the scanners producing less-hard dots offer more versatility for manual correction by a color artist.

There are many different scanners available, and all have slightly different capabilities. Some will handle separations up to 11 inches by 17 inches, while others are limited to 10 inches by 12 inches. One scanner may separate a single color in 20 minutes, while the next will scan four colors simultaneously in the same amount of time.

Because color scanning is so highly automated, it is the least expensive separation option on the market. (Inexpensive for the buyer, anyhow. The supplier might have a $300,000 outlay to get a small scanning department set up.) And given the recent technical advances in the field, the quality of scanned subjects·is meeting the expectations of more buyers every day. As of this writing, about 70 percent of all separations are done on scanners, and the number is still rising.

How do these three techniques compare to one another in relation to limitations, quality, and cost? Let's take a look.

Limitations

All three techniques will separate either reflective or transparent artwork. However, each technique (and more specifically, each machine) has its limitations. For example, one camera might be capable of enlarging a 35-mm slide up to 1,200 percent, while another has a limitation of 300 percent.

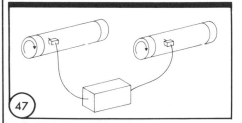

The color scanner uses a computer to interpret what the light sensor sees on the original material. The image is processed electronically and exposed onto the separation film.

DIRECT SCREEN AND SCANNER SEPARATIONS

There are only a few basic rules covering physical specifications. For conventional and direct methods, any work that will fit on the camera copyboard can be shot. That includes thick illustration board, tissue paper, and so on. Some shops can even separate three-dimensional objects, thereby eliminating the need to photograph them beforehand. Size is not a critical problem because if your regular vendor can't do an extremely large separation, you can always find one who can.

Scanners, though, have some built-in, rigid limitations. Currently there are no large scanners on the market. An original-art limitation of 12 inches by 18 inches is typical and 20 by 24 is pretty much the top limit.

In addition, scanners cannot accept flat artwork (illustration board, books, and so on) because all material to be separated must literally be wrapped around the scanning drum.

Quality

Generally speaking, you can get high quality separations using any of the three systems discussed here. The results depend, of course, on the skill of the camera, the scanner operators, and the amount of corrections you need to make.

While some of the finest separations have been done with conventional techniques, equally good material has been produced with direct processes and scanners. It takes quite a bit of training to detect—with the naked eye—subtle differences in dot structure produced by these methods. But there are a few significant differences. The first—and most notable—is cost. Nonscanner methods tend to take more time, and therefore cost more money.

Black details

One area to pay attention to, though, is that of "fine black detail." Both conventional and direct-camera techniques have the inherent problem of bouncing light off the art, through the lens, and onto the film. By using various filters, three of the printing primaries can be reproduced quite faithfully. But the fourth, black, presents a problem. Because black pigment is basically the presence of all reflective primaries (magenta, cyan, and yellow), it is a tough one to break out.

Sometimes you'll hear the term "ghost black" mentioned. This simply means that very little black ink will be printed on the final piece, and only to add a little punch to the color reproduction. But that can create a problem.

Suppose you have a number of fine black lines (cross-hatching arrows) in the original art. A light black possibly will help the general appearance of the piece, but it won't provide detail where you want it. In addition, the other three primaries will have a light dot structure in the "fine black line" area. The result on the finished piece

140

could be that your black line will appear quite fuzzy. It will be composed of a little black ink and a little of the other three colors.

This is one area in which scanners that incorporate lasers excel. To demonstrate this point, review Illustrations 48 and 49. We've enlarged two portions of offset printed artwork. One of these pieces was separated with the direct-screen method, while the other was scanned. The same piece of original art was used for both separations. Our enlargement is a line shot, which means it shows only red and black ink. Both printed pieces were in very good register. (We can't, of course, print a sample of the original because we would have to separate it with one of the three systems, so you wouldn't actually see the original piece.)

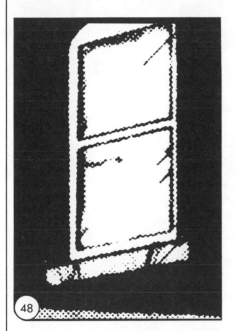

The scanner has the ability to extract more black detail from the photo than the camera. Here we see fine hairline black inklines around the window, enlarged for illustration purposes. The weaker outline around the window was produced by separating the photo on a camera, while the thicker, cleaner outline was produced by the scanner.

As the enlargements show, there is a significant difference in the quality of the black lines. The direct-screen version shows a strong dot pattern in the window area. The scanned version has almost no evidence of a pattern, and the line itself is cleaner and thicker. On the original art, these were simply crisp hairlines.

So what does it all mean? Basically, it means that scanners do have something to offer that you can't get on a camera. They have no lenses, so they don't pass the reflected light across a six-foot span, through the lens, and onto the film. Because they have direct-reading color-sensing heads, electronic-quality controls, and sophisticated, computerized color interpretation, you can expect to get much more detail from your photos or art than you'd get with any other technique—but only if your vendor has a quality state-of-the-art scanner.

Making a decision

Selecting the "best" separation method for your magazine is a

DIRECT SCREEN AND SCANNER SEPARATIONS

subjective decision. In the long run, though, you will probably find yourself choosing a scanner because the process is taking over quickly. Additionally, price dictates where many production people can spend their money. If that is your case, the scanner is your best bet. □

*Wrong reading photostats shot from
Magenta (left) and Cyan (right) color
separation negative films.*

THE ECONOMICS OF COLOR SEPARATIONS

Most production managers are deeply involved in the four-color explosion. The more color you use, though, the more you spend on separations, color corrections, and stripping, which are all expensive. But the number of separations needn't push your final costs up proportionately. Rather, the more you have, the less each should cost.

Those cost reductions don't just happen. The buyer/manager must be aware of the techniques that make things happen. By combining available techniques and negotiating volume prices with your separator, you can be sure you'll get the most from your color-separation dollar. There are many traditional and innovative methods that you can put to your own use.

Color separation, by any method, is a service business. Your material may get electronically scanned in 20 minutes or hand-corrected for hours. Generally, this means that the cost of materials has little to do with the final price. So, if you're after economy of any sort, gone are the days of getting a single-slide conventionally separated and handworked for hours.

Today, we hear a lot of talk about common-focus separations, which are similar in theory to group-shooting halftones described earlier. We also hear about dupes, mounts to position, and single-page strips. Any or all of these methods can be used, depending on the type of material and number of subjects that you have.

Group separations

One of the basic economic tricks of the trade is common-focus separations. Common focus means that more than one subject will be separated at the same time at a given scaling (enlargement or reduction). The only limiting factor here is the camera your job is produced on: How large is the copyboard and how large is the filmboard? If you check with your separator for specifications and prices, you will probably learn how much you can get on the camera at one time and what the savings will be.

Common-focus techniques apply to all separation systems: conventional methods, direct screening, and scanning. Common-focus grouping has the following advantages:

•*Economy:* Since you're making fewer total separations, your total cost and your per-subject cost will both be reduced.

•*Speed:* Because you save time (a factor implied by economy), you get an additional benefit: When you reduce total separation time, you can work closer to the deadline.

•*Simplicity:* There are no mechanical tricks for you to learn. Your only activity in grouping photos is to let your color separator know what you intend to do.

Requirements for group separations

Not just any group of subjects can be separated together.

144

They must meet these requirements:

•*Category:* You can't group a transparency with reflective art. One is lit from behind, the other from the front.

•*Percentage:* Naturally, all subjects in a group must be shot at the same camera setting.

•*Density:* You'll need to develop an eye for this. For example, a pale white-on-white photo of a dozen eggs can't normally be grouped with a dark campfire-type scene. As with B/W halftone shooting, exposure compensations must be made to faithfully reproduce a photo with highlight and shadow densities that vary from the norm.

•*Size:* Although you may have a group of subjects that meets the above requirements, you're still limited by the size of the camera copyboard, which must hold your material, and the vacuum board, which limits the size of final film. (Note: In the case of scanners, you're limited by the circumference and length of the machine's drum, its reproduction limits, and your material's flexibility to wrap around the drum.)

If you exceed size limitations with a group, you're automatically into another camera setup, so you're free to change the percentage of your next shot.

Compromises and costs: group separations

Naturally, grouping photos doesn't get you something for absolutely nothing. A small compromise will be made in the quality of the separations. Your separator knows this and will probably advise you that he goes for "best overall color" or "your preference," in which case you tell him the most important photo in the group. Of course, if you grouped a cover photo with a small filler shot, you'd give preference to the cover.

Usually the cost saved by grouping subjects is significant. Therefore, you can make, and pay for, more color correcting and still come out ahead. On the other hand, if you need flawless color, you could find yourself spending more on correction time than you've saved on separations. In that case, you'd be better off paying for individual separations.

Finally, you may be charged for each additional photo you add to a camera shot. This charge usually covers the time required for inspection, balancing, and possibly nominal corrections. These charges vary from one shop to the next, but they are usually somewhere between nothing at all and 25 percent of the single-subject separation cost. Sometimes the charge is there just to make sure that you don't get something for nothing.

When you try to put group separations to work, you may find that your art director (or the others involved in producing your material) will have several photos—all within a percentage or two of each other—that simply "must" be shot at those exact settings. In

CHAPTER 27

some cases, it will be true. In other cases, you will just be up against a bullheaded fellow employee, and you'll have a better chance of winning the argument if you can show that person the bottom line.

Here's how the prices of a typical four-subject group separation might look compared to individual shots. These prices existed in 1983, but at the time you read this, you may (and justifiably so) pay more (or less) in your area.

	Grouped	Individual
First subject:	$150	$150
Second subject:	30	150
Third subject:	30	150
Fourth subject:	30	150
Stripping:	100	100
Proof:	35	35
TOTAL:	$375	$735

Why have we added stripping costs to the above? For this reason: Subsequent techniques that we will discuss will save vast amounts of stripping time, which costs money. Stripping, by the way, can never be totally avoided. It includes the time required to position the four negatives, crop them, and ensure that, when the printing plate is made, all the four colors will print their inks in the same place to produce the illusion of the original photo.

As the above shows, with a little bit of compromise, you might well be in a position to cut your separation costs by nearly half.
□

DUPLICATE TRANSPARENCIES

The most troublesome limitation of common-focus separating is that all photos (artwork) in a group must be shot at the same percentage. That shortcoming can be overcome by having each subject duplicated to its ideal reproduction size before it is separated. When that's accomplished, your photos can all be separated with one camera setting (usually 100 percent), thus taking full advantage of the money-saving qualities that common-focus groups offer.

That intermediate step is known as duplication, or the making of a "dupe." Each of your photos will be placed in a camera (for reflective art) or enlarger (for transparencies) and shot at the individual percentage you require.

The result will be a color transparency of each subject at its eventual reproduction size ready to be separated with other material on the separation camera at the same time. In effect, you are creating a common-focus group even though the percentage requirements of the originals were initially different.

The economic factor that allows you to save money (although you are adding an additional step) is that dupes are much less expensive to produce than individual color-separations. Although making each dupe may cost you an average of $20 to $30 per subject, the same percentage changes could cost you something like $100 to $150 on the separation camera.

Requirements for dupes

You'll have much more versatility when using the dupe technique as a preliminary to common-focus shots, but once you've duped your art and photos to reproduction size, you still have two of the limitations that apply to common-focus grouping:

•*Density:* Even though you may have two transparencies (of photos, art, or mixed) duped for a 100 percent shot, their densities should be similar. Very dark scenes may separate very poorly when grouped up with those brilliantly lit.

However, each color separator makes these judgments individually, and you'll find that each opinion will be different. After working with your separator for a while, you'll get a feel as to what he or she thinks is acceptable.

•*Size:* All separation methods have physical limits. If the scanner drum is 12 inches by 18 inches, then that's the area limit for material to be color separated at one time. So if you have a batch of material that, when laid flat, measures 14 inches by 20 inches, you will need two separations and your average cost per separation will rise.

Compromises

There is little information available to the separation buyer about color compromises that result from separating duped transparencies. There is also little agreement among separators concerning the final quality of such work.

The reasons for the confusion are that some color separation houses are better than others, and some dupe houses are better than others. A very good photo lab can dupe and balance your work beautifully, only to have it messed up by a crummy separation. Or a batch of poorly made dupes can be saved by a conscientious separation firm.

As you can see, there is room for mistakes, arguments, and bad feeling. But by shopping around and getting involved in the problems as they arise, you can eventually create an excellent working relationship with vendors.

So back to the question: What are the compromises? Some say there are none; others point out that the duplication process, by its nature, increases the contrast of the original photo, and that the subsequent group separation adds to the deterioration of fidelity. You must answer the questions yourself, based on your own needs and experience. If you're really curious (and have a few dollars to spend), you might consider having several photos separated as originals, and then having the same material duped and separated again as a group. The color proofs should provide you with a very satisfactory comparison.

In the long run, the only real problem dupes will give you is that they demand lead time and often require that you deal with another vendor. Sure, they save separation time, but you must get the originals to the dupe house up to a week early. Is it worth it? That depends on the nature of your deadlines, the early availability of your color material, and the time you will subsequently save with fewer separations.

Suppliers of duplicate transparencies

Put your "test work" at a local color lab that does its own processing. (You can also work through the mail with an out-of-town firm, but you will eventually be more comfortable with a close working relationship with your dupe supplier.)

In getting a 35-mm slide or small transparency duped, make it clear to the lab that you will give them an exact reproduction size and that they should not add a safety factor. In any case, be sure that you add whatever slight oversizing that you will need to fill the reproduction area. For example, you might have a slide that will reproduce at five-inches wide duped at five-and-one-eighth-inches wide, thereby giving you a margin of error for final insertion into position.

Reflective artwork can be duped, too, by being placed on a litho camera and exposed to transparency film. The same scaling advice applies: Determine exactly what size you want the dupe to be (including oversizing) and make it clear to the lab that you have already added a safety margin. If you allow them to take care of safety margins, they may either make the dupe a shade too large or a shade too small. Control it yourself and you'll have less trouble.

Costs

Here again you'll find variations among suppliers. Your best bet will be to shop around, get an idea of the price structures, place sample orders, check the quality, and put the picture together. You'll find the following points will often come up:

Color dupe houses may 1) charge more for reflective art; 2) have a floating schedule based on your final film sizes; 3) include some color balancing, or 4) charge for even the slightest color alteration.

Separation houses may 1) charge for each additional photo in your group (or maybe they won't); 2) charge for inspection and control of density, regardless of additional color correction; 3) charge for color correction either on "unit time" or per subject. In rare cases, a separation house may refuse to accept your dupes at all. This can happen when the firm doesn't really understand your position as a buyer, or when they see too many poorly made dupes come in the door. Rarer yet is the separation house that's just too greedy to let you save money through your own initiative.

Bottom line comparisons

The bottom line, naturally, best describes the advantages of duping to size. Let's say that you have eight originals. For some reason, each must be reproduced at a different percentage, and your schedule allows you to get the work done over a two-week period. Local color dupes cost $25, and your separator charges $20 for each additional subject. His separation charge is $150. Strips (four colors, four pieces of film) are $25. Here's the final comparison:

	No Dupes Made	Dupes Made
Dupes (8)	-0-	$200
Separations	$1,200	150
Strips (8)	200	200
Additional subjects	-0-	160
TOTAL:	$1,400	$710

That's $690 in the bank. True, the above example is in strong favor of dupes, but that's because such situations do come up. Catalogs, for example, use thousands of separations, and their costs are staggering.

The point is, when you get into multiple-percentage work, dupes are a very viable option. Before eliminating them based on rumors about quality, examine the potential savings and give them a try. They have their place in prep.

Mounting to position

Now, let's take dupes one step further and examine what can happen next.

Each of those four-color photos must be stripped into proper position. And since stripping is virtually an all-man-hours operation, you are paying for the time it takes to position your material.

The separation procedure

Let's say that you have a total of eight photos for the same page of a magazine. Each four-color photo has four separation negatives: magenta, cyan, yellow, and black. Thus, the eight photos will require the stripper to accurately position 32 pieces of film.

Prices for stripping these photos are normally based on the number of pieces of film that must be handled by the stripper. Let's use the figure of $25 for each photo (each four pieces of film).

A procedure closely related to dupes, called mounting to position, can be used to reduce the number of strips required. While this is not true in all cases, keep in mind that for this example we want all eight photos to appear on a single magazine page. Mounting to position can cut the required number of strips to four.

Here's how it is done:

The secret is to get your dupes into "page position" (meaning the positions in which they will later be printed) *before* they get separated. In our example of the eight photos on a page, the photos will print in the positions specified by the art director who created the job. If those positions are known before the material is separated (as they very likely are), the actual-size dupes of the photos can be placed (mounted) in their exact relative positions on a sheet of acetate, which will later be put on the camera or a scanner.

The entire mounting procedure will normally have little or no effect on your group separation prices (although in odd cases, it can), but because it will later reduce the number of strips, those charges will be significantly lower. In our example above, if the eight photos were separated in their proper relative positions on four pieces of film, you'd be paying for only one strip. This dollar difference is significant.

The mounting process presumes a few things: 1) that all your photos are of similar densities (as they would be with any other group-separation procedure); 2) that they are of the same category (transparency); and 3) that you know exactly where they will print. The first and second points are no problem because the same rules apply to common-focus separations and the duping processes.

Point three won't cause trouble either; that is, *if* you're work-

151

DUPLICATE TRANSPARENCIES

ing on a "normal job," which means that you have the original photos, accurate layout (or completed paste-up), and enough time (usually about three working days) to dupe and to mount (an hour or less, in this example).

If your color lab offers mounting services, you will simply send in one more set of instructions with your material. Rather than provide the lab with just percentages or measurements for your dupes, you will also "key" each photo (with a number, letter, or some other means of identification) to your paste-up or layout. After the lab makes the dupes, they will mount each photo on a sheet of acetate. The result will be that you'll see the dupes in their exact positions relative to each other, and it will coincide with the paste-up or layout.

On the other hand, maybe the color lab doesn't have mounting facilities, but your printer or separator does. In that case, you'd supply the loose dupes and the layout to either one of them. They would mount and separate, and the next thing that you'd see would be a proof of the color work. What you see will depend on your separator's facilities and whether or not you supplied the complete paste-ups, art, and instructions needed to fully mount, strip, and proof the job.

Mounting is a versatile procedure, but there can be problems if you need to butt photos. This situation occurs when one photo's edge must touch the edge of another. The person mounting photos that butt must slice each common margin precisely and then actually glue the photos together. For simpler mounts, tape can be used to position dupes.

A sample dupe/mount job

Let's take a look at the sequence of activity for the eight-photos-to-a-page example mentioned earlier.

1. You send your photos to the lab for duping. When they're returned to you, the color looks fine.

2. You mark the dupes, keying them to the same numbers that you've put on the paste-up. Dupes are normally delivered in plastic sleeves on which you can write with a marker or grease pencil. ("Page 1, Photo A" is a nice keying notation to use.)

3. You send the paste-ups and dupes to your printer, who in this example is also your color separator.

4. The printer mounts the color work, separates and strips the mount (instead of individual photos), shoots the paste-ups, and combines all the negatives—such as color, black-and-white headlines—into the finished film.

152

5. A proof is pulled and sent to you for approval.

Naturally, this sequence can vary. If your printer doesn't mount or separate, you'd need to coordinate those activities with an outside source and be very sure that the printer's specifications were followed exactly.

For that matter, you could take all the work—separations, stripping, and proofs—to a prep house and then supply your printer with negatives and a proof.

Duplication and mounting of color photos can have a dramatic effect as compared to conventional single separations of material. Disregard the prices; they fluctuate with time and geography. The point is, there is money to be saved with duplicate, mounted transparencies.

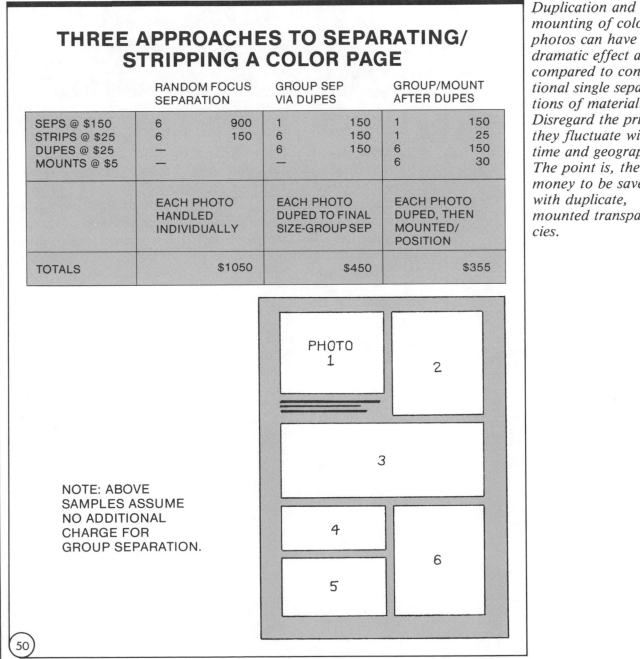

THREE APPROACHES TO SEPARATING/ STRIPPING A COLOR PAGE

	RANDOM FOCUS SEPARATION		GROUP SEP VIA DUPES		GROUP/MOUNT AFTER DUPES	
SEPS @ $150	6	900	1	150	1	150
STRIPS @ $25	6	150	6	150	1	25
DUPES @ $25	—		6	150	6	150
MOUNTS @ $5	—		—		6	30
	EACH PHOTO HANDLED INDIVIDUALLY		EACH PHOTO DUPED TO FINAL SIZE-GROUP SEP		EACH PHOTO DUPED, THEN MOUNTED/ POSITION	
TOTALS		$1050		$450		$355

NOTE: ABOVE SAMPLES ASSUME NO ADDITIONAL CHARGE FOR GROUP SEPARATION.

PHOTO 1

2

3

4

5

6

Cost effects

What can dupes/mounts do to the bottom line? Our example uses these factors. Dupes cost $25 each, the mounting procedure costs $5 per dupe and strips are $25. The example compares eight mounted dupes to eight loose photos separated and stripped individually (no grouping or other economies attempted). Separations are $150.

	Dupe/Mount	Individual
Dupes	$200	-0-
Mounts	40	-0-
Separations	150	$1,200
Strips	25	200
TOTAL:	$415	$1,400

Looks pretty good, right? But it is not automatic and universal. Keep in mind that in our example each of these photos appears on the same page. If they all appeared on different pages, the stripping costs would not be affected. And if the art director had taken pains to make them all fit at the same percentage in the first place, the dupes, too, would be ineffective. Eight grouped photos are cheaper than eight-duped-and-mounted photos in some cases.

Your job is to keep these techniques in mind, solicit prices, and gain enough experience to know when it makes sense to use them for both your quality minimums and budget requirements.□

PROOFS: A DEFINITION

What's a proof? Nothing more than a representation of what is on a set of negatives or positives. The proof is generally used to show the buyer what something will look like when it's printed. The idea is to get the buyer to say, "That is okay," *before* printing takes place.

As you already understand, the paste-up, photos, and other materials spend a good deal of time at the preparation stage before the plates are made. Proofing a job, part of this prep stage, confirms that all the procedures were done correctly.

More often than not, it is the customer, and only the customer, who has the knowledge to confirm that "everything is okay." Let's say, for example, that you publish a book on raising hybrid rabbits. Your printer certainly doesn't know as much about bunnies as do you. Therefore, who is to say that all the photos are in the right place? That they are not flopped? That all the rabbits on page 69 are female? You, the customer—because you have special knowledge (which the printer probably cannot even comprehend).

But even in other cases, the customer is the final judge of proofs. Suppose you wanted a tint to print over a panel of type. You specified this appropriately on your paste-up, but the printer's proof shows that no tint was placed there. Is that special knowledge? No. Did he follow the instructions? No. Is he responsible if the job goes to press without that tint? Again, the answer is no.

Printers have enough to worry about without attempting to learn everything about your whims, graphic desires, and instructions. While you can look at a page and instantly recall what you had in mind, the printer deals with many customers who have many more whims. Thus, the proofing stage is your opportunity to confirm that the job was done to your specification and satisfaction.

Customer responsibility

Before we get into the various types of proofs available to the magazine customer, let's discuss your responsibilities in reviewing a proof. Although the entire formal version of Printing Trade Customs is not universally enforced, one area that is considered sacred is the section on proofs. Whether it is found in a printing contract or is in force because of a handshake agreement, it goes something like this:

> *PROOFS. Proofs shall be submitted with original copy. Corrections are to be made on "master set," returned marked "O.K." or "O.K. with corrections" and signed by customer. If revised proofs are desired, request must be made when proofs are returned. Printer regrets any errors that may occur through production undetected, but cannot be held responsible for errors if the work is printed per customer's Okay or if changes are communicated verbally. Printer shall not be responsible for errors if the customer has not ordered or has refused to accept proofs or has failed to return proofs*

with indication of changes or has instructed printer to proceed without submission of proofs.

If that language is new to you, read it carefully as many times as necessary to understand its wide ramifications. It means that the printer is never responsible for something that you have okayed at the proofing stage. It means that you can ask the printer to fix something, but that if you do not also ask for another proof and he goofs up the fix, it is your fault. It means that if you forget to ask for a proof, all errors are your fault.

Sounds a bit rough, doesn't it? It is, and for good reason. The printer is not an art director, editor, or publisher. He is a manufacturer. For practical purposes, consider the printing plant a factory. If you order the wrong bumper design for your auto plant, send the wrong specifications, inspect the prototype, give it your okay, and then find that the bumper doesn't fit—tough luck. That is precisely what the prototype was for. Proofs are printing prototypes, and you are the buyer who must confirm that the specifications match.

What to look for: Nonprocess page proofs

Just what does the buyer look for on a dummied, magazine proof? Here is a basic checklist.

1. *Pagination:* It is quite possible for the stripper to put page 10 where page 12 should be. The printer's own copy checkers should catch such gross errors, but check it yourself. Quickly flip through each page of the proof to check that the numerical sequence is correct before you go any further.

2. *Page position:* Each page is somehow put in place, often by an individual prone to make errors. Therefore, you could find one page higher than the others or further to the right. Study the position of each page in relation to the others and confirm that there is consistency and that this consistency matches the ideal position of the copy on the page (per your original paste-ups or specifications).

3. *Copy:* When manual stripping is performed, masks of some sort are normally used around each page negative to prevent unwanted light from reaching the proof, the printing plate, and so on. These masks could also accidentally prevent a caption from printing, or they could even "chop off" a row of letters in a column. Check to see that what you had on your paste-ups (that which was supposed to print) is actually there.

A helpful tip for a page of text is the "four corner" check. Look at the outermost areas of the paste-up and compare them to the proof. Although the proof might "look good," a page could very well be missing the top two rows of type—something that is otherwise hard to notice *unless* you *proofread* your proofs. (Don't! See below.)

4. *Photos:* Be sure that each photo on the proof is the right one, since all faces look alike to printers. Be sure it is not flopped. Film can be laid in place the right way or flipped over and placed the wrong way. The proof will show the error. The artist or designer must "know" it and check for it. And be sure it is the right size. If you scale your own photos, you should check to see that the printer followed your instructions. Generally, this is easy. If it isn't as large or small as you wanted, you will probably notice it.

Of course, also check for any other instructions that you gave. It is best to have handy your original set of notes or the transmittal sheet discussed earlier.

What not to check for

Unfortunately, many buyers don't understand what they should *not* check for. After the negatives are made, the editing is over. The page is hard as a rock in terms of copy, punctuation, and so on. These changes absolutely must be made prior to the proofing stage; otherwise you will never get along with any printer.

Proofs are made after the film is shot, which means that to make a correction, the film will probably have to be shot again. Imagine this: A customer sends out the okayed paste-ups. The printer shoots, strips, and proofs. The customer passes the proofs to the publisher, who then reads the magazine for the first time. The publisher makes a change or two on each page, then signs the proof.

What a disaster! Now the printer must reshoot the entire magazine, restrip it, and proof it again. Why didn't the publisher read the *paste-ups?* Please, if you get anything out of this section, get this: Proofs are not for copy editors. They are for the person whose job it is to check that what was asked for on the paste-up is what the printer has on the proof. If you asked for "Phred," don't change it to "Fred" on the proof unless you want to pay for it.

Alterations versus corrections

The above type of change (let us call it an arbitrary change) is called an alteration. The customer has simply changed his mind—and changed it too late for it to be inexpensive.

The rabbit problem described earlier would be called a correction. If the printer can't tell one end of the rabbit from the other, he will fix it at no charge (as long as the instructions were clear). But if the publisher can't tell "Phred" from "Fred" until after the paste-ups have been okayed, it is an alteration.

Printers must charge for alterations. They can work like crazy to avoid corrections, but everybody makes mistakes. Printers pay for corrections, but customers pay for alterations. More than one large printing job has been booted out the door because of the customer's inability to understand this.

Checking color proofs

Color proofs are a different ball game. Generally, there are two categories of color proofs that the customer will see—"scatter" and final-color.

"Scatter" proofs are what the printer would show *after* the color separation has been made, but *before* the material has been stripped into page position, cropped, and finalized into its printing version. In other words, the scatter proof shows what the color separation process produced.

At this stage, the customer is asked to confirm that the colors in the separation itself are close enough to the original photo. Because color separation in most cases, particularly in magazines, is not a perfect process, a close approximation (pleasing color) is normally good enough.

If the work was very critical, such as an elaborate food photo in a high-quality cookbook, the customer might mark up the scatter proof with his requests. "Match beans better. Bluer tablecloth." These types of changes are related to the arrangement that you have with the person who does your separations. If you are ordering high-quality, expensive color work, these corrections may be included in the base price of the separation. If you are ordering the most economical color separations that you can find, these changes will probably cost you money.

Once the scatter proof is okayed, the color separation is put back into the prep cycle again. It is stripped into page position and cropped to fit the layout.

All checks done on the black-and-white-type proof are also done on the final-color proof. This proof will include a color representation of the photos (full color), the typesetting, any color tints, combination tints, or any other stripping work that you have requested, and so forth. The full-color proof is considered a very close representation of what the final printed magazine page will look like.

However, this is not the time to make the corrections or alterations that should have been done on the scatter-color proof. It is only the time to check that the instructions for the stripper were followed.

The color-type proofs are not normally delivered to the buyer in book form. More often, they are delivered in the same configuration as the press will print them. If the press prints eight pages on one side of a sheet (before cutting and folding), the color proof will probably be delivered as an eight-page, flat sheet. When this is done, it is also common to deliver a simpler proof—the black-and-white variety—trimmed to the final size and folded into book form. This is used for the pagination and positioning check described earlier.□

THE VARIOUS
TYPES OF PROOFS

How are proofs made? This will be short and sweet. Proofs are made via the contacting procedures outlined earlier. The negatives or positives are placed in contact with the proofing material, and vacuum pressure is used to force them into tight contact. The appropriate light source is turned on, and the proofs are developed according to their respective needs.

The light sources and development procedures, which vary with the proof being used, will be described below.

Later, depending again on the type of proof, it may be folded and cut to its final size for presentation to the customer. This folding/cutting process is limited generally to thin, inexpensive proofing materials and is unsuitable for most full-color proofs.

Now, let's discuss the various types of proofs most commonly available. We will describe the manner in which they are made, the kind of proofs they are, their general quality, and the relative costs of each.

Some typical black-and-white and two-color proofs

Name: Dylux
Type: Plasticized paper
Appearance: Blue on yellow paper (typical)
Quality: Moderate
Cost: Low
Color Representation: Simulated two-color
Made from: Negatives
Development: None

The Dylux, a DuPont product, is an extremely popular proofing material. It offers moderate quality, although it might be difficult to determine the dot sizes in halftones. For straight text, it is more than adequate.

Dyluxes are commonly put into magazine form; that is, they are often trimmed to size and stapled together. They are also a two-sided proof, meaning the trimmed book feels quite normal and is easy to check.

When more than one color is being printed, the printer can use a shorter exposure to burn the supplemental colors. For example, if a headline was to print in red, the Dylux could be burned lighter when the red negative was in contact with it. The result would be a pale headline, and darker images for the other material.

This can take some getting used to because it is not always obvious to the observer. So as a double check, the printer will often make notes on the Dylux for the customer, such as, "Headline prints in red."

At this writing, the typical cost for a magazine-page Dylux (in book form) is between 90 cents and $1.40. Part of the reason for the low cost is that Dyluxes are exposed under ultraviolet light, but need no processing or development. They "set" the image with any room light. Be cautioned, though, that exposure to sunlight or any other source high in UV wavelengths will eventually destroy the image.

Name: Brownprint, BP, VanDyke
Type: Paper
Appearance: Brown, blue on mottled background
Quality: Moderate to low
Cost: Low
Color Representation: Poor
Made from: Negatives
Development: Machine (ammonia vapor)

This category includes all the paper-type proofs that are processed via the ammonia-vapor method. As you might guess, their quality could be compared to that of a blueprint, another name for this category.

Checking halftone quality is as difficult as checking color representation. Therefore, this proof could be used when there are few areas in which to make mistakes: The type is clean, the pages are generally straight text, and there is no reason to check photo quality, and so on.

These proofs can cost the same or less than the Dylux. If the price is the same, the buyer might prefer Dylux because of its generally better quality and color ability (the two-color light burn). However, if brownprint is all the printer has, it will suffice.

Other black-and-white possibilities

Before we go into color proofs, let's review some of the other possibilities for black-and-white and simple checking. Office copy machines can be an adequate method of proofing straight text. An advantage here is that the proofs can be made before the negatives are shot and developed.

Also, the color-proofing methods that we will describe below can be used for single-color and simple multicolor proofs. Suppose you are highly critical of halftone quality. What kind of proof would you order?

Not one of the above. Rather, for a true check of halftone quality, you would order the *black* portion of a color proof. As we discussed earlier in the color separation and halftone sections, all photos and copy are made from negatives or positives. If you need a superb proof, you could use a proof designed for process color, but order only the black (not the magenta, cyan, or yellow). Or for two-color work, you could use one of the process-proofing systems with the second color matched to the ink that you will print with later.

Name: Color Key
Type: Acetate layers

THE VARIOUS TYPES OF PROOFS

Appearance: Full color, gray cast
Quality: Good
Cost: Low (for a color proof)
Color Representation: Adequate
Made from: Negatives or positives
Development: Single chemical, by machine or hand

The Color Key System was introduced awhile back by 3M, and many printers still use it.

Basically, Color Keys can be used to show a proof of anything: colored type, panels, black-and-white halftones, or full-color photographs.

The Color Key is one the least expensive proofing system that shows, in a composite fashion, how a printed job will look in full color. Many ad agencies use it to proof expensive advertisements—and lots of publishers use it to proof magazine pages.

Physically, a Color Key is simply a sheet of clear acetate that has been sensitized with a pigment (such as magenta), exposed, and developed. The result is a translucent image of the original. When four Color Keys are stacked up (magenta, cyan, yellow, and black), you can see a pretty good image of the eventual printing job.

But there are some limitations to using Color Keys as proofs of four-color separations (photos). They are prone to operator error if they are not machine processed. And, depending on the light source used to expose them, their dot resolution (quality) can seriously affect the image. Also, because they are composed of stacked acetate, they give a gray cast to the subject matter.

Like some other proofing systems, the Color Key is manufactured in "standard"-process colors, along with a range of PMS (Pantone Matching System) colors. This is not considered a limitation for most work. However, there are other systems (notably, the Cromalin) that can be modified to match the specific ink hues being used at a given printer. For the most critical color quality, the Color Key would not be selected.

Cost for a magazine page can range from about $12 to $25, depending on how many are made at one time (eight pages at a time are less expensive than one at a time), and the printer's pricing system.

Name: Transfer Key
Type: Lamination
Appearance: Full color on white background
Quality: Excellent
Cost: Moderate
Color Representation: Good to excellent
Made from: Negatives
Development: Machine

The Transfer Key, a registered trademark of the 3M Company, is related closely to the Color Key. Both use the same exposure and development procedures. However, the Transfer Key is a lamination product. Instead of using the layered acetate, this system laminates a far thinner sheet to a piece of plastic carrier. The result is that there is no gray buildup.

Otherwise, many of the qualities are the same. The system uses "stock" colors (not mixable or matchable to a given printer).

One aspect of Transfer Keys is that they produce a much finer, or more accurate, dot image than do Color Keys. Some printers say this is an advantage because the proof will show exactly what is on the film. Others say the proof is literally too good: The typical press cannot reproduce such a perfect dot. As long as there are two printers, this debate will go on.

Cost varies from the same as Color Keys to a premium dictated by the printer. The added expense of the lamination machine is a justifiable reason to charge more.

Name: Match Print
Type: Lamination
Appearance: Full color on a variety of backgrounds
Quality: Excellent
Cost: Moderate to high
Color Representation: Unique
Made from: Negatives
Development: Machine

The Match Print, also a registered trademark of 3M, is virtually the same as the Transfer Key, but with one spectacular exception: It can be proofed on any paper rather than just on the plastic base. This is unique, and is used when the need arises. If you were considering a change in printing stocks, you might have the same material proofed on both stocks via this system, to check any notable differences. Or, if you were considering either a special project or a magazine section that required a four-color process to be printed on colored stock, this is the proof to order.

Name: Cromalin
Type: Powder/Lamination
Appearance: Full color on white background
Quality: Excellent
Cost: Moderate to high
Color Representation: Modifiable, excellent
Made from: Negatives or positives
Development: Complex

Cromalins, a registered trademark of DuPont, when properly made, have often been called the next best thing to an actual press proof. While that statement could be argued forever, most people agree with this one: Cromalins give you a very good idea of what is on the film from which they were burned, and that is something even a press proof might not do.

CHAPTER 30

163

A Cromalin is simply a sheet of paper on top of which an extremely thin sheet of photo-sensitive film has been applied. It is exposed and then a pigmented powder is dusted onto the tacky film. Since this powder can be mixed to match a printer's ink it can get very close to what will appear on the press

Depending on the job, then, more exposures can be made (and different powders applied) until the finished product is shown in full color. A color photograph, for example, will be made up of four separate Cromalin exposures and pigment applications and topped off with a sheet of protective film.

Cromalins were originally designed to work from positive film only. Later, negative-acting material was introduced. There is still some disagreement about whether the negative-type provides as good a proof as the positive-acting version.

Cost can be the highest of the pre-press proofs. A charge of $30 to $80 per page is not unheard of. And, if the positive type is the only version used at the printer, there is the distinct possibility that contacts will need to be made to make the proof, again adding to the cost.

Name: Press Proof
Type: Printed
Appearance: Printed
Quality: Depends on the press
Cost: High
Color Representation: Good to accurate
Made from: Negatives or positives, and plates
Development: Printed

There is still controversy over the value of press proofs, and for good reasons: They are very expensive to make and sometimes don't tell you as much about the material as they supposedly "prove."

A press proof is a "preprinted" printing job. Proofing presses normally run slowly and have the ability to register colors almost perfectly. They can also proof "wet" (ink on top of ink) or "dry" (colors allowed to set between applications).

In theory, a press proof is the ultimate. It doesn't show you how the job will look in a single color, or how it will look when made into a Cromalin, but it will show you a printed version of the job itself.

In practice, there are two main areas where the press proof can fail: First, it is almost always "pulled" (printed) on a slow, sheet-fed press while the actual job may be printed on an ultra-fast web press. Second, it may be created from original film while the printer will be working from a duplicate set. So color shifts are to be expected.

Also, another area for potential error is the ink itself. Few proofing houses actually take care to match their proofing inks to the final printer's ink, which is absolutely essential if a "perfect" proof is to be made. And few magazine printers make their own press proofs. So, inconsistency is common.

Before the invention of Cromalins, Transfer Keys and Match Prints, press proofs were the only way to get a true, accurate idea of film quality. Today they are often the cause for heated debate, but they do have uses.

Choose a press proof if you meet all of the following requirements: 1) you have money to spend; 2) you want better than a first-class job; and 3) *the printer that pulls the proof will also run the job.* If these requirements aren't filled, there is a good chance that a press proof is not required for your material.

Costs can be staggering when compared to the other procedures. Rates between $300 to $600 are routine.

Finally, because there is disagreement over the uses of press proofs in today's printing world, discuss them with your printer. Some printers throw press proofs on the shelf, and make a prepress proof to use at press. This tells them what is on the film rather than what was produced on the proofing press. Others will use the press proof like a bible and attempt to follow it on press. Get your printer's preferences and take his account into consideration if and when you must choose between press proofs and the less expensive pre-press types.□

CHAPTER 30

SECTION V: COMPLEX COLOR STRIPPING

INTRODUCTION TO COLOR STRIPPING

Black-and-white stripping and proofs are not horribly complicated. But that is not to suggest that stripping is a simple task: When color is added, particularly process color, the chore can become a nightmare. No attempt will be made to pack a 10-year apprenticeship into this book. It would benefit few readers to know as much as a journeyman knows about stripping. But in order to assist you to comprehend at least the more complicated aspects of stripping, let's again follow a job through its production cycle. This process is often referred to as "prestripping," or "building up."

Although this job will be a process-color sample, including tints, reverses, and other more complicated matter, keep this point in mind: Any type of multicolor stripping will involve the creation of different plate negatives for each color. If a job is to print in red and black, it will need a red negative and a black negative to burn the respective plates. Process (four-color) printing automatically brings the minimum number of plates to four, meaning that there will be four negatives to strip and to register before plate time.

"Fake" color

Process printing also brings up the topic of "fake" color. If the "red" ink on the press is actually magenta, how does a process magazine page show a truly "red" panel? By printing red and yellow ink in the same place.

If you remember your primaries from grade school, you know that other combinations produce predictable colors. Magenta and cyan produce something in the purple range; full yellow printing with 50 percent magenta will give an orange effect. These ink combinations are often called "fake" color. Why? Because they are generated on the stripping table. They are not the product of color separation, which is "process color" in the truest sense of the word.

Getting "fake" color on the paste-up

Remember that the use of overlays and panels for stripping purposes was described in the paste-up section. Suppose you want a pale orange panel to overprint an area of type. How do you do it?

First, the paste-up person tapes a sheet of acetate over the paste-up. Then, a red or orange sheet of paper is cut to the exact shape that the panel will print and is pasted (or waxed) onto the acetate. Later, the printer will shoot a negative of the acetate overlay. It will have a clear "window" where the red or orange panel appeared on the overlay, which will then be used in the stripping process. Appropriate tints of process colors will print with the dimensions of this window area.

Specifying tints and color matches

There are two ways to print a special or "matched" color:

fake color and matched ink. When it is done literally by using the appropriate color of ink (such as having a deep blue ink put on the press), it is specified as a PMS (Pantone Matching System) color. In this case, the overlay just mentioned would simply be used to create the deep blue negative, which later will create the plate to run that ink.

PMS inks are the purest way to achieve a specific color, but they are not inexpensive. When a matched ink is used, the printer must wash out the fountain that held the old ink and put in the new color before continuing with the job. So when process-color printing is being used and the match is not critical, it is fake color techniques that are used.

The "deep blue" that you are after might be something like 100 percent cyan, 10 percent magenta, and 30 percent black ink printing in the same place. In that case, the printer would use the overlay on the paste-up to create negatives for those colors. He would add the proper tints during the stripping stage.

The use of panels for color will be described as we follow the sample page through the production cycle. Regardless of whether you are working with a single color, matched ink, or fake color, the panels are handled the same way. They are put on overlays, with a clearly marked tissue to indicate what will happen later.

As was also mentioned in the paste-up section, multicolor paste-up preparation is often handled with overlays. If a headline is to print in color, it may be put on the overlay. This would make it simpler for the printer to handle later on. The more complicated your color breakouts (such as running a portion of the numbers in a chart in color), the more it makes sense to use overlays to separate the material before it is shot on camera.

Picking colors

If you use matched colors at all, you will want a PMS color booklet. This lists hundreds of special inks and has samples printed on both coated (slick) and uncoated (dull) paper. On the other hand, for picking fake color, you should ask your printer for a copy of the color chart he uses. Generally, this is a large sheet with hundreds of process-color tint combinations.

Finally, you may want to purchase a color wheel, which has acetate sheets that carry color tints. By rotating the various wheels of colored acetate, you can more or less fabricate any hue that is available with the four process inks.□

A SAMPLE COMPLICATED PAGE

The following sample job is one of the more complicated stripping jobs generated by the typical magazine: the separation and stripping of the cover itself. For less complicated work, the only difference would be that *some* of the following methods are used, not all. But also keep in mind that this is merely a "typically" complicated sample: Other projects can become far more complicated, to the point that you would need years of exposure to stripping procedures just to understand them.

The subheads in the following material relate directly to the illustrations that show what is being done. Refer to them as you read the text, and you should be on your way to understanding the somewhat complicated world of magazine preparation.

1. Paste-up and overlays

•Paste-up: The paste-up is a black-and-white representation of all the elements that will appear on the page. Even though type will reverse, print in colors, and (in this case) be blocked out by panels, the normal procedure is to stick with simple black-on-white images. The reverses and other work will be done by the printer.

On this paste-up, a keyline (a thin, black line) is drawn to indicate that the photo will bleed (Illustration 51). Why not use a window? Because for complicated prep, the main window is often not wanted by the printer. Rather than shoot a huge blank page, he will later cut a mask on stripping film.

The paste-up also has a light blue drawing of the photo to be printed on the page. Blue is used because it doesn't photograph as a line shot. The cover, then, contains only elements that will print (even though they may be reversed). It is not generally a good idea to clutter it up with black line drawings for position indication or with any other material that is not supposed to print.

Also note at the top of the illustration the instruction that overlays will be taped to the paste-up board.

•Overlays: Illustration 51 shows two overlays. One is simply a panel in the upper right of the page; the other is the type that will print in that area. The overlays are acetate sheets (Mylar is popular, too) on the paste-up exactly in their proper positions. The printer will shoot these sheets like any other material.

Why didn't we put the panel material right on the paste-up? First, the type and the panel print in the same area, so if we put the type on the paste-up, the panel can't go there. Second, the magazine logo will later be partially blocked out by the panel. Because this is a very meticulous fitting procedure, it is not usually wise to attempt to do it on a paste-up. It is better left to the skills of an experienced stripper.

So, we use overlays because all this material will interact, with extremely tight fits, in the final piece.

170

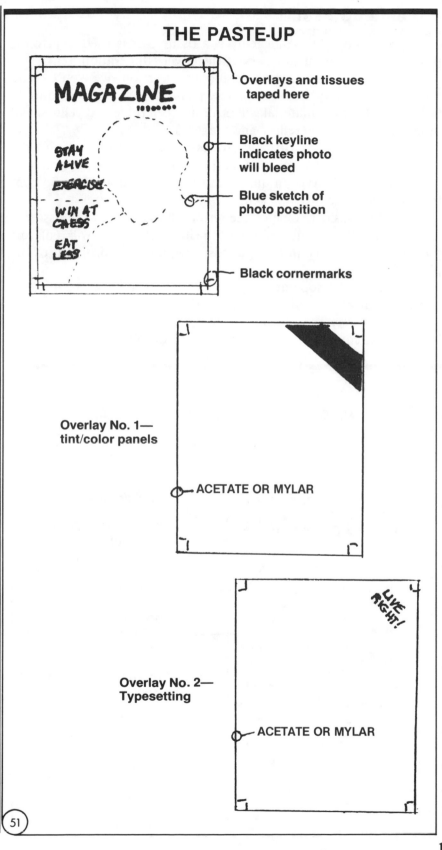

THE PASTE-UP

MAGAZINE

STAY ALIVE

EXERCISE

WIN AT CHESS

EAT LESS

Overlays and tissues taped here

Black keyline indicates photo will bleed

Blue sketch of photo position

Black cornermarks

Overlay No. 1— tint/color panels

ACETATE OR MYLAR

Overlay No. 2— Typesetting

LIVE RIGHT!

ACETATE OR MYLAR

CHAPTER 32

Complex stripping, also called prestripping or buildup, can be a time-consuming chore. These illustrations demonstrate the basic steps in creating a complex page—a magazine cover.

In the beginning, there was the paste-up—and overlays, too. Generally, the paste-up person should attempt to use the minimum required overlays for complex color work. The rule: If it can't be placed on the paste-up (conflicts in position with other elements), put it on an overlay.

2. Paste-up tissue

Also taped to the paste-up is a tissue that is used to give the printer detailed instructions about the cover (Illustration 52).

Because we are not discussing art direction, we won't spend time explaining why these colors were picked. However, the notes do indicate that certain material will print in green (blue and yellow) and other material in red (yellow and magenta).

Color choice is virtually always dictated by the color of the photo itself. If the background of the photo were blue, it would be foolish to print the type in blue because it would not show. So contrasting colors are often picked.

Let's consider some of the terminology used on the tissue:

• Drop out: This means that the item referred to will replace a portion of the photo. In other words, the panel will drop out of the photo.

• Print: "Drop out and print yellow" means that the material will drop out of the photo and then print in yellow.

• Reverse: This means that the material will be white. Reverse is also often considered a synonym for "drop out."

These notes on the tissue should tell the stripper everything he needs to know about the intended use of color, photo position, and so forth.

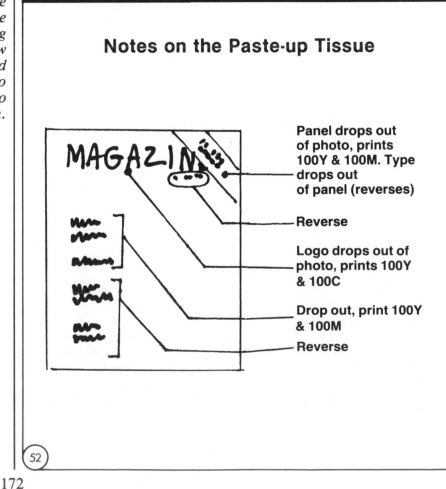

Notes on the Paste-up Tissue

Panel drops out of photo, prints 100Y & 100M. Type drops out of panel (reverses)

Reverse

Logo drops out of photo, prints 100Y & 100C

Drop out, print 100Y & 100M

Reverse

52

3. Camera shots

As described in the chapter on line shots, the paste-up and its overlays are normally shot as line negatives. Each is shot separately, producing the material shown in Illustration 53.

The first step is to shoot film negatives of the paste-up and overlays.

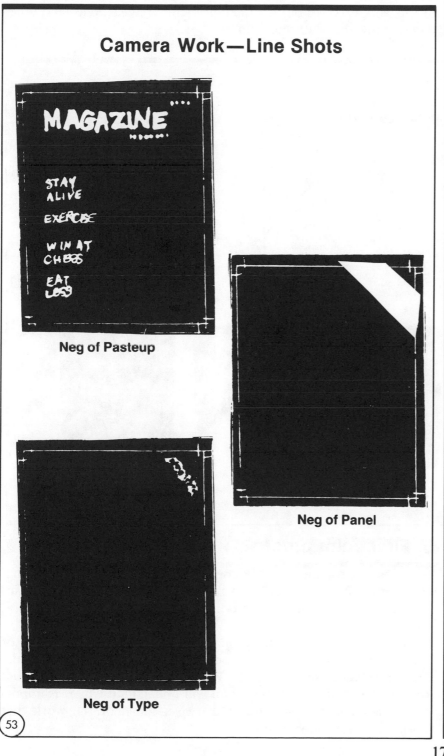

Camera Work—Line Shots

Neg of Pasteup

Neg of Panel

Neg of Type

53

4. Color separation

Now the color is separated. If you asked for it to be enlarged, reduced, or somehow cropped, that would happen at this stage.

As you can see in Illustration 54, the separation process (negative, in this case) produces four pieces of film. Much of the rest of the work involves putting the typesetting, panels, logo, and other material together with this film.

Although not truly a stripping activity, the color separation produces fun working (stripping) negatives or-depending on personal preference of the prep shop or printer—working positives.

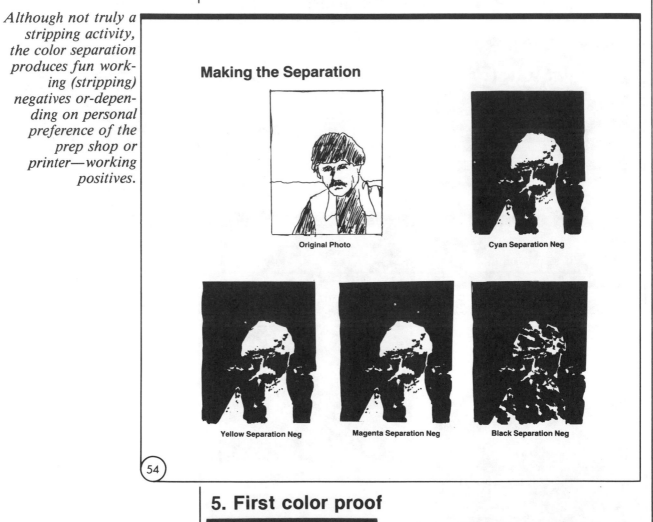

Making the Separation

Original Photo

Cyan Separation Neg

Yellow Separation Neg

Magenta Separation Neg

Black Separation Neg

54

5. First color proof

Before too much else happens, you are normally shown a first proof of the color separation. This may be a Color Key, Cromalin, Match Print, or some other proof available to the printer (Illustration 55).

It is at this stage, based on your displeasure with the color of the photo as separated and proofed, that you should make any necessary changes or corrections. When you see how much work goes into the photo after this stage, you will understand why it is important to ask for changes *now*. Otherwise, much of the work that follows will be wasted effort.

6. Chokes and spreads

Now for something a little strange. The reason for this discussion is that, in general, magazine presses and lithography are far from perfect: They simply cannot "hold register" (or, in plain English, fit) too well.

Have you ever noticed "white" typesetting on a dark full-color photo? Have you ever noticed type, which was supposed to be white, with a little red or blue around it that made it hard to read?

The fact is, a full-color reverse (white type on a process-color photo, which means no ink where the type is) is the most difficult of all lithographic tasks. Therefore, it is the one that has the most room for error. If any of the printing plates deposit their images slightly off register, the legibility and appearance of the type will be damaged.

Now, suppose we have a full-color photo and we want to drop out some type—and then print it in another color, such as yellow. One way would be to have the yellow print in the exact shape of the character and then to reverse that exact character shape out of the process colors. But then we would have an "exact fit" problem, one that is not easily solved by the press.

So, what if we take that light yellow type, which will drop out

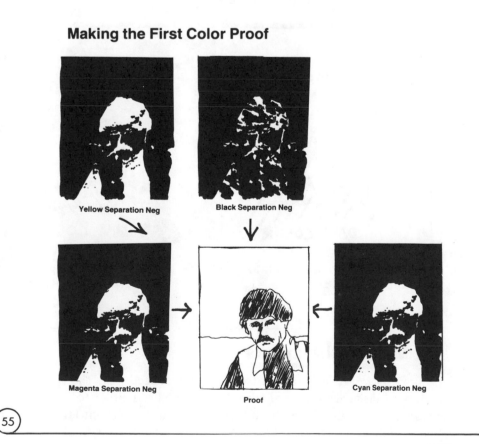

Making the First Color Proof

Yellow Separation Neg

Black Separation Neg

Magenta Separation Neg

Proof

Cyan Separation Neg

A first proof is made of the separation before any stripping work is done. At this point, the customer either approves the color quality or asks for color corrections to be made.

55

of a dark background, and make it a little fatter than the original type? Then the dark background colors would have a clean reverse image of the type, but the color that we lay in would be slightly oversized. If the press misregistered by a hair, nobody would notice. But if both background and type used the same exact area, any misregistration would show up as a white line around a part of the type. This is called a "fatty," or a "spread." When type is to print in a lighter color than the background, it is reversed out of the background, but it will actually print (or overprint) slightly larger than its own reverse image.

What if the background is a light color and the type is to print darker? Then we would want the type to maintain its perfect shape. But to aid in registration, we would want the area that it drops out of to be slightly smaller or skinnier than the type image. There would be a little overlap, but it would normally go undetected. This is called a "choke," or a "skinny."

Illustration 56A shows an exaggerated picture of a choke, or skinny. The light colored background slightly eats into the area occupied by the dark colored letter.

Illustration 56B shows the opposite approach, the spread or fatty. In this case, the lighter-colored letter sightly overextends the "drop out" area of the dark-colored photo, increasing the press's ability to register the inks properly.

Preliminary contacting and stripping produces chokes, spreads, and masks that either allow certain colors to show or block them out. The choke and spread procedures are an aid to subsequent optical registration on press. If printing were a perfect process, no chokes or spreads would be required.

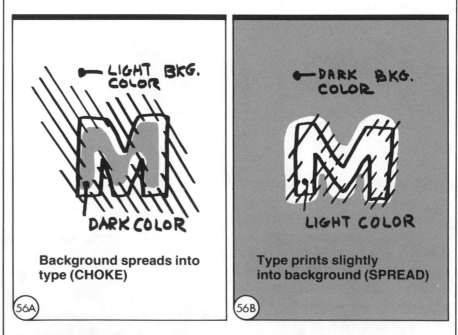

Background spreads into type (CHOKE)

Type prints slightly into background (SPREAD)

7. Making the masks

Now, using standard contacting procedures, the masks are made. Masks are sheets of film that will be used either to prevent unwanted portions of the photo from being duplicated onto the final set of negatives or to introduce other material into the final negatives (such as type, panels of color, and so forth). In other words, the masks will serve the purpose of combining images into the final, cropped, single-composite (complete) blue negative, magenta negative, and so on. Therefore, certain masks are common to all separations. For example, when we modify the cyan negative so that the photo will not print where the logo goes, we will also use the same mask on the red negative because no part of that photo should print where the logo is.

To create the mask, contacts are made from the paste-up negative. Illustration 56C is a positive contact, while 56D and 56E are a few generations away, meaning they were created either from duplicates of this positive or from a combination of duplicate positives and negatives.

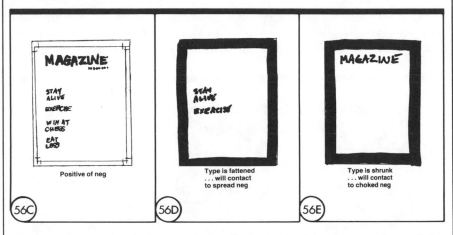

The choke and spread are also required in the creation of the masks. Let us assume that the logo prints on a light blue sky background. The logo must be shrunk, or skinnied up, to allow a portion of the photo to overlap into it, and then it must be kept intact so that the blue and yellow printing negatives can be made.

Thus, the skinny, or choke, will be created in a film-positive form, which will interrupt the photo from printing where the logo goes. The film positive is a mask used to prevent all of the photo from duplicating when contact duplication negatives are later made.

But the type in the lower left corner will be printing in a dark background (for sample purposes). So this type, which must be spread for the yellow and magenta printers, will then slightly overlap the photo background.

Chokes and spreads are made with one or more of the following techniques: overexposure, out-of-contact exposure, or sidelighting. Suffice to say that what normally makes a "bad" contact makes for a good choke or spread. More contacting is done to generate the final masks.

The contacts shown in Illustrations 56 C, D, and E are all intermediate pieces of film. They will be used to generate the final masks (56F, G, and H).

8. Final mask making

From the intermediate masks the printer can now create the final masks. Illustration 56F is the red and yellow printer (Mask A). This negative, along with the photo, will be duplicated into the final red and yellow contacts. The copy on the left, along with the panel in the upper right, will become one with the photo negative. Since the copy on the left was supposed to be spread (because its background photo is dark), it is slightly fatter than its corresponding reverse in Mask B (Illustration 56G).

The photo negatives themselves (the separation negatives) must not have copy in those areas. Therefore, all of the separation negatives will be duplicated with the master mask (Illustration 56H) lying over them. This master mask is a positive image of all material that should either reverse or drop out of the photo. If it drops out and prints in a color or colors, then masks A and B will correspond later by carrying an image in the appropriate negative.

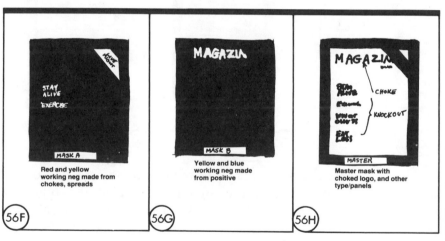

Red and yellow
working neg made from
chokes, spreads

Yellow and blue
working neg made
from positive

Master mask with
choked logo, and other
type/panels

9. Final contact: Yellow negative

We now have the separation negatives and the other negatives with type and material to print in various colors (Illustration 57). Let's see how they are combined.

The yellow separation negative has images where we don't want them. Let's put the master mask on top of it. Then let's contact it to duplication film. What will the result be?

If we are using duplication film, then the negative will be a perfect replication of the separation yellow negative, but it will not have any images where the mask interrupted the light from hitting it.

Now, let's remove the mask and remove the yellow separation negative, but leave the duplication film in place. Then, let's take mask B and make another exposure. The light (clear) areas from mask B will also be duplicated onto the film. So now both the clear areas of the separation negative and the mask will also be clear on the duplicate.

Finally, we expose mask A onto the duplication film.

What we have done is to make a duplicate image of all the yellow-printing material, including the photo itself, onto a final yellow negative.

(For your information, there are ways to do this entire procedure with positives rather than negatives, but unless you want to be a stripper, don't bother trying to learn it all. It is the general procedure that you pay for and need to understand.)

Similarly, each of the other color's final negatives—magenta, cyan and black—are contacted from the master mask, along with the other masks that will supply the color for the panels, the copy, and so on. (Illustrations 58, 59, 60).

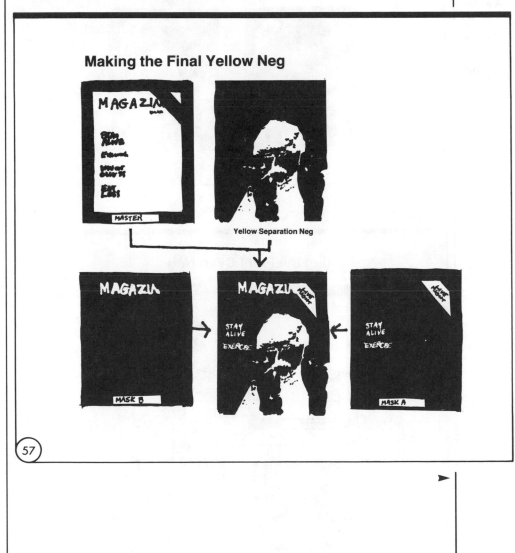

Making the Final Yellow Neg

57

A SAMPLE COMPLICATED PAGE

The masks and negs are now exposed either singly or in combinations to produce the desired result on the final composite (one-piece) film. Again, the process may be done positive or negative, depending on technical preference.

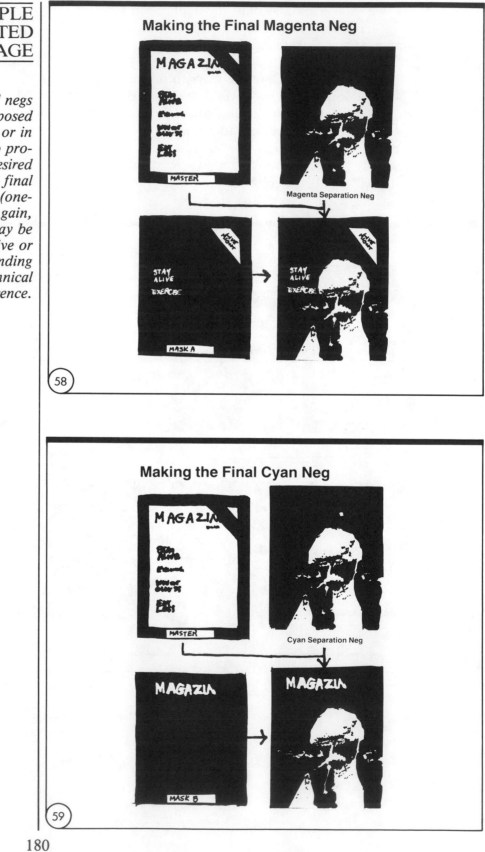

58

59

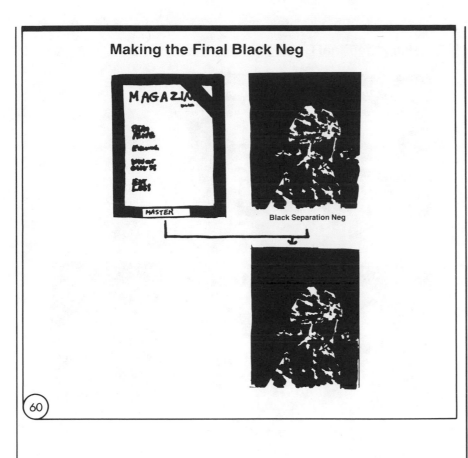

Making the Final Black Neg

MASTER

Black Separation Neg

60

10. Final color proof

At last, we can take a look at the cover (Illustration 61, next page). The four final contact duplications are called "one piece film" because they carry all the images required, which neither the separation negative nor the intermediate masks did.

Now, a proof is made to show you how the colors were inserted to your specifications and to give you a chance to change your mind.

Just remember that at this point an arbitrary change will back up the system quite drastically. It is rare that a final contacted one-piece negative can be modified with customer alteration. Rather, it will more than likely have to be "rebuilt" from the working film.

A SAMPLE COMPLICATED PAGE

The four final negs or positives are now used to expose the complete color proof, with all elements—panels, type, photo—in place. Color corrections and/or attractions of any sort after this stage can range from the simple to the absurd, so it is to your advantage to accurately visualize this proof early in the process—right at the paste-up stage.

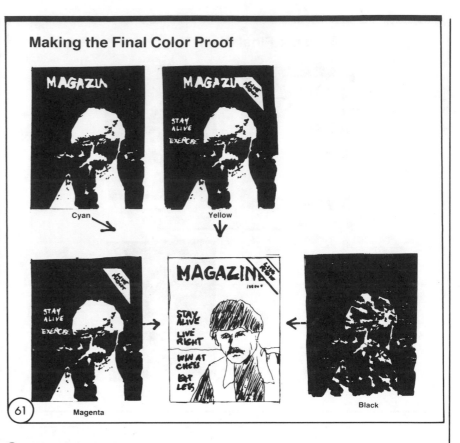

Making the Final Color Proof

Cyan

Yellow

Magenta

MAGAZINE
STAY ALIVE
LIVE RIGHT
WIN AT CHESS
EAT LESS

Black

61

Summary

If nothing else, you can understand why stripping takes time and money. But I hope that you understand more than that: It is not *impossible* to understand just what will have to be done when you ask for a reverse, an overprint, and so on.

If possible, ask your printer to let you watch an issue being stripped. After a few hours, you'll have a much better understanding of how your printer works, and, more importantly, how clear your instructions were and what they meant to the stripper, the contacter, and the separation technician.□

UNDERCOLOR

One of the more mysterious areas faced by the production person is known as "undercolor." It is mentioned by many printers, all color houses, and magazines themselves (in rate cards). Just what is it, and does it concern you?

What undercolor is

Before we go any further, let's be sure we're all discussing the same creature. Total ink density (in four-color printing) is simply the sum of all the ink in a given area. For example, if you decide to print 100 percent magenta in the same area as you are printing 100 percent yellow, you would produce the color red, and you would have a total ink density in that area of exactly 200 percent.

Similarly, if you combined 30 percent yellow, 30 percent blue, and 30 percent magenta, you'd have a rather odd looking color, and a total density of 90 percent. But the total ink density isn't used solely to determine the percentages of color panels or tints. It is also used to determine the maximum densities that are printable in color photographs.

If the photo that you intend to print is color separated, the separating technique (be it camera, scanner, or whatever method used) will be manipulated to control the total density of ink in all the portions of the picture. Undercolor addresses a special problem: Can the press reproduce all of what the proof can show? Meaning, can a printing press, particularly the magazine type, print 400 percent color saturation just because it happens to be in the negatives and on the proof?

The question, then, concerns the dark portions of the separation—the shadow areas. In those areas, the printed picture will be a combination of all the primary colors (magenta, cyan, and yellow), plus a percentage of black. And, as mentioned both in the Standards for Web Offset Printing and in the printer's specifications, that total density generally should not exceed 260 percent.

It's not easy to determine the total ink density in a separation photograph without special equipment. When you use fake color, of course, you are specifying exact percentages, such as 100 yellow, 80 blue, 50 red, and 20 black (totaling 250 percent, so in theory it should print well).

In measuring separation film, a densitometer (a machine that reads the amount of transmitted or reflected light) is used to read each piece of film separately. When reading the shadow areas of a photo, all film will be read at the "darkest" part, and the four separate percentages will be added to deduce the total density of the printed pieces. In theory, anything beyond 260 percent will provide press problems. In fact, that may not be true, but we'll get to that later.

There are a variety of opinions about undercolor. We combined several interviews with printers along with our own research to compile this brief history of undercolor problems—how they came to be, and what they've become in the past 20 years.

CHAPTER 33

A bit of history

First of all, undercolor was "invented" with modern lithographic printing. At the turn of the century, lithographers were manually creating "full-color" printing. After tedious hand drawing on stones by skilled craftsmen, the press-ready stones might require eight or more printing colors to achieve the desired result. Each color was printed and dried, and the paper was stored until the pressmen were ready to apply the next color. At that time, undercolor was not a problem. The reason? The ink was allowed to dry between applications of color.

Today, the parallel is the small sheetfed press that prints one color at a time, allowing each to dry before the next is applied. With these methods, the press *can* print virtually anything that is on the film, regardless of the total ink density.

Then came four-color lithography and separation procedures. It became accepted that most of the visual color spectrum could be adequately reproduced with three primary colors, along with black for added punch. The color separation process, though, was not all that accurate. Only one color, yellow, actually separated "well." Cyan and magenta tended to be contaminated by all other colors, with the result that camera-type color separations (with no corrections for "cleaning up" the magenta and cyan) would carry too much color. Masking processes (a filtering technique, in this case) were developed to control that *extra* color, and the procedure was called undercolor removal.

Trapping

This was the state of the art until "wet" printing took over. Undercolor removal until this time was basically a cure for camera problems. The camera saw more color than it should have, and the masking process brought the densities back down without losing detail. Without undercolor corrections, color separations of any type would look muddy, details would be lost, and middletone colors would tend to be gray.

But because one layer of ink was dry before the next was printed, the trapping ability of the ink was not a significant factor. Trapping is the quality of an ink that allows one layer to "stick" to another layer, which is critical for multicolor printing. Therefore, the old process, along with single-color (and drying time) sheetfed printing is called dry-trap printing.

But as time marched on, it made more sense to print all four colors at the same time. That meant inks that would "wet trap" had to be developed. In other words, before the yellow ink was dry, it would have to accept (trap) a layer of red ink, then the red and yellow would have to trap the blue, and then the three combined wet inks would have to trap the black.

Undercolor removal began to take on new dimensions because the wet layers of ink weren't particularly prone to having another layer of goo applied to them.

Whereas dry-trap, sheetfed presses had no trouble laying thick layers of ink on top of ink, the wet-trapping press couldn't force the same amount of ink onto paper. The wet layers didn't accept each other in the same way dry layers did. The solution was to modify the separation process: While dry-trap separations could pile on the three primaries to create dense shadow areas, wet-trapping required less of the three primaries in the shadow areas (to reduce the amount of ink), and more black. The slow, dry, sheetfed press could produce excellent color with very little black in the shadows (called a ghost black), while the wet process needed considerably more black in the shadow areas to compensate for the reduced amount of other colors.

Printing is less than perfect

If that sounds like a fancy solution, keep in mind that it never quite worked. The 260 percent total is the acceptable amount of ink that will properly trap in a wet situation, using the general industry standard. That doesn't mean 310 percent wouldn't look better, and it doesn't mean that undercolor corrections are overridden because of camera limitations (as just discussed). It simply means that the wet-trapping ability of ink will probably deteriorate at 260 percent total density. This deterioration would appear to the naked eye as "muddy" or low-detail shadow areas, or just a plain, dirty-looking page of color.

For a quick review, then, undercolor removal has two objectives. One is color balance, which requires manipulating what the camera sees in order to match the original. The second relates to wet-trap considerations to make the piece printable. You can be sure that even if a Cromalin proof looks spectacular, with 350 percent density in some areas, the inks will not trap in the shadows and that the job is not reproducible on a wet-trapping (or web) press —although it might look great produced on a single-color, dry-trapping press.

While ink makers continue to search for the perfect inks, which would, in theory, trap up to a full 400 percent coverage, web-press standards will be written with current technology in mind. Thus, the 260 percent figure is the most recently published standard for wet-trapping performance.

High-speed trapping

So far, only the factors that affect sheet-fed and web presses have been discussed. But there are additional problems to consider with web printing. Four-color, wet-web (rolls of paper rather than sheets) lithography introduced a few more troublemakers: The presses were now running significantly faster than the old sheet units, thus creating the true high-speed trap situation. And they were now running the inks through an oven, which resulted in high-speed, heat-set lithographic printing. The ink makers had to compensate for these two new variables by adjusting, experimenting, and taking the blame. Why? Because contemporary web printing was developed and marketed before suitable inks were invented.

The state of the art

With that background, we can return to the present. Inks have improved remarkably during the past 10 years and get better every year. A few years ago, based on the maximum ability of the average web ink at the time, the figure of 260 percent total density for web printing was selected.

That's where our interviews with printers take over. While one major printer's technical rep said that the 260 percent maximum produced "flat" (or dull) printing, another said he wouldn't attempt to go beyond that limit without fear of affecting quality. The first said that 310 percent took full advantage of today's inks, while the second said 300 percent would definitely show deterioration in the shadow areas, muddy the photo, and destroy middletone detail.

How do you know if your printer is concerned with undercolor, and is it important? For starters, you can assume that any printer who produces four-color material will have the proper equipment (densitometers and the people who use them) to check film, and will also be able to tell you the history of that problem in the plant over the past several years.

Trapping and undercolor go hand in hand, and all competent printers are constantly striving to make improvements in this area. As the inks are upgraded, the standards will follow. Your printer should certainly be aware of his position today.

Importance to the buyer

If your printer has color separation abilities and you use him for those services, consider yourself lucky: It means that the printer controls the amount of density on the film and uses his own experience and internal standards when doing separations.

Thus, if your printer has a limit of 280 percent in the shadows, he will make color separations that do not exceed that limit.

However, you may buy color separations from another vendor, and you may accept four-color, final negatives from advertisers. In ordering separations, you must relate your printer's requests to your separation house. They must control the total density in the shadows, keeping them within limits. Sometimes this may produce a

187

UNDERCOLOR

"flat" looking photo on the proof, but that is not the concern. There will be gain and other effects at press time, and the result should be photos that actually print better than the flat-looking proof.

As for your supplied color separations (those sent by ad agencies), you must be sure to at least advise them of maximum allowable densities. In the event you anticipate a problem, or simply want to know if your specifications are being met, your printer can inspect the film when it arrives.□

SINGLE-PIECE FILM

The complex stripping process described earlier demonstrated how many individual pieces of film can be brought down to only four pieces, one for each primary color.

There are alternatives. It's just as feasible to take 20 or 30 different pieces of film and burn the plate in the same sequence as would be used to create duplicate film.

Generally, this is not a good idea. There are reasons for this: 1) errors could be made when burning the plate, 2) the material used in prestripping (or building up the page) may not be composed of hard dots, and 3) whenever masks are used, there is the possibility that the plate will pick up additional images because of light scattering through the stripping material.

So, for many pages, the printer may decide to prestrip the images—the goal being one-piece negatives per color.

But even when the need for stripping isn't readily apparent (such as in a complex buildup), there are times when it is still used. Let's suppose you have two full-bleed advertisements to print on the same sheet as a printer spread. The printer must somehow crop these advertisements (they are almost always slightly oversized) and get their gutter edges to perfectly butt one another. One way to do this would be to slice off the edge of the film itself. You can imagine the problem if someone slips with the blade: The ad would be ruined.

Then there are instances when one photo must be stripped within the printing area of another. Although this would be simpler than the cover strip described, it would almost certainly entail prestripping to final film.

Illustration 62 shows the general scheme of building up two oversized ads into one final set of negatives. Both of the negatives

If for any of a number of reasons, the printer desires to have single-piece final composite film (or put another way, desires to have one master set of film with which to expose the printing plate), then as final composite is exposed from more than one original. In this example, both photos A and B were oversized. Rather than attempt to crudely cut them and splice them together, each would be separately exposed to the final film. After those exposures, the final film is processed and then used to expose the printing plate.

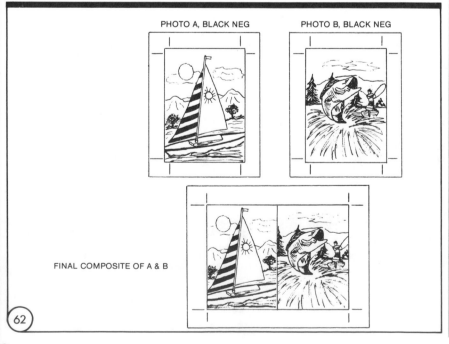

PHOTO A, BLACK NEG   PHOTO B, BLACK NEG

FINAL COMPOSITE OF A & B

62

(they might be from color separations or simply black-and-white ads) are oversized. In the same manner as discussed in the complex strip, masks are made. These will block out the oversized portions of the negatives when they are exposed to duplication film. Each exposure will be made independently with the appropriate blockout mask.

The result is the third, final composite negative, which now has the ads ready to print in their cropped dimensions. The butt at the fold will be virtually perfect if the procedure was done properly.

Positive plates

If you happen to know that your magazine is plated from positive-reading film (rather than negatives), you may be somewhat confused at our heavy concentration on negative stripping. How is a magazine stripped in positive?

Often as not, when positives are required for plates, the magazine is still stripped in negative. There are many reasons.

First, advertisers generally supply negatives. They must be stripped as such. Second, the negative stripping procedure works nicely with standard paste-ups. A conventionally prepared paste-up is easily shot on camera as a negative, and stripped as such. Halftones are normally shot as film negatives and are conveniently stripped that way. Thus, if positive film is required to burn the plates, it is common to strip the entire project as negative, make the proofs from the negatives, and then do the corrections and alterations. When everything is finalized, one master contact is made to positives. Then the plates are burned again, but from the positives.

Cost effects

There is a cost effect when positives are required. In most cases, the cost for preparation work will be higher than it would have otherwise been. Why, then, would a buyer consider allowing his printer to convert to positives at all?

Keep in mind that the printer is making this decision for plate-burning reasons, not for preparation reasons. Some printers burn exclusively from positives because they have converted their entire process to that system (rather than offer both kinds).

The decision might be based on the general belief that positive-acting plates last a lot longer than negative, so they are cheaper in the long run (in spite of the added film cost).

The total cost increase for positives, then, should not be significant on the bottom line. What is spent on prep should be saved on press because the plates won't wear out as quickly as a negative-acting plate.

Other considerations

There is one key consideration for the buyer, though. If you

CHAPTER 34

191

SINGLE-PIECE FILM

have all of the material converted to positives, it means that you will never burn a plate from advertiser-supplied film. The contacting procedure allows room for error here.

Worse yet, many buyers do not understand the different requirements for emulsions and don't know whether their printer takes care of this potential problem. If an ad is supplied as a right-reading, emulsion-down negative and then contacted to a positive, it may well be that the contact will be made with the emulsions wrong (out of contact).

It is important, then, for the buyer to understand which plating procedure will be used. Knowing that, you can advise your advertisers of your requirements.□

SECTION VI: LITHOGRAPHIC PRINTING

THE TWO COMMON PRINTING PROCESSES

Although this book concentrates on lithographic offset printing, a short review of today's most commonly used printing methods will be helpful to the novice production director. I will begin with lithography, the most common printing process in use.

Basic lithography

Lithography was originally achieved by printing from the surface of a smooth, flat stone. The concept was a chemical one: Grease and water do not mix well. The image was placed on the stone using photographic chemical techniques. The areas that were to be printed held (or attracted) ink and repelled water. Conversely, nonprinting areas would hold water and repel ink.

Today, the stone has given way to a flexible plate made of paper or aluminum. In modern lithographic presses, the image to be printed is "offset" onto a rubber-coated "blanket" and then transferred to paper. "Offset" simply means that the plates do not print on the paper, but on the blanket—which in turn contacts the paper. Thus, the modern term for lithography has become offset.

Offset printing is an excellent way to get high-quality printing on runs of up to a million or more without having to go to the added expense of changing plates, which wear out in time.

Speaking of time, the time it takes to give the printer the necessary material and get a job on press is called "lead time." For offset printing, this lead time is (in most cases) shorter than for other processes. Because of this relatively short lead time, offset lends itself to weekly magazines and other timely printed matter.

Another advantage to offset is that, when printing color, you have the opportunity to "proof" the job before it goes on the press—to check that it will print exactly as you want it to. Offset prepress proofing methods are the fastest and least expensive in the business.

Sheetfed and web-offset litho

Two types of offset printing are used for magazines today: sheetfed and web. In sheetfed, a sheet of paper is fed into the press, printed, sprayed with a drying powder, and delivered whole (uncut). Sheetfed printing is most commonly used for magazine inserts on card stock, business forms, one-color jobs, small printing runs and covers.

Sheetfed offset generally produces a higher quality than web offset, and is sometimes selected when quality is more important than speed. Sheetfed, by nature, is a slow operation. Also, sheetfed presses can usually handle heavier paper stock than can web presses.

In web-offset printing, a continuous roll of paper is fed through the press, printed, dried with heat, folded, cut and delivered (in any number of configurations) ready for the bindery. (There are many variations, of course: Some web presses have no dryers, and some are equipped with "sheeters" that deliver a flat, unfolded piece. Also, there are many different types of folders available.)

Web offset lends itself to the high-speed printing of publications, books, catalogs, and complex bindery jobs. This brief introduction won't cover the complexities of folding options, imposition, or any other lengthy topics.

Rotogravure

Two basic physical concepts make the gravure process work: absorbency and surface tension. The image to be printed is placed on the cylinder by etching an arrangement of hollows (called "cells") below the drum surface. (The etching is done either chemically or mechanically.) During the printing process, ink is deposited in these cells and drawn out when put in contact with the paper.

Rotogravure (so named because the printing cells are on cylinders that revolve) is a very consistent, high-speed method of producing excellent, four-color printing via a paper web. Because of the high cost of cylinder preparation, however, it is uncommon to find jobs of less than one million being produced by gravure.□

CHAPTER 35

HOW LITHOGRAPHY WORKS

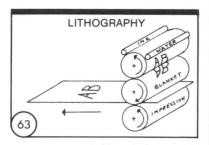

LITHOGRAPHY

63

Offset lithography uses the principle that "ink and water don't mix." The image on the printing plate is ink receptive in areas where the image should print, but water repellent. In areas where there should be no image, the plate is water receptive and, consequently, ink repellent. The image is reproduced on the rubber roller called the blanket, which comes into contact with the paper. This simple drawing represents a sheetfed press, which uses an impression cylinder.

In preceding chapters, many aspects of preparation were discussed. The eventual result of this preparation is usually a set of film negatives or (depending on the type of printing plate to be used) film positives. It is these negatives or positives that are used to expose the printing plate itself—and it is this step that marks the beginning of the actual printing process. As we describe lithographic printing in general, refer to Illustration 63.

Assuming that a conventional-size press is being used, an eight-page "flat" (an assembly of pages that will be printed from one plate) is placed in contact with the printing plate. A controlled exposure is made, and if there are additional burns or exposures on the same plate (see prep section), they will also be made.

The plate is now developed. Years back, the only way to develop a plate was to apply chemicals by hand, rub the plate to develop the image, and then make several other treatments to protect and preserve that image.

For today's magazine print buyer, it is far more typical for plates to be developed by machine. A plate-developing unit performs all of the necessary processes faster, and with greater consistency.

The plate is a positive-reading image of the material to be printed. Those areas that are to print (and carry images) are compatible with oil-based material (ink, in this case). Those areas that are not supposed to print (and carry no image) are compatible with water. Actually, the water is a special "fountain solution" on the press.

Therefore, the image areas attract ink and repel water, while the nonimage areas attract water and repel ink. That, in a nutshell, is how lithography works.

The plate is then wrapped around the (plate) cylinder on the press, and, assuming that everything goes well, what takes place is the following: the plate rotates on its cylinder and comes into contact with both the fountain-solution rollers and the inking rollers. After a few revolutions, the area that will print has picked up a microscopic layer of ink.

As we mentioned in the short review, lithography is called "offset" printing because the printing plate doesn't actually come into contact with the paper. Rather, the plate puts the image onto a rubber roller, called the blanket, which in turn deposits the ink onto the paper. That is the "offsetting": plate to blanket to paper, (rather than plate to paper).

On a simple lithographic press, the blanket cylinder is pressed into contact with the paper by the impression cylinder. On more sophisticated presses (such as web-fed, or roll-fed magazine presses) the entire plate/blanket/ink/water system exists both above and below the sheet of paper. Thus, on a web press, the two blankets act as each other's impression cylinders. This is sometimes called blanket-to-blanket printing, but it is so common on web presses that the term "web" covers it all.

Four-color printing

That simple description of lithography covers the basics and would only apply if the job at hand were merely a black-and-white printed page. But what about four-color (process) printing?

Even a simple press can reproduce a four-color image. First, the yellow printing plate would be exposed and mounted, and yellow put in the inking fountains. Then, after the copies were printed, the yellow ink would be removed, magenta ink put in, the magenta plate installed, the press run again—this time printing *over* the yellow ink.

The subsequent two colors, cyan and black, would be handled the same way.

Obviously, all this plate and ink changing is expensive. Therefore, most process-color jobs find their way to printing presses capable of printing four colors at one time.

While still discussing sheetfed, we can consider a more complicated press: a four-color sheetfed press, *i.e.*, one that can print a maximum of four colors during one pass.

This makes the press capable of printing a full-color image in one pass. The main advantages are that 1) all the colors can be manipulated in harmony (meaning each can be adjusted while the press is running), and 2) the paper passes through the press fewer times. Using this press, if a portion of a magazine were to print in full color on one side of a sheet and in single color (say, black) on the other side of the sheet, the paper would go through the press twice. This contrasts with the five passes needed if the press could deliver only one color at a time.

But even two passes can be too many, which is why the web press is used for volume printing. By its very nature, the web press (for magazines) prints *all* jobs in one pass (a job meaning four, eight, 16, or another multiple of four pages at one time).

Illustration 64 shows a simple web-press setup. Each printing section of the press is called a unit. Each unit is capable of printing one color on the top of the web (meaning the roll of paper) and one on the bottom.

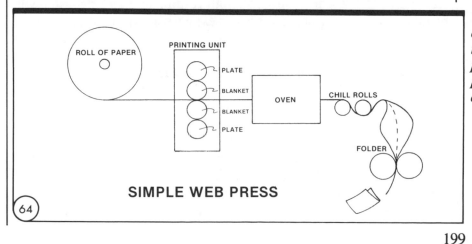

This simple side view of a web press shows its main sections: the paper roll (web), printing unit, oven, and folder.

199

A standard magazine web press would have at least four units, giving it the capability of printing four-colors on the top of the web and four-colors on the bottom. Naturally, the press must be capable of holding the paper. This is done by reel stands at one end of the press. The reel stands are regulated by infeed controls, which dictate the tension that will be placed on the paper during printing.

Because the paper moves through the press at high speed, the ink never has time to dry. So, afterward it goes into the ovens, which set the ink. And, because rapid drying tends to heat the paper, it passes over chill rolls, then over moisturizing rollers, and, finally, goes into the folder.

The variety of folders on the market allows for many printing options (which will be discussed separately in the section on imposition). For now, suffice it to say that if the press were printing a 16-page signature, the folder would cut and fold the paper into the appropriate 16-page format.

Key differences: Web vs. sheetfed

The significant differences between web-fed and sheetfed presses are summarized below:

1. *Makeready costs:* Makeready is the activity required to get the first "good" copy off the press. Because web presses are more complicated, they require a lengthier setup.

This fact is one consideration when deciding whether to put a job on a sheet or web press. Although there is no specific formula, a standard job requiring 100,000 copies would be placed on a web press, while a standard 5,000-copy job would be run on a sheetfed press. Why? Although it may cost thousands of dollars to do the makeready on a web, that cost would be absorbed over the length of the run. The added economy of single-pass printing and automatic folding makes the web highly competitive.

On the other hand, the sheetfed press has a relatively low makeready, giving it an automatic, several-thousand-dollar head start on the 5,000-copy job. Although folding and cutting costs will be incurred later, the net effect is less expensive printing on the sheetfed for smaller runs.

2. *In-line folding:* The web press virtually always has a folder attached to it, while the sheetfed doesn't. Therefore, the web picks up tremendous speed relative to sheetfed presses.

3. *Multicolor ability:* As described, the sheetfed press can make several passes, even to the point of applying all colors individually. Therefore, if cost were not a factor, the sheetfed has unlimited ability to apply different colors of ink to the same job.

The web has this built-in limitation: The total number of

printing units dictates the maximum number of colors that can be used on a job (unless the fountains are split).

4. *Speed:* The web press is far faster than the sheetfed because a sheetfed press must use grippers to pick up a stationary piece of paper, accelerate it to press speed, and then slow it down to place it on a stack.

The web uses a roll of paper that is turning at press speed, and a folder that can be considered moving in harmony with the rest of the press. This results in much higher printing speeds.

5. *Inking method:* The speed and configuration of web presses never allow one color to dry before the next is applied. This means that all the inks must be capable of interacting "wet." For example, if yellow is the first color printed on a web and magenta the second, the magenta ink must be capable of printing onto "wet" yellow ink (while the yellow ink need only be capable of printing on a dry sheet of paper).

Web presses, then, are always "wet trapping" presses. This means the inks must be able to trap, or hold, another layer on top of them before any ink is truly dry.

Now comes the sticky part. Sheetfeds can be either wet- or dry-trapping. On a four-color sheetfed press, it is obvious that wet-trapping will occur. But when a four-color job is printed in four separate passes on a small sheetfed press, the inks would dry between applications and the job would be produced via dry-trapping.

Some sheetfed presses are two-color, meaning that they print two colors via wet-trapping, have a drying period, and then print the subsequent two colors via wet-trapping—but onto a layer of dry-trapping inks.

Still, in both cases, the bottom line remains quality. If you are quality-critical, then you must be sure that all the prepress activities discussed earlier conform to the type of press on which you will run your job. Your color separator will make the appropriate changes in the way he prepares film, based on the type of press (web or sheet) and the actual color printing sequence (rotation). In this way, the densities of color in the film will conform to anticipated trapping later on.

Press controls

Offset lithographic controls can be broken into three major areas that are all critical to producing an acceptable job. They are mechanical position; the dampening fountain; and the inking fountain. The first major control, mechanical position, affects the registration of color, the position of the images on the paper, and the position and accuracy of folds, and so forth.

Errors in mechanical position of the printed image are quite obvious. In Illustration 65, we demonstrate poor registration (positioning of colors). In four-color printing, this can be particularly obvious when an image "reverses" out of a full-color photo. If all four colors are not printing in register, then you will notice one of the colors "shadowing" the image. In other words, the type will be mostly white, but will also have a partial outline of the color that is out of register.

(65)

Poor registration. Originally printed in full color, the type was to have printed in tints of black, magenta, and cyan on a yellow background. This is an extreme example.

Similarly, when a four-color photo is printing very "fuzzy" but the separation and proof appear to be in order, poor press registration is usually the reason.

The dampening fountain and rollers are the second major control area (Illustration 66). By varying the speed of certain oscillating rollers, the pressman can control how much water reaches the plate. This is critical because if too much water reaches the plate, it will emulsify with the ink and work its way into the inking rollers.

Conversely, too little water will upset the ink/water "no-mix" rule of printing, and the plate will pick up ink in all areas. Thus, the dampening fountain and rollers must be set up and monitored to meet rather critical limits. Either too much or too little water will break the rules of lithography, and the press won't print.

Typical fountain on a lithographic press. By varying the speed of the ductor, fountain, and vibrator rollers, the pressman controls how much fountain solution ("water") reaches the plate, thereby controlling the plate's ink receptivity.

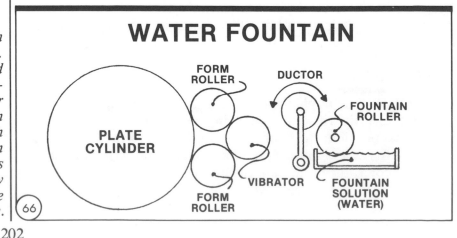

WATER FOUNTAIN

(66)

PLATE CYLINDER

FORM ROLLER

DUCTOR

FOUNTAIN ROLLER

VIBRATOR

FOUNTAIN SOLUTION (WATER)

FORM ROLLER

The third major control is the inking fountain. Of all the press controls, this is the one to which customers become most sensitive. While in theory there should be no "artistic" talent to printing, the inking fountain seems to make printing a creative skill.

On all offset lithographic presses, the inking fountain has a row of "keys" (Illustration 67). All these keys apply pressure on a plate that more or less allows ink to pass onto the roller system. The plate, which is somewhat flexible, also gives some local control as to how much ink will pass to the rollers.

Setting the inking fountains, part of the makeready on a press run, entails starting the press and getting it in rough register. Then the inking fountains are opened or closed to match the total applied ink to the amount required for the total job. For example, if a portion of the press sheet requires almost no cyan, those keys that control that area must be almost entirely shut. Otherwise, too much ink would build up and eventually show up as too much cyan.

Inking keys allow more or less ink to reach the plate, which directly relates to the intensity (or lack thereof) of the printed image. Opening the keys allows more ink to print in an "alley" (two pages in a row). Closing them will restrict ink in that area.

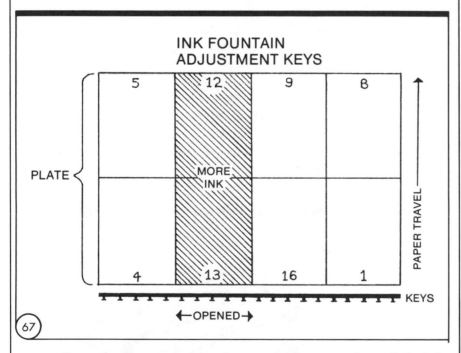

So, even when switching from one job to another, all the inking keys might need adjusting. Then, in order to meet the needs of a given press layout, a given customer's preferences, and the temperature and humidity of the pressroom on a given day, the ink keys are "fine-tuned" to match the proof as closely as possible.□

203

SHEETFED PRINTING FOR MAGAZINES

Although most magazines are printed on web presses, there probably will always be a handful that better fit the sheetfed environment. For the buyer, the choice of web or sheetfed is usually based on price. As said in the preceding chapter, because of the high cost of "gearing up" the web press (doing the makeready), sheetfed printing is competitive for magazines with runs in the lower range.

Sheetfed advantages

Some people regard the sheetfed press as small potatoes, but in a few areas the process does have advantages over web printing.

As mentioned, the makeready costs are low. Imagine the typical, medium-size sheetfed press being operated: One person handles the back of the press, another the front. Whenever trouble arises, the press has to be immediately shut down and the problem corrected. When switching from one job to another, the operators merely change roles from pressmen to plate changers to fountain cleaners, and so forth.

The web press (in the typical magazine environment) is operated by four to eight individuals, and changing from one job to another could consume four hours or more. Getting the press set up for new paper, new inks and new plates could consume thousands of dollars in labor and materials.

One of the obvious strengths of sheetfed printing is the option of running extremely high-quality work. Depending on the given press's ability, a job could be printed one color at a time, with drying periods between applications of ink, or it could be printed four colors at a time. The web press offers no such choices.

A simple sheetfed printing unit. Paper can be ordered or cut to fit the needs of a specific job. The notable difference between sheetfed and web printing is implied by the name: Sheetfed presses print only upon cut sheets of paper, and cannot print from rolls or webs.

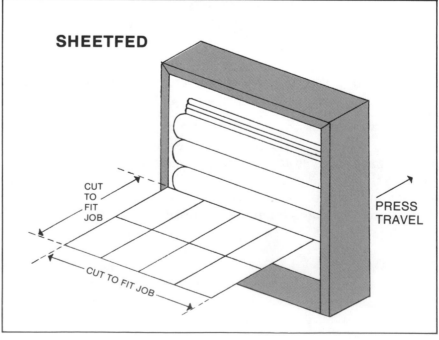

SHEETFED

CUT TO FIT JOB

CUT TO FIT JOB

PRESS TRAVEL

In summary, the four strengths of sheetfed printing are the following:

• *Unlimited color ability:* The same paper can pass through the press any number of times.

• *Economical makeready:* Overall manning requirements are lower and job changes easier.

•*Lower capital investment:* Sheetfed presses are generally less expensive than web presses to purchase, install, maintain, and run.

•*Variable paper dimensions:* Unlike the web press, a sheetfed can accept a wide range of paper dimensions. Although the web press can accept various widths of rolls of paper, the sheetfed press can also accommodate various lengths of sheets. While the web has a fixed longitudinal cutoff for a roll of paper, the sheetfed unit can accept a "short" sheet, which just may have to be cut to fit the exact dimension of a particular job.

Types of sheetfed presses

Sheetfed printing is the granddaddy of offset lithography. It accommodates a wide range of products, which has naturally led to the development of a wide variety of specialty sheetfed presses.

For magazines, sheetfed presses can be categorized with the following parameters:

1. *Maximum paper size:* The smallest press on which you are likely to have any material printed will deliver a sheet measuring 11 inches by 17 inches. Folded, that would be four magazine pages.

Larger presses would accept paper up to 17 inches by 22 inches or 20 inches by 24 inches—allowing for "bleeds," or material that prints beyond the actual page and is later trimmed off in the bindery.

More common for the magazine is a sheetfed press capable of accepting a sheet up to 23 inches by 35 inches, or 25 inches by 38 inches. This would allow eight pages to be printed on each side of the paper, or a total of 16 pages per press run.

2. *Number of printing units:* A printing unit is a section of a press capable of putting one color of ink on one or two sides of the paper. The number of units is important for this reason: Suppose you have a job printed on a single-unit sheetfed press, but your work requires two colors (black and red) to be printed on each side of the sheet. That press would have to run the paper through four times —once for each color on each side.

Although sheetfed presses have reasonably inexpensive makereadies, the above situation would require four makereadies and four passes for a single sheet of paper.

And what if that job required four colors on each side? That would mean eight passes through the press. This is poor economy: More printing units could produce the same job in fewer passes.

So let's assume that you need two colors on both sides of the paper. What if the press had only two printing units?

The number of passes would be cut in half. In addition, because both of the colors would print at the same time, any conflict between them (a mistake, in other words) could be identified before the damage was complete. If the two colors didn't register, the press could be stopped. But on a single-color press, it is possible that one color would be laid down *before* the problem was identified.

A sheetfed press with four printing units might be considered a "stripped down web" because it would be printing with web-type wet-trapping and allow the operator to balance all four colors together.

3. *Perfecting ability:* Perfecting presses literally turn the sheet over while it is running through the press. For example, a four-color perfecting sheetfed can print any of the following:

- Four colors on one side of the sheet.
- Two colors on each side at the same time.
- Three colors on one side and one on the other.

The obvious advantage to a perfector is that the press can take on a new personality, depending on the job. It could produce a two-color job (two colors on each side) in one pass, or a four-color job (four colors on both sides) in two passes, or any other feasible combination.

A typical sheetfed-printed magazine

In order to demonstrate the sheetfed press in action, let's use a magazine as an example. Suppose you publish a magazine with a press run of 5,000 (5M). It includes some four-color, but is primarily black and white.

Let's assume that we have available a 25 inch by 38 inch, two-color, perfecting sheetfed press.

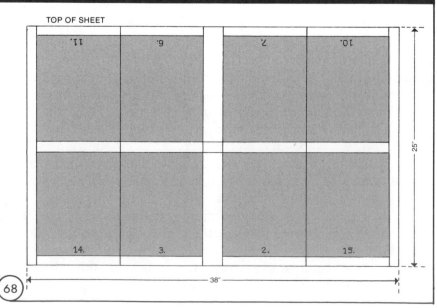

Imposition for a 16-page sheetfed signature, showing the images to be printed on one side of the sheet.

As shown in Illustration 68, we will print 16-page signatures. (A signature is a section of a magazine that is folded to the configuration required at the bindery stage).

We'll say that one signature will be printed in four colors on one side and in two colors on the other. The other two signatures will be single color only.

Here's how the job will run.

First of all, either you or your printer will make "fold-downs" of the magazine. If you take a horizontal sheet of paper and fold it in half three times (as shown in Illustration 69), you will come up with a 16-page signature.

The fold-downs will tell you which pages will appear on which signatures (as shown in Illustration 70). Obviously, the first page of signature one is page one. The first page of signature two is nine. To determine which numbers fall on which portions of the signature, the fold-downs are assembled into a dummy.

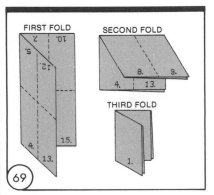

FIRST FOLD   SECOND FOLD

THIRD FOLD

69

Illustration 68's imposition relates directly to this folded signature.

A fold-down or dummy. In planning a magazine, the printer or customer creates a numbered dummy from folded sheets of paper. They can then be unfolded to show the imposition, or relative positions, of the pages in the magazine.

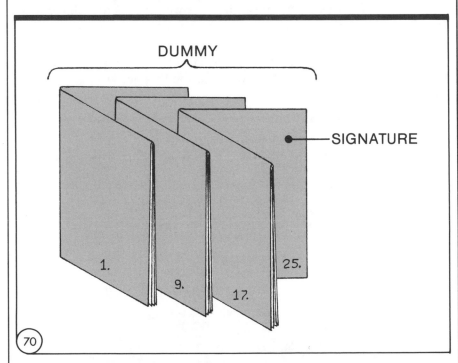

DUMMY

SIGNATURE

1.   9.   17.   25.

70

After the pages in the dummy are numbered, the signatures are unfolded and used as a guide in stripping the magazine to press imposition. This brings us back to Illustration 68, which shows one side of the 16-page signature. For clarity, we have numbered Illustration 68 to represent a single 16-page "magazine" so that you will be better able to see what happens during the folding operation.

But let's get back to the printing. Assume that Illustration 68 shows the four-color side of the signature. Because our hypothetical press is limited to two colors, we will assume that the magenta and yellow inks will be printed first. That takes one pass through the press. Next, the plates and the inks are changed and then the blue and black inks applied. Finally, the inks and plates are changed, the sheet is turned over, and the two other colors are printed on the back side.

So much for signature one, which is still flat sheets of paper stacked on a skid. Signatures two and three are much easier to print: Black ink is put into both printing units, and the perfecting ability of the press is brought into play. We run 5M of the second signature and 5M of the third. Note that these two signatures combined took far less effort to print than the other single signature.

At this point, we have three skids of flat paper that must be folded. Illustration 69 shows a typical fold for 16-page signatures. If you take a piece of scrap paper and duplicate the folds, you'll immediately see the logic to the page numbering shown in Illustration 68.

For saddle-stitched magazines, folding requires that a lip of paper be available for the bindery operation. (We will discuss this in more detail later in the bindery section).

At this point, the sheetfed press has produced—with the assistance of an off-line folder—just what the web press could have produced all in one pass. (Not just any web press, but a web nonetheless.)

Now, for the covers. One of the strengths of the sheetfed is its ability to "work and turn." As we describe this activity, refer to Illustration 71.

Typical work-and-turn method of printing covers or other four-page signatures. The main advantage is that a single set of plates applies the image to both sides of the paper.

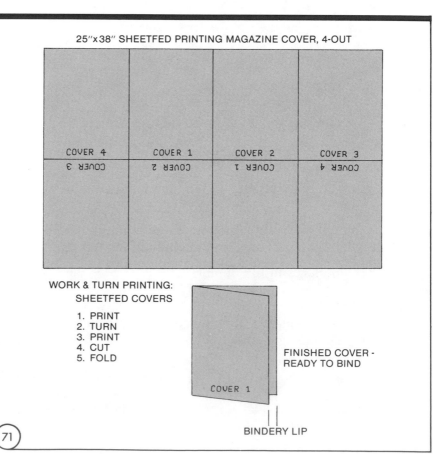

25"x38" SHEETFED PRINTING MAGAZINE COVER, 4-OUT

| COVER 4 | COVER 1 | COVER 2 | COVER 3 |
| COVER 3 | COVER 2 | COVER 1 | COVER 4 |

WORK & TURN PRINTING:
SHEETFED COVERS

1. PRINT
2. TURN
3. PRINT
4. CUT
5. FOLD

FINISHED COVER - READY TO BIND

COVER 1

BINDERY LIP

71

Suppose we print the eight pages shown on the 25 inch by 38 inch sheetfed layout. We'll print cover one two times since all the other pages will print two times on this side. So we will print the red and yellow inks on our two-color press, and then we'll turn the sheet over and print the same red and yellow again. If you take a sheet of paper and number it as is shown, you will see that page one will be backed up by page two, and so forth.

Then, we'll switch the plates and inks and print the blue and black on the front side, and again flip it over, printing the same on the back side. Now, with only two makereadies, we have printed a sheet in four colors on two sides. That's pretty economical compared to the three makereadies it took to print signature one (and with only two colors on the back side of that form).

So that's the economical secret of sheetfed, work-and-turn printing. It requires only four printing plates and, on this press, only two makereadies. Why? Because the same plate prints the front and back of the sheet. Better yet, it is often possible to use the same film to make the exposures in the different areas. This is called "step and repeat" plate exposure and will show up as economical printing bids from printers who propose it.

The bottom of Illustration 71 again shows the bindery lip on one of the four-page covers printed using the above method. Naturally, after printing they are cut and folded to this configuration.

The final advantage of this type of work-and-turn printing is this: Each sheet of paper delivers four covers for the magazine, meaning the press run is cut to 25 percent of the total required quantity. This is called printing "four out." There are also such creatures as two out, eight out and 16 out, depending on the job and the size of the press.

Limitations and penalties

Sheetfed has its place, but it also has its limitations. All the material printed in the preceding example is stacked and then taken to the cutter (if necessary). It is then folded and finally restacked to await binding into the final product. Compared to what happens on a web press, this means that the paper is handled at least twice.

Handling means time and materials. Thus, the penalties of sheetfed printing include lengthier production time and more waste allowance. Each time a sheet of paper is handled, it could be damaged, meaning that the press run is kicked up in anticipation of subsequent damage and loss of a few signatures.

But quality cannot be overlooked. Consider this: The sheetfed press can print colors singly and allow them all to dry. This means that an unlimited amount of ink can be piled layer upon layer. The results can be spectacular. Additionally, the finished job can be allowed to dry and then given a heavy application of varnish. (On a web, the varnish—when used to add "gloss" to a cover or another critical piece—is often applied over wet ink so that little of its potential benefit is realized.)

So the economy of small runs on a sheetfed press is hard to match. For the short-run magazine, both the quality and cost of running sheetfed are mighty hard to beat.□

WEB PRINTING

The lithographic web press is easily the winner for magazine production. Although sheetfed meets the requirements of the short-run magazine, and gravure presses (another type of web) take over for the long-run magazines, the litho web covers the very large middle market. Statistically, it is likely that if you are the production director of a magazine, you print via lithographic web.

So, it makes sense to spend a good deal of time describing just how the litho web works. In this section, we will cover the various types of webs, their abilities, the basic theory of their operation, and their minimum and maximum output of printed products.

And from now on, when we use the term "web," it will mean lithographic offset web press.

The roll-fed web

You know from the previous chapters that sheetfed presses start with a cut-to-size piece of paper and deliver it at the other end of the press without altering its size. Naturally, the web press has a different set of rules. It starts with a roll of paper at one end and delivers a folded product at the other. So, it is both a press and a piece of bindery equipment.

While the complexities of folders and imposition have a section of their own in this book, a few activities performed in the folding end of the press must be related directly to the printing units before a discussion can ensue.

A web printing unit. The circumference of the printing plate cylinder dictates the cutoff, or the dimension at which the paper will be cut to by the folder. The width of the roll of paper is specific at the time it is ordered, and should conform to the minimum width needed to print the job.

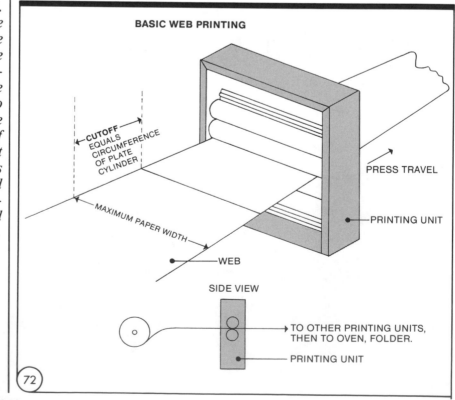

BASIC WEB PRINTING

CUTOFF EQUALS CIRCUMFERENCE OF PLATE CYLINDER

PRESS TRAVEL

PRINTING UNIT

MAXIMUM PAPER WIDTH

WEB

SIDE VIEW

TO OTHER PRINTING UNITS, THEN TO OVEN, FOLDER.

PRINTING UNIT

72

212

In Illustration 72, a single printing unit of a web press is shown. By printing unit, I mean a section of the press that will print one color on the top of the web (or moving sheet of paper) and one color on the bottom. It must be understood that the web is not cut while it travels through the printing units and folder. Rather, it will be cut perpendicular to its direction of travel *at a fixed dimension* when it goes through the folder. The dimension to which it will be cut is called the *cutoff* of the press. This is a mechanically fixed measurement that cannot be altered after a press is constructed. The cutoff is the first key (critical) dimension on a press.

Referring again to Illustration 72, you will see that the cutoff of the press is equal to the circumference of the plate cylinder (onto which the printing plate is mounted). On most presses, the plate cylinder and the blanket cylinder have the same circumference (although in a few cases, the blanket cylinder can be double the circumference of the plate cylinder to allow a longer blanket life).

What is the importance of cutoff? Illustration 73 demonstrates it. Keeping in mind that the cutoff is a fixed figure, but that the height of different magazines is a variable, examine the drawing.

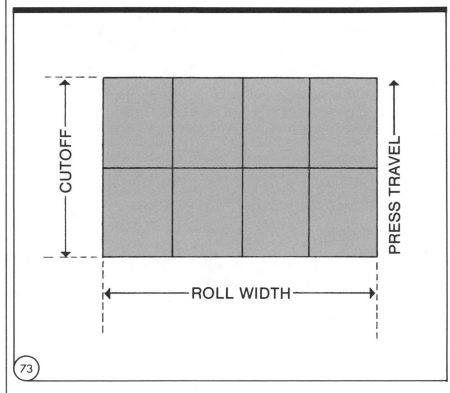

Cutoff and roll width work together in saving paper. A magazine that trims at 8-3/8" in width needs a roll slightly wider than 34 inches (slightly more than four page widths). If its trim height is 10-7/8", a cutoff of 23-3/4" (slightly more than two page heights) would suffice.

It reflects a web printing plate capable of printing eight pages on one side of the web (and eight on the other side, of course).

For a magazine that trims at a full 11 inches, the cutoff on a web of this size must be approximately 23-9/16 inches. This figure takes into account the small, dead space where the plate meets itself after wrapping around the cylinder, and the required bindery trims after the product is folded. The importance of this to the buyer is that it is quite common to find yourself printing with a cutoff of 23-9/16 inches, while producing a magazine with a trim height of 10-3/4 inches. What is the effect?

There is no way around the cutoff, and more paper will be used than necessary. Later, in the bindery, although the cutoff accommodates a full 11-inch trim, the magazine will be chopped down to a height of 10-3/4 inches. The excess paper is simply trimmed off and disposed of as waste.

In summary, keep two things in mind about cutoffs: They are not a variable and they should relate to the magazine being produced to keep your paper usage at a minimum.

Roll width

The second key dimension is roll width. Refer again to Illustration 73. On a typical press that could produce this product (eight pages per web side), the maximum width of a roll of paper could be approximately 38 inches. But what width would actually be required to produce a book that trimmed to 8-1/4 inches? Possibly a 34-1/4-inch roll. It would be a tremendous waste to run a roll that is 38 inches wide on a press if it were producing a standard-size magazine. Similarly, what if your magazine is currently trimming at 8-1/2-inches wide, and you are contemplating a change to 8-1/8 inches? Sure, you would save in postage and shipping costs, but what about paper? If your printer did not change the paper order for a narrower roll, there would be no paper savings at all. Again, the excess would be trimmed in the bindery and sold as scrap.□

VARIOUS KINDS OF PRESSES

Did you notice that we were careful to state that the cutoff and roll widths, as described above, relate to a press that prints eight pages per side? The reason for this is that there are several different types of web presses. On some presses, the cutoff affects the height of a printed page. On others, it affects the width of the page. Naturally, the roll width reflects the opposite of the cutoff.

Now, as we discuss the four common types of web presses, be sure to pay attention to the press travel (direction) as it relates to both cutoff and roll width. If the page travels through the press from top to bottom (head to foot, or foot to head), then the cutoff will affect the maximum page height. And if the page travels through the press sideways, the cutoff will affect the maximum page width.

In your purchasing activities, attention to this relationship is critical to your paper costs. You will most likely want to ensure that the press is suited to your job—meaning that neither the cutoff nor roll widths are causing excessive paper waste.

Let's now describe the four common types of web presses, starting with a single printing unit and then progressing to multiple printing units and multiple roll stands.

The half-web

Illustration 74 (page 218) shows a simple drawing of a printing unit on a half-web. It is called such because, for practical purposes, it runs a width of paper that is approximately half the width of the most common web press (conventional or full-web).

As shown, the cutoff on the press would be approximately 22-3/4 inches. We emphasize—for this drawing and those to follow—that this is an *approximate* figure for illustrative purposes only. The press itself has a fixed dimension. In this instance it is somewhere around 22-3/4 inches, but it could be as small as 22-1/2 inches, or as large as 23-9/16 inches.

Although the difference between these figures may seem minimal, it can reflect up to a 5 percent difference in relative paper consumption. Why? Because if a magazine needs only 22-1/2 inches in cutoff to meet its needs, up to 5 percent in paper could be wasted by running the product on the "wrong" press.

Back to the drawing. On the half-web press, the maximum paper width would be around 18 inches, with 17-3/4 inches more likely. The half-web produces eight pages per web by printing four pages on the top and four on the bottom. Remember, we are examining only one printing unit. The typical magazine-type web press has at least four printing units to deliver a full-color (process color) product.

You can begin to familiarize yourself with imposition by noting the page numbers on the paper in Illustration 74. If you were to take a sheet of paper and number it as shown in the illustration, and then turn it over and number the back side logically (page two on the back of page one, and so on), you would have a simple press imposition for this half-web press. Thus you can see that imposition is noth-

216

ing more than the position of each page on the plate in relation to how the cut sheet is folded.

One of the key differences you will notice between one press and another is the "rotation," or "pulling," through the press. These terms describe exactly how the sheet is printed: side to side or top to bottom. If you have ever read complex specifications, you will remember that rotation was mentioned. Why is it important to the magazine buyer? For this reason: Web presses are not perfect. For example, in Illustration 74, the ink used to print page five could possibly have negative effects on the amount of ink required for page eight. This is normally not critical for simple, single-color printing (black). But when page five is a paid, full-color advertisement and page eight is another one, the careful production manager wants to know that the press can deliver the same quality on both ads.

The technical term for this relationship is called "ghosting." It means that pages that run "in line" (one in front of the other), or items on the same page that are in line (in relation to their travel through the press) have a relationship. Normally, the relationship is not good, and one page will have a slightly adverse effect on the other.

Ghosting problems and solutions will be discussed in a separate chapter. However, for the purpose of perspective, we can say a few general things about each of the four major presses that we will describe.

First, on the half-web now being discussed, the direction of travel is the most common direction in the litho-web world. Pages are printed head to foot or vice versa. There are minimal relationships between pages four and five and one and eight in the illustrations, and maximum relationships between five and eight and one and four.

Second, the web will later fold against the grain of the paper. What is grain? Grain is the general orientation of the fibers in the paper itself. Paper fibers are long, slender, microscopic bits that tend to become oriented in the direction in which they travel while the sheet is being manufactured.

For the magazine person, and particularly for those who have a saddle-stitched product, grain can have a noticeable effect. In the case of all presses that print head to foot, the paper will be folded with the grain. In the case of magazines printed side to side, the fold will be against the grain.

The difference is in the quality of the fold. Paper always folds better with the grain. When folding against the grain, the paper fibers at the fold can break. In addition, a fold against the grain will not lie as flat as a grain-fold, which means that the magazine may have a tendency to loft up when lying on a table.

So, looking at the drawing, it is obvious that the press is printing in the most acceptable direction and that the fold will (later) be with the grain. Now, let's move on to the next type of small web press and see everything change.

The mini-web

Illustration 75 shows what is commonly called a mini-web, and like the half-web, each printing unit prints eight pages on the moving web. The big difference between the half-web and the mini-web is that the mini prints side to side rather than bottom to top.

Is this press "better"? We won't pass that kind of judgment, but we will point out the differences.

For discussion purposes, suppose this printed product reflects an eight-page magazine. Page one being the cover, it is obvious (when speaking of press travel) that the back cover and front cover have a printing relationship. And it might be quite uncomfortable for a given magazine to consider compromising its two most important pages. Plus, the paper grain will be folded "wrong."

Other than those two key differences, the mini- and half-webs produce similar products. The mini has a cutoff of about 17-3/4 inches and a maximum width of about 26 inches.

Illustrations 74-77 demonstrate the relationships between roll width and cutoff for four types of presses: the mini-web, half-web, standard web, and one version of a wide web.

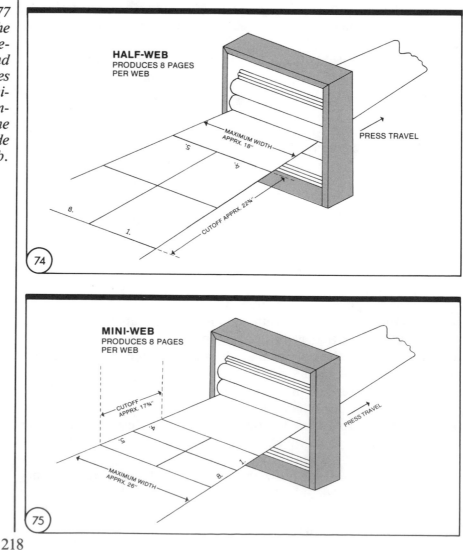

HALF-WEB
PRODUCES 8 PAGES
PER WEB

MAXIMUM WIDTH APPRX. 18"

PRESS TRAVEL

CUTOFF APPRX. 22¾"

74

MINI-WEB
PRODUCES 8 PAGES
PER WEB

CUTOFF APPRX. 17¾"

PRESS TRAVEL

MAXIMUM WIDTH APPRX. 26"

75

Note in these two cases, mini-web and half-web, that any compromises made on the press are only between two pages. This will also be the case with the next kind of press.

CHAPTER 39

The conventional (or full) web

Illustration 76 shows a conventional web printing unit. In this case, the cutoff is about 22-3/4 inches (and within the range mentioned earlier); the maximum roll width is about 38 inches.

Because of the direction of travel, head-to-foot printing and grain-folded paper, this type of web is considered standard. It produces eight pages per side, or 16 pages per web.

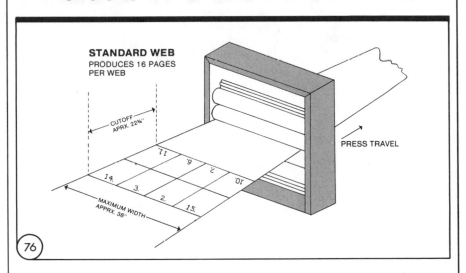

Years ago, the standard common height for a trimmed magazine was 11 inches—even more in some cases. The conventional web with a 23-9/16-inch cutoff was designed to print these magazines.

As years went by, postage costs and paper costs rose dramatically and publishers attempted to trim their magazines as small as possible without creating any noticeable visual effects. While the transition is not complete (many magazines still trim at 11 inches), the trend has been generally established.

Thus, printers began having presses delivered with shorter cutoffs. The newer presses today have cutoffs of 22-1/2 inches or 22-3/4 inches, which limits them to printing magazines with today's shorter trim height. Note that word—limits.

A stroll through the web printing shops in this country is an education in this transition. Almost all of the 23-9/16-inch presses are old. Virtually all of the newer presses trim at a shorter dimension. The smart publisher is aware of the logic here and of the potential paper savings (or loss). Although the maximum amount of waste is truly 4.72 percent, the average "mistake" made by the unwary publisher is 3.57 percent. This average figure represents the difference in paper consumption between a press cutoff of 22-3/4 inches and one of 23-9/16 inches.

Also, generally speaking, the newer the web press, the faster and better it prints. So, by combining the appropriate cutoff and gaining from a higher-speed press, the publisher can see significant economic gains.

The wide web

Illustration 77 shows a wide web, so named because it is a good deal wider than the more common conventional web. Its cutoff is approximately 38 inches, and the maximum width is usually about 45 inches, though often as wide as 50 inches.

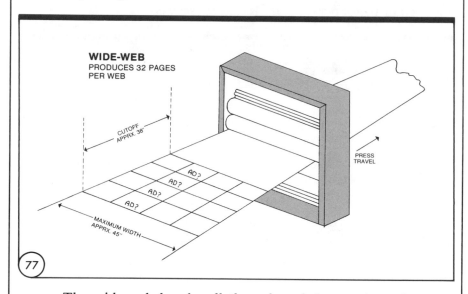

WIDE-WEB
PRODUCES 32 PAGES
PER WEB

CUTOFF
APPRX. 38"

PRESS
TRAVEL

AD?
AD?
AD?
AD?

MAXIMUM WIDTH
APPRX. 45"

77

The wide-web breaks all the rules of the previous three examples. With the half, mini, and conventional web presses, no single page has a critical printing relationship with more than one other page (again, for practical purposes). But the wide-web diagram shows a more serious relationship: Each printed page has three companions on the plate (relative to press travel). Assuming that you occasionally see four paid advertisements running in a row (in line), what can you expect?

Without even addressing the problem of having quality materials (properly prepared advertising film) to work with, you can expect that the pressman must find some sort of average balance for each ad's color requirements. If the first ad on the plate requires a good deal of magenta ink while the others cannot tolerate it without going out of balance, what is the solution?

Often, the solution is to have the customer on hand specify a preference. Or, before printing commences, some printers will contact the customer for a decision on which pages, if any, to favor and which to let slide.

It is only fair to criticize the wide-web for its major weaknesses. We are not advising against this type of press since it does fit the needs of high-volume weekly magazines and certain long-run jobs, and so forth. But beware of the often-serious compromises. They follow:

1. Each page may compromise the quality of three others.

2. The paper will fold grain-wrong.

3. Registration will consistently be a problem for two reasons: First, the plate is larger than a conventional press's plate so it is more likely to misregister, and second, because 16 pages print on each side of the web and are physically harder to handle, many printers with wide-web presses strip in eight page flats, which again creates an area of possible misregistration when the final, one-piece plate is exposed.

Which press for you?

Now that you have a general idea of the types of webs and of the abilities of sheetfeds, you may be asking the most often raised question in the magazine production world: Which type of press fits your product?

Let's say up front that there are simply no rules. Each printer and magazine is unique. All the variables must be considered, including frequency of publication, average issue size, color usage, and so forth. So please do not accept the following discussion as bible truth. Use it only as a guideline in your own investigations.

We will concentrate on 1) the length of the press run (rather than on color usage or frequency), 2) makeready costs (getting the first good copy off the press), and 3) quality.

Sheetfed presses

Sheetfed presses are competitive, generally, in the lower press run area. Quantities can be as little as a thousand and can reach into the 30 thousand range or higher.

Makeready costs are generally far lower for sheetfed than for web presses. The sheetfed is often operated by just two men or women and the pace seems more relaxed because these presses cost less to install and have a lower hourly rate.

In the quality circle, sheetfeds can be real winners, depending on their basic design. A small, single-color or two-color sheetfed can produce spectacular quality for technical reasons: While the web press must always "wet trap," sheetfeds can "dry trap" (allow the ink to dry before applying the next color). This means a virtually unlimited capacity to apply process inks.

Mini and half webs

Run lengths for these presses generally start at 10M to 15M and reach 30M or, in a few cases, 100M and up. The difference depends more on the printer's marketing strategy than on the press's ability to print economically.

Makeready costs are higher for mini and half webs than for

most sheetfed presses, but are usually far lower than for conventionally sized webs. Why? The plates are smaller, so the press requires fewer people.

Quality on small webs has always been a topic of debate. Suffice to say, the small web, when installed to conventional-web specifications, should be able to deliver better quality on the final printed product. It registers only four pages on each side of the web rather than eight, and the more pages on a side, the greater the problem of consistent registration.

Conventional webs

In terms of range, the standard web usually gets competitive at 20M and up, with its limit being a million or two. Again, the printer's marketing strategy sets the top and bottom limits.

Makeready costs can vary dramatically because of the wide range of configurations in which you can order the press itself. A small, two-color standard web can have a makeready cost competitive with that of a half web, while an eight-color standard web can run many thousands of dollars more.

The quality of the standard web is, more or less, the standard of web printing. While some mini and half webs produce better work, the larger webs (wide webs) are generally inferior.

Wide web

For most purposes, the wide web is considered a tool of speed rather than of economy or quality. Its most obvious use is in producing weekly newsmagazines. On such magazines, there is an obvious need for speed, at which the wide web excels.

Quantity is not an easy topic to address. You can use the figures of 50M to a million if you like, but on this type of press there are more exceptions than rules.

Makeready costs are understandably high. Because of the sizes of the plates, which are very large and costly, initial registration can be time-consuming.

Quality, as discussed earlier in this chapter, could be called "what's left after the compromises have been made." If that seems rather harsh, do keep in mind that the half web must get only four pages per side working in harmony. The wide web must deal with 16.

Cross bidding

You should have noticed some obvious crossovers in the preceding descriptions. There are cases when sheetfed presses compete with conventional webs, when half webs compete with wide webs.

It is important to realize that marketing strategy can affect the press that you will be on. Therefore, when it comes time to solicit bids from printers, don't make the mistake of automatically excluding a printer based on his equipment. Your concern is that the ultimate bottom line and the quality of the product meet your needs, and that the product is delivered on time.□

CHAPTER 39

WEB PRESS CONFIGURATIONS

The preceding discussion on web presses concentrated on the basic mechanics of a single printing unit. Part of the personality of the web press is the cutoff and the maximum roll width. There are a few more fundamentals that, when examined by the production director, start to create a truer picture of what the web press can do. So, assuming that you now understand the importance of a single printing unit and its variables (plate size, cutoff, maximum roll width), you can look at the other variables that make up the press's total character. They are as follows:

1. *Number of printing units:* This will dictate the maximum number of inks that can be applied at one time on the press (split fountains not being considered).

2. *Number of roll stands:* Depending on how it is ordered, a magazine web press can hold one, two, or more rolls of active paper (or webs). A conventional web press delivers 16 pages per web, but the total number of pages produced on the press equals the number of roll stands multiplied by 16 pages each.

3. *Type of folder:* This is the final ingredient in understanding just what a press can do. It combines all elements so far mentioned and dictates the positions available for each page. Because the folding operation is complex and has ramifications that affect virtually all other parts of the press, it needs to be discussed separately. For now, we will look at the printing units and roll stands and how they interact with one another.

The typical press

Let's call Illustration 78 the side view of a typical conventionally sized web press. And before going further, a few observations:

Web presses are generally ordered to meet the market needs of a printer. One of the major questions is, what should the maximum roll width and cutoff dimensions be on a single printing unit? Then, how many printing units should be installed? (Obviously, for a full-color magazine, a minimum of four printing units will be needed. But more might logically be added, as this section will demonstrate.) The final question is, how many roll stands should be installed?

Although we will describe the many configurations available for a conventional web press, all the parameters and possibilities will apply to all presses: mini-webs, half-webs, conventional webs, and wide webs. But, for the sake of clarity, in the illustrations, we will consistently refer to a conventional web.

As Illustration 78 shows, a web might be installed with four printing units and a single roll stand. Viewed from the side, you can imagine the roll of paper being fed into the press, through the printing units, and into the oven for drying. After the oven, it enters the folder, which we will cover separately later on.

In this drawing, we see the web going through the press, but only through one printing unit. Why?

224

Suppose this was a 16-page, black-and-white section of a magazine. What purpose would it serve to crank up three more printing units—magenta, cyan and yellow? None whatsoever. For this reason, our first drawing shows one of the common uses of a full-color web—the printing of a single-color signature, or form (16 pages in this case).

Under the drawing, we see the language of conventional web technology. We say "one reel, four-unit press running 1/1." That means, one reel of paper is being run, with one color (black) printing on the top and one on the bottom of the web. Then the paper enters the oven.

How does the paper get past the first three printing units? It moves over a series of grater rollers located above the press. We have not shown the graters in any of these illustrations, nor any of the hundreds of (possible) rollers that allow paper to be strung through the press in numerous ways.

One consideration for the buyer, then, is color itself as it relates to press capability. If this press has only one roll stand and four printing units, its market is already apparent: It was designed to run 16-page signatures in full-color on both sides. The print buyer looking at this illustration could make the assumption that this press is being underutilized. If a magazine printed no full-color at all, this would not likely be the most economical press on which to print the job. You would constantly be "dragging" (not using) three printing units, whose cost is somehow reflected in the overall operating cost of the press.

Illustration 79 shows the same press running 4/4, or four colors on the top and the bottom of the web (full color). Now all printing units are being utilized and the press is running at its maximum ability: 16 pages in full color per press run.

CHAPTER 40

One of the primary strengths of the web press is its versatility. Illustrations 78-94 show progressively more complicated presses. The addition of reel stands (to hold rolls of paper), printing units, and ovens dictates whether the press—in this case a standard size web—can print 16, 32, or 48 pages in one pass.

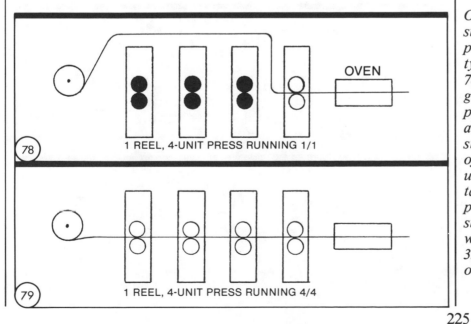

78 — 1 REEL, 4-UNIT PRESS RUNNING 1/1

79 — 1 REEL, 4-UNIT PRESS RUNNING 4/4

225

Two reels, two ovens

Illustration 80 shows some different thinking on the part of the printer. What if there were, in fact, many jobs that required less than full-color printing?

By ordering the press with two roll stands, the press can now deliver a maximum of 32 pages per run. Of course, any time a roll stand is added, an oven must also be added. In this drawing, we demonstrate using a four-unit web press to print two webs, with two colors on the tops and the bottoms of the webs. Thus, the notation: two-reel, 2/2, 2/2 (meaning, two rolls of paper with the first and second being printed two colors over two colors).

This two-roll arrangement should strike you as much more efficient than what could be done in the arrangement shown in Illustration 78. Without the second reel stand, the press simply cannot deliver more than 16 pages, regardless of how much or how little color is demanded of the printing units. This means two complete make-readies would be required to produce 32 pages. This would entail putting the plates on the press and running it until good copies were achieved. Then, if the run were 50M, the press would produce the job, another makeready would be performed, and another 50M run.

The press in Illustration 80 kills two birds with one stone. Although the makeready is a bit more expensive (adding a roll of paper means more controls, more coordination), the press will deliver 50M copies of 32 pages in one pass, rather than 50M copies in two passes. You could say that the setup in Illustration 80 is roughly twice as time-efficient as that in Illustration 78.

And, to top it off, Illustration 80 shows two colors being applied to both sides of the web.

Other variations are possible, of course. Illustration 81 shows

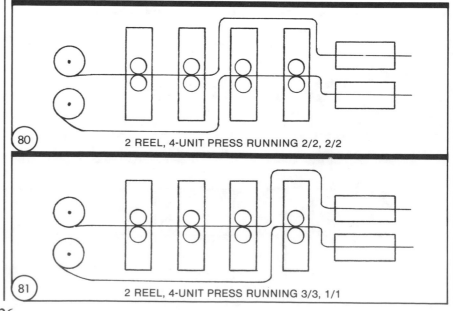

80 2 REEL, 4-UNIT PRESS RUNNING 2/2, 2/2

81 2 REEL, 4-UNIT PRESS RUNNING 3/3, 1/1

226

the same press configuration as that in Illustration 80. The difference is that three colors are being applied to the top and the bottom of one web, while only one color is being applied to the top and the bottom of another. This type of printing arrangement would be common to a magazine that runs many ads needing matched colors (such as Pantone Warm Red on one ad, cyan on another, and so on).

You may have already figured out one of the critical points of consideration for the production director and the printer—maximizing the press. Starting with an underutilized press in Illustration 78, we have progressed to full-utilization in Illustrations 80 and 81. What does that mean? The press is designed for a market. Running it at full capacity suggests that you happen to fit the market for which the press was ordered. In other words, when you find the right printer, the right press, and fit the market, you should be saving money.

Five units

Illustration 82 shows another installation. This time the printer ordered a press with five units and one reel stand. Why?

Perhaps he specializes in printing covers with this press and needs the fifth unit to apply varnish. Or maybe he prints many jobs that require a special, fifth ink (such as metallic silver for a General Motors ad).

In any case, the utilization in Illustration 82 is adequate. Having only one reel stand, this press was not meant to print more than 16 pages at a time. The fifth unit is available, if required, but it is not the critical factor in determining the economy and market area of the press. If anything, it should be considered an "escape" route for problem jobs requiring another color (in addition to the four basic process colors).

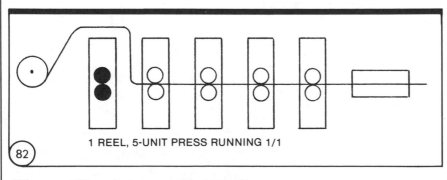

1 REEL, 5-UNIT PRESS RUNNING 1/1

82

Five units, two reel stands

But in Illustration 83, the same press with a second reel stand becomes very powerful. For process-color work, one web can be run four colors on the top and four on the bottom. For problem work (five-color), it can be run 5/5. But to really see economy, the press can also run 4/4, 1/4 (one web with full color and one web black).

What for? For this: If a magazine needs limited four color intermingled with black pages (text, for example), then it makes perfect sense to have a five-unit press. The delivery will be 16 pages in full color and 16 pages in black. Depending on the type and number of folders at the other end, this can make for very economical printing. The black-only signature (or section) requires very little additional effort for makeready purposes, yet a full 32 pages can be delivered in a single press run.

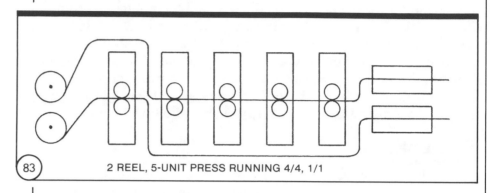

83   2 REEL, 5-UNIT PRESS RUNNING 4/4, 1/1

Compare that to Illustration 78: If 32 pages are needed on that press, with half being full color, the press needs two makereadies and two press runs versus one of each for the press in Illustration 83. If you were to have your magazine bid by competitive printers with configurations as shown in Illustrations 78 and 83, and if you used four color for part of the magazine, what would you see? It would be virtually impossible for the single-reel printer to be competitive. He would require nearly twice the effort and twice the time to produce your work. No contest at all!

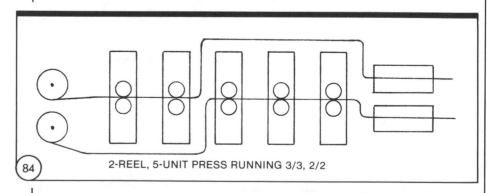

84   2-REEL, 5-UNIT PRESS RUNNING 3/3, 2/2

By now you should be able to look at Illustration 84 and see what we did. Using the previous press, we are running 32 pages, 3/3, 2/2. Again, this kind of configuration would be handy to a magazine running many two-color, matched-ink ads.

Six units, two reels

Let's add another printing unit. Illustration 85 shows a press with six units running 4/4, 2/2. For what purpose? Obviously, four color is required for 16 pages. But what if two colors are required on the tops and the bottoms of the second web?

In some cases, a printer with a five-unit press would have no option but to run the job as two separate 16s, meaning two make-readies and two press runs. But in this case, the two-color requirement on the second 16-pager is easily accommodated. Again, this demonstrates running a press at its maximum capacity, which translates into maximum economy for the buyer.

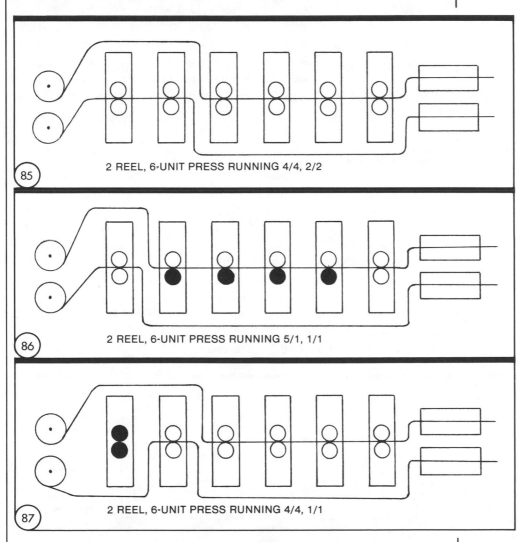

85   2 REEL, 6-UNIT PRESS RUNNING 4/4, 2/2

86   2 REEL, 6-UNIT PRESS RUNNING 5/1, 1/1

87   2 REEL, 6-UNIT PRESS RUNNING 4/4, 1/1

Illustrations 86 and 87 show slightly different uses of that same six-unit press. In Illustration 86, four of the blankets are darkened to indicate that they are not being used. The press is printing 1/1, 5/1, which means that one web is being printed in one color on both sides, and the other with five colors on one side and one color on the other. This might occur if the magazine needed only a maximum of eight pages with full color, plus a special matched ink, but in this example, the bottom half of that web really didn't call for any color.

This example shows two economies: The press is again being

CHAPTER 40

229

used to its maximum, and, in addition, the buyer is not paying for the cost of the four printing plates on the bottom of the full-color web. Printing plates are doubly expensive. They cost money to make, to install, and to run. And the more plates, the more registration problems. There is nothing wrong at all with running full-color on the top of a web and partial or B/W on the bottom.

Illustration 87 (page 229) shows still another way of running that same web. This time, because one 16-page web requires only black, a unit of the press is not being used. True, one unit is dragging, but this slight underutilization of the press has little overall effect on selecting a printer. In fact, if the press generally meets your needs, you can expect to frequently use less of it than is available—that is, as long as your maximum color needs are in line with the press's maximum delivery capability.

Three reels

Let's add another roll of paper to this same six-unit press. Illustration 88 shows this monster printing three webs of paper, one in full color, and the other two in black only.

The economics of this arrangement should bang you over the head. Now we're delivering a full 48 pages of the magazine, a third of which are in full color. Compare this to Illustration 78. Can you see the difference? Three makereadies versus one? Three press runs versus one? What if the job were running at 30M impressions (signatures) per hour and had a press run of 300M? It would take 10 running hours with the press in Illustration 88, and 30 with that in Illustration 78. That's quite a difference.

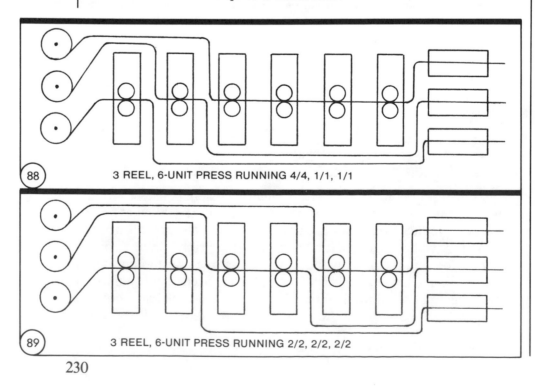

88 3 REEL, 6-UNIT PRESS RUNNING 4/4, 1/1, 1/1

89 3 REEL, 6-UNIT PRESS RUNNING 2/2, 2/2, 2/2

Illustration 89 shows the same press printing 2/2, 2/2, 2/2. For a magazine that prints in two color throughout, we have another winner here. This six-unit, three-roll press will be virtually impossible to beat by any of the other presses described so far.

And, to keep you thinking, Illustration 90 shows the same press running 2/1, 1/2, 2/1.

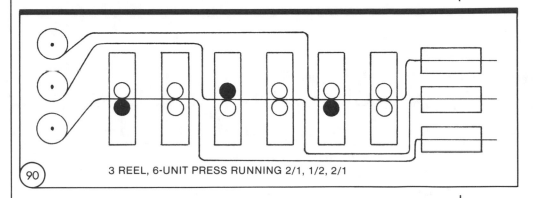

90 3 REEL, 6-UNIT PRESS RUNNING 2/1, 1/2, 2/1

Eight units, two reels

Now let's back off a bit. Three webs of paper are pretty hard for some printers to handle. Illustration 91 shows a rather novel approach to web presses, based in part on the reaction to the ever-increasing use of four-color printing in magazines.

We have two rolls of paper and eight printing units. This allows full color to be printed on an entire 32 pages at one time. But is it economical?

Assuming that you need full color throughout the magazine, it is certainly a good option. Consider any other of the example installations: Not one single press discussed could print 32 pages in full color in one press pass. Since four color makereadies are the most expensive, this press can do something that the others can't. It can deliver the 300M, 32 pages in full color in about 10 hours. The other presses would require twice that time, plus another makeready.

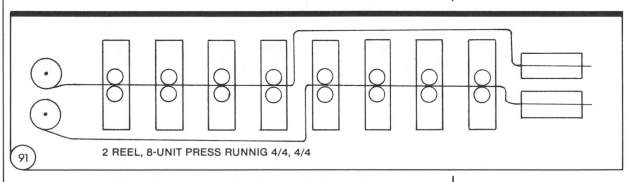

91 2 REEL, 8-UNIT PRESS RUNNIG 4/4, 4/4

But what if a printer had *only* this press? Illustration 92 shows the uneconomical results. While the machinery was obviously installed for jobs requiring full color, this publisher is running only two units: 32 pages, all black. This would be highly uneconomical and brings up a larger point: A good mix of presses at the printer could be economical to the publisher with a variety of printing needs. Dragging 75 percent of a press will be more expensive than using, say, a two-reel, two-unit press for the black-and-white work. And many printers have small presses around for just that reason. Why run the new, powerful monster just to print a simple easy signature?

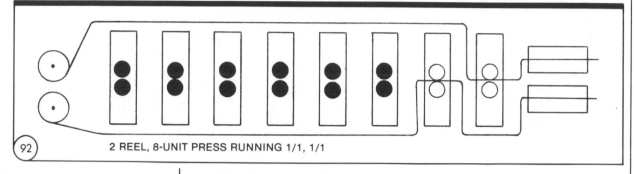

92 2 REEL, 8-UNIT PRESS RUNNING 1/1, 1/1

Four-reel possibilities

Illustration 93 takes this press to a further extreme. What about running four reels, giving you 64 total pages, 2/2, 2/2, 2/2, 2/2? Or run four reels, 4/4, 2/2, 1/1, 1/1.

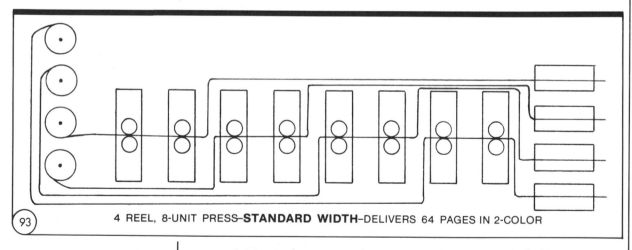

93 4 REEL, 8-UNIT PRESS—**STANDARD WIDTH**—DELIVERS 64 PAGES IN 2-COLOR

Apparently, most printers recognize that at this point the conventional web loses ground to the wide-web press shown in Illustration 94. Running four rolls of paper requires a very expensive press, long makeready, and constant attention to the tensions of each roll of paper as it is printing. The press in Illustration 93 will most likely be plagued by web breaks and folder problems.

The press in Illustration 94 is a better approach. If, in fact, the job's economics require delivering 64 pages at a time in two-color, it might best be run on a wide web. Now only two rolls are running through four printing units, so all controls and problems have virtually been halved.

And note this: Previously I described the wide web as having more registration problems than the narrow web. But in this comparison, we are talking about two-color work, which is much easier to register. Only two plates must be registered to the blacks, so we can forget about most of the registration worries.

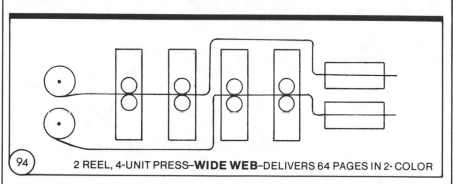

94   2 REEL, 4-UNIT PRESS–**WIDE WEB**–DELIVERS 64 PAGES IN 2-COLOR

Summary

This discussion should raise more questions for you than it answers. Presses come in any number of sizes, with any number of printing units, and with from one to four roll stands. And this discussion was limited, for the most part, to conventionally sized webs. These same variations occur in the arena of half-webs, mini-webs, and wide webs. The number of units, rolls of paper, and the customer's needs must all be considered when you look for the "right" press for your magazine.

And since your magazine is certainly unique in many ways, only you can conduct the appropriate investigation to find the right printer and the right press.◻

GHOSTING

If you haven't yet run into ghosting problems in offset printing, you're either lucky or you're not paying attention. Ghosting effects can be seen in several variations, and can be avoided in some situations. All offset-press users, and consequently most magazines, run into these problems.

Press ghosts

The term "ghost" is not a universally accepted description of a press problem. But to keep things straight, we will use it to describe the problem that results from taking too much ink from the inking rollers. The ghost occurs when you can see a visible difference in ink coverage. Let's look at the two basic types of ghosts.

Single-page ghosts

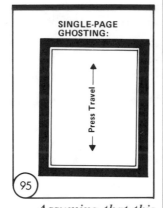

SINGLE-PAGE GHOSTING:

◀— Press Travel —▶

95

Assuming that this page will travel through the press as indicated, the color stripes on the side will remove much more ink than the stripes at the top and bottom.

Illustration 95 shows a solid-color border, the kind that might print around a photograph or an article. This use of color should already warn the art director (or production person) that a ghost will occur—and in this particular situation, there is no way to prevent it on an offset press.

Look at Illustration 97, and you will see why. The two "border stripes" around the photo will, for practical purposes, constantly pull ink fron the inking rollers during the press run. But since the rollers won't constantly be using ink when printing the horizontal stripes, the result will be two areas on the roller that won't keep up with the rest of the press.

How will it affect the printed piece? If the ghost is pronounced, you will notice that the color of the vertical rules will be weaker than the color of the horizontal rules, and that a visible "break" (or shift from weak ink to strong ink) will be apparent in all four corners of the page.

This might not seem to make sense when you assume that a 100 percent blue will print at a full 100 percent strength, no matter what. But the fact is that a press can lay down either a little or a lot of ink. And the thinner the film of ink, the paler the final color. Thus—even with the same ink—one press can be running a brilliant solid, while another will print the same solid in a weaker tone.

This first ghost in Illustration 95 shows that you needn't print more than one page to have trouble printing a border with even consistency.

In-line ghosts

This second ghost is the bane of magazine production directors. If you've ever wondered why pressmen will "favor" one page while making another suffer, this is one of the reasons. As shown in Illustration 96, we have one page running above another, with both using a good deal of a particular color (blue, for example). Because

234

so much ink is being pulled off one side of the page (Illustration 97, again), the ghosting will be apparent on the bottom of the page —which will show a stronger amount of ink on the left side, then a visible shift half-way across the page, and finally a lighter coverage on the right side.

This effect can be minimized to an extent by the pressman, who can open up the "keys" to allow more ink on the right half of the page. But this will not solve the problem of the "break" because the point at which more ink is required will still show in the form of a vertical, washed-out line.

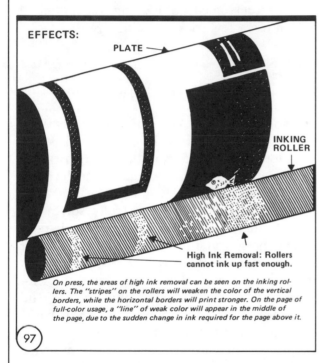

EFFECTS:

PLATE

INKING ROLLER

High Ink Removal: Rollers cannot ink up fast enough.

On press, the areas of high ink removal can be seen on the inking rollers. The "stripes" on the rollers will weaken the color of the vertical borders, while the horizontal borders will print stronger. On the page of full-color usage, a "line" of weak color will appear in the middle of the page, due to the sudden change in ink required for the page above it.

97

Identifying ghosts before presstime

Now, into the problem. The question is: Before running the job, how can you tell if and when ink will create severe ghosting problems on the press?

Oddly enough, most of us don't have the luxury of seeing first hand just what will happen. The reason is that most buyers get either Cromalin proofs, Transfer Keys, brownprints, or Color Keys—and not a single one of these proofing systems will demonstrate ghosting. Press proofs would show the effects, but almost nobody buys them for magazine or catalog printing, at least not in full-press layouts.

The reason none of these proofing methods shows the ghosts is simple: All of them are based on laying an unlimited amount of pigment (color) on any size area and, because the job is not being printed, there are no inking rollers to cope with. As an example, an original color photograph will show you as much red, yellow, or blue as your heart desires. No pigment is being "pulled away" from any

IN-LINE GHOSTING:

96

In this case, the material on the "top" page will remove ink on half the page's width . . . while the bottom page needs a great deal of ink across the entire page.

235

GHOSTING

In illustration 98 "color bars" are used to remove ink beneath the center rules. This is usually not practical unless you happen to be printing with a lot of "waste" paper. At the far right, the ghosting problem is minimized by simply changing the layout, which evens up the amount of ink required across the two pages. No hard ghosting line will show. Better yet would be to move the top page to another location entirely.

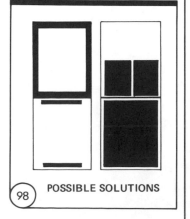

POSSIBLE SOLUTIONS

(98)

part of the proof. In short, these pre-press proofing methods don't show you a thing about what will happen on the press. They simply show you what was on the original film, not what might happen later.

But that doesn't mean these proofs are useless. They will show you where ghosting might occur if you know what to look for.

In Illustration 96, even if you're a novice, you should be able to predict a real problem on press. And in Illustration 95, you should be able to use the basic rules of ghosting to determine that any border printing in a solid will not reproduce without a ghosting problem.

And, once you get accustomed to looking for potential ghosting problems, you can use a few tricks to minimize them.

Some ghost busters

Let's start with Illustration 95. If, as we just said, the problem should be obvious, what are the options?

Well, you should avoid using these kinds of layouts. By eliminating either both horizontal or both vertical borders, you would eliminate a ghosting situation. Or, by reducing the strength of the rules from 100 percent to 50 percent, the ghost would at least be minimized.

Unfortunately, neither of these solutions really solves the problem: Offset presses are limited creatures, and the single-page ghost is a problem that no press can fully correct. So, whenever possible, try not to print a layout like this.

In Illustration 96, you have several choices. This type of in-line curse haunts advertisers and often results in makeovers for paid ads. Let's say that the top page and the bottom page use a blue background and that both are important (paid ads).

If you did a press proof, you'd first notice the ghosting stripe in the middle of the bottom. The pressman might ask which ad is more critical and then attempt to favor it, but the problem would not be solved—only minimized.

It could, though, be almost totally avoided with a layout change. The first, and best, option would be to move one of the ads to another page position. It's as simple as that.

Second, if there happened to be any leeway, which you would have if one of the pages were "house" or editorial, you could stack the photos differently (Illustration 98). By evening up the total usage of ink across the page, you could have more control over both pages, and if the two smaller photos were to butt, you could certainly eliminate the pronounced "break" of color usage in the center of the bottom ad.

Gravure presses and ghosts

The one cure-all for ghosting is to switch to gravure printing. Gravure presses don't use a roller-applied ink, but rather ink is applied from the fountain directly into the printing "cells."

But, unless you're running a million or more impressions, you will still do better to cope with ghosting and minimize it whenever you can.□

SPLITTING THE FOUNTAIN

Said my printing associate: "Customers who don't split fountains are foolish." "I resent that," was my reply—and the beginning of a discussion on the economies of splitting fountains. In case the meaning of the word "fountain" temporarily escapes you, here's a quick refresher. With any offset press, the ink (whatever color it may be) is held in and applied from a trough (fountain). Directly beneath the fountain are adjustable "keys" that selectively control the amount of ink being released and applied to the inking rollers.

And "splitting" a fountain simply means that a mechanical device, a splitter, is placed in the fountain, and different inks are poured into either side of it. In certain cases, this simple press operation can save hundreds, or even thousands, of dollars for the buyer. The reason is that a split fountain can save the cost of using an entire additional press "unit" (to apply a special color ink), or even save the cost of a complete additional pass through the press.

We'll discuss some of the common situations in which the "split" is a good bet, and then describe the process itself.

PMS ink matches

If you are involved in any type of publishing that accepts advertising, you'll often be requested to run a special matched ink. PMS colors are the normal reference, and stand for the Pantone Matching System. In the case of two-color web printing, you might not have a problem because you can use your flexibility to change one of the colors on one side of the web. But what if you're doing two-color work and you get one more request than you can handle for a special ink? All units of the sheet have been taken, and there's no room for the final matched color. Your options are 1) to use another unit on the press (and pay a substantial cost) or 2) to split one of the fountains, run two inks in it, and save one large chunk of money.

The PMS match problem occurs for four-color web users, too. Let's suppose you are printing a 16-page, four-color project and, for some reason, one little section needs a matched green ink. As in the case above, you could use one more press unit, if it's available. But you might be on a press that is running at capacity when printing 16 pages in four color—and, if so, you wouldn't have this option. Instead, you'd have to switch to a different press or printer. Or you could split one of the fountains. The compromise here would be that the split would affect at least one other page of your product, which is something that you'll quickly learn to work with.

Sheetfed splits

Fountain splits are not limited to web presses. In fact, they can save even more relative costs when used in sheetfed situations.

238

Another example: Your short-run, sheetfed brochure runs eight pages, and four-color is used on both sides. Your best price was supplied by a printer with a two-unit press (meaning that he prints only two colors at a time and then runs the paper through the press again). At the last minute, you need a special color ink for a logotype. What happens to the price?

Press costs could go up a fat 25 percent if the ink required an additional "pass" through the machine; or you could get another printer to do the job on larger (and more expensive) equipment; or prices could remain approximately the same with your current printer if you split a fountain and worked with the subsequent minor limitations. The actual cost of the split varies. On a web, you might pay as little as $100 (1984 dollars) plus the cost of the colored ink, while at a small sheetfed operation, it could be half of that. You'll have to check.

How splits work

There's nothing terribly complicated about splitting a fountain, but there are a few limitations to be aware of. Violate these simple rules, and you'll get into deep trouble.

We'll describe fountain splits by following a typical situation step by step through production. It doesn't matter whether the job is being printed web or sheetfed—the basic rules don't change.

First, the problem. The job depicted in Illustration 99 (next page) is a 16-pager, four color on both sides of the sheet. Four color material is being used on one side of the sheet, as indicated in the illustration, but one piece of material happens to be a black-and-brown duotone (two-color halftone photo) that simply must have a specially matched ink. This problem piece appears in the lower right corner of the illustration.

The goal is to get the color on the page at the lowest possible cost. So, if an additional printing unit or an additional pass through the press can be avoided, that's the route we'll take.

First, an editorial decision must be made: If we split a fountain on page five, can we live without process color on the page above it (four)? If not, are there another two pages of in-line material that would allow the split? (And, if not, forget about saving money.)

Next, the printer must be contacted. The first question is, how much of a "clear area" is required between two inks in a split situation? This clear area is required for an obvious reason. If the same inking roller is applying two different colors, then at some point on the roller those colors will tend to mix a bit. Mixing can be reduced somewhat by closing the keys, but it cannot be eliminated. In our example, let's assume that the printer requires a five-inch clear zone, but keep in mind that some printers will go down to three inches, while still others will demand full-page separation between ink changes.

Now, back to the editorial question: In our drawing, the photo on page 12 is on the left side of the page. What if the art director wants to put it on the right side? There goes the clear zone, which requires five inches, and there goes the money-saving fountain split. So, we'll override the art director and tell him or her just where that photo is going to go. (Good luck on this, by the way.)

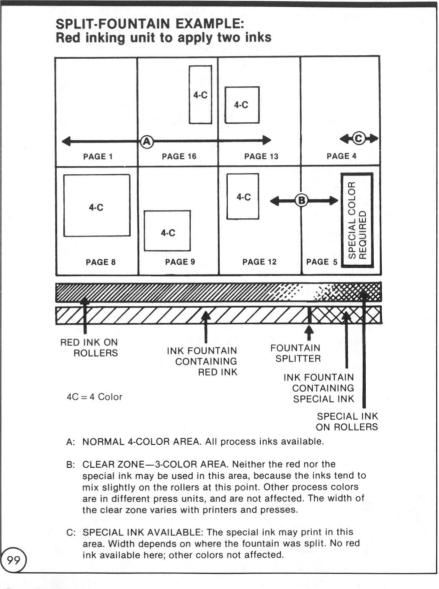

SPLIT-FOUNTAIN EXAMPLE:
Red inking unit to apply two inks

A: NORMAL 4-COLOR AREA. All process inks available.

B: CLEAR ZONE—3-COLOR AREA. Neither the red nor the special ink may be used in this area, because the inks tend to mix slightly on the rollers at this point. Other process colors are in different press units, and are not affected. The width of the clear zone varies with printers and presses.

C: SPECIAL INK AVAILABLE: The special ink may print in this area. Width depends on where the fountain was split. No red ink available here; other colors not affected.

Savings

Basically, that's about it. The job, if it meets these requirements, can be printed much more economically than by any other means. Just how economically varies from printer to printer, but can range up to thousands when the split can save a complex web makeready.

The only "loose end" is which color is best for the fountain split? Should you split red, black or yellow? The only general rule is, don't run any other color in the yellow fountain. The slight "mixing" of inks will possibly show up and contaminate the light colors (yellow being one). Black splits are usually out of the question because the ink is needed for test material. That leaves red and blue, and we suggest splitting red because it is a fairly dense color and so won't suffer too much from a little contamination.

Now that you've got the basics of fountain splitting, answer the question yourself: Is the customer who doesn't use fountain splitting foolish, misinformed, or merely uninformed?□

IN-LINE PROBLEMS: WHAT TO DO

Printing full color on each available page can lead to color compromises (lower quality). Each two pages "in line" above (for example, pages 12 and 13) will interact somewhat with each other, possibly necessitating compromise in the amount of ink applied in the "alley."

An in-line problem can occur any time one page prints from the same printing plate above or below another. Ghosting, which we have already discussed, is one form of an in-line problem, even though it can occur internally on a page. But just as troublesome is this routine situation: A page running above another needs a different setting of the ink fountain. Or when one page is in color balance, the other is not.

To put it bluntly, an in-line problem simply cannot be totally solved on the press. That's one of the basic limitations of the modern web. In trying to come up with some sort of on-press compromise, the pressman must decide whether to "favor" one of the pages to get the best color or to compromise both pages. Obviously, either decision can cause a problem with an ad and, therefore, a problem with a paying customer, such as an advertiser.

When an in-line problem originates in the production department, it doesn't go away. The conventional web press simply cannot accommodate two critical-color pages, one above the other, without sacrificing something. The only solution, then, is to avoid creating the problem in the first place.

The press imposition

Let's look at a typical eight-page press form, as the press sees it. Illustration 100 shows a side of a 16-page signature. To create the worst of all possible in-line problems on press, all one has to do is put a four-color ad on every page of this press pass. Would anyone do such a crazy thing?

Yes, actually a lot of publishers do. Unaware of the limitations of printing fully saturated signatures, these publishers assume that all eight of the color ads might as well be printed with the greatest possible economy. That "economy" can be deceptive because if a single advertiser gives you heat about poor reproduction quality, you could well lose any or all possible savings.

Possible solutions

Because avoidance is the only answer, your production department needs to be equipped to properly plan for good reproduction. It's not enough simply to know which pages have available color and which ones don't. The imposition itself must be viewed in its printing format.

All web printers have imposition layout sheets available for customer use. So it's merely a matter of planning the book out, dropping the pages into their respective positions, and then redoing the entire procedure until you get something that will print, with little or no in-line color conflicts.

Illustration 101 shows one solution—the "checkerboard" method of laying out a form. With this solution, no advertisement will run in-line with another. But to make use of the color available, you might choose to print editorial color above or below the ads.

There are two points to consider if you use this approach: First, you must put it in writing to your printer that all advertisements take priority over all editorial pages.

Second, be prepared for some terrible printing on your editorial pages. True, many times you will luck out. But occasionally, when the printer favors a given ad, the editorial will look as bad as an early makeready throughout the run.

There is an even better solution to in-line conflicts, however. Illustration 102 shows that instead of checkerboarding color ad and editorial, you could just checkerboard color itself. In this example, the publisher has decided to use only four pages of process color per eight-page side.

Is such a solution practical? This would depend on just how critical you arc about your color and what you want to spend. Taken to the extreme, this solution could double your four-color makeready costs.

All of these examples use an eight-page side, which makes sense because most magazines are printed on standard-width webs. But if you think these in-line problems are troublesome, consider the poor production managers who use wide-webs. They have 16 pages to work with on any process-color side. The possibility of having to compromise on four ads running in-line can drive a veteran production manager to polish his or her resume and send it out.

On the other hand, you might envy the person who plans forms for a mini-web with only four pages to worry about at a time. This means that even if that person checkerboards to accommodate two ads, only two pages of the form will be lost.

The more effort you put into avoiding in-line problems, the less often you'll have to resort to some of the standard explanations: "Gee, none of our copies were like that. You must have been accidentally shipped a makeready copy."

"Your film was _____. (Choose one: full, weak, or out of register). We did the best we could."

"Bear with us. We're switching printers as soon as we can."

"We fired that production director. It will never happen again."

"What color problem?" □

CHAPTER 43

One solution to color compromise is to plan the book so that critical pages—often advertisements—run in line with non-critical pages, such as editorial. Ink is adjusted for best appearance of the ad, and the editorial may be allowed to print with less than ideal color control.

Another solution is to checkerboard the imposition, so that no color page has another running in line with it. This is often expensive, necessitating more color printing, but very effective.

PRINTING PRIORITIES, OR QUALITY WHERE YOU WANT IT

Does this sound like you? "I like to run my process color on the heavy side—and I mean heavy! When I order something from my printer, I want to see that ink layer upon layer, pigment upon pigment, until the pressman screams, 'No more!'"

On the other hand, some publishers like to run their color on the lighter side, achieving pleasant—even somewhat pale—reproduction.

Printers, of course, have absolutely no way of knowing what kind of reproduction you are most pleased with. And presses, for good or bad, are just as adept at printing too heavy as they are capable of printing too light.

The situation becomes even more complicated when you add the variables of advertising, editorial photos, and preference (*e.g.*, giving more attention to a photo of a model than to one photo of your local tax assessor). Because so many variables are involved, many purchasers choose to perform the traditional press check.

Press checks aren't enough

Many buyers like press checks. They feel that printing is, for good or bad, a publisher's lifeblood. If you publish a magazine today, you are involved with printing. Assemble the words in any sequence that you like, but they must still roll off the press. However, a representative at press-side can do no more than tell the printer whether the product meets the publisher's expectations.

Let me offer an example. Years ago, I began making a regular trip to a particular printing plant for a specific customer. With each visit, the printer and buyer were a little more in sync. On visit number three, they had a better feel for my whims because they had remembered the decisions that we made during the first two visits. After a half dozen press okays (over a six-issue span), things became much easier for everybody. Whereas on day one my penchant for heavy process color was looked at with a bit of apprehension, six months later the pressmen would be piling the ink on thick long before my phone rang.

In addition, it took some time before certain publisher-optional preferences became clear to the operators. For this magazine, the publisher chose to let the editorial material suffer whenever a conflict arose between house material and paid advertising. That seemed like an obvious decision to me, but little did I know that some of this printer's clients actually favored their editorial and let the advertising suffer. How were the pressmen to know which was more important?

We finally got the priorities straight. But what if I had written my expectations down at the outset and presented my idiosyncrasies in memorandum form? Wouldn't that have given the press personnel some direction and saved a lot of aggravation?

244

Put your instructions in writing

CHAPTER 44

Memo writing can be one of the most productive steps that you can take to obtain uniform, customer-pleasing printing. It can either complement or replace the chore of standing next to those noisy, overgrown duplicators.

Suppose the printer had the following memo sent to him before I had ever stepped through his door:

> *"We tend to run our process color on the heavy side. We prefer glossy color over perfect matches to the proof. Advertising always takes priority over editorial. Advertiser-supplied proofs take priority over subsequent proofs. Full-color advertisements take priority over partial-color advertisements. Double-truck (two page spread) advertisers have absolute priority."*

Although the instructions are quite simple, keep in mind that the printer may have a hundred customers to deal with, each of whom has a slightly different set of rules.

Let's review each simple sentence from that memo and point out the possibilities.

• *We tend to run our process color on the heavy side:* The fact is, some buyers run their color on the light side. They prefer a clean, crisp dot to dense, shiny color. Others crave lots of ink. The printer should know what you want.

You can test this out by doing a single press check, asking the printer to demonstrate the difference between a light application of ink and an extremely dense one. If you've never done this test, you will be surprised at the versatility of a press in producing a wide variety of results from the same printing plate.

• *We prefer glossy color over perfect matches to proof:* This clarification can be extremely important to the press operators. Some customers are absolutely fanatical about coming as close to the proof as possible. Others show up at press side only to say, "Hey, that looks better than what we gave you. Run it."

Of course, if the customer states that glossy color is preferred over perfect matches, that preference should not be interpreted to mean that glossy color cannot be achieved along with a perfect or close-to-perfect match. If both a good glossy and a good match are possible, both should be achieved.

• *Advertising always takes priority over editorial:* You might think that everybody in the business knows this. Well, it isn't true. There are many publishers who prefer to concentrate on their editorial photos—even at the expense of paid advertising. Printers must cope with these widely different methods of producing a pleasing

PRINTING PRIORITIES, OR QUALITY WHERE YOU WANT IT

product, and you simply cannot expect a printer to read your mind.

Worse yet, you could be one of the publishers with a hybrid preference. Consider the following: ''Advertising always takes preference over editorial unless the conflicting editorial is a full-page photo of a human face.'' Don't laugh; that's a direct quote from one publisher's preference memo.

• *Advertiser-supplied proofs take priority over subsequent proofs:* This statement implies that there may be a difference between what the advertiser gave you and what you are getting from your film. Again, it is entirely logical for the printer to assume that you wish to print what was on your film. It is no secret that the difference between a supplied press proof and a subsequent Cromalin (or Color Key or Transfer Key) can be extreme. It is also just as logical for the printer to assume that you want to match the supplied proof. With both solutions falling nicely within the sphere of printers' logic, you would be doing everyone a favor by putting your directions in writing.

• *Full-color advertisements take priority over partial-color advertisements:* This statement covers those situations where the printer has no way of knowing which advertiser to favor when you run into a compromise problem.

However, what if you had been working for years to land a national advertiser—who just happens to run two-color ads—and that ad happened to conflict (on press) with a full-bleed, old-faithful, full-colored account? In this instance, since you would be more concerned with the two-color printing, you'd have to alter your own instructions.

• *Double-truck (two-page spread) advertisers have absolute priority:* This request says that no matter what happens on press, the printer is to favor the advertiser occupying the most space.

Consider the following: A two-page ad is run on two different signatures (sometimes because of a need for a stitched-in insert between two pages). On the printing of the second signature, in-line problems suggest to the printer that a compromise is necessary (to save some of the quality of the competing ad.

In this situation, the publisher's memo would clearly tell the printer to let the one-page ad go down the drain, if necessary, to save the color balance of the two-pager.

If this all sounds complicated, just remember: As a production person, a publisher, or an observer, you have preferences that are not always the same preferences as your printer's other customers. By putting those preferences in writing, your printer will be able to give you exactly what you want, and with a minimum amount of fuss.□

CUSTOMER PRESS CHECKS AND "GOOD" COLOR

t's no secret that some magazines look better than others. Sometimes it is the press itself that can affect appearance; other times paper or color-separation quality is the culprit. Worse yet, sometimes all three combine unfavorably to produce an inferior job. So let's address some of the many variables that can affect the appearance of the finished piece.

Quality of originals

Process-color quality will directly relate to the quality of the original material you have chosen to print. It isn't uncommon for a customer to be completely dissatisfied with the press output because the photos are printing in a washed-out manner. The theory of "garbage in, garbage out" holds true here: For practical purposes, the press cannot deliver better quality than you have supplied to the separation house. If the press sample matches the supplied proofs, your job is running well—even if it looks terrible.

Method and cost of separations

In addition to the quality of the original subjects, keep in mind the system used in getting them separated for press. Did you buy "pleasing" or inexpensive color, or did you drop an arm and a leg to get a critical match? As an example, I have seen customers spend $10,000 for color work that could easily have been purchased for $3,000. The more expensive route provided many quality control options, but the cheaper separations would have been adequate for most publications or commercial work.

Also, the amount of detail on press will relate to the type of separation. Scanners, for example, will generally pull much more fine detail from a photo than will conventional camera separations.

Paper

After the above questions are settled, you can get into the really critical area of producing decent color: getting the ink onto the paper.

The paper itself has a lot more to do with the final quality than many buyers suspect. For example, some assume they will get faithful reproduction merely because they run their four-color work on coated stock. That can be a far cry from the truth.

First, the opacity of paper depends on both the thickness of the sheet and the surface coating on it. Opacity affects the amount of "show through" that you can expect. When running a job on a sheet of less than 40-lb. basis weight, opacity (show-through) can alter the page's color balance. That usually occurs when a good deal of ink is applied to both sides of the sheet. A bright red panel on a page that is backed up by a solid yellow panel will cause obvious problems because the red will "show through" and change the hues of the yellow.

This gets even more critical when you need a light tint to appear on a two-page spread. If there is no color backing up one page, while the other is backed up by a large, dense halftone, the tints cannot be faithfully cross-matched on very light stock.

What can you do about it? You can either 1) consider a heavier stock (which most of us won't do), 2) plan the product carefully so that the show through is either anticipated or designed out, or 3) decide to live with it. One thing's certain: You can't expect the pressmen to help you solve show-through problems. By the time it reaches them, it's already out of their hands.

Whiteness and amount of coating

Also, the whiteness of the sheet will either enhance or alter the color reproduction. Again, it's not enough to sit back and think, "Well, we have coated stock. so the job should run okay." One sheet might be a dirty, dull blue while another is the result of heavy bleaching and thick surface coating.

What it boils down to is this: Some papers accept ink better than others, and some papers are whiter than others. You can't expect to get more quality than the sheet was designed to produce.

This brings up the question of just how closely the press can match a proof. Example: Two jobs are ready for press and both were prepared and proofed the same way (Cromalins are used for the press okays). Now, although the printer might generally say that he can almost perfectly match a properly prepared Cromalin, what happens when the first job runs on a cheap 40-lb. stock and the second on an expensive 70-lb. sheet? The second job will more faithfully match the original, that's what.

The press itself

All the variables so far discussed are pretty much under the direct control of the buyer. But there are also problems that are only indirectly controlled by the buyer. To be blunt, there are good presses and bad presses. One printer's ATF will not print quite the same as the next, even though the units are theoretically identical.

The reasons are many. Presses are very complicated creatures —and they age. It is easy for the press-erecting firm to get lax in installing a unit or to overlook a small adjustment problem. Several of the adjustments on presses cannot be performed by the printer. Some adjustments are so esoteric that he may not even suspect where tiny quality problems come from.

And, you should also be aware that there are different *types* of printing presses. Do you know which type of dampening system is used on your "favorite" press? Are you aware that the system in use cannot be altered, but that it affects the machine's printing quality?

Or, to take it to an extreme, one customer might get his work printed on a "CIC" (common impression cylinder) press and another on a conventional litho unit. Each press has an entirely different ability to register the job.

The pressman

The scene continues to get more complex when you combine all the variables of lithographic printing and put them under the control of one man: the press operator. Experience will show you that some pressmen are hard workers who know and enjoy their business and who want to please the customer. But the next time you walk into a shop, you just might run smack into a pressman who couldn't care less about the job, who isn't ambitious enough to help you get what you need, and who doesn't care to troubleshoot any old or new problem.

In other words, there's no way to tell what kind of person you're dealing with until you've worked with several. And once you find that shining star who truly cares about your product, it's almost impossible to ask the company for this person to run your job at all times. But you could give it a try.

If you keep in mind that some pressmen can make the same machine work better than others, which ultimately affects your work's quality, you'll begin to understand why the job can look crisp one hour and flat the next.

The color okay

Let's suppose that all these variables are now under control. You may choose to do a simple color okay, which amounts to asking for either more or less of a given ink, right? Basically, that's right, but I've seen customers get so far over their head that keeping a straight face was all the pressman could do.

Let's re-create this classic bungle: The buyer, new to okays, walks into the pressroom with a "snappy color" in mind. He realizes that "snap" is primarily the result of light bouncing off the ink, and thus, the more ink, the more snap.

The first corrections are made to bring the match close to the original. A little red is added for fleshtones, a little blue for the field of grass. Now the color is basically good, but it still lacks the "snap." So the customer says, "Bring up some black to give it a punch, and a little blue for some more gloss."

The pressman smiles, shakes his head, and adds the ink. And now the customer says, "Hey, now you made the fleshtones too muddy." So the customer asks for less blue, and the glossy look again subsides. "How about some yellow, or some more red again?" The scene becomes embarrassing for the buyer, who truly knows what he wants but doesn't truly know how the press works.

There's no need to get yourself into this kind of trap. It's a simple matter to walk into the pressroom with a stated objective:

250

Either you want a healthy, snappy, glossy print, or you want a precision match to the originals—and if you're lucky, you'll get both. But do let the pressman or supervisor know exactly what your priorities are. Without experience in press okays, it is totally unnecessary for you to ask for a specific color to be brought up or down. When you ask for a touch of blue, remember that the person to whom you are talking may have 20 years' experience in adding that color, and he may well know that the photo's color balance will be destroyed with a bit more ink.

It's much safer to ask, "Can you get that fleshtone closer?" And if the pressman says, "Yes, but it will change the balance on the automobile," then you make the decisions that only the customer can make: Is the face more important than the car?

That is one of the strongest arguments for customer okays: When a compromise must be reached, you cannot expect the printer to "know" what your priorities are—that is, until you tell him.

The big picture

If you do press okays, you'll learn something every time you go to the plant. That means that, based on experience, one customer will do better okays than the next. For newcomers, I suggest the "help me out" approach, rather than specific requests for color changes. Old hands may be seasoned to the point that they can ask for exactly the right increase or decrease, which is also fine—if you're an old hand. But in any case, the press okay has a lot more variables to it than simply adding or subtracting ink. If you keep those variables in mind, you'll have a better chance of understanding exactly why your color either meets or falls short of your expectations. □

SECTION VII: IMPOSITIONS AND FOLDERS

UNDERSTANDING IMPOSITIONS AND FOLDERS

You may find it odd that impositions and folders are discussed as a single topic. There is a reason for that. But first, a few explanations. What is imposition? It is the answer to these questions: On which printing plate does each page go? In what position on the plate? And what color (process, B/W) will be available for that page? An eight-page printing plate is the result of selecting the imposition that dictates which page goes where.

Neither the buyer nor the printer ever "invents" impositions. A web press is delivered in a specific configuration, with one or more folders, and is capable of a predetermined number of impositions. That number may be large, but it is not flexible. A number of variables will affect the total number of impositions. These include the following:

- The number of reels on the press (see press section).
- The number of folders on the press. (A press may have one, or more different folders, one of which is used during a given job.)
- The number of internal modifications to the folders. Normally, this means the number of extra "turning rollers" a printer installs when the folder is built. A turning bar, for your purposes, is a roller that creates more imposition variations.
- The number of printing units. As more printing units are available, variety increases. That will become more apparent as we get deeper into this discussion.

The folder on a web press is the device that mechanically organizes a signature into its proper order. On some folders, there are only a few ways to organize the paper during the folding operation. On others, there are almost an unlimited number of ways to organize multiple webs during folding. That, of course, is what we're going to discuss: both the types of folders available to the average magazine and what each folder is capable of doing.

Variety of presses and impositions

Unfortunately, there is no standard for impositions from one printer to the next. For that matter, it isn't uncommon to see the same press in two different plants running impositions that the other can't duplicate. This is because a press is ordered by the printer to deliver a certain variety of folds, which affects imposition.

We will cover the fundamentals of sheetfed imposition (a good introduction to web imposition) and then two common folders —the combination and the double-former—and their relative imposition effects. And in order to keep this book less than a few thousand pages, we will limit our review to a standard-web press (38 inch maximum roll width, 22-3/4 inch cutoff—see press section).

But the good news is this: This entire section on impositions is meant to help you learn to learn. In other words, if you can follow our discussion here, limited to two types of folders on one type of press, you will soon be able to understand any imposition that a

CHAPTER 46

printer gives you. Your printer knows the impositions that are available to him and should have a stock booklet of the impositions available on his presses.

Don't forget: The following information and demonstrations of folds are for a given press with a given set of folders, and even at that, we are only exploring. The object is to be able to understand how folders and impositions work and to be able to dissect the information supplied to you by your printer.

Who does the imposition?

To prepare a magazine, someone normally sits down and determines which folders and impositions will be used. This will ultimately result in 1) a series of drawings that indicate where on each printing plate each page of the magazine falls, and 2) information about which pages have color available and what that color is (process or two-color, and so on).

Whose job is it to determine all this? It is common for the magazine production manager to make these determinations, and for an important reason. The production director generally works with the advertiser to come up with a magazine "plan" that minimizes four-color makereadies while meeting the magazine's needs. For example, you may need to run a good number of color ads up front, but you may want to keep them from facing each other on spreads. Or, you may need several color spreads on one signature (printed section of the magazine), but none on another.

There are two ways to get the versatility necessary to do either. First, you could simply run four-color throughout the magazine and use it as necessary. Although there would be no planning to speak of, there would be a staggering increase in your printing costs.

Second, you could learn as much as possible about your available impositions and then select from them as your advertising and editorial color needs dictate.

The printer's job is to keep his presses rolling and make some money while he's at it. Although many printers are very helpful in teaching you how to keep your costs down, such a task is neither in their realm of responsibility nor in their immediate best interest. Would you teach a printer how to reduce your gross revenue? Should he teach you how to reduce his?

The answer is that a printer is more likely to keep you as a longtime customer if he does, in fact, help you reduce his own gross revenue. But in the short run, you are the person who has to try to save money. That is what imposition is all about. If it were a terribly obvious topic, like shoe-tying, it would need only minor mention here. But it tends to be a complicated, overlooked area that can have significant effects on a magazine's overall costs. So, learn what you can. This will be a good start. By necessity, we will rely heavily on illustrations to demonstrate just what's going on.□

255

SHEETFED IMPOSITION

Let's start with sheetfed press impositions. First, it's a good introduction to just what imposition is and does; second, many magazines have their covers and inserts printed via sheetfed. For the newcomer, a review of some sheetfed economics will be instructive.

An eight-page sheetfed signature

Illustration 103 shows the simplest of impositions: a single sheet of paper that will be folded into an eight-page signature. (Any complete product, such as this eight-page folded press sheet, will be considered a signature that is later assembled with other signatures in the bindery.)

A simple eight-page imposition. The sheet is printed on both sides with pages appearing where shown. When folded, they fall into magazine sequence.

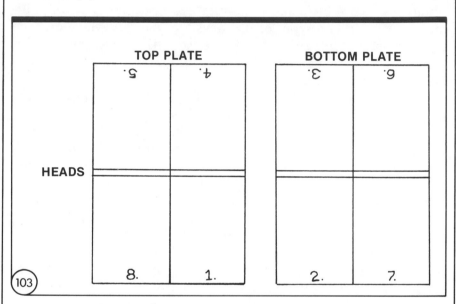

Note that we have a drawing for the top of the sheet and another for the bottom. The pages will appear on the printing plates just as they do on these drawings. (Again, refer to the press section if you haven't already read it.)

Of course, any imposition for a single sheet of paper must reflect what's going on on both sides of the sheet. Page one is never printed on the back of page one—that's where page two would go. So, unless we are talking work-and-turn (the next topic), the top plate (the one that prints on the top of the sheet of paper) will be different from the bottom plate. Therefore, assuming that one of these plates prints on the top of the sheet and the other on the bottom, we will have page two printed on the back of page one, page seven on the back of page eight, and so on.

The term "heads" refers to where the top of each page is. In this case, the signature is printing "head to head," meaning that the tops of the pages are toward the center of the printed sheet.

The left side of Illustration 104 shows the first fold being made. Because this is a sheetfed job, it is made on a folding machine (rather than on the press, which is what the web press does).

The right side of Illustration 104 shows the second and final fold. At this point, you may want to take out a piece of paper, number it as we have done in Illustration 103—being sure to number both sides of one sheet, not two separate sheets as the drawing may suggest—and fold it down as we have done. If you feel confident that you understand it, fine. But later on, as it gets more complicated, do get your paper and Crayolas ready. It is far easier to understand if you watch the folds being made.

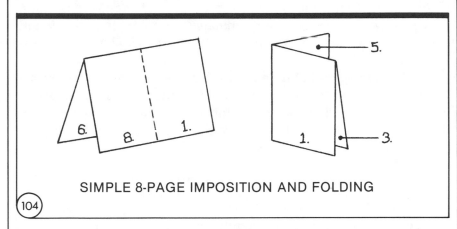

SIMPLE 8-PAGE IMPOSITION AND FOLDING

(104)

There is nothing too dramatic about what we have done so far. The result is an eight-page, closed-head signature. Closed head?

As we said, the imposition was for head-to-head printing. The final product now has the heads of the paper at the top, where they belong. The "head" of the signature itself is a fold—and this fold is called "closed head."

If you want to know the significance of closed-head folding, do this: Stack up eight sheets of paper and fold the entire stack twice, as you have just done with the single sheet. Now unfold only the second fold and look at the creases in the center of the two pages. It is wrinkled and distorted. You and I might call this "sloppy folding." Printers call it "gusseting," which is inherent to any closed-head folds. For practical purposes, though, it is important only when we use either 32-page signatures or very heavy paper stock. (You have been warned!)

Now, before we go further, let's look at the practical result of the eight-page folded press sheet. Can there be any creativity in this simple fold?

Sure. Suppose you needed a full-color spread for an editorial and you happened to print this eight-pager via sheetfed. As you know from the press section, each printing plate costs money. If you wanted to spend only what was necessary and wanted to have a full-color spread on pages four and five, you would run only the top half of the signature in four-color (four printing plates) and the bottom half in single color (one printing plate).

Look at your folded sheet again. By doing the above, you will have a color spread on pages four and five, and color available on

257

pages one and eight. All of the other pages will be black and white. By simply making the *opposite* side four-color instead, all that changes. Now, pages two and three and pages six and seven will have full-color, meaning that there are two color spreads rather than one.

So the result is this: Even on a fold as simple as the one shown here, one might have to consider imposition. Sure, we could just run the entire form in four-color, and sure, the fold is as simple as it can be. But this example was a practical one: The number of printing plates required for a job is a direct result of studying the imposition of that particular job. Once we eliminate four-color on a side (or add it), we want to know how the signature is affected and where the color is going to fall.

Keep in mind that if an imposition as simple as this can be affected so dramatically merely by running one side of the paper in black and white and the other in color, then all the other impositions that we discuss will have dozens of variations, based on the usage of color, or plates.

Sheetfed work-and-turn imposition

Let's look at Illustration 105 and get a bit more complicated. In the preceding example, we didn't actually say it, but the imposition used was designed for a press that could print only four magazine pages per printing plate. Otherwise, why not run a larger sheet of paper?

If a sheetfed press is capable of printing eight pages to a side, then we would be using it to its full ability, even though we were printing only a four-page signature. But eight pages to a side is 16 pages total, which we wouldn't want to fold down into a signature because we'd have too many pages!

The work-and-turn imposition is a good option and has some interesting strengths. Let's suppose this time that the entire eight-page section must be in four-color. That would normally mean four printing plates for the top of the sheet and four for the bottom. Right? Not necessarily. Take a sheet of paper and number it as we have in Illustration 105. Then turn it over laterally (left to right) and number it again. Finally, cut it right down the middle. You will have two signatures to fold, and each will be replicas of what we achieved with the first sample, numbered one through eight.

The benefits of using work-and-turn printing are significant. First, it is a "two-up" printing method. If we needed 20,000 signatures and used the first example (Illustrations 103-104), we would print 20,000 signatures. But this two-up method (two signatures printed on one sheet of paper) means that we print only 10,000 sheets of paper and then cut them apart into 20,000 signatures, which reduces press time by half.

Second, we had a different printing plate for the top and bottom of the sheet in the first example. In this example, we use the same plate—and with one plate for each process color, that means we are now using four plates instead of eight. That, too, is a significant benefit and saves time and money.

Now, let's briefly elaborate on "two-up." This second example shows an eight-page running two-up, or two-out, via work-and-turn. Web presses cannot work-and-turn because the paper can only go through the press once (while sheetfed paper can be turned over and passed through again). And two-up printing is not the limit.

If we were printing magazine covers on this eight-page to a plate press, we might run them four-up. This would be very likely if the outsides of the covers were full color while the insides were black and white. In that case, we'd make the eight-page plates for the top of the sheet (four plates), and one plate for the bottom (black). We'd run four front covers and four back covers on the top; eight inside covers on the bottom. The press run would be 25 percent of the total amount required. And the advantage of this over work-and-turn would be that we wouldn't waste four-color plates on black-and-white pages.

Moving back to the web again: Although the web can't run work-and-turn, it can often be used to run "multiple-out" signatures. To do this on the web, we'd run the same four-out cover configuration just described—with the same advantage as sheetfed printing. But where sheetfed work-and-turn is practical, it is simply not available on the web. Web printing cannot print both sides of a sheet with one plate—and that is that. □

A work-and-turn imposition, whereby the same plate is used to print the top and bottom of the sheet. This is feasible only on a sheetfed press.

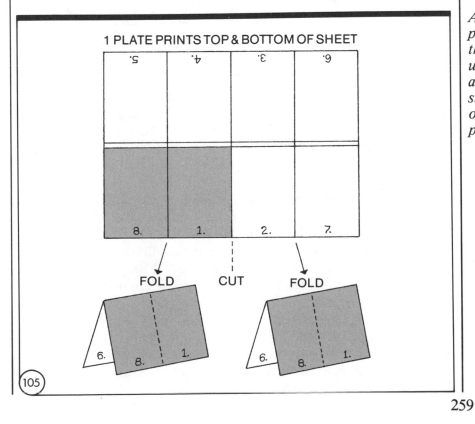

1 PLATE PRINTS TOP & BOTTOM OF SHEET

SHEETWISE PRINTING AND FOLDING

The workhorse of the industry: the combination fold.

Now we get into the transition area of folders. Let's discuss the sheetwise printing and folding performed via the sheetfed method, which relates directly to the 16-page combination (or chop) fold done on a web press.

Illustration 106 shows a sheetwise layout for a sheetfed press. Sheetwise means that the job will need different plates for the top and the bottom of the sheet. In one-color printing, of course, that would be a black plate for the top of the sheet and a black plate for the bottom. In web printing, it would mean at least one printing unit.

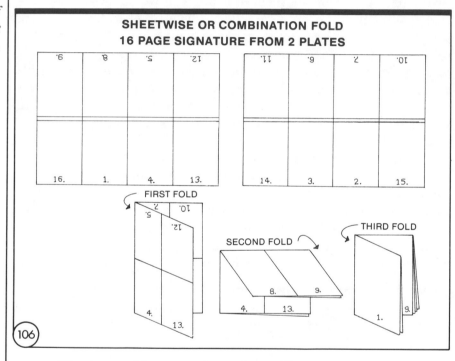

The top and bottom plates shown illustrate where each of 16 pages would fall on this particular signature. I suggest that you take a sheet of paper and number it as shown in the illustration, and make the folds as you read. By following the first and second folds, you should come up with a 16-page signature that is numbered the same as the third fold.

The first eight pages of the signature, along with the entire top of it, are "closed," as described earlier. That brings up "gusseting" again, which again is inherent to this type of fold.

Other than that, the same general possibilities exist. What if we printed the top of the web in four-color? Where, in our printed signature, would the color fall? Similarly, what about printing only the bottom of the web in four-color?

Unfold your signature and, with a marking pen, put a colored "x" on one side of the sheet (one x on each numbered page). Then fold the page and see how that x is distributed. You will be looking at exactly how you can vary the color imposition of this simple sheetwise job by running only half of the signature in full color.

Relating the printer's imposition to your own

Now's the right time for an interruption and an explanation. In the few impositions discussed so far, all the printer's plates (or drawings of his impositions) have been numbered beginning with one and ending with the highest number of pages (eight or 16). Unfortunately, your magazine can't restrict itself to those numbers. You may have 96. How do impositions relate to you numerically?

To illustrate, let's suppose the job at hand is a saddle-stitched product. (Perfect-bound products react differently to imposition and arc described in dctail in thc chapters on bindery. Once you understand both bindery and imposition, you will be able to construct more complicated examples, including perfect-bound examples.)

Illustrations 107 and 108 use the same 16-page numbering system shown in the previous example, but now we'll renumber the plates to fit your magazine. Suppose, for example, that we have a 32-page magazine and are using sheetwise (or combination) folding on two 16-page signatures.

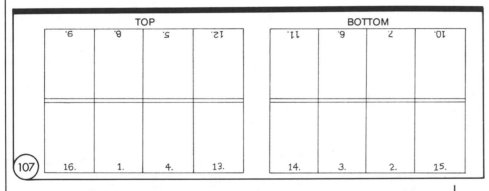

This shows how the combination fold relates to page numbers of the magazine. The printer's imposition doesn't change; only the page numbers do.

Folding down the sample in Illustration 107 will produce a signature numbered similar to the drawing on the left of Illustration 108. But suppose that this particular signature belongs in the center of the magazine. It can't start with page one. Rather, it should start with page nine. And the latter half of this center signature should be page 17. Finally, the latter half of the outer signature should be numbered from pages 25 to 32.

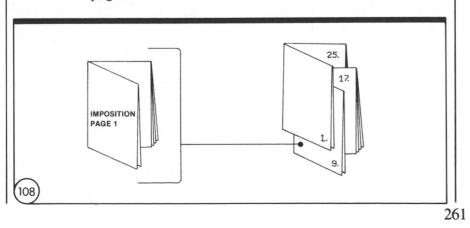

SHEETWISE PRINTING AND FOLDING

Most people solve this renumbering problem mechanically. You will see how if you fold two 16-page signatures the same way as before and then snip off the corners (so you can turn the pages more easily), and number them. Put the two of them together as shown on the right of Illustration 108. Number the pages, one through 32, as they will actually appear in the magazine.

Now, unfold the signatures. Illustration 109 shows how the middle signature relates to the printer's imposition. Where he had page one, our signature has page nine. Therefore, where he had page two, we will have page 10, and so on. In the latter half of the signature, the printer's page nine becomes our page 17, page 10 becomes 18, and so on.

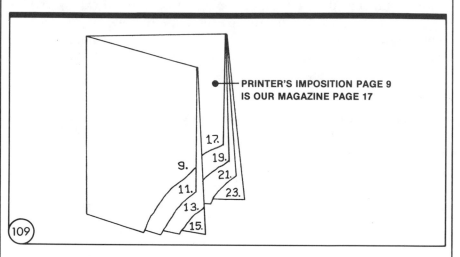

PRINTER'S IMPOSITION PAGE 9
IS OUR MAGAZINE PAGE 17

17.
19.
9.
21.
11.
23.
13.
15.

(109)

By "unfolding" the signature in Illustration 109, we get a view of what appears on the printing plates for the top and bottom of the sheet.

Moving on to Illustration 110, we are now looking at the renumbered imposition. Because we have the magazine's pages in their proper printing positions (derived from the original printer's impositions, starting with page one), we can see what the printing plate will actually look like.

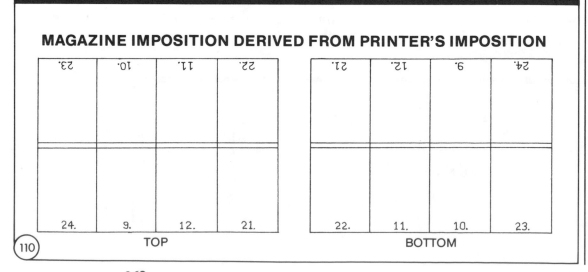

MAGAZINE IMPOSITION DERIVED FROM PRINTER'S IMPOSITION

23.	10.	11.	22.		21.	12.	9.	24.
24.	9.	12.	21.		22.	11.	10.	23.

TOP BOTTOM

(110)

That is important to us for a few reasons. First, we may want to send "completed flats" (eight pages at a time) to the printer, rather than everything all at once. Having the actual magazine imposition is the only way to know what makes a "complete" flat.

Also, if quality is a problem with advertisements, having the true imposition is the only way to know whether there is a likelihood of one ad competing with another for ink (see ghosting section).

And, of course, even if you didn't want to know the true plate imposition, you would accidentally discover it if you were interested in reducing makeready costs. Why use color where it isn't needed?

□

THE COMBINATION FOLD

As mentioned, the sheetfed "sheetwise" fold has a lot in common with the web press "combination" fold. The 16-page signature just illustrated can be produced by either the sheetfed or web press method. What, then, is the difference between the sheetwise and combination folds?

Mainly this: The sheetfed press, when running a typical eight-page-per-plate signature (16 pages), is usually at its limit. That is often its maximum plate size. What happens when two 16-page signatures are needed? Then the sheetfed printer needs two press runs and two passes through the folder. And the sheetfed press can't stack up two sheets of paper and fold them into a single 32-page signature.

And voila, that is the critical difference between the sheetfed and the web method: A web press can stack up two webs and fold them together into a single 32-page signature.

Before we describe it, let's answer the obvious question: Why is the combination folder named as such, and why is it often called a "chop" fold?

Combination refers to the three distinctly different mechanical ways of making the required folds. The first one, called a "former" fold, is achieved by passing the moving web over a triangular-shaped board (called the "former" board). The second, called the "jaw" fold is made with two cylinders. The third, called the "chop" fold (because that's the way it looks), is made by whacking at the signature with a blade.

Rather than bore you with the actual mechanics of these folds, let's discuss the total effect of the combination folder itself. (If you are interested in the technical specifics of how they are done, any web press book can satisfy your curiosity.)

Illustration 111 shows segments of two moving webs traveling together. The mechanics of the combination folder stack one on top of the other. As we describe this folder, imagine that one of the webs has been printed in four-color and the other in black and white.

Illustration 112 shows the first fold, the former, being made. Illustration 113 shows the second, the jaw fold. And Illustration 114, the third, the chop fold, along with a representation of the result.

If the shaded web was in full color, we can now see how it would be distributed throughout the signature itself. Pages one and two are color (no color spread). Pages seven, eight, nine, and 10 are color, and if you study the drawing (or your own fold-down), you will see there is one color spread, pages eight and nine. Finally, page 16 is in color. (The back of the signature will have the same distribution of color.)

The result is that this signature has two internal color spreads. All other four-color is in a single page format. (Keep in mind that we are describing the folds in relation to saddle stitching; perfect binding produces different results.)

Now, what if we assume that the nonshaded portions are full-color and the shaded portions black and white? By studying the signature, you will quickly see that the 32-pager now has four internal four-color spreads. Quite a difference. And, if the signature runs at the center of the book, the center spread will now be black and white.

Virtually all presses capable of delivering this 32-page combination fold can run the signature either way. It just depends on which web is "stacked" on top of the other before the folds are made. However, when delivering a 32-page signature, that's about it for creativity. One of the two distributions of color can be used, but the signature cannot be delivered with any other imposition.

Which brings up a point. We talked earlier about a press having more than one folder. What if this press happened to have two combination folders? That would mean two independent folders capable of producing the combination fold.

We would then have one more imposition possibility: By running one web through each folder, we could have one four-color 16-page signature and one B/W 16-page signature. They could be placed together in the magazine or separated by still other signatures. Their impositions would be eight pages in a row with the same color: B/W for one signature and four-color for the other. A press may have one of several different kinds of folders or several of the same kind of folder. You don't know which until you inquire at the printing plant. So make sure that you do inquire. □

The web press often prints on more than one roll of paper. In this case we see two webs being combination-folded. The shaded web might be four-color, the un-shaded web black and white, thereby dictating where the color falls in this signature.

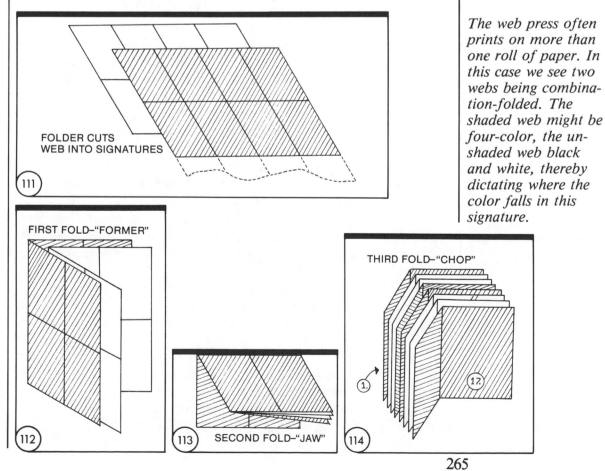

FOLDER CUTS WEB INTO SIGNATURES

111

FIRST FOLD–"FORMER"

112

SECOND FOLD–"JAW"

113

THIRD FOLD–"CHOP"

114

265

DOUBLE-FORMER FOLDERS

The imposition, or relative page positions, of a double former delivering two eight-page signatures "the same." If the magazine run is 50,000, this situation will produce that amount with 25,000 press impressions.

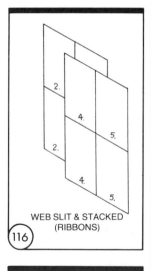

WEB SLIT & STACKED
(RIBBONS)

(116)

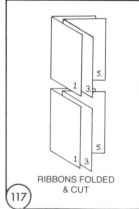

RIBBONS FOLDED
& CUT

(117)

We said that we'd discuss the two common web folders. The first was the combination folder; the second is the double-former. Double-formers are simple enough to describe, but can offer tremendous variety in color distribution. For starters, let's look at one of the possibilities: running a 16-page web in a configuration that delivers two similar eight-page signatures.

Illustration 115 shows the top and bottom printing plate configuration of such a signature. The first noticeable difference is that we are now printing head to foot rather than head to head. The second is that, because we are going to deliver two eight-pagers that are "the same," we see that page two runs in-line with page two (known as a two-out or two-up delivery).

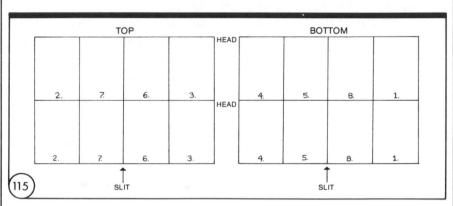

(115)

Pause a moment. Remember the discussion of in-line problems, one page affecting another? Isn't this a refreshing change? If the ad on page two has routinely generated complaints because of the difficulty of balancing its color with anything running below or above it on the press, we have an interesting solution here. Run the problem ads in line with themselves. Then, you can start concentrating on getting the color exactly as you want it on the press without any compromises. Don't forget this. It's one of the least discussed solutions to one of the biggest problems in magazine printing.

Back to the mechanics of the double-former. The first radical departure from the combination fold is that what *would have been* folded first, the former fold, is not folded at all. Rather, a slitting wheel cuts the web into two parts—each half is now being called a "ribbon."

Illustration 116 shows the folder stacking one ribbon on top of the other. And, Illustration 117 shows the only fold made by the folder at all, the former fold. The final function is to cut the product into two signatures (Illustration 117).

Because we set this example up as a double-former, two-out "the same" delivery, we now have two signatures that are the same —and the press run has been cut in half.

Another oddity: The double-former delivers a totally open signature: open head, open low, or high folio; everything open. It's just a bunch of folded sheets that stay together because that's the way they were "stacked." The main difference to the buyer? No gusseting. It cannot occur on a double-former.

If you haven't already done so, I now strongly recommend that you get some paper and scissors. Watching these folds is crucial for most people; otherwise it might be hard to follow the various convolutions. Illustration 118 takes the exact same printing and folding configuration that we just used but delivers two eight-pagers that are different. "Page one" of the first (Illustration 117) might be page one of the magazine, while "page one" of the second (Illustration 120) might be page five. Again, we are addressing the differences between the printer's generic impositions with the customized imposition that is important to the buyer.

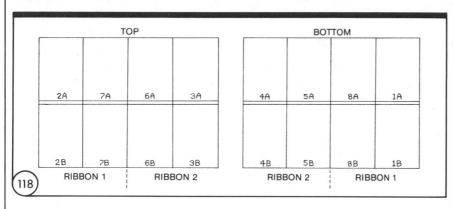

TOP				BOTTOM			
2A	7A	6A	3A	4A	5A	8A	1A
2B	7B	6B	3B	4B	5B	8B	1B
RIBBON 1		RIBBON 2		RIBBON 2		RIBBON 1	

(118)

To make things more comprehensible, we will now identify the top and bottom halves of each plate as either A or B.

The ribbons are stacked as they were before (Illustration 119) and cut as they were before (Illustration 120). The difference is that we now have two eight-page signatures that have one similarity: The

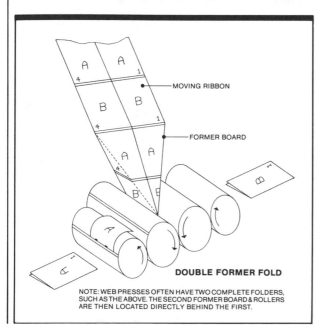

DOUBLE FORMER FOLD

MOVING RIBBON

FORMER BOARD

NOTE: WEB PRESSES OFTEN HAVE TWO COMPLETE FOLDERS, SUCH AS THE ABOVE. THE SECOND FORMER BOARD & ROLLERS ARE THEN LOCATED DIRECTLY BEHIND THE FIRST.

CHAPTER 50

Although the press doesn't run any differently than shown in Illustrations 115-117, the two eight-page signatures could be "different." The impositions might look like these. In this case, 50,000 press impressions will deliver the two eight-pagers.

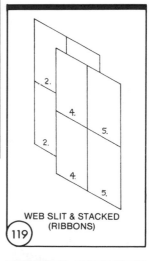

WEB SLIT & STACKED (RIBBONS)

(119)

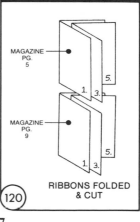

MAGAZINE PG. 5

MAGAZINE PG. 9

RIBBONS FOLDED & CUT

(120)

color distribution throughout each signature is identical. If we ran color only on the top plate, then that color would be distributed through signature A in the exact same way it is distributed through signature B.

One thing should be obvious to you by now: The double-former always delivers at least two signatures. That's where it got its name. They may be two identical or two different signatures, but the point is—a double-former cannot deliver a single product. If it could, it would lose its name and not be called a double-former anymore.

Complicating the double-former delivery

That should make sense, but now I hope you've been playing with your scissors because now we're going to complicate the double-former fold.

Illustration 121 shows a much more typical application of the double-former. Rather than running one web, we'll run two: one with color (full process) on both sides and the other in black and white. (Naturally, whatever results we get will be different from those obtained if we were to set this test up with four-color only on one side of one web. You can run through the variations on your own.)

So, Illustration 121 shows four printing plates rather than page numbers. Web 1, at the top, is all four-color and is broken (horizontally) into its A and B deliveries, as was the previous example.

Web 2 is all black and white but also has A and B deliveries. What we will do is cut these webs into ribbons and stack them into different configurations to see what will happen.

A somewhat complicated look at the printing plates (impositions) for a two-reel press with a double former. The paper will be cut into ribbons as indicated.

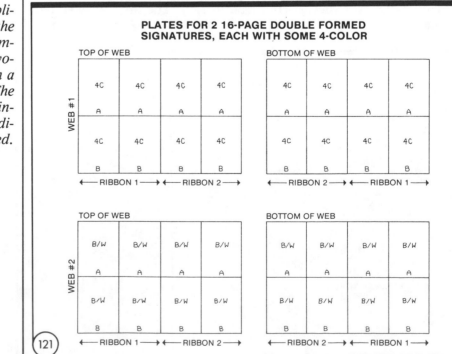

PLATES FOR 2 16-PAGE DOUBLE FORMED SIGNATURES, EACH WITH SOME 4-COLOR

Illustration 122 shows the two webs cut into four ribbons. Two ribbons are full-color, two are not. On a versatile double-former, there are no restrictions as to how we must stack the ribbons before we fold them. So, let's go to Illustration 123. The ribbons are stacked so that the two four-color ribbons are lying on top of the two B/W ribbons. As you know, we must deliver two signatures, and they may be the same or different.

Let's look at a schematic for this delivery. Using the printer's pagination, pretend you are looking at a top view of the folded sheets in Illustration 123. It might look like this schematic, with the slashes and page numbers indicating which page is which.

Because ribbons 1 and 2 are from the four-color web, they will have full-color on them. So, looking at the schematic, we can see how that color is distributed through the signatures. This particular fold (or delivery) will provide two four-color spreads in each of the two signatures (pages two-three, and 14-15).

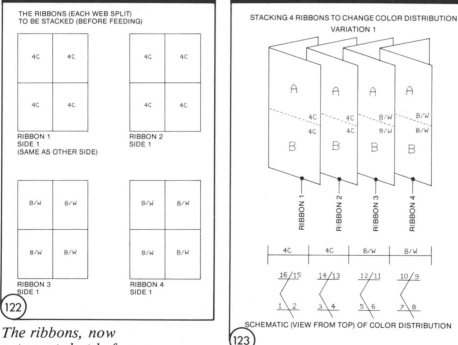

The ribbons, now cut apart, but before folding.

The real strength of the double former is its ability to intermingle the full-color portions of the signature with the black and white or two color. These illustrations (123-128) show how the color is distributed differently with each variation of the "stack." In other words, after the webs are split into ribbons, they are stacked at the discretion of the pressman (under the direction of the customer or magazine planner) to distribute the color as needed.

Remember, we said that a double-former like this one will normally allow you to stack the ribbons in any order. Thus, we are looking at only one of six possible impositions available on this folder. Let's review one more of them before you wander through the balance at your leisure.

Illustration 124 represents the exchange of positions of a four-color ribbon with a black and white. The imposition effects are significant. Suddenly the signatures have no four-color spreads. This might be critical to a publisher who must separate several competing four-color advertisers.

269

DOUBLE-FORMER FOLDERS

Keep in mind also that with all six of these variations (Illustrations 123 through 128), we may be talking about either two-out "the same," or two-out "different," meaning that if a particular imposition for a 16-page section of the magazine had merit, we could run it quite nicely on the double-former—without affecting the 16 other pages with the same imposition. And, because imposition variations

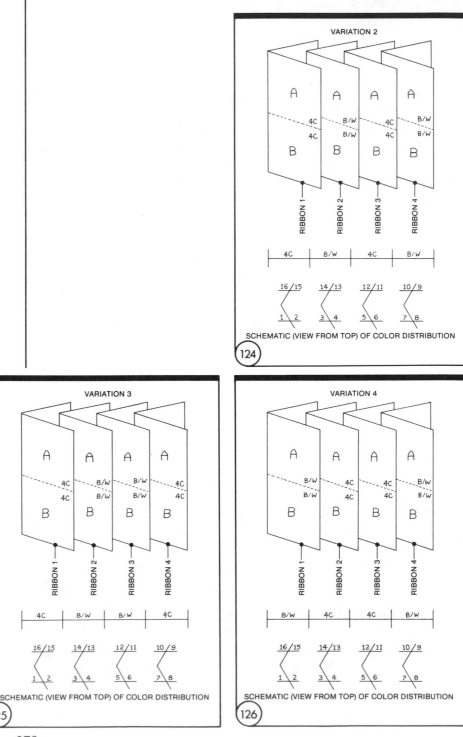

VARIATION 2

SCHEMATIC (VIEW FROM TOP) OF COLOR DISTRIBUTION

124

VARIATION 3

SCHEMATIC (VIEW FROM TOP) OF COLOR DISTRIBUTION

125

VARIATION 4

SCHEMATIC (VIEW FROM TOP) OF COLOR DISTRIBUTION

126

are wider on the double-former, we could find ourselves using it to solve various problems ranging from in-line quality control to the need for a unique imposition. The combination folder usually cannot solve these problems.

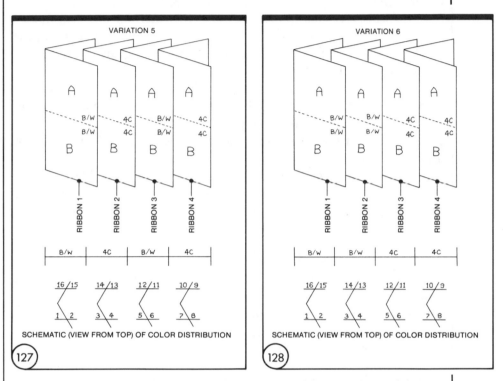

Now, let's get into the real world. If you can see the attractions of this double-former folder running two webs, consider the following:

•Many conventional webs have two double-formers that can run four ribbons over one former board, or any combination over two boards. Possibly three ribbons over Board 1 and one over Board 2, or any other arrangement.

•Some webs have two double-formers and three reel stands, allowing any combination over any former board. This might be six ribbons on one board: five and one, four and two, or three and three. This would result in dozens upon dozens of deliveries. One extreme would be to deliver two four-page signatures and two 20-page signatures in the same press pass. The variations boggle the mind of the double-former or combination-folder addict.

•All of these variations change when you add enough printing units to supply two-color to one or more of the nonprocess-color webs. Similarly, if you were running a variety of two-color material on any of the above options, you would find an unlimited ability to get the color where you wanted it and with good economy.

•Some presses have a double-former and a combination folder, thus offering the customer fantastic imposition selections.

271

Other comparisons

Imposition is only one of the comparisons that you must consider when deciding which folder best suits your product. There are other technical aspects that must be weighed.

As already mentioned, the double-former delivers an "open" signature. If you happened to be using a rather thick paper stock, the double-former might be more attractive simply because it is free of gusseting effects.

But the double-former does (at times) have a penalty. When a signature is delivered as two "different," then the double-former (in some cases) would require two pockets in the bindery (one for each 16-pager) rather than the single pocket needed for the 32-pager. (For a detailed discussion of pockets, see the bindery section.)

As we said much earlier, the topics discussed would cover only saddle-stitching effects of impositions on a few given presses. Your knowledge of the principles of folding (and their effects on imposition) must be coupled with the peculiarities of the specific presses at your printer.

Or, when you are soliciting printing bids, you must certainly be able to compare the way an imposition change can affect your costs. While any given magazine can be run on any given press, the one that does it most economically will almost always have the most versatile interplay between the available printing units, reel stands, and the folder (or folders) on the press.

Other folders and presses

Finally, there are many other folding options available on a press. If you happened to print a magazine that trimmed to five-and-a-half-inches by eight-and-a-half inches, then the double-parallel ability of the combination folder would be critical to you. The same would apply to a tabloid-size magazine.

Or, your press might have a ribbon folder, which tends to combine the mechanical abilities of both the chop folder and the double-former folder.

Then too, the press itself is a consideration. A wide web (45-inch to 50-inch web) with several double-formers is a far different creature from either a standard or mini-web with the same folder—if for no other reason than more pages are affected by each choice of imposition.

As stated earlier, little is written on the topic of folders and impositions. Perhaps you now understand why: Even a single press can have hundreds of imposition variations. Each press is slightly different from the next. Each printer must supply you with the particular details of what each of his presses can deliver. And you, the production director, must sort it all out. Get curious, play with your scissors, learn to read your printer's imposition charts, and you'll not only have some fun, but be dollars ahead for your efforts.

Folder variations

Just what can a folder deliver? Although each press may be set up somewhat differently, let's take a look at a hypothetical press with the following folding equipment. Although you're not likely to find all these abilities on one press, it is an example of just how far a printer could go with just one of many presses.

The parameters: a six-unit press, three reel stands, one double-former folder (two former boards, four deliveries), and two combination folders.

Illustration 129 demonstrates some of the possible deliveries. Note that we are discussing only the number of pages delivered in each signature. If we were also to attempt to dictate the possible variations of where color would fall in each signature (assuming one web were running in four-color), we could devote the rest of this book to diagrams of all of the possibilities.

As an exercise, you may want to practice folding sheets of paper and rearranging color distribution, as the folder would. Check with your printer to find out whether all the variations are available to you.□

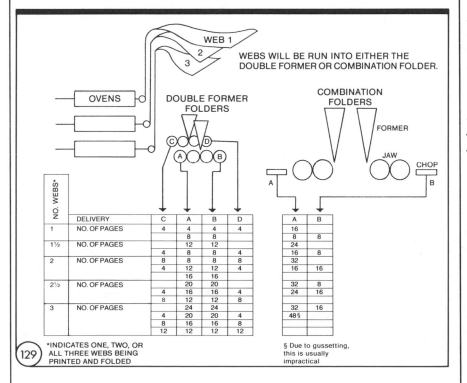

DOUBLE FORMER FOLDERS

NO. WEBS*	DELIVERY	C	A	B	D
1	NO. OF PAGES	4	4	4	4
			8	8	
1½	NO. OF PAGES		12	12	
		4	8	8	4
2	NO. OF PAGES	8	8	8	8
		4	12	12	4
			16	16	
2½	NO. OF PAGES		20	20	
		4	16	16	4
		8	12	12	8
3	NO. OF PAGES		24	24	
		4	20	20	4
		8	16	16	8
		12	12	12	12

COMBINATION FOLDERS

A	B
16	
8	8
24	
16	8
32	
16	16
32	8
24	16
32	16
48§	

WEB 1

WEBS WILL BE RUN INTO EITHER THE DOUBLE FORMER OR COMBINATION FOLDER.

(129) *INDICATES ONE, TWO, OR ALL THREE WEBS BEING PRINTED AND FOLDED

§ Due to gussetting, this is usually impractical

A comparison of a double former to a combination folder. Actually, we are looking at two double formers on a press, which is a frequently-seen configuration. They are compared to two combination folders on a press, which is also common. The purpose of this comparison is to show the number and types of deliveries available with the double former. Practical application of the double former often reduces color makereadies, because color can be placed where required. Makereadies are the most expensive single activity in printing a magazine.

SECTION VIII:
PAPER
AND THE BINDERY

INTRODUCTION: SIZES AND SAVINGS

Much has been written on paper (most everything, if you don't mind the pun). It is not within the scope of this book to discuss the complexities of paper manufacture, nor all the varieties of paper. And fortunately, it isn't necessary. There are dozens of reference books available through any library. In addition, all the paper manufacturers publish vast amounts of promotional literature, which—aside from promoting their product—also helps the newcomer learn just what it is that he or she is buying. (One such handy guide is the *Warren Paper Estimating Guide*, available from the S.D. Warren Company, 225 Franklin St., Boston, Massachusetts 02101.)

The purpose here is to set forth the fundamentals, but first, I want to drive home a point made in the chapter on web printing: No matter who orders paper—you or your printer—it must be ordered in a size that relates to your publication. Ordering sheetfed stock can, at times, become a problem. Because the sheets are delivered in predetermined sizes, they cannot always be "cut out" to a press dimension without waste. Web stock, however, can generally be ordered in a roll width that suits your product.

Paying attention to the press's cutoff and to roll width—as compared to blindly ordering (or having your printer order) the wrong roll width—can save nearly 4 percent of your total paper consumption.

Couple the above with a potential savings of an additional 2 percent to 3 percent based on press performance and you could approach a magical 10 percent savings on paper—that is, given the right circumstances.

What "press performance" means is that some presses are better than others. Generally speaking, a new press (or one that has been retrofitted with automated controls) will use less paper than an older, manually operated press.

But you can achieve savings only if you are aware of how the roll of paper (or sheet), the press, and the bindery all interrelate. So don't isolate your paper figuring. It is integral to all other major printing activity.□

CHAPTER 51

Photo courtesy of Weyerhaeuser Co., Paper Division

BASIC MAGAZINE STOCKS

Several categories of paper are commonly used today in the production of magazines. Your choice of paper will depend on your magazine's particular needs. A brief description of some of the papers available and a look at their major attributes should help you decide which paper is best for you.

•*Coated groundwood:* This term describes a relatively inexpensive stock which, for all practical purposes, is newsprint that has been bleached and coated.

Why is "groundwood" part of its name? Because its major ingredient is groundwood pulp. This material is the result of chipping logs into tiny pieces, adding water, grinding the mixture into a smooth consistency, and passing it over a machine that squeezes out the water and produces a sheet of paper. Bleaching during manufacture does what its name implies: It whitens the stock. Coating is the process that puts a shiny surface on the paper.

The popularity of coated groundwood has more to do with its price than its printing ability. Given the fact that the basic stock is similar to newsprint, manufacturing coated groundwood starts with the least expensive materials on the market. The coating, applied to give the paper better printing ability, results in the crisper appearance of coated-paper printing, as compared to printing on newsprint or uncoated stock (Illustration 130).

However, one cannot overlook the fact that, as usual, you get what you pay for. Coated groundwood is an inexpensive sheet of paper and prints as such. It doesn't have great qualities on press—just adequate. Don't think, though, that only "cheap" magazines use it. The major newsweeklies, most monthlies, and thousands of trade journals print on coated groundwood.

In comparing coated stock printing to uncoated printing, there are two chief differences. One is the absorption tendency of the stock as shown here. The other is more obvious to the naked eye: Coated stock allows "glossy" printing.

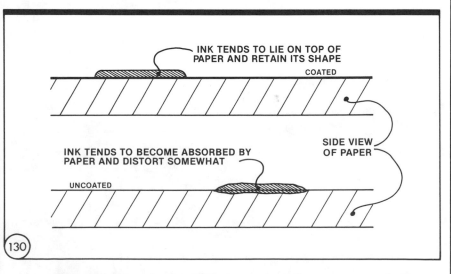

INK TENDS TO LIE ON TOP OF PAPER AND RETAIN ITS SHAPE

COATED

INK TENDS TO BECOME ABSORBED BY PAPER AND DISTORT SOMEWHAT

UNCOATED

SIDE VIEW OF PAPER

130

•*Coated free sheets:* This term describes a paper similar to coated groundwood, with one major exception. The paper is called a "free sheet" because it is free of groundwood pulp. In the manufacture of coated free sheets, the pulp (the mixture of chipped wood and water) is chemically treated numerous times to take out impurities in the logs (such as resins).

CHAPTER 52

This mixture is called chemical pulp (rather than groundwood pulp). The sheet will be much purer and whiter. It will also be given a coating (as is groundwood) of clay and other fillers to produce a shiny printing surface.

But a stiff penalty is paid during the manufacture of coated free sheets. When the impurities are removed from the pulp, approximately half the pulp volume is lost, which is the main reason that free sheets are so much more expensive than groundwoods.

•*Uncoated paper:* Both of the above two sheets could be manufactured as uncoated sheets. In the case of groundwood, the result would be newsprint. In the case of a free sheet, the result would look like a page from an expensive hardbound textbook. Books are often manufactured on uncoated free sheets because 1) uncoateds are easier to read, 2) when halftones are not used, fine detail ability is not a necessity, and 3) free sheets are considered much more permanent than groundwoods. You know that newspaper will discolor in a few days. That same deterioration happens to typical magazine paper, but because of the coating, it takes a while longer.

•*Matte finishes:* When a sheet of paper is coated but not "ironed" or polished (so to speak), it will have a far better printing ability than uncoated stock, but will not be quite up to par with a normal coated sheet. Many people find a matte finish attractive because it doesn't have the glare (or shine) associated with a fully coated sheet.

•*High-bulk stocks:* In a primer on paper, this stock wouldn't be discussed. But in the magazine context, it should be. Why? Because magazines often use insert cards that are torn out and mailed as postcards. The United States Postal Service has requirements for minimum thicknesses for a card in the mail, specifically, seven mils (seven thousandths of an inch). High-bulk stock is a paper that has been designed to be thicker than usual, but without adding appreciably to the weight of the pulp used to make a sheet.

In simple terms, an attempt is made during manufacture to fill the paper with air to make the sheet more bulky. Without going into detail, it is enough to say that for an average quality insert card, seven-mil (also called seven-point) high-bulk, uncoated paper is the normal choice.

Most printers who produce insert cards will have a stock sheet of high-bulk paper "on the floor" or available for customers to use.

How paper is measured

Paper is sold by its weight. There are a half-dozen ways to figure the weight of a sheet (called the basis weight), but only two common methods for magazine purposes: text weight and cover weight. Text weight (also called book weight) is the unit you would use to answer this question: If you were to cut 500 sheets of paper to the dimensions of 25 inches by 38 inches, how much would that stack weigh? If it weighed 50 pounds, you'd have a stack of paper with a 50-pound basis weight.

Basis weights of 45 pounds or less are generally called "lightweight" stocks. If they are coated (as most magazine stock is), it would be called a lightweight coated, or LWC.

As the basis weight of a stock increases, so does the thickness of the sheet itself.

One of the advantages of web printing is that the web press can handle much thinner sheets than the sheetfed press. Although a printer may not print anything less than a 50-pound stock on a sheetfed press, some magazines are running as low as 34 pounds on a web. Naturally, webs use far less paper (by weight, which is how you pay for it) than a sheetfed press, which results in substantially lower paper costs. In addition, the less a magazine weighs, the less it will cost to mail (if it is a conventional second class publication).

There are economic advantages to using the thinnest sheet available, but there are also penalties. The two most significant are "see-through" and "show-through."

"See-through" is an effect that you *want* in tracing tissue: You literally want to see through the sheet. But when a paper is thin enough (even a magazine grade), "see-through" can be a minor distraction—one you *don't* want.

"Show-through" is similar, except more problematic and typical. If you print something on one side of a sheet, will you be able to see its image from the other? To a degree, all LWCs have some show-through, the very lightest of them can cause readability problems.

With uncoated sheets, a very light stock will have more show-through problems than a comparable coated stock. This is because uncoated stock absorbs the ink slightly, while the coated sheet tends to keep the ink on its surface.

Cover weight

If you followed the description of basis weight, you'll understand this: Cover weights are based on 500 sheets of paper cut to 20 inches by 26 inches.

Imagine two sheets of paper, both called 50-pound, but one is cover weight and the other is text weight. Which is the thicker, heavier sheet?

The cover weight is thicker. If you have two stacks of paper weighing 50 pounds, and one of the stacks has been cut to much narrower dimensions, it should make sense that these smaller sheets of paper must be much heavier (and thicker) to weigh the same as the larger-dimensioned stack.

Just because you print a heavier cover than text (or body) doesn't mean you must print on "cover paper" or on a sheet measured by cover basis weight. You may print the body of your magazine on 45-pound basis, 25 inches by 38 inches and then print the cover on 80-pound basis, 25 inches by 38 inches.

If you wanted, you could also describe the cover as 44-pound basis, 20 inches by 26 inches. But it so happens that cover paper isn't manufactured in that basis weight!

That may seem to make no sense at all, and it doesn't. The standards of measuring paper have little significance. For the average magazine, it may be more practical to describe all your papers in text or book basis weights. And by asking your printer or paper supplier for a sampling of text basis weight sheets, which is the quality you are probably most interested in, you'll have a ready method of ordering a sheet by "feel." If you are curious, the following table compares the common basis weights for text and cover weights.

Book basis weight, 500 sheets, 25″ by 38″	Would compare to cover weight, 500 sheets, 20″ by 26″	Cover basis weight, 500 sheets, 20″ by 26″	Would compare to book weight, 500 sheets 25″ by 38″
30	16	55	100
40	22	60	110
45	25	63	115
50	27	65	119
60	33	68	124
70	38	80	146
80	44	90	164
90	49	100	183
100	55	110	201
120	66	120	219

So, if covers are "not manufactured" in a 50-pound weight, what does it mean to you? It means that you will technically order a book weight for your cover. In one sense, there is no such thing as a 44-pound cover. But in another sense, any 80-pound text will have the thickness and the feel of a 44-pound cover. To be accurate (and prevent the printer from chuckling), you would specify something like this:

Body Paper: 25″ x 38″ basis 50-pound coated groundwood.
Cover Paper: 25″ x 38″ basis 90-pound coated free sheet.

Those basic parameters would be great starters. The next step would be to pick from the dozens of coated groundwoods and hundreds of coated free sheets on the market. Your printer will have a representative sample of what is available and at what price.□

SELECTING AND PURCHASING PAPER FOR YOUR MAGAZINE

Just how would a newcomer select paper for a magazine? Let's hope someone had your job before you so that you have a place to start. But some people do have to start from scratch. The following general parameters may be helpful to the beginner.

•*Uncoated groundwood:* Least expensive sheet available. Suitable for text and for somewhat crude printing of halftones. Several grades available, with varying degrees of bleaching. Magazine will tend to discolor, possibly within a year. Assumes web printing.

•*Coated groundwood:* Least expensive of the coated stocks. Provides very adequate B/W halftone printing and adequate full-color printing. Used by most major magazines. Generally assumes web printing.

•*Uncoated free sheet:* More expensive than any groundwood. Suited to a good quality magazine where the halftone printing is not absolutely critical, but must be good. Prints either web or sheetfed.

•*Coated free sheet:* Highest priced stock for magazines. Provides best halftone and full-color printing on either web or sheetfed.

•*Matte free sheet:* Approximately the same cost as coated free sheet. Very good quality for halftones and text. Unique, low-gloss quality for full-color work.

Other possibilities: Paper and press

For some magazines, an extremely heavy cover stock is used, possibly coated on one side only. For these very thick sheets, the paper is described in "points." A point, in this case, is 1/1000th of an inch. A paper company might describe a sheet as being eight-point, coated one side, with a weight of 150 pounds per thousand sheets, measuring 20 inches by 26 inches. What would that compare to? Well, first of all, 500 sheets must weigh 75 pounds. So it would compare to a 75-pound cover weight sheet. That would compare to a text sheet of 130 pounds (as the charts in the previous chapter indicate). If it were coated one side, it would have a shiny coating (normally for the outside cover) on one side and no coating on the other.

So, an eight-point sheet, coated one side would be abbreviated eight-pt., C1S, and would compare to a 75-pound cover sheet, or a 130-pound book sheet. Such a sheet would be destined for an atypical magazine, one that needed a very thick cover. Along the same line, this atypical magazine might need exceptional quality and appearance. So we might couple this sheet of paper with press varnishing, or actual lamination.

Varnishing is the application of a printing varnish (which acts somewhat like the varnish you'd put on your table) to give a printed sheet a shinier, more durable finish. A sheet can be varnished "wet" or "dry." On a sheetfed press, the covers might be printed and allowed to dry before the varnish is applied. This would allow for a heavy, shiny coat of varnish, resulting in an exceptional finish.

In other cases, and always in the case of web printing, the sheet could be varnished while the ink is still wet. This would not result in as dense an application of varnish. Rather, it offers a flatter finish—although still a shinier finish than what you would get using no varnish at all.

Lamination is far more expensive than varnishing, but offers the ultimate in "shine" and protection. In this case, a thin film of plastic is laminated, or glued, to the sheet after printing. What results is an almost glass-like reflectivity, which some people interpret as the ultimate in quality.

Although a few magazines use the above techniques, most do not. The reason is that eight-point stock (and heavier) and varnishing or laminating dramatically increase the final cost. In that most magazines are designed to be discarded in a month or so, it is more common to see the production director select the least expensive materials that will adequately transport the message to the reader.

Who buys the paper?

As mentioned earlier in this discussion, paper is no small topic. If there are hundreds of books about the raw material itself, there ought to be several on how to purchase it. Unfortunately, that is not the case. Worse yet, the topic would easily fill several volumes. But the good news is that there is space here to briefly review how paper is purchased by large and small publishers.

Paper can be bought in two general ways: by the customer (and supplied to the printer) or by the printer (and sold to the customer during printing). There are advantages to both methods.

Printer-supplied paper

Having the printer supply your paper has both financial and technical implications. If the printer purchases your stock, he gets the original invoice. This means your money won't be tied up in a physical inventory. In addition, the printer is likely to be much more adept at making the decisions involved in ordering stock. He will know whether the paper was delivered according to specifications, whether it is inferior (poor finish, web breaks on press), and how to resolve any of these problems with the paper company or broker.

Just as important, keep in mind that most magazines are produced by somewhat small firms. While you may publish two titles, your printer may print 50. He is in a strong bargaining position, ordering the paper for 50 magazines, while you are in a less strong position, ordering paper for two. This leverage can be important when it comes time to resolve a complaint, deal with a late shipment, or negotiate paper supply during one of the cyclical shortages that we are subject to.

But, as always, there can be hidden costs. Printers normally

283

mark up the cost of paper before they bill the customer. For a small publisher, this markup can reach the outlandish height of 25 percent. Given that paper might represent 25 percent of your annual gross, a severe markup can be quite significant to your overall profit.

Larger magazines generally suffer a smaller markup. A total of 3 percent over the true cost might appear on the invoice. Or the printer may simply bill the customer exactly what the paper cost and then tack on a handling charge to cover the paperwork, inventory, insurance, and so forth. But it is hard to conceive of any printer providing paper at no markup at all. After all, the printer must have warehouse space, insurance, and equipment to handle stock. If there is absolutely no direct way that you are billed for these costs, you can assume that the overhead is padded somewhere in the printing costs themselves.

And this is *not* an accusation. Printers simply must cover their costs, and how they happen to cover them can sometimes be creative.

One of the nicer things about printer-supplied paper is that it doesn't cost you anything until you get your magazines. Although the printer may have to order $100,000 worth of stock a month prior to your magazine's printing cycle, and may take delivery of stock that far in advance of a printing job, your invoice won't show the paper cost until the magazine is on your dock. This can effectively look like "interest-free money," but it isn't, really. After all, as I said, the printer must recover his costs from his customers. But it is definitely reflected in your cash flow since you won't have to pay for inventory before the magazine is printed.

Publisher-supplied paper

On the other hand, many publishers purchase their own stock direct from the mill or from a paper broker. This also has advantages and disadvantages.

One of the immediate possible benefits is that the publisher can order stock that is exactly suited to his or her needs. If the printer has a "standard" roll of paper that is used for all titles, the publisher might save several percents of his costs by ordering a roll suited exactly to his particular magazine's trim size.

Regarding paper shortages, which as noted before seem to pop up from time to time, publishers who purchase their own paper may have more freedom to maneuver. If you use printer-supplied stock, a shortage puts you at the mercy of your printer/supplier in terms of price and selection of stock. The publisher who buys his own paper, however, has a working relationship with a mill or broker. In the event of a shortage, the publisher can take his paper allotment and find another printer, if need be. That can be hard to do if the other printer can't get the kind of paper you need.

Regarding markups, publisher-supplied stock is generally

handled by the printer at a fixed rate, say per roll or per hundred pounds of paper. However, there is no flat markup based on the price of the stock. The publisher, then, can save whatever profit the printer would have made by selling the stock to the customer. But the publisher would likely have to pay a separate handling charge, which somewhat offsets this savings.

Because all printers and publishers work out their own pricing and contracts, it's not possible to say here just how much can be saved by supplying your own stock. The only way to find out for sure is to get paper prices from an independent source, and then find out what your printer would charge to handle it. At the same time, be sure to get other printing prices, too: It may just be that your printer happens to have his paper handling charges built into the printing costs, which could lead you to believe you are saving money when you are actually being charged—or even double charged.

There are many disadvantages to buying your own paper, particularly if you are a small firm. Up front, of course, is the cash-flow effect. Your paper will probably have to be paid for either before or during the printing cycle, draining your piggybank before the advertisers even think of paying you.

On the other hand, if you are cash-fat, you could possibly negotiate a 2 percent net 10 arrangement with the mill or broker. This could be significant in reducing your costs, but, again, also in draining the pocket.

If you are small, you will not need much paper. The mills and brokers set up their own discounts, depending on the volume the purchaser buys. The smaller publisher hasn't enough volume to get the discounts available to a typical printer.

There are other considerations to supplying your own stock: Once paper is shipped, it is your responsibility. This means that defective paper, paper lost in shipment, paper delayed because of a lost train car, or any other problem is your legal responsibility. Your printer may be helpful in identifying a bad lot of paper, but he is under no obligation to negotiate with the mill for you. So, you will need either muscle (as a large buyer) or technical expertise (your friendly printer, or your own knowledge) to solve such problems.

Finding the reasons for technical defects can be a chore, too. What if the paper lints (picks apart) during printing, or breaks (the web), or wraps up inside the press, causing damage and slowdowns? Is it the fault of the printer or the paper? (For an explanation of these problems, see the chapter titled "Paper Problems.")

It may be hard for you to tell. A printer may have the tendency to blame the stock if he didn't purchase it. That can lead to technical meetings at the plant—with a paper mill representative, the printer, and you all trying to figure out who (or what) the culprit is. These situations aren't necessarily unpleasant, but they do consume time and energy.

Another factor: If you purchase stock, you store it at the printer. He must keep accurate records not only of how much is there, but of how much he used compared to what he estimated he needed. This can be a complicated relationship: If the printer estimates 100,000 pounds of paper for your magazine, but actually uses 110,000, who pays for the overconsumption? And what if he uses only 90,000 pounds? Finally, what if all goes well, but at the end of two years you are missing 50,000 pounds of paper that was consumed on your publication, but not taken out of the books?

Any of the above situations can occur. For the publisher to gain maximum benefit from purchasing paper directly, all such situations must be anticipated.

The printer and publisher should agree up front how much paper should be required. If the printer overconsumes for no reason, it is likely that he should pay the publisher for that overconsumption. If the printer underconsumes, the publisher should either get the full benefit or work out a relationship whereby they share the savings. But the consumption standards (estimates) for future issues should then be lowered.

In all cases, a highly accurate inventory is required. You can imagine the disaster to a publishing firm if the paper inventory were suddenly reduced by a half-issue's inventory, honest mistake or not.

Again, all the above requires detail work. For larger publishers, the savings from buying direct offsets the energy and cash-flow effects. For intermediate publishers, only experimentation and price solicitation will demonstrate whether savings are available. As for smaller publishers, they do buy paper direct, but with much less frequency.

How is paper sold?

With all the preceding discussion about buying paper, let's answer a technical question that you may have. Just how is paper measured and sold? You may have heard of the term "CWT." These initials stand for hundredweight ("C" in Roman numerals means 100). And that's how paper is sold.

Going back to weights, if paper is 25″ x 38″ basis 50-pound text and sells for $45/CWT, what's the relationship? It means that for every 100 pounds of paper you buy, the price is $45, plain and simple. By using ordinary math, you can also figure out approximately how much paper (by area) you will get in a 100,000-pound shipment.

But before you figure out how many magazines a 100,000-pound shipment of paper will make, the subject of paper waste should be addressed.

If you are a novice, these numbers (generated by an independent group in 1979) may shock you. If you are experienced, just skip this section. It is unpleasant reading. But in either case, take heart: As of this writing, the numbers are five years old. That may not seem like a long time, but since 1979 many new web presses have been installed. The newer webs will generally waste less paper than the older ones.

CHAPTER 53

Paper waste in action

When paper reaches the web, it is wrapped in a protective sheet. This sheet is weighed and sold with the stock as if it were usable paper.

After the wrapper is removed, some paper is stripped off because the outer layers are damaged somewhat in shipment.

After the roll has been almost completely run, a splice is made to the next roll. What is left over is called core waste. Furthermore, the splice may cause the web to go out of register, thereby creating waste during the run.

The makeready uses paper, too, of course. This paper is tossed into the waste bin and sold as scrap.

During the press run, a web break or a quality problem of some sort will be reason to toss out some more paper.

In the bindery, there is another makeready. Waste occurs here, too. During the run, any machine problems will damage some press signatures. The web press run itself may have been increased by 1 percent to 3 percent in anticipation of makeready and running waste in the bindery.

Finally, three sides of the magazine are trimmed—and this "trimmed" paper is sucked up the waste tubes and into the scrap bin.

What is the result of all this?

On a two-web run, one web in four-color on coated stock, with a press run of 25,000, the total stock waste can be 20 percent.

On the same web run, with a 200,000 count, the waste falls to 11 percent—demonstrating just how the makereadies in both press and bindery consume large amounts of paper.

Although you can't do much directly about eliminating the waste in the printing industry, you can certainly keep an eye open for printers who are very conscious of converting your paper dollars into paper scrap. As the industry strives to lower the conventional waste patterns, you want to be part of the party.

Paper has two sides

Before closing this chapter, one of the oddities about paper that can affect the quality of printing should be discussed. It is the *side* of the paper being printed.

For background, you must understand just a little of the manufacturing process of the sheet itself. Therefore, let's discuss the

287

SELECTING AND PURCHASING PAPER FOR YOUR MAGAZINE

manufacture of a typical sheet of coated groundwood. It starts out as a pile of logs. This pile of logs is ground into chunks. The chunks are mixed with water, ground some more, and finally blended into the soupy mixture called pulp. The pulp is passed over a series of screens (wire meshes) and the water is more or less sucked out—a process that will eventually result in a fairly water-free sheet of paper.

It is the wire mesh that creates the paper's different sides. The side from which the water is sucked is called the wire side, and it has a rather firm texture. The other side, called the "felt" side, was not in firm contact with the wire during manufacture; it has a slightly softer finish. Even after coating, the sheet can retain its two different characteristics—firm texture or soft finish. The problem is that the felt side may not hold ink as well as the wire side.

If the press happens to have the type of folder that prints felt-side up from one roll and wire-side up from the next, you may see the color change markedly for better or worse right after a roll change (splice). This type of folder uses a festoon of paper and does what is called a zero-speed splice.

But if the web press has what is called a flying paster, it probably will not print on either side of the rolls from a given batch of paper. Thus, you would not necessarily know whether you had a press problem or a paper problem if you detect a printing quality problem.

Finally, it must be mentioned that there are such creatures as "twin wire" paper machines. These do put both sides of a sheet in contact with a wire mesh. The result is that they tend to produce a sheet with consistent printing qualities from one side to the other.□

PAPER PROBLEMS

Whether you press-check your work or not, chances are that you will—at some point—hear sob stories from your printer about "what went wrong." (And, according to Murphy's Law, anything that can, will.) Your printer's explanation will be an attempt to calm you down while you live with either 1) late delivery or 2) poor quality.

But as a buyer, you will need more then calming down. You will need the answers to a few questions. Whose fault was it? Was the problem avoidable? Will it happen again? And finally, should you attempt to get credit for the error—either in the form of money or as a rerun?

One of the major causes of printing problems is the paper itself. Given the light weights commonly used (which don't perform as well as heavier ones), it is not uncommon to experience all sorts of printing problems—some of which are related to weight, others to the type of sheet itself. When price is a prime area of concern, the publisher may find himself using a very inexpensive sheet, one that comes with no guarantee as to runability. The paper is simply delivered—and the paper company believes it has done its job. The paper won't necessarily be consistent or run well or be free of a tendency to break.

With this in mind, let's review a few typical paper problems and see what possible action you can take. Keep in mind that your ability to act and your general position will depend on whether you purchase the paper yourself or have it supplied by the printer. This difference will be especially important in the event you get into credit situations. If you supply stock to the printer, you will need accurate records and reports in order to proceed with credit claims.

Those who have their printer supply their stock needn't be too concerned with this discussion as long as the stock is a common one and readily available. But those whose printers supply an odd or unique stock will be interested in the following material—the reason is that paper problems could possibly mean that you don't get an issue out when you should. It would be wise to become familiar with what can happen and how to anticipate it.

Damaged roll

It's possible to run into problems even before your job is on the press. Rolls may have internal or external damage, which will either make them unprintable or result in excess waste before they can be mounted on the press. Or sheets may be curled or have damage in the side of the stack.

For those of you who don't supply the paper to the printer, this is not usually a problem. The printer will negotiate with the paper company, and the problem will be solved perhaps without your even hearing about it. But in certain cases, for example, when a special stock is ordered and there's no adequate backup, these buyers, too, would want to know what happened and how to proceed.

If you do supply paper, the first thing to find out in a "damaged roll" situation is when the damage was reported in relation to when the paper was received by the printer. Here's a typical example. You have a shipment sent to the printer on the first of the month, to be printed 45 days later. Just as your job goes on press, you get a call. The printer says that half the rolls were damaged in shipment, and you'll either have to replace them or allow the printer to unwrap the rolls until they are free of cuts and bumps. Then later, you'll have to arrange for a credit with the railroad or trucking line. Does this sound logical?

No. In the above example, the printer should have reported the damaged shipment immediately. Delaying the report 45 days raises the question of who actually mishandled the stock. You will have a tough time getting a credit for it, too; the railroad will claim that, because you didn't report the problem earlier, the damage must have occurred at the printer. You'll be in a mess.

As we've said many times, most printers and buyers are honest, but some (only a few, we hope) are not to be trusted. Then, too, it's not the president of the printing company who actually handles the rolls of paper. (The author once saw a roll-truck driver literally ram a railcar separation door into six rolls of paper because he was mad at his girlfriend! And no report was filed.)

•*The solution:* The way to handle the above case, if you own the paper, is to ask the printer to cover the loss. The reason is that you had no knowledge of the damage and, consequently, no way to claim a credit. If the printer states that the rolls were crushed in shipment, you must ask him how he knows this to be true. (Our friendly roll-truck driver may have dropped two rolls onto two others, for example.) And if the printer is still convinced that the fault is not his, ask him to deduct the cost of the claim from your bill and, as your representative, settle the credit directly with the railroad.

•*Prevention:* This sort of situation can be avoided if the printer thoroughly examines the paper before putting it into storage. Any damage found at this point should be reported to you at once, and if you own the stock, you can then start a claim. A trustworthy printer will have no qualms about this setup, while a shady printer (with a crazy roll-truck driver) might tell you that all paper problems are your problems.

The situation is generally less complicated for those who don't purchase their own paper. If you don't, and your magazine is run on a conventional grade paper, the printer should be able to replace it instantly if necessary. But if you run on a unique stock, you might very well want to have the printer fill out inspection reports at the time of delivery—simply so you know that there will be material for your next issue.

Web breaks

In this case, the printer can't foresee the situation. The paper is put on press—and suddenly it's breaking every 20 minutes. Then the press must be stopped, rewebbed, and restarted. This takes time, which equals money, and "someone's going to pay." It might be the paper people, if they actually guarantee the stock (which isn't always the case with less expensive papers), but it just might be the printer's fault. Read on.

•*Solution:* Before you part with a dollar, you would be wise to get more facts. Again, in most cases, the printer will not be trying to take you for a ride, but it never hurts to find out for sure—especially with a new job or new printer. Make sure that the printer knows ahead of time that you personally want to inspect web breaks when they occur. Then keep in mind that you shouldn't, according to the odds, see a break during a splicing operation—that is, when one roll expires and another is started without stopping the press. The reason is that splices are usually 95 percent (sometimes 98 percent) "good."

If the splices are not the problem, the printer might show you an area of the web that flutters wildly when the press is running. That could indicate a poorly wound roll, an oval-shaped roll, or any of a number of problems. Don't simply agree that "Yes, it's fluttering like mad." Take a look at the other presses running with other stocks. If there's no difference, get suspicious. All web presses must critically control paper tension; if the press isn't doing its job, breaks are going to occur.

Note, too, that there is another kind of splice on web paper: It is produced at the mill. The average roll of paper has no mill splices. If the pressman can show you one on every other roll, the mill is at fault. If you don't have the technical knowledge (or detective ability) to identify the culprit, don't hesitate to call in a pro, even if it costs you a few extra dollars for his consulting services.

•*Prevention:* Expect to have web-break problems at some point in your career. To keep control over them, anticipate them: Ask the printer to provide you with a continuing report on all breaks, which he probably reports already on an internal basis. When you see a change in the pattern, even though it might not be a serious one, contact the printer and get his opinion. Visit the plant if you're concerned, get help if you need it, and experiment with other papers (even a few rolls might do it) to see if the pattern changes.

Picking

Picking is the action of the printing blanket (and the ink on it) pulling tiny fibers and loose particles from the paper. When these particles accumulate on the blanket, the result is poor printing quality. Excessive picking during the run causes frequent press shutdowns to allow for cleaning.

Picking can occur with any type of paper, but it is most common on uncoated stock—and the cheaper the sheet, the more likely that it will be "picked apart" on press. Why? Because the ink itself must have a property called "tack," which is its ability to stick to the sheet, and "tack" facilitates "picking."

As more publishers use uncoated sheets, the problem of picking is becoming more frequent. And although there are several ways to control it, many printers have no experience with these lower-quality stocks—consequently, their first reaction might be "This stuff won't run."

•*Solution:* Before you try to trace the problem, then, you should determine whether the paper itself is different from what the printer normally runs. If he runs coated, slick sheets 99 percent of the time and you ask him to run an uncoated, which you paid little for, you can expect start-up problems.

If no test data are available on the sheets (many printers perform tests on all sheets delivered to them), have them done—preferably at an independent lab. Compare the results with the paper mill's specifications; if they are far apart, you've probably got a bad lot of paper. If the tests show that your paper has the proper picking resistance, it's back to the printer.

The tack of ink can be tested and controlled. Your printer surely knows the tack of his current ink, but it is quite possible (and probable in this case) that a different tacking ability will be required to print the sheet that has been subject to picking.

So it is possible that you can solve this problem with minimal hassle—unless the tests showed that the paper was well off the specs. In that case, go for a credit from the mill. But if the printer was at fault, he should eat the loss and chalk it up to experience.

•*Prevention:* Again, it pays to keep in constant touch with your printer. If he's curious enough to do tests on all the stock that he runs, you should be curious enough to monitor the results. Paper is extensively tested for several variables at certain plants, while others wait until a problem occurs on press. The above example will not happen to you if you know that your printer will not go to press with a high-picking paper. He would spot the trouble ahead of time and save you the worry. However, if your printer doesn't have the ability or inclination to test your paper before running it, you should ask for representative samples to be sent to you or to a lab and get the testing done yourself.

Paper's bad side

One of the most baffling problems that the newcomer sees in the pressroom is the "bad side" of paper—a situation discussed at the end of the last chapter. As said, most paper machines do not produce the same finish on both sides of the sheet. And whether you purchase paper directly or not, this effect can confound you at first.

PAPER PROBLEMS

Uncoated sheets have the most pronounced top-to-bottom difference when produced on any of the older paper machines in the country. The "felt" side tends to have more fibers on the surface, while the "wire" side is smoother. The result is that full-color printing will look better on the wire side. These differences can also show up with black-and-white printing, but it is usually not as noticeable.

Coated stocks can also have felt and wire-side differences, although the effect is usually not as pronounced. When it does occur, it can be hard to spot.

Imagine doing a press okay with your printer and having great difficulty getting anything on one side of the sheet to meet your expectations. Then, when you're about to give up, a roll change is made (using a specific type of roll-change machine), and suddenly the "bad" side looks good, and the "good" side looks bad. This invariably indicates a sheet with a pronounced problem with "wire" and "felt" sides.

This situation cannot be corrected at press side without using a different lot of paper. But it will, if it occurs frequently, tell you that you are buying a bad sheet of paper and that you will have to move up in price and quality.

Of course, this brief introduction to paper problems isn't conclusive. There are hundreds of variables involved in the manufacture of paper, and each has its own subtle effect when the job reaches press. Just keep in mind that for each area in which paper can cause a problem, it already has. Pre-press tests can identify many such problems. Then on-press samples can be pulled for subsequent examination by the paper supplier or a laboratory.

If and when you are confronted with a major or consistent problem, I advise you to contact either an independent paper consultant, the paper mill, or the quality control department at the printing plant—maybe all three. With their combined knowledge, you will at least learn how to avoid such problems in the future.□

THE WAR ON WASTE

Several years ago, a graphics arts industry group thought up the term "War on Waste" (WOW), and the name has stuck ever since. Basically, WOW is concerned with paper waste, particularly in those cases where the customer furnishes paper to the printer.

Ten years ago, it wasn't uncommon to see a roll-tender (the person who feeds paper into a web press) strip away the outside one-quarter inch from every roll. And if he (she) had any question about making the next splice, he'd simply strip away some more until the roll looked smooth.

Now, it's not uncommon to see a paper handler examine each individual layer of paper that he takes from the roll, making sure that what goes in the waste bin is, in fact, scrap. And, at the other end of the press, the person in charge is highly aware of when the job is of "acceptable commercial quality," and when the counter is stopped in order to regain color or registration. The WOW program, when it's developed and accepted in a printing plant, can have dramatic effects. Total waste of 18 percent might be cut to 13 percent, with everyone benefiting.

Well, everyone should benefit, but do they? Take a look at the first-run skid. At what point is the decision being made to save? Is it made too soon? If it is, the first-run load may not be acceptable to you; it may look more like the scrap you've seen going to the shredder. Which means you're not benefiting—you're losing.

The only way to get a real feel for this is to arrange, in a friendly manner, to watch the job on press for several production cycles. All printers and all pressmen are unique, and the decision of when and where to "save" varies from one to the next.

If that's not practical, or if you want to go a bit further, you can try the "time-stamped" sample technique. Many printers use this as a matter of routine for internal quality control, and just as many customers are unaware of it. Here's how it works: The pressmen take sample signatures (folded sections) each hour or each 5,000 impressions (or more or less, depending on the situation). Each signature is stamped with a timeclock in the pressroom, and the total run is noted. (A sample might read "March 9, 18,600, 8:35 p.m.) If your printer already uses this trick, he shouldn't object to supplying you with a full set of samples taken during the run.

True, you have no way of knowing whether the samples were really taken at the time stated, but if you can't trust your printer to be honest about this, you've got more problems than we can possibly discuss here.

After you're satisfied that the printer's WOW program isn't costing you quality, what can you do to save money? One of the simplest things you can do is to get involved in an incentive program. Keeping in mind that quality normally comes first, and realizing that printers are just people who need some sort of motivation to do a good job, it's easy to see how these programs can provide a mutual incentive for printer and customer to reduce consumption of customer-supplied paper.

CHAPTER 55

An incentive program is based, first of all, on thorough breakouts of how much paper the printer has used in the past and how much he is using during current production. Say, for example, that your magazine (catalog or book) project has been realistically estimated to consume 500 tons of paper annually (based on prior use and down-to-earth current consumption).

With various paper-saving techniques, assume that the printer uses 490 tons of paper during a production year. With a WOW agreement, that 10-ton saving will be shared equally between the printer and customer. If the printer supplied the paper, that means the buyer will pay for more paper than was actually consumed. The printer pockets the cost of five tons, while the customer, in effect, does the same. Without the incentive to reduce consumption, the customer would have paid for the full 500 tons of paper (probably).

If the paper was supplied by the customer, the situation still works: He (she) can give half the savings to the printer in either paper or money.

Now comes the real saving: For the next production cycle, the consumption estimate is rewritten. The new standard will be 490 tons —and the customer is almost guaranteed to save a lot more during subsequent years of production. (Some printers reduce the estimate by only half the savings in order to compensate for "accidental" underconsumption. It varies from plant to plant, but if you can win a full reduction—that is, an estimate fully lowered to the actual paper savings, you'll be dollars ahead.)

During the second year, then, the standard is 490 tons. For the printer to make any money on the incentive program, he must work much harder to lower consumption. Eventually (after, say, three or four years of usage reductions) the pattern should show little activity unless technical advances or equipment changes make more savings possible. For example, a new press could mean an automatic 3 percent to 5 percent further savings.

Again, be very conscious of quality. Know what you'll accept before you enter into a WOW incentive program, and monitor your product closely. And as you move into the subsequent years, keep in mind that reductions in usage will be harder for the printer to achieve. Also remember that a "good quality" first year on the program doesn't ensure that your product won't slip as production goals become more elusive.□

THE BINDERY

When a magazine is printed via the sheetfed method, it exits the pressroom the same way it entered—as a stack of paper sheets. It then must be folded into signatures, a task that is considered a bindery function. For that matter, any handling of the printed sheet after it exits the pressroom falls into the bindery area.

Web presses have, in a sense, a piece of bindery machinery hanging on their delivery ends. Rather than wind the paper back onto a roll, the folder arranges the moving paper into cut-and-folded press signatures.

In either case, before a magazine is actually bound or assembled, the portions of the magazine are sent to the binder as signatures, as shown in Illustrations 131–135. The bindery function will collect these signatures in their proper sequence and attach them together, along with the cover and any insert cards destined for the magazine.

There are only two common binding methods for magazines today: saddle and perfect. Let's first discuss saddle stitching (or stapling, which is what "stitching" means).

Saddle binding

Again referring to Illustration 131, assume that this signature represents 16 pages of a magazine. The magazine will be composed of

The web press delivers a folded product called a signature. It may be composed of four, eight, 12, 16, 20, 24, or 32 pages.

(131)

The signature is delivered with a "lip" or "lap" or, to put it more simply, it is folded off-center. This allows mechanical fingers to open the signature.

LIP OR LAP

(132)

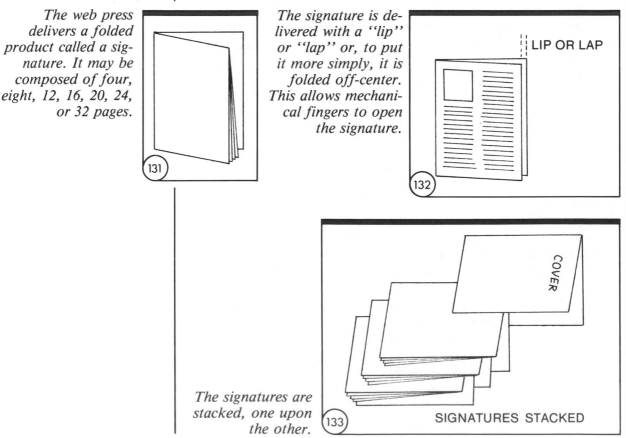

COVER

The signatures are stacked, one upon the other.

(133)

SIGNATURES STACKED

298

three of these signatures, plus a four-page cover signature.

You can imagine that if, as suggested by Illustration 133, these signatures must be opened at their centers and placed one on top of the other (thrown onto the saddle, so to speak), then there must be some way of grabbing them. This is done with mechanical hands that are called grippers.

The grippers need something to grab, of course. So in folding the signatures, either on press (web) or off-line (on a folding machine after sheetfed printing), either the latter half or the front half of the signature will have a "lip" or "lap." You can simulate this lip by simply folding a sheet of paper slightly off center: One half will be slightly wider than the other.

It is this lip (Illustration 132) that allows the grippers to grab the signature, open it up, and throw it on the "rail," which is sort of a conveyor belt on the saddle stitcher.

So, the magazine proceeds to be formed as a collection of signatures, one being tossed on another (Illustration 133). When it has all of its parts, it is stitched, or stapled (Illustration 134).

Finally, the three unstapled edges of the magazine are trimmed with a series of blades, resulting in the finished magazine (Illustration 135). It can now be labeled, or wrapped and labeled, or packed and shipped.

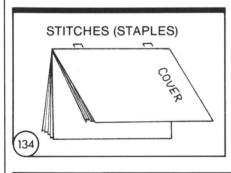

STITCHES (STAPLES)

COVER

134

Staples—or more technically, wire stitches—hold the magazine together.

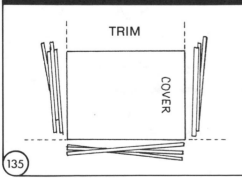

TRIM

COVER

135

After stitching, the magazine is trimmed on three sides. In many cases, the same machine that performs all this activity will now apply a mailing label, stack a quantity of magazines, and tie them for mailing.

Perfect binding

In perfect binding, the signatures are not opened and stacked on each other. Rather, the signatures are placed side to side and held together by mechanical clamps, as shown in Illustration 136. If there

THE BINDERY

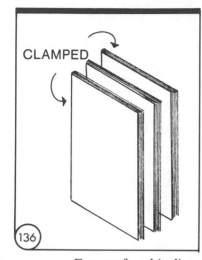

136

For perfect binding, a lip or lap isn't necessary, because the signatures need not be opened prior to binding. They are clamped together.

is to be a separate cover signature (as shown in Illustrations 133/134 in the saddle example), it is not applied at this time.

Next, rotating blades (called skives) slice the folded edge of the signatures completely off (Illustration 137). Were it not for the clamps at this stage, you'd have a mess of pretty loose signatures. After skiving, devices called "roughers" (not shown in the illustration) grind away at the smooth skive cut to prepare the edge for an application of glue.

In Illustration 138, the cover is being glued to the assembly of

Blades, called the skives, slice about 3/16" off the signatures while the clamps hold them together.

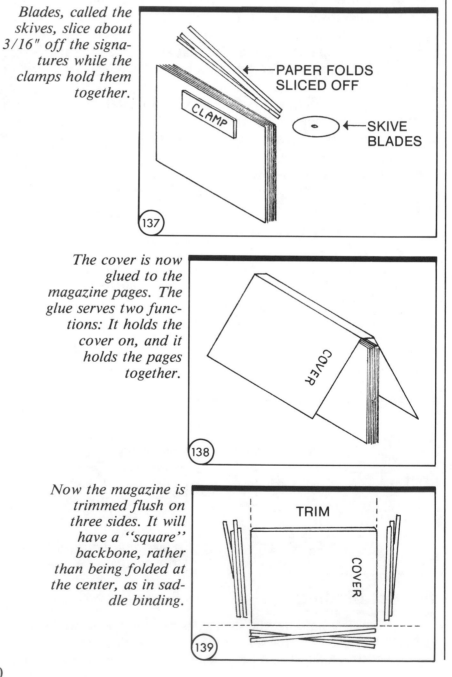

137

PAPER FOLDS
SLICED OFF

CLAMP

SKIVE
BLADES

The cover is now glued to the magazine pages. The glue serves two functions: It holds the cover on, and it holds the pages together.

COVER

138

Now the magazine is trimmed flush on three sides. It will have a "square" backbone, rather than being folded at the center, as in saddle binding.

TRIM

COVER

139

signatures. In perfect binding, the cover is always delivered to the binder flat rather than folded. The equipment is designed to accept only flat covers, which it folds during application to the body of the magazine.

Finally, in Illustration 139, the book is trimmed in a similar manner to the saddle magazine.

By the way, if you are curious about why perfect binding is so called, it was merely a vain reflection of its original inventors. They thought it was that good.

Some common aspects

These two bindery methods have a few mechanical points in common—for example, pockets. A pocket is the section of a binder that holds a stack of the same signature, ready to be bound. Generally speaking, a given binder has a limited number of pockets.

To you, this can be a limitation. Suppose you have a magazine composed of 10 eight-page signatures, plus a cover. That would require a total of 11 bindery pockets. But if the machine happened to have only nine pockets, you would have a problem.

In saddle binding, that problem can be circumvented by doing a "precollation," which is nothing more than simply stitching several signatures together so that they can all be placed in one pocket. In the above example, we could stitch three of the eight-page signatures together, then put those three in one pocket, and get by with the total available nine pockets. Such a practice is rarely economical because it means that, for practical purposes, the magazine makes two passes through the binder: one for precollation and one for final assembly.

On the perfect binder, it is not as easy as making the above fix. Putting two signatures together prior to binding would have effects reaching as far back as the preparation and printing stages. Although it can be done, it is not so often a problem for this reason: Perfect binders tend to have more pockets than saddle binders because they were designed for larger magazines in the first place. So unless you have an unduly large magazine, you will not likely tax the upper limits of a perfect binder.

Another area of commonality is the method of inserting cards (reader service, bingo cards, etc.) and preprinted inserts (such as supplied advertising material).

Illustration 140 shows a saddle-stitching operation that includes a small, four-page insert card. This card could be handled by the machinery in one of two ways. If fed from a normal binder pocket, it would have a lip (as would a full-size signature) and would be picked up by the grippers and tossed onto the preceding signature. Or, it may be fed from a "card feeder," a device that takes a flat four-page insert (an unfolded, four-page card in this example) and folds it as it places it on the saddle.

Why bother with the card feeder? The answer relates to the

CHAPTER 56

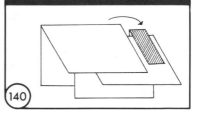

In saddle binding, an insert card appearing in the front of the magazine means there will be one appearing in the back.

301

THE BINDERY

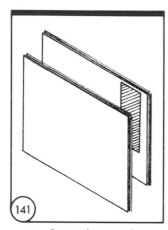

Inserting an insert card into a perfect-bound magazine is simply a matter of locating it between any two signatures. It doesn't create the front-back problem inherent to saddle binding.

number of pockets. Many saddle stitchers have a pocket limit, which can be problematic for many of the printer's customers. The card feeder allows the binder to use all or most of its conventional pockets for actual magazine signatures. The feeder, more or less portable, can not only be moved to any position on the binder, but also can be interchanged between similar binders. This also allows much flexibility at the printing plant and lower cost for the customer because precollation can often be avoided when the printer has a suitable number of card feeders.

In addition, the card feeder can eliminate the folding cost, which would have been incurred had the cards been prepared for insertion at a normal bindery pocket.

Perfect bindery insertion of cards is handled just like any other material in the magazine. The card is placed in a pocket and fed along with the signatures. As you can already see, there is a key difference between perfect and saddle inserts: The perfect binder is inherently capable of inserting a two-page insert (Illustration 141), while the saddle stitcher requires a four-page insert. There are ways to circumvent this limitation on the saddle stitcher (called "tipping," or sometimes the gluing of a bindery strip to a sheet of paper), but they are never inexpensive. These differences will be discussed in more detail shortly.

Another common area is that these binders "jog" the magazine. Jogging, in Illustrations 140 and 141, means that the signatures and inserts will all be shuffled into alignment, the same way you would align one side of a stack of dissimilar sheets of paper.

Look at the two illustrations: Is the insert card being jogged to the top or the bottom of the book? You can't tell.

Depending on how the signatures were printed, it could be either way. In other words, the insert cards will be mechanically restricted on the binder, and you may literally have printed the book upside down, thereby reversing the jog. Your printer has the information you need on this.

But it does matter in either case: If your binder jogs to the top, your insert cards will appear there, and you will need to order them with the additional paper that will be trimmed at the top of the book. Similarly, if you jog to the bottom, your advertisers may want to know that, and your insert cards will need excess paper at the bottom to be trimmed.

Many printers (to make things complicated) can offer either a top or bottom jog for the signatures, and also a "floating" position for insert cards. In this case, you would probably not have a very accurate idea of just where on the page the card would fall, but neither would you have a requirement for having the cards printed with additional paper for bindery trim.

That, in brief, is the simple comparison between saddle binding and perfect binding. If only it could be that simple. True, the main effect to the casual observer is that perfect binding has a backbone and saddle does not.

But the bindery has a powerful rippling effect: It can dictate both major and subtle changes felt all the way back to the preparation stage, and can impact on paper consumption, press costs, and virtually every other area discussed in this book. The next chapter will briefly explain just why the binder has such power, and in the process will complete this general discussion of the bindery function. □

CHAPTER 56

SADDLE AND PERFECT BINDING COMPARED

Of all technical areas of magazine production, bindery probably suffers the most from misinformation. You may have heard any or all of the following: Perfect binding is more expensive than saddle binding. Saddle binding is much faster than perfect binding. Perfect binding is suited only to very high-page-count magazines.

Although the reasoning behind these statements is sound and based on good logic, that logic is nevertheless narrowminded and overlooks many other variables in magazine production. In this section, the bindery question will be approached with an open mind. As a result, after reading through the information, you should be able to make a truly intelligent bindery choice for your own magazine based on total price and total effect.

Keep in mind that the differences must be discussed as independent variables. However, your final choice of binding method will be based on the total effect of all variables. It will be your job to identify priorities and make the choice.

It is often said that perfect binding is a desirable option only when the size of the magazine becomes too much for the saddle stitcher. The reasoning here is that saddle binding is more aesthetically attractive than perfect binding. (That decision, of course, must be left to the observer.) The reasoning also assumes that perfect binders cannot handle the smaller page counts. That is not true, but again may be related to how a perfect-bound, low-page-count magazine happens to please the eye.

There are magazine plants doing perfect-bound products with as few as 32 body pages, plus the cover. The visual impact of the backbond is not the fat, square-finish that you would expect—but the binding method, in these cases, is not selected for visual appeal but rather for the total economy of the magazine.

Regarding high and low limits, there are no hard and fast figures. However, it is common for the average printer to carefully consider whether a magazine with 200 or more pages will suitably saddle-bind. At that page count, several things happen. For example, the binder pockets are pushed to their maximum and the other binder components taxed.

So, generally speaking, virtually any magazine could be perfect bound. But some magazines, because of their high number of pages, are more suited to perfect than saddle. The perfect binder was designed to handle high page counts; the saddle binder the opposite. While a 360-page saddle-bound magazine is an improbability, a 32-page perfect and a 360-page perfect can be logical possibilities.

Cost

The subject of cost is brought up rather early to make a point. When you hear the old line, "Perfect binding is more costly," regard it as no more than rumor. Although it is generally true that the mechanical charges for perfect binding are higher than those for saddle, so what? Bindery costs have routinely been looked at as independent of the other printing functions. But they are not. They are closely related to all other activities, and each affects the other. The cost of perfect binding must be evaluated after the costs of printing, paper, ink, and so forth have been considered.

Speed

Here there may be a case for the saddle binder. Depending on your deadline needs, saddle binding can be faster than perfect binding, and thus give you better turnaround.

However, when we discuss critical deadlines, we are talking about magazines that are timed to the hour, such as a newsweekly, which might have severe distribution problems if it left the plant eight hours late.

For a monthly magazine, speed would not be as critical a factor. Then too, the printer may have an adequate number of perfect binders, allowing him to run the magazine "across" several machines, literally doubling or tripling the speed at which it would run on a single binder. But one perfect binder sitting next to one saddle binder will run more slowly than the saddle. In fact, saddle binding is mechanically faster than perfect binding, sometimes by 50 percent to 100 percent. This may change as perfect binders are improved, but as of today the comparison is valid.

Cover printing and costs

At last we get to a clear-cut difference between binders. On a perfect-bound magazine, the cover must be taken care of as a separate item. It is normally printed either on a sheetfed or sheeting-type web. Then it is cut and probably scored along the areas where the spine will be folded. This cutting and folding itself is an off-line procedure, meaning that the press cannot do it in one pass. This alone adds time and money to the job.

More important for comparison purposes, at least for some magazines, is that a perfect-bound magazine cannot be a self-cover item. Look again at Illustrations 140 and 141. The saddle magazine might well have the outer 16 pages function as body and cover pages. In other words, it is possible to print the cover right on the outer signature and avoid handling it as a separate item. Keep in mind, however, that not all magazines could tolerate a self cover: The more pages in the magazine, the more important the protective, heavier outer cover paper.

But let it be said again: The perfect-bound magazine requires a separate cover. On top of that, the cover preparation is much more expensive than the preparation of either a conventional saddle-

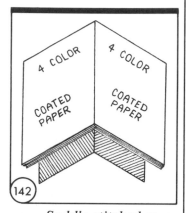

Saddle-stitched magazines can have the problem of running many four-color pages up front, thus creating many opportunities to use four-color in the back of the book. However, if there is no need or use for color in the back of the book, it can be wasted.

stitched cover, which can be web-printed and folded, or the less-conventional saddle-stitched self cover, which is in fact no cover at all.

Paper and color distribution

Illustrations 142 and 143 show the very significant differences in the distribution of both the type of paper used in the magazine and the color usage on that paper (ink).

In the saddle magazine, front-back distribution is the rule. Because all signatures are equally distributed in both the front and back of the magazine, the respective halves of the book are similar. That means that if you need a lot of four-color space in the front of the magazine to accommodate advertising and editorial material, that same four-color distribution will be available in the back of the magazine (where you normally may tend to run only black-and-white material). It also means that if you need coated stock in the front of the book, you will also get it in the back, where you may not need it (for classified ads, simple black-and-white ads, etc.).

This can directly affect both printing and paper costs. Full-color printing is generally much more expensive than black-and-white printing, particularly in the press makeready stage. Often a saddle magazine is designed by the front half only—say, 12 pages needed for four-color advertising, four pages for four-color editorial, meaning 16 pages of four-color are needed. Then, the back of the magazine, with the same distribution, often goes underused (or the advertisers who find themselves back there complain).

At worst, this means that some magazines find themselves paying for up to twice the four-color makereadies they really need. With a color makeready sometimes twice as costly as a black-and-white makeready, this can be a very significant expense—and one that saddle binding cannot truly solve.

With reference again to paper distribution, a similar limitation exists. The saddle magazine cannot put ''cheap'' paper at the back of the magazine, where it might be useful, without putting it in the front, where it usually isn't wanted. Therefore, you tend to see most saddle magazines making limited use of alternative paper stock and inefficient use of color makereadies. This is not to say that this variable stands alone, either. It merely suggests that, for some publishers, this particular negative aspect of saddle binding is outweighed by other factors.

Perfect binding has an entirely different and more versatile way of handling color and paper. In Illustration 143, you can see that while the front 16 or 32 pages of this magazine are on coated stock running in four-color, the next signature is black and white on uncoated paper (generally less expensive). You can arrange any usage of color and paper by picking where you want each signature inserted. It's that simple.

As you can probably already see, the ability of the perfect binder to dictate press makereadies and paper selection ("cheap" versus expensive) could be important. Suppose a magazine does need to put advertisers up front, and they do run in color, but the balance of the book is largely black and white? The perfect binder would allow such an arrangement without penalty. There would be no wasted paper or color makereadies in the back of the book.

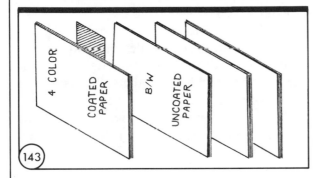

Insert card material

Sticking with our illustrations, consider a supplied two-page insert from an advertiser, which arrives as single sheets of paper trimmed to 8-1/2″ x 11″. If this insert belongs in a saddle magazine, it would have to be glued to the front of one of the existing signatures. This is an off-binder procedure that could cost from $10 to $20 per thousand applications—and that only if the printer could do it at all.

Or, if the insert is a four-pager and has to run in order (four pages in a row), it would either be restricted to the center of the magazine or have to be tipped to another signature.

The perfect binder can perform either insertion without penalty. A two-page insert is handled just like any other signature and can fall between any other two signatures. A four-pager, handled no differently, can appear between any other signatures and keeps all four pages in order.

Now, let's suppose that we don't have full-page inserts, but small insert cards. The saddle magazine must put something in the back of the book if it puts something in the front. Sometimes, this is simply a blank flap of paper, but more often, the magazine production and ad people decide to use another card—perhaps another advertising card or even a "filler" subscription card.

Again, the perfect binder has an easier time with the single-page card. If only one card is needed, only one is inserted. Nothing deeper in the magazine changes because a card is being inserted up front. However, what if you actually need both cards? In that case, the perfect binder would suffer because each card would require a pocket, and pockets cost money. Thus, depending on your particular needs, either binder can be a winning or losing proposition.

CHAPTER 57

The perfect-bound magazine tends to be able to use both color and paper effectively. Creating a special black-and-white section (for directory listings, as an example) doesn't automatically put a black-and-white section elsewhere in the magazine, as would occur in saddle binding.

SADDLE AND PERFECT BINDING COMPARED

Aesthetics

Now, to a silly question. Which looks better, saddle binding or perfect binding? The saddle magazine offers a flatter book for the reader. When it is opened, it lies relatively evenly on a table. The perfect-bound magazine can never lie truly flat because it is squarely glued at the spine. So what's the answer? Some people like saddle and some like perfect. There seems to be a heftier feel to one of them, but people disagree as to which one.

Speaking technically, though, when a photo is to print across two pages, the saddle book allows a more controlled presentation because it isn't so violently bent open at the center. Material at the gutter (center) is more visible on the saddle book, which allows more of the photo to be seen and is easier on the viewer's eyes.

The question—"Which looks better?"—should definitely be put to the magazine's designer or art director. The answer could very well dictate just how a spread is laid out.

Stripping effects

At first glance, you might not think that a change in bindery could affect stripping costs to any significant extent. But it is possible and worth looking into.

If you read the prep section, you know that two full-bleed ads that print on the same printer spread must be "built up" into final film. This is the norm. In some cases, multiple plate burns are an option, but many printers avoid the practice.

Perfect binding never requires body pages to truly butt at the fold. Why? Because the fold is sliced off during binding. This means that there is a clear space of paper between any two pages on the same printer spread.

It could mean, then, that the stripping department could complete the flat stripping procedure without having to duplicate film because of the butt-at-fold (gutter) inherent to saddle stripping.

In a few cases, it is possible that perfect binding could eliminate the need for advertising film buildups and contacts, possibly saving thousands of dollars in a given magazine. This particular benefit isn't available to all magazines, though, and requires that you investigate to see whether there would, in fact, be a significant (or any) cost benefit based on how your prep house or printer handles your work.

Physical effects

There are, finally, several physical differences between the perfect-bound and saddle-bound product.

"Lofting" describes a saddle-stitched magazine's tendency to stay somewhat open at the fold. In other words, it won't lie truly flat; there will be a little air where the pages meet.

This normally doesn't bother anyone, but a magazine with a high page count tends to loft a lot and may thus fall over when placed on a newsstand. Similarly, this physical aspect will make the magazine hard to trim properly. When a magazine is thick enough, the saddle binder will squish it slightly out of shape as it applies pressure before trimming. This could give the magazine a slightly off-square trim, with the front of the book having a different dimension than the back (or other slightly noticeable effect).

Creep or shingling

The last aspect of binding to discuss is an oddity for some magazines, but of concern for others because it has a slight potential to create some paper waste. It is called "creep" or "shingling."

Illustrations 144 and 145 show saddle-bound and perfect-bound magazines from the top edge. The saddle magazine requires that the outer paper, exaggerated in this drawing, travel further to get from point A to point B than the inner paper travels from point C to D. What does this mean?

It means the outer signatures, when laid flat, will have a total width that is greater than twice the page size. You would think that by trimming a magazine at eight inches, any two pages together would measure 16 inches, but the cover in this case will have its two pages total more than 16 inches because of the "creep" or "shingling" effect.

In the same way, the inner pages will total less than 16 inches. The truth is, there are very few pages in the saddle-stitched book that are the same dimension.

The perfect-bound magazine, on the other hand, trims all pages to the same dimension.

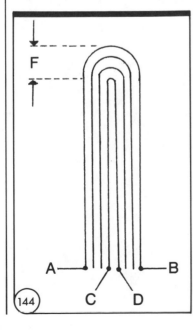

Saddle-bound magazines have "shingling" or "creeping" effects, as shown in the end view of a magazine. Because of the fold at F, the pages will trim at different widths. Pages A and B will be wider than pages C and D.

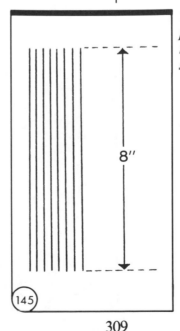

The pages in a perfect-bound magazine are all the same width.

Visual effects of the two methods of binding can be noticeable. In a sample 200-page coated-stock magazine shown in Illustration 144, the dimension at F is one-eighth-of-an-inch, meaning the center (inner) pages of the magazine are one-eighth-inch narrower than the outer pages. In the stripping department, this must be accounted for; the pages of a saddle-stitched book must be pulled in toward the center.

At the extreme, if a magazine is very thick—say, with a one-quarter-inch dimension at F—you might want to compute the amount of excess paper needed for the cover and outer signatures versus the amount of paper needed for the center signatures. In this case, it might be wise for the production director to order different width paper rolls (for a standard web) and possibly achieve another percent or more of paper savings.

Bindery summary

By now you should be getting the picture. In some ways, bindery is the simplest aspect of magazine printing. But because it can affect the economy of all other aspects—press usage, paper roll width, stripping procedures, and makeready costs—it needs to be handled in a logical, systematic, thoughtful way.

It is not easy to answer the question: How expensive would perfect binding be for my magazine? To come up with a solid, logical figure, you would have to look at how a change in bindery would affect your unique magazine—not mine, and not your competitor's.

The preceding points are a good beginning for an honest and productive evaluation of your bindery needs and costs.◻

SECTION IX:
IN PURSUIT OF QUALITY:
PROBLEMS
AND SOLUTIONS

DEFINING QUALITY IN PRINTING

Are one hundred minor irritations the equivalent of one major headache? The question comes up often when checking the performance of a printer. One month, you may have a few eyesores in an issue, along with a generally inferior printed piece. Next month, bang: An entire insert might be missing.

There are also the gray areas: Exactly what is a serious defect in a printed magazine? Which errors by the printer should result in a credit, and which should be thrown on the back burner?

And here's a critical question: Just how does your printer learn what is really important in the production of your magazine—what your priorities are? He has to be able to distinguish your real concerns from general, routine complaining. And he has to be able to do this *before* your magazine goes into production.

In a U.S. Government Printing Office Technical Report (No. 19, February 1979) is the Equivalent Defect Rating System (which I stumbled upon) that includes a five-level definition of quality. Rather than use it in its very general nature, I adapted the report more specifically for magazine production people and their publishers. The result covers the following areas of printing quality: printing; color separations and proofs; defects; and guidelines for the bindery. Revenue loss is a necessarily related subject, and needs to be considered as well.

Each of the first four areas should be discussed with your printer before your magazine goes into production. Such a discussion gives your printer a clear understanding of what you want, and consequently increases the chances that that is what you will get.

Printing

In a discussion or analysis of printing, the following levels of quality will apply.

•*Level 1, Best quality:* Requires the best available materials, printing, workmanship and quality control, and commensurate production time. All films to be inspected and certified before printing. Maximum fidelity in detail, color, and resolution to original copy and/or films is required. (Example products in this category: 300-line halftones, reproductions of detailed engravings, and so on.)

•*Level 2, Better quality:* Requires high quality printing, materials, workmanship and quality control, and commensurate production time. Close fidelity and resolution to original copy and/or film is required. (Example: 150-line halftones and exceptional printing.)

•*Level 3, Good quality:* Requires above average materials, printing, workmanship and quality control, and commensurate production time. Above average fidelity and resolution to original copy and/or film. (Example: Halftones up to 150-lines and crisp, clean four-color printing.)

•*Level 4, Basic quality:* Requires average quality printing, ma-

314

terials, workmanship, and commensurate production time. Reasonable fidelity and resolution to original copy and/or film. (Example: Up to 133-line halftones, pleasant-looking process color.)

•*Level 5, Duplication quality:* Requires no information loss from original. (Example: Xerographic copies, ''instant'' printing.)

For most of us, levels two through four are the only options. There are a handful of magazines in the field that do indeed have Level 5 quality, but they pay the price with a shoddy-looking newspaper appearance. There are even a few at the bottom end that border on suffering information loss because of poor quality of printing.

Color separations and proofs

This second area of quality rating applies to color separations and proofs. Although not in the Government Printing Office report, this three-level system is used, with a variety of modifications, by many buyers and sellers across the country.

•*Level 1, Matched color:* I hesitate to use the word ''perfect'' when describing matched color because there is no such thing. Four-color printing will not perfectly match original dyes in photographs. Process printing simply doesn't have the range.

The match can be quite close, though.

In asking for a Level 1 color separation, you should expect the subject to be separated as an individual piece (no grouping or ganging separations). The film should be inspected, proofed, corrected (with either dot-etching or reseparating), and proofed again. Then either a press proof, Cromalin, Transfer Key or a Match Print should be made. Press inks or proofing pigments and papers would be the same as the finished piece.

•*Level 2, Good color:* Here you could expect the subjects to be group separated, but with special attention to compatibility and quality control. The color shifts resulting from the group separation technique would be largely compensated for in the correcting stage. It is unlikely that a second set of corrected proofs would be made, and just as unlikely that a press proof would be pulled.

•*Level 3, Pleasing color:* As one publisher aptly put it, ''Make the sky blue and the grass green.'' Pleasing color often goes totally uncorrected unless the balance is so dramatically wrong that the photo is unprintable. The proofing method could be Color Keys or Transfer Keys, both of which are made directly from the separation negatives. (Note: Since this manuscript was submitted, DuPont introduced CromaCheck, which is similar in quality and price to Color Keys.)

Pleasing color is suitable for many magazines that have neither the need nor the desire for better quality. Publishers using newsprint, for example, are already in the marginal quality reproduction range and may have little to gain by correcting their separations.

With these two quality levels in mind—color separations and proofs, and printing—let's look at a practical example of how they can be used.

Fred publishes a magazine that runs hundreds of photos per year, all of which are small pictures of new products (machinery, tools, and so on). He sees no reason to spend the proverbial arm-and-a-leg to ensure that a tractor is printed with the proper hue of yellow or that a company logotype is "Crimson Red." Yet he will not tolerate plugged or wash-out editorial halftones, poorly trimmed magazines, or any other noticeable printing errors. So, Fred asks for Level 3 color separations and proofs, but Level 2 printing. He *is* willing to pay a premium for a nicely printed product, but *not* for elaborate work on his separations.

Classifying defects

The third quality rating applies to defects. Again, I have adapted the GPO report for magazine or catalog usage.

•*Critical defect:* This is a defect that renders the product unfit for its intended use. Information loss is the key factor here. Examples would be missing components (signatures, insert cards, etc.) or unreadable material.

•*Major defect:* This type of defect is one that would be noticed by readers (for example, grossly poor color balance) and would likely result in complaints (from readers and/or advertisers). Nonetheless, a major defect does not make the product unfit for its intended use.

•*Minor defect:* In this case, the problem would be noticed by the average reader or advertiser, but would not result in complaints.

Guidelines for the bindery: Trim variations

The fourth quality rating defines the guidelines for the bindery. Regarding trimming deviations, the GPO report suggests the following rating system for "Good Quality" products.

•*Critical defect:* Variation that results in information loss.
•*Major defect:* Variation greater than one-eighth of an inch.
•*Minor defect:* Variation from one-sixteenth of an inch to one-eighth of an inch.
•*No defect:* Variation of one-sixteenth of an inch or less.

Of course, you can set your own standards for bindery trim. For a magazine publisher, a trim of one-eighth inch too large could result in a tremendous increase in postage costs. Thus, you might decide that any defect that adds weight to your product is critical, while any undersize trim problems are minor or major (unless they result in information loss).

316

Now, before actually using the Equivalent Defect Rating System to evaluate an issue of a magazine, let's add one more vegetable to the stew: revenue loss.

Errors that cause revenue loss

Magazine publishers have a unique problem when it comes to print quality—the unhappy advertiser. An advertisement prints poorly, the publisher gets a phone call, and the negotiations begin. It isn't unheard of for an advertiser to cancel a contract because of poor reproduction.

A situation whereby a critical defect leads to revenue loss is not limited to advertising revenue, however. What if, for example, the printer binds a publisher's insert card backward? There is no information loss, which would automatically make the mistake critical. The error might not even be noticed by the average reader (and anyway, notice by readers doesn't classify a defect as major). However, the result could be decreased revenues for the publisher if readers can't find the house ad's appropriate order card.

For rating purposes, then, any revenue loss—either potential or real—will be considered a critical defect.

Charting the system

The Equivalent Defects Rating System is based on a simple premise: Some errors are worse than others.

In the accompanying chart (Illustration 146), I've listed the various classifications of errors and added that all-important aspect of relativity. In the value column, each type of error is given a number ranging from zero to five.

By using an objective method of evaluating printers' errors, you can take a good deal of emotion out of the relationship. Note that we classify an error "noticeable by staff only" as no error at all. You might disagree with this philosophy, which basically states that "if it doesn't hurt anything, why get excited"?

Classifying Printer's Errors			
Classification	**Description**	**Example**	**Value**
Critical	Any information loss, real or potential revenue loss.	Missing page or pages; reverse type not readable; lost advertising revenue, lost subscription sales.	5
Major	Noticeable by average reader and likely to result in complaints; trim variations greater than 1/8″; complaints from advertisers.	Complaints received regarding printing, but no credits given.	1
Minor	Noticeable by average reader, but not likely to result in complaints; trim variations of 1/16″ to 1/8″.	Skin tones on photos off balance; correction inserted crooked.	.2
None	Noticeable by staff only. Trim variations of less than 1/16″; other errors.	Wrong color used in headline; photo flopped.	0

146

DEFINING QUALITY
IN PRINTING

You'll note that the bottom entry on the chart gives no weight at all to certain problems. Even though the printer may make a mistake, this system apparently lets the printer "get away with" certain mistakes. Why?

Let's be practical. You sell information. Even if your printer makes a minor mistake, such as using the wrong combination of colors for a headline, your product is hardly affected. No reader will notice the error, no information is lost, and all advertisers are happy. Why go for blood? Printers are human, too, and this rating system takes that fact into account.

In addition, the rating system itself is not designed to prove anything or to punish the printer. It is designed as a vehicle of communication for quality control. It can also be used to compare one printer to another. But it isn't intended to give you rock-solid evidence that your printer is good or bad.□

318

HOW TO RATE AN ISSUE

Now that the fundamentals of the system have been explained, you can put them to work by rating a given issue. Begin by selecting an appropriate representation of your total printed product. There are several ways to do this:

1. Have copies mailed to "dummy" addresses so that you will get a representative cross section of what your readers are seeing.

2. Work out an arrangement with your printer whereby you will receive hourly "pulls," or a single copy for every 10,000 bound, for example.

3. Take a quantity of random samples from the material shipped to you by the printer.

4. Stand in the bindery and grab a magazine every 20 minutes.

Which of these methods is best? It depends on the relationship you have with your printer (trust or no-trust), the total quantity printed, and how deeply you want to get involved in accurate quality monitoring.

The next obvious question: How many random copies do you need? In the original government version of rating printing, the author suggested 100 pieces. However, because magazines have different press runs, 100 may be either too many or too few. In addition, you will have time constraints to work with. Your objective is to select a sample large enough to provide an accurate summary of quality, but small enough to be manageable (because you or an employee will be critically evaluating each magazine, page by page). For practical purposes, a random sampling of 50 books seems appropriate.

A sample review

Having collected 50 magazines that represent the overall quality of your magazine, get comfortable. Now comes the hard work. You will need to examine each printed page of each magazine (partial insert cards count as a full page). Let's take a walk through one of the 50 copies.

The first thing we notice is that the cover is slightly out of register and the color balance is out of whack. This counts as two errors. But because neither error is likely to result in complaints and because no information is lost, we assign two minor errors (total: .4 points) to the cover. (Later, we may want to go over each book with the printer.)

Next, we notice that a four-page signature is missing—a critical information loss, to be sure. Each missing page is given a rating of five, for a total of 20 points. The missing signature is not counted as a single mistake because all errors are later summarized and converted into errors per thousand pages, not errors per magazine.

Moving along, we notice (just as we described earlier) that a special insert card has been inserted backward. Readers won't have a convenient way of ordering our super-saver on Florida oranges, and by next issue the oranges will be rotten. We'll lose money, so the error gets a critical rating of five. Because the back half of the card didn't relate to anything in particular, it gets no error rating at all.

Pages 32 through 39, along with an equal number of pages in the back of the book (it's saddle stitched), were apparently folded poorly. Each page is positioned slightly more than one-sixteenth-of-an-inch high. The 16 pages get a total error rating of 3.2 (.2 x 16) (each counts as a minor error).

Fortunately, that's all we notice in our evaluation of this particular copy, and there are only 49 more to check out before proceeding to the next step!

Summary report

At long last, we have 50 random magazines, each with notes on the pages with errors and each with a summary clipped to the cover. (Keeping a chart of the errors would be easier than keeping the magazines themselves, but then you'd have nothing to show your printer.) The final step is to total all the error ratings and divide that number by the number of pages reviewed (in thousands).

The first copy that we rated had a total rating of 28.6 relative (or equivalent) points. The other 49 copies may be higher or lower, but assuming that each one had the same total rating of 28.6, the final tally would be 1,430 points.

We then determine the total pages reviewed. If each book had 120 pages, the review totals 6,000 pages. Divide 1,430 by six (the number of thousands of pages reviewed). Finally, we have the number that we've been shooting for all along: This magazine has an Equivalent Defect Rating of 240 per thousand pages.

That number, standing alone, is useless. It merely tells you that, based on all the viewing, rating, and adding just done, that particular printing had a score of 240. How do you make the "useless" number valuable? The secret is to develop an Equivalent Defect Rating System and use it month after month. If the prior issue had a score of 116, and the one before that a score of 77, something—quite obviously—is wrong.

This system, as we said earlier, isn't perfect. But it is a helpful, easy-to-use tool to monitor quality. And better yet, it can be an extremely valuable tool for reducing the error rate. You'll never have to use that nebulous, wishy-washy statement: "The printer is getting worse and worse, but we don't know exactly how to nail things down."

Using the system

Now comes the communication. If you have been as objective as possible in examining the sample issues, you will have the tools to show the printer exactly what the problems are, why they are important to you, and how the score for each issue was determined.

HOW TO RATE AN ISSUE

There are several ways to use an issue's rating to communicate. The first is simply to compare grand totals.

Let's say, for example, that over a six-issue span, your magazine had Equivalent Defect Rating scores of 100, 105, 112, 121, 138, and 145. If you have been objective in your ratings—and if you have kept the 50 sample issues—there will be little doubt that quality is on the downslide.

However, as I said earlier, this system isn't intended to "punish" your printer. Don't even consider taking copies to the plant and asking for credit. Instead, use the scores to demonstrate quality in order to improve it or maintain it.

The totaled scores are an effective device that print management can use to communicate directly with those who produce the job. Poor quality isn't always the result of simple mistakes. If the general attitude in a printing plant is that "good enough" is equal to "great," for example, quality will slide. Also, it may well be that a deteriorating company morale is the reason for consistently rising Equivalent Defect scores.

The totals aren't the only tool you have, however. By keeping records of the errors, you will also be able to pinpoint specific problems. For example: Suppose your scores were on the rise because of ever increasing bindery errors. You would be able to aid the printer by identifying not only the general problem area, but also the specific machine at fault, which part of the machine to concentrate on, and possibly even which individual in the plant is making the mistake.

In addition to defining a problem area or machine, you want to watch for repetitive mistakes. Take the example of an insert card being stitched backward. If that error continued issue after issue (and kept the Equivalent Defect scores high), you'd be able to help the printer devise a correction, perhaps something as simple as a visual reminder for the absentminded card feeder in the bindery.

Keeping accurate records of the types of mistakes is very important. It becomes critical when you use the rating system to compare printers. Suppose, for example, that you are choosing between two printers with similar capabilities and you have the opportunity to develop a rating system for both. If both printers had remarkably similar total Equivalent Defect scores for several issues, and all other factors were equal, which printer would you choose? By referring to your records, you'd pick the printer with the lowest Critical Error score. It's as simple as that.

Of course, most publishers find it impossible to have their magazines printed at two different plants before making a decision. But the system can still be used if the printer will give you just a slight bit of cooperation. Simply ask permission to spend several hours at the plant—preferably in the bindery. Once there, take a quantity of random samples of another publisher's magazine as it comes off the machine, inspect it, make notes, and put it back. Look for errors such as poor registration, missing signatures or inserts, varying trim, and all the other variables we discussed. Do the same at the other plant—and voila: months or years of guesswork boiled down to a few days of observation.

How will printers react to your using a standardized system for rating quality? Ideally, they will support it. It is a far better system than most buyers use today (such as "I heard they have crummy quality, so let's print somewhere else"). Any method of objectively reviewing quality should be welcomed.

And keep in mind, the Equivalent Defect Rating System should not be used solely to criticize the quality of the finished piece. If your printer cooperates, helps you out, and reduces your headaches (all of which will show in declining Equivalent Defect ratings), be sure that you put your compliments into written form—just as you do with your complaints.□

RESOLVING
A BAD
PRINTING JOB

Regardless of how careful you are in dealing with your printer, the inevitable must occasionally occur: At some time, you won't get what you asked for. If the blame is yours—because of poor instructions or bad material—you can't expect the printer to rectify the situation. You can either pay to have the job rerun, or use it as it was produced. In either case, you take your medicine and learn from the mistake.

At other times, though, the printer will be at fault in producing an unacceptable product. The specific headache might be poor ink laydown, or a bad color match, or an accidental omission, or a backward fold, or any of a thousand other errors that can occur along the line.

Typically, the customer wants to get a fair shake. To do so, he demands some sort of compensation for the bad job. Several ways of settling up will be discussed in this chapter.

How good is good?

Simple complaints include four-color work with very poor color balance, two-color work with a bad color match, and black-and-white printing with plugged halftones or light coverage. But before you start making noises, you should consider two factors:

1. If the job was press-checked, be sure that it wasn't delivered per the okay. It has been known to happen that, after the customer's company has sent a representative to watch the job run, someone at the main office later decides the job isn't good enough. This person then files a complaint and expects action from the printer.

Obviously, if the job is delivered in the same form as it was okayed, you don't have a leg to stand on. A few of the more unscrupulous buyers realize this, but try to squeeze that extra nickel out of the supplier anyhow.

2. If the work actually is of very poor quality, you must consider what was eventually done with it. Was it delivered to readers or clients? Was the problem obvious enough to prompt complaints from advertisers? In other words, be sure the error is significant before you sit down at the negotiating table.

Assume then, that you have received a product that does warrant some kind of compensation—and that you're not playing games with the printer. What can you expect in the form of a settlement?

Reruns

Based on the assumption that you don't think the work is acceptable, the first consideration should be to scrap the material and do a rerun. Although that sounds a bit drastic, reruns have several advantages. First, they give you exactly what you wanted (and paid for!), which should make you happy. Second, your printer gains—in the long run—by producing first-class work and keeping his customers satisfied. Also, he won't have to worry that you're trying to get something for nothing. (More on reruns at the end of this chapter.)

Makegoods

There are times, though, when a rerun cannot be realistically asked for. They include the following:

•*"Aggravation-type" errors:* When an error simply doesn't warrant disposal of valuable paper, you will choose to use the job as printed.

•*Material already delivered:* If your magazine or catalog is in the mail, there's not much you can do. Mailing it a second time is useless.

•*Tight schedules:* Even though you might notice a serious problem, you don't always have time to fix it. When you're already late, the logistics of reshooting, restripping, replating, and rerunning can be just too much.

Which brings up the makegood. Basically, the makegood is an economical method of correcting an error.

Let's assume, for example, that because of some gross negligence at the print shop, a two-page, four-color ad is run with the yellow negative where the red should have been and vice versa (it's happened). If those two pages are part of a 100-page magazine, the printer would not expect to print your next 100-page job for free. But he might offer to reduce your bill by 2 percent or even print and bind an additional two pages into your next production at no charge.

Naturally, if an entire section of your book (such as a 32-pager) has a bad error that makes each page unacceptable, then you'd be talking about more pages for a makegood.

Getting a reduced price

Sometimes you won't be in a position to accept a makegood. When that occurs, consider the last resort: a cash settlement.

I consider this a last resort because it is the most abused method of settling a printing dispute. Some buyers complain about each and every job they receive. They want to get a portion of the cost knocked off for the most insignificant of problems, and they're not happy unless they see the printer grit his teeth. (I've heard of one publisher who actually "teaches" his protege that all printers are crooked and that the only way to stay in business is to take your money back any way you can.) So with that bit of editorializing out of the way, here we go.

A price reduction, like a makegood, is normally limited to the relative amount of damage. If the printer messed up half the pages, you can realistically try to get half the price knocked off. There are problems, though:

CHAPTER 60

RESOLVING A BAD PRINTING JOB

1. Remember to consider what was done with the product. If you are complaining about bad register on half the run, but you mailed them anyhow, you are asking the printer to absorb the cost of something you actually used. Sure, you might believe that the bad printing damages your reputation, but what is that damage worth? The printer has no way of knowing if you will actually suffer a financial loss because of bad printing. He might logically argue that you're asking for too much.

For example, what if the four-color shot of your product is out of register and the photo is used in a promotional piece? The buyer might say, "We've lost a half million in revenue because of this poor registration." If the job cost only $5,000, the printer will hardly be interested in covering your estimated half-million-dollar loss. Nor does he have any legal obligation to do so. His liability is specifically limited to the cost of the goods and services that he sells.

2. At other times, though, an advertisement is printed so poorly that the *advertiser* refuses to pay. Again, the printer will not usually agree to cover that loss with a price reduction. Some publications get $30,000 per page, while others get $300. Why should a bad reproduction cost the printer $300 one day and over $30,000 the next?

In practice, the settlement is limited to the actual area of the mistake. When the printer causes you to lose revenue from a one-inch ad, he'll frequently agree to settle on a pro-rated amount of the bill. And one inch of your product could be as little as 3/100ths of a percent of the invoice, which won't cover your loss.

Whether you've lost fifty bucks or your best advertiser most likely won't affect the amount of final settlement. In summary, then, the "cash reduction" will normally be related directly to the amount of badly produced work.

Advantage of the rerun

Now, back as promised to the subject of reruns. It seems obvious to the author that the rerun has a great many advantages. In addition to giving both parties a fair deal, it is free of the problems just mentioned. The buyer is less likely to inflate his gripe, the advertiser will never see the bad reproduction, and the cutthroat customer doesn't have an opportunity to set the stage for an artificial, cost-cutting complaint.

Naturally, there are times when the rerun won't be the best bet. And any time that you do ask for it, you must remember that the printer is eating both the lost press time and paper. So don't ask for it too often. But when you're sure the product won't do the job for you, you may want to start with the most powerful suggestion: "Don't do it cheaper. Just do it right." Then if the printer suggests a cash alternative, keep an open mind.□

KEEPING TABS ON SCHEDULES

One of the many elusive areas that must be examined by the print buyer is the daily flow of material in relation to established schedules. As you already know, timely delivery is as important as overall quality—indeed, it is a vital aspect of overall quality. So delivery should be examined closely. In fact, you should be as aggressive in controlling it as you are in other areas of the job.

How do you keep tabs on the schedule? The answer might be a daily progress chart that will give you a permanent record of production.

By keeping a daily record of production, you'll gain in two important ways: The first and most obvious way in which you will gain is that you will have a daily "show and tell" of where your job stands. It's not uncommon for the small-publication manager to be in the dark for several days as to the status of his (her) material—such as whether or not the entire job was on and off press according to schedule, or exactly how much of the work was bound and delivered on a given date. Large publications have the same problems, too.

There are many reasons why this information isn't transmitted on a timely basis, or even supplied at all.
- The printer doesn't realize that you need or want the data.
- The printer doesn't have a system for reporting the information on a regular basis.
- The printer would rather not release the information.
- The customer asks for figures on a sporadic basis.

The second way in which keeping a daily record of production will help is in control of long-term patterns: You will not only be able to demonstrate a one-year (or more) pattern of timely (or late) deliveries experienced at one plant, but you'll also have a "fact sheet" that will allow you to compare one printer to another on a long- or short-term basis.

Recording the information

Use of the "Press and Bindery Progress Report" (Illustration 147) will vary from publisher to publisher. But basically, there are two ways to update it on a regular basis.

The first—and most desirable—method is to have your representative at the printer complete the sheet. Such an arrangement would require that the following conditions be met:

1. The printer has the time. (Some customer representatives are completely overworked and additional paperwork is just too much to ask.)

2. The printer is straightforward. In other words, you'll have to trust the person completing the sheet.

3. The printer is detail-oriented. The information you request must be updated on a regular basis. If the printer's representative lets it slide for a few days or shoves it aside when the work piles up, you

won't have complete records. Again, some people have more than enough to do, and this sheet might strike them as a low-priority item.

In practice, when the printer completes the form you can either get the information passed on to you on a daily basis (copies in the mail) or wait until the job is complete before requesting the sheet.

A systematic approach to keeping tabs on a job while it is being printed and bound. An interesting legal sidelight: Internal notes such as this one can be used as evidence to help prove in court that the printer did or did not live up to his promises.

PRESS & BINDERY PROGRESS REPORT

Publisher _____ Total Ordered _____

Printer _____ Total Delivered _____

Issue _____ Over/Under Percentage _____

Press_____

ON PRESS: Scheduled _____ Actual _____ _____

OFF PRESS: Scheduled _____ Actual _____ _____

FORM	DATE ON	DATE OFF	NOTES	REPORTED BY (Initials)

Bindery/Delivery_____

IN BINDERY: Scheduled _____ Actual _____

DATE	DESCRIPTION	DAY TTL.	CUM. TTL.	NOTES	REPORTED BY (Initials)

ALL COMPLETE: Scheduled _____ Actual _____

Notes: _____

_____

_____

_____

(147)

Which way is best? That depends on how critical it is for you to get the facts quickly. In some cases, it also depends on whether or not you're convinced that daily production is up to par.

The second method is to complete the records yourself by checking with the printer by phone or in person on a daily basis. This will increase your workload, but it will also assure you that the job is getting done.

329

If you want to get the facts over the telephone, your job will be a little easier if the printer agrees to call you on a daily basis. Then, even when you're out of the office, someone can simply jot the figures down in the appropriate columns.

Evaluating the report

As mentioned, the report can be examined on both a long-term and short-term (single-job) basis. The sample shown, Illustration 148, relates to a single production cycle only, but it also demonstrates the key points of comparison.

A completed press/ bindery progress report, with notes as to what happened, who said what, when the job was completed, etc.

PRESS & BINDERY PROGRESS REPORT

Publisher _PG INDUSTRIES_ Total Ordered _80,000_
Printer _J.R. RANK_ Total Delivered _86,012_
Issue _MAR-79_ Over/Under Percentage _+7.5%_

Press
ON PRESS: Scheduled _2/1_ Actual _2/2_
OFF PRESS: Scheduled _2/5_ Actual _2/7_

FORM	DATE ON	DATE OFF	NOTES	REPORTED BY (Initials)
A	2/2	2/2	LATE START — NO EXPLANATION *	JM
B	2/3	2/4	" "	JM
C	2/5	2/5	" "	JM
D	2/6	2/7	TWO DAYS LATE... LOST ANOTHER DAY SINCE LATE START	RWW JM

Bindery/Delivery
IN BINDERY: Scheduled _2/6_ Actual _2/8_

DATE	DESCRIPTION	DAY TTL.	CUM. TTL.	NOTES	REPORTED BY (Initials)
2/8	SUBS "A"	26M	←	BOUND & MAILED	RWW
2/8	SUBS "B"	5M	31M	" " "	RWW
2/9	NEWS "A"	6M	37M	SHIPPED TO STANDS	JM
2/9	BAL. SUBS "B"	25M	62M	BOUND & MAILED	JM
2/11	NEWS "B"	3M	65M	SHIPPED... STARTED 5 PM... **	JM
2/12	BAL. NEWS "B"	3M	68M		JM
2/12	CAN, FOREIGN	10M	78M	SHIPPED **	RWW

ALL COMPLETE: Scheduled _2/9_ Actual _2/12_ _RMH_
Notes: * PRESSROOM HEAVILY BOOKED... NO LOGICAL EXPLANATION.
** BLOW-IN & BIND IN CARDS LATE FROM PUBLISHER (OUR FAULT).
→ PRINTER CAUSED 2 DAY DELAY, WE'RE AT FAULT FOR 3RD.

1. The figures in the upper right show the total ordered versus the total delivered. In this job, a fat 7.5 percent excess was delivered, which might not make the buyer happy. He could immediately try to negotiate that overage (unless it is within an agreed-upon limit), and then watch that percentage in the future: If it is consistently high or low or if it fluctuates, something is probably wrong at the print plant. Ideally, the percentage should remain stable unless something changes the nature of the work (different paper or bindery procedures, etc.).

2. For obvious reasons, the scheduled press date is compared to the actual press date. Again, a pattern of late pressroom start-ups would point out a problem, and you'd be wise to investigate before

pointing any fingers. If you are consistently late with your material, this sheet will incriminate you (and not the printer). But if you are timely with your deliveries, your suppliers should be too.

If there is a problem (you were late with negatives or you tried a new sheet of low-grade paper), jot it down in the "Notes" area. And, although you might not "buy" it, write down any excuse your printer has for falling behind.

The "Reported By" column might be especially useful if your printer has several persons assigned to your account. At least you'll have a record of who told you what when.

3. The bindery operation can be critical to many publishing operations. It can affect your relationship with advertisers. For example, if half your run mails on time while the other sits for a week, it will affect direct-mail response to coupon-type advertisers. And it can affect your readers, too, if half of your readers get a "hot" story while the others get "week-old" news.

So, on this portion of the chart, pay particular attention to what type of material was shipped when. You might notice a problem that could easily be solved merely by changing bindery priorities.

4. In the "Final Evaluation" (bottom of the chart), be fair. If you created the most significant scheduling problem, admit it. Then, next time, you'll have ammunition with which to goad your staff. But if the printer is obviously at fault, the chart will give you detailed facts about what patterns developed (over a long period of time), what "new" problems cropped up, and exactly what the entire situation did to your schedule. It's a lot easier to refer to facts like these than it is to "remember" why each of the last six issues got into the mail later than scheduled.

Resolution

If you do notice a pattern of late deliveries or if you do suffer some sort of financial loss because of the printer's schedule mess-ups, what's the next step? Discussion with your printer is the first —and maybe the last—step to take. When discussions don't work and the problems are significant enough, it may be time to change printers.

It is not my intention to sound eager to point you to the court-house, but keep in mind that your daily records and notes are acceptable as evidence in a court of law. And if you've ever sat on a witness stand, you can imagine how handy it would be to have all your information recorded through your daily duties as a production director.

Notes such as these can be powerful tools in proving that your printer has truly let you down. Should you find yourself being sued or countersued, you will find them extremely valuable. The main point is that since magazines are highly time-oriented, some sort of production-level record keeping is called for if you are sensitive about delivery to your reader.□

ESTIMATING THE PRESS RUN

Estimating your press run may be quite easy or nearly impossible, depending on the nature of your publication. If you are publishing a stable product—such as a catalog sent to a limited number of people—you may only need to order a quantity that will meet your mailing list requirements. But when you attempt to estimate the printing requirements of an unstable product—such as a growing publication—the picture can get complicated. Because correctly estimating a press run is, in part, a reflection of *your* quality as a production manager, I'm including some tips on how to go about it.

Who selects the quantity?

First of all, who actually determines the press run? If you have the ultimate responsibility, good. At least you won't constantly be second guessed. You will, though, need to consider all available factors—and this means you will have to coordinate several opinions.

Let's say that you do your homework: You discuss the requirements of newsstand versions with one person, subscriptions with another, and promotional needs with a third person. And then you place your printing order and ship and mail the job—only to discover that you ordered a 15 percent excess.

Naturally, you will try to find the errors in the estimates. The trouble is, the guilty party may claim that he had the proper information all along, but simply wasn't asked to produce it.

An estimate technique

One way to resolve the situation is to design a rather rigid system of coordinating your estimates. Such a system should immediately do two things for you: provide a single-source compilation of each contributor's figures, and second, provide a framework for those figures to be in writing.

The "rules" can be quite simple. You might state that an initial estimate will be needed from all parties one month before press time and a final estimate one week before press time. Adjustments made after your cutoff date would not be guaranteed. (The actual time limitations must be geared to your own particular work.)

The sample Estimate Sheet shown here (Illustration 149) is obviously geared to a magazine-type situation. In actual use, only one master sheet is circulated to the individuals providing the figures. There are several reasons for using one sheet rather than sending a memo-request or sending duplicate sheets from which numbers will be compiled. The single-sheet system allows each party to get a feel for what the requirements of the others are; more important, it requires that each person "fill in the blanks" and initial the document.

One simple method is to put the master estimate request in a standard "route to" envelope. This will work only if your staff pays attention to interoffice memos. If not, you might want to personally deliver the sheet to each person.

332

Naturally, this type of estimate is for internal use and may have to be modified, depending on the printing contract or terms.

Suppose your printer has the leeway to deliver as much as 5 percent over or under your printing order? That 10 percent spread would have to be anticipated in the final print order. It demonstrates why overage and underage are such hot topics for large-circulation magazines. If exactly one million copies are needed for all departments, one could hardly tolerate receiving only 950,000 or 1,050,000.

So the contract or purchase order will be drafted by both printer and customer to get the overs and unders to a mutually agreeable percentage. The customer wants no overs or unders; the printer wants 10 percent both ways. Whatever figure is agreed upon will dictate what final print order is derived from this estimate sheet.

```
PRESS RUN ESTIMATE          ISSUE NO. _____

                 Preliminary   By          Final      By
                 (1 month):    (Initials):  (1 week):  (Initials):
SUBSCRIPTIONS

    Main Run     _____    _____   _____  _____
    Supplemental _____    _____   _____  _____
    Misc.        _____    _____   _____  _____

NEWSSTAND

    Gross        _____    _____   _____  _____
    Misc.        _____    _____   _____  _____

ADVERTISING

    Promotion    _____    _____   _____  _____
    Misc.        _____    _____   _____  _____

HOUSE USE

    Inventory    _____    _____   _____  _____
    Departments  _____    _____   _____  _____

OTHER

    _____   _____    _____   _____  _____
    _____   _____    _____   _____  _____

TOTAL

    From Above:  _____                 _____

    Press Run:   _____                 _____
```

A bindery flow chart

The chart shown in Illustration 150 (next page) may seem too simple to be of any use. To my surprise, however, it was a smash hit with the first printer who saw it. Here's how it was developed and what it does.

CHAPTER 62

Some sort of systematic approach to estimating your press run must be used. If you need to solicit information from various department heads, why not formalize the project?

ESTIMATING
THE PRESS RUN

For several years, I had been typing out our bindery and shipping instructions and hoping for the best. For some reason, though, it seemed that nobody read them. I'd spell out exactly where code 6422 went, for example, how many were there, and where they were to ship—and bang, it would get messed up.

I finally deduced that my instructions weren't as clear as I thought. In order to verify a code, the bindery foreman was having to scan the complete typewritten message. So I developed a chart that put all the information at his fingertips in a logical sequence. And I also labeled my priorities so that he'd know what to ship first.

The chart begins with the total bindery count and then breaks into the smaller components of the run.

According to my printer, the chart was easy to read and almost foolproof: All the counts added up. Although it was developed for a magazine, this system should work well for any job that has split runs, multiple codes, different drop dates, or more than one method of shipping (mail, freight, UPS, etc.).□

Sometimes, it's better to say it with a picture. This bindery flow chart graphically tells the printer just how this somewhat complicated consumer magazine breaks up.

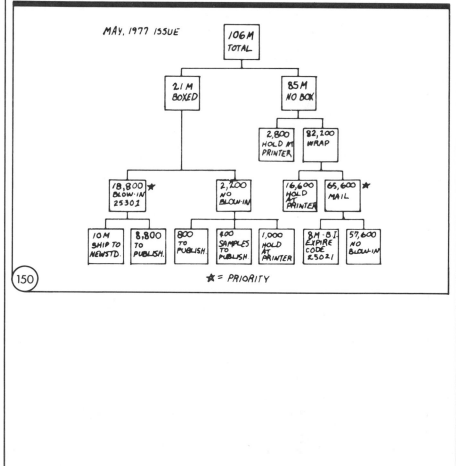

RATE CARD'S MECHANICAL SPECIFICATIONS

If you get involved with rate cards and mechanical specifications, this graphic approach might serve your purpose well. It literally shows the reader what a given ad size will look like in the magazine.

With all the technical talk about printing in this book, it should go without saying that your rate card (Illustration 151) should be technically accurate. But, in a way, rate cards are like heirlooms. As far as mechanical specifications go, one production director hands it down to the next until finally it has almost no relevance to the current magazine's actual standards. Let's spend a moment to review the situation.

Positive or negative?

When specifying how an ad should be supplied, nearly every rate card calls for either positives or negatives. And, because of the common stripping practices employed around the country, most printers prefer to work with negatives. Why?

Even though many magazines are plated from positive film, most printers still start out with negatives. The negatives are easier to work with, for one thing. For another, the positives required to burn plates must be spotless, with no cut marks. So much for positives. I haven't seen too many magazines make this error, but it is closely related to another common error: Are emulsions up or down?

Emulsions up or down?

If your magazine is plated directly from original negative film, the only suitable negative would be right reading, emulsion down (RRED). The reason is simple: For proper contacts or plate burns, emulsion must always be in contact with emulsion, ensuring maximum fidelity during exposure. (Plates always have their emulsions "up.")

But what if your magazine is one of many produced via positive-acting plates, which are burned from positive film? As mentioned, the typical printer will still strip the job in negatives and then contact those negatives to the plate positives.

It boils down to this: If you are printed via positive plates, your printer would more than likely prefer that your supplied negatives be right reading, emulsion *up*. Then, when the printer contacts to the plate positives, emulsions will be in contact. And when the positive is burned to the plate, emulsions will *still* be in contact.

In other words, if yours is one of the many magazines being printed via positive plates, you are probably requesting your film from advertisers *the wrong way*. What's the difference? To find out, wait until you can't match an ad and somebody points out the reason—your emulsions were requested wrong and you are to blame.

Maximum densities

Many freshmen production directors write their technical information by reading other rate cards. One of the most esoteric items is maximum density. Let's briefly review.

Process color magazines print with four colors. In order to create a "full-color" image, a photo must carry varying amounts of magenta, yellow, cyan, and black. In the dark areas of the photo, a percentage of all colors will print. The maximum amount of color available is 100 percent of each of the primaries, totaling 400 percent. But the maximum that can be reliably printed on a modern press might be more like 285 percent.

The reason most magazines mess this up is that they tend to copy each other's mistakes. Any printer worth his invoice knows approximately how much ink he can plaster onto a page. It might be 275 percent or it might be 320 percent.

Avoid the density dilemma: Don't copy this information from other publishers. Don't blindly follow SWOP standards. Your printer might be able to do better. Just ask him what he can do and put it in your rate card.

RATE CARD'S MECHANICAL SPECIFICATIONS

Color rotation

Does your printer really print his inks in the classical color rotation (or sequence) of yellow, red, blue, black? Many lay the black down first. Some start with red. Find out what those guys are doing and put the facts in your rate card.

By the way, rotation is a cocktail-party topic, good for production directors who've had a few too many. Some "know" rotation doesn't matter and that the printer takes care of overall balance and trapping (the ability of one ink to accept another layer on top of it). Others "know" it is terribly important and that, depending on your printer's quality standards, it should be a significant factor.

Press proofs

What kind of proofs do you ask for? In my career, no other topic has caused me more arguments than this one. I personally happen not to be fond of press proofs. Others disagree, and with good technical reason.

The answer isn't for you to sit down and decide whether a production writer is to be trusted. The answer, again, is to ask your printer what he prefers. In the experience of some printers I've talked to, press proofs are about as valuable as bad-pay ads. Yet others swear by them.

If your printer *prefers* a Cromalin or a Transfer Key, he is probably paying little attention to any press proofs supplied by you or your advertisers.

Ask his opinion as to his preferred material, and then request it from your advertisers.

Line screens

Finally, there is the question of line screens. I've seen magazines blindly ask for a "maximum of 150-line for process color, and a maximum of 120 line for black-and-white halftones." Hold on. First, unless you print on two types of paper, you need only one maximum screen, not two. Second, I don't know a publication printer in the country who would *request* 150-line separations for web printing.

For reliable printing—no muddy color and no dirty halftones —most printers will go with a maximum screen of 133-lines to the inch. Many I've talked to would prefer 120-lines, but few publishers, and fewer advertisers, would tolerate it.

The answer, again, is to ask your printer for the facts. If he says "go 150," bless him. That's pretty good.

If you've caught my drift so far, you know that it is the *printer* who should be largely responsible for the specifications in your rate card. Publishers who arbitrarily decide on specifications are merely opening the door for remakes, reruns, and serious hassles from advertising agencies.

True, you are the production director. But you are not the manufacturer. You shouldn't sit down and draft the mechanical specifications any more than you should attempt to redesign the rack-and-pinion steering mechanism on your Porsche.□

SECTION X: SOLICITING AN ACCURATE PRINTING ESTIMATE

SETTING
YOUR GOALS

Reading through the many technical aspects of print purchasing described in this book, you may have noticed that in most cases a rather light emphasis has been placed on something very important: printing costs. In this section of the book, the subject will be tackled head-on. Each of the six chapters will deal with a specific aspect of printing costs via the process of soliciting an accurate printing estimate.

The first chapter begins with *you*, because *you* must take the first step. In this case (or for that matter in any aspect of performing your job), the first step in getting an accurate bid is to clarify and record your goals. (That may sound a bit basic, but a careful look at the situation can prove otherwise.) This chapter will outline what some of those goals may be.

A price double check

A common reason to solicit one or more estimates is to ensure that the prices you are currently paying are not too high. You might be prompted into action by a substantial price hike at your current printer or by a general dissatisfaction with what appears to be relatively high costs.

In any case, if a "double check" is your main objective, you could have a problem. Your search could provoke negative reactions from printers. After all, they sell printing, not information—and what you are actually seeking *is* information—not necessarily a new printer.

Your own printer, for example, might not be aware of what you're up to initially. But it's likely that he'll hear about it through the very effective "printing grapevine." What will his reaction be? He would have no way of knowing that you are simply checking prices—that you are not necessarily serious about moving the account. On the other hand, he's probably no dummy and realizes that you won't be overlooking the possibility of lowering your costs by giving the job to one of his competitors.

The reaction from the competition is also important. If you don't appear to be serious about moving the job, other printers won't be serious about giving you an accurate bid. You must at least appear to be a potential customer or they won't want to spend time on your account. Once they get the idea that you're playing a price game, you will have very little chance of getting a good look at their capabilities. You might also earn a reputation as a tire kicker, and that stigma could be with you for years.

But if you are successful in keeping your price hunting quiet, you'll probably get an honest estimate from the printers you contact.

Are there any options in this game? Sure. If method number one is to keep things under wraps, then method number two would be to tell all your suppliers what you're trying to accomplish.

If you have good reason to believe that certain prices are high, you must first tell your printer that you need some objective answers —that you're happy with the work and you don't intend to move the printing unless you are forced to do so—but you just want to be sure that you're paying the right prices.

Then you could go ahead and tell other printers the same simple truth: You don't want to move the printing unless your current bills are simply much too high. You'd like to give them the opportunity to look the job over—and if they'd like to bid, they're welcome to take a shot at it.

The "honest" approach does two things for you: 1) Your present supplier will realize that you are concerned with prices and will very probably examine the figures in question and 2) because other suppliers will know what's going on, there should be no hard feelings. If they think they can bid effectively against your printer, they'll take a look at the work; if they don't think they can bid low enough to snatch you away, they won't waste a lot of time working up an estimate.

Finding a printer

Another common goal is to select a printer for new work. Your company might be printing a new catalog or adding a publication to its list—whatever. In these cases, you'll probably want to consider several printers before you make a final selection—even though your regular supplier might be fully capable of doing the job. No hard feelings here, either: Getting a comprehensive bid is normal, and most printers will expect you to do it.

Or maybe you are buying printing for the first time. Again, nobody would think you'd get only one bid, and you shouldn't run into opposition from potential suppliers.

Sometimes the goal will be very clear and rigid: to switch printers. This could happen for many reasons, some of which follow:

•*Capacity:* You simply may have outgrown your printer. If his expansion can't keep up with your growth, a switch is definitely in order. The situation should be as obvious to him as it is to you, and —if he can face the facts—he'll realize that you must put the work elsewhere.

•*Quality:* This is a touchy subject. Quality is very hard to define and can be (and mean) different things to different people. Many buyers expect too much from a printer, while just as many printers deliver too little. If you are sure that you have a significant quality problem and are equally sure your printer can't (or won't) solve it, move the job. But if there is any doubt in your mind, slow down. In most cases, you're better off solving an existing quality problem than finding a bunch of new ones at another print shop.

•*Communication:* A communication problem can often look like a quality problem. One morning, you might call your printer and explain a complex shipping procedure. Then a few hours later, you might discover that he messed up the whole project. But what if you had written the instructions and either mailed them or sent them over a facsimile machine? Technical communications between buyer and seller must be specific and should be written whenever possible. If you do write all instructions clearly and the printer *still* bungles every job, you might have a communication problem that can be solved only by moving the job someplace else.

•*Personality conflicts:* Unfortunately, some accounts are moved just because of simple personality conflicts. That shouldn't be. What difference does it make if someone in your company doesn't get along with someone at the printer's plant? Yet the situation often gets out of hand—and the only alternative can appear to be moving the job. But if you can tactfully intervene, do it. You'll be spared the trouble of needlessly switching suppliers. And, if you can't resolve the situation, you might at least go on record and vote for reconciliation.

Record your goals

It's a good idea to keep a record of all your solicitation activity. That includes recording your basic goals. As mentioned, your objective might be a simple comparison of prices, or the placement of new work, or a desire to move the printing regardless of any other factors.

When you state the purpose in black and white, your boss might announce that he's in total disagreement with you. Find that out early, and you'll avoid complications later.

Your statement of purpose might read something like this:

> *The objective of our estimate solicitation is to find a new printer for our catalog and to discontinue our relationship with ABC Printers by the middle of the calendar year.*

You can immediately see the goal in that statement. It's not to investigate prices or to take the lowest bid and run with it: The purpose is to put the account somewhere other than at ABC.

Naturally, there are many other factors to consider in the solicitation of a printing bid. But unless your main objective is clearly stated in writing, those factors will be hard to focus on, much less to identify.□

BASICS OF THE BID PACKAGE

Now that you've addressed the main goals of the price solicitation, you can get into the more specific details involved in working up a bid package. To begin, you should establish a list of technical priorities. You are already aware of certain obvious factors. For example, a long-run job might not be suitable for sheetfed printing, so you'd automatically limit yourself to shopping for web reproduction. But some of the other technical factors aren't so obvious, as you'll see.

Naturally, not every possible variable can be listed in this chapter. Needs vary from one publisher to the next, and your own experience will tell you what is important. This sampling, though, may give you an idea of how to tackle the task.

Quantity

When considering the quantity of your publication, you must evaluate two numbers: what you are printing now and what you might be printing in the future. Let's assume that you have a press run of 50,000 at this time. That single fact could slant your entire solicitation: You probably would not want to consider dealing with a very large printing firm where your work would take a back seat. On the other hand, you wouldn't be in the "quick-print" bracket either. But you might be planning to boost that press run from 50,000 to 250,000. (It happens.) In that case, you would want to place the work with a larger firm capable of handling your growth.

Establishing the base quantity, then, gives you a starting point. You can immediately begin to use that number in an elimination process. You might decide to be neither the largest nor the smallest customer of any printer (which is a safe decision in most cases), and this parameter can be used to help you decide whether to bother getting bids from literally hundreds of firms.

Frequency

The frequency factor can be viewed in the same way that you look at quantity. If you produce a monthly publication, for example, you want a printer who knows the problems of a monthly magazine. Again, you might logically decide that you don't want to be the only monthly publication produced at the printing plant you select. There are exceptions, of course, but in most cases you're better off sticking with a proven system.

Page count

If the number of pages in your product varies, keep in mind that although a certain printer produces 96 pages very economically, he might not be very competitive producing 104 pages. That will show up in the actual estimate.

346

More important, though, is the logic used in examining quantity and frequency: Will you be the fattest production at the plant on a regular basis? The smallest? Would your job be taking advantage of the equipment or pushing it to its technical limits?

Without elaborating too much, it's again safe to say that, as a rule, you are smart to stick with a firm that produces material similar to your own. You'll have enough problems in simply moving the work at all, and if you can avoid any potential additional trouble, more power to you.

Trim size

Your material's trim size is probably well established. However, a change in printers often opens the door to a slight change in trim. If you currently run 8-1/2″ x 11″, ask whether you really need that historically popular size. Could you live with 8-1/4″ x 10-1/2″? Or something other than the current trim?

It's a good idea to discuss this factor with your bosses/co-workers before you look for estimates. If the smaller size is acceptable (at the right price), you'll have a larger group of printers to choose from. If not, you will be committed to spending more, wasting more, and making your final selection from a smaller group of companies.

If there is potential for a dimensional change, you will later draw your specs in "range" form. That is, the width will be between X and Y; the height between A and B. This versatility can be very economical.

Paper

You've probably got the hang of this by now. Don't accidentally become the first customer to run uncoated stock, very thin paper, or a very thick sheet at your new printer. True, the company might be dead right in saying that your work will not pose any significant problems. But if you can, let some other customer handle those insignificant details that occur with the first use of anything. Let someone else do that work—and you reap the benefits.

The question of whether you should purchase your own stock is always complicated (as noted in other parts of this book). If you decide to supply the stock, be sure to state that fact in your initial contacts with printers. Some of them rely on more substantial markups than others, and if your work is bid on the presumption that the printer will supply the paper, you might not get accurate, competitive estimates. (Consider this example: A printer who has a heavy paper markup probably charges relatively less for other items in the estimate. If you suddenly decide to supply the paper, he might have to rebid the entire job.)

Bindery

As mentioned earlier, the size of your product shouldn't push any equipment to its limits. If you are saddle stitching, under most circumstances you want to avoid "precollating" your product. (Precollation is a makeshift way of getting more from a stitcher than it was designed to give. When an extra pocket is required, two portions of the work are stitched together before being placed into the same pocket.)

Other options you need to check out include tippers, card feeders, blow-in stations, and so on. If these functions are important, they could later be the basis for choosing one firm over another.

Geography

If you have a specific geographic location in mind for your work, you again have a handy tool for eliminating many printers. That's simple enough in the 25-mile range, but more complicated in the 2,500-mile category. So temporarily use your geographic preference as a screening tool. Later on, the convenience of one location over another will show up in each printer's total "score."

Total control

Depending on your work, you may want a single source to handle all aspects of your product. That means you might not want the printer to rely on outside sources for insert cards, covers, mailing functions, and so on. On the other hand, some publications simply must spread the work out. Still others like to farm out components to save money.

You must decide whether the printer must run a "full shop." Do you need color separation facilities at the plant? Small sheetfed presses for inserts? If so, also use these factors to eliminate potential suppliers.

Getting samples

The preceding areas cover some of the big questions that you might have regarding a new plant. In your preliminary investigation, you'd be wise to get samples from potential printers, along with a list of their clients. That way you can begin forming an idea of each printer's quality and get a feel for the type of work they're performing and looking for (such as weeklies, monthlies, and so on).

Preliminary checklist

The broad parameters outlined here can now be used as your initial checklist. If you have been consistent, each factor discussed represents an absolute priority. If the printer can't handle the job as sketched out on this list, you want to scratch him from the group of "possibles." As the sample list shows (Illustration 152), some printers make it and others don't.

The initial evaluation might seem quite simple. It is. This first step is used to weed out those firms that are unqualified even to bid the work. This black-and-white approach will probably cut your list to 10 percent of its original size.

So you've gained two important benefits from creating your absolute priorities: First, you have narrowed down the list of suppliers to those who, for technical reasons, appear best qualified to produce your job. Second, you have created a record of your decision-making process. A few months from now when someone asks, "Why the heck didn't you get a bid from XXL Printers?" you may not remember why. Your checklist will refresh your memory.

CHAPTER 65

PRELIMINARY CHECKLIST / PRINTER & LOCATION	QUANTITY Typical of other customers	FREQUENCY Typical, no scheduling problems	PAGE COUNT Within normal press capabilites	TRIM SIZE Within range of specs	PAPER	BINDERY Stitchers, card feeders, blow-ins as required	LOCATION Within 500 miles	COLOR SEP Facilities in house	OTHER No "farming" of work required	PROCEED WITH BID	TENTATIVE	NEGATIVE
Pub & Press Assoc.	30-50M	OK	OK	✓	OK	✓	460	no	OK			NO COLOR SEP ✓
Modern Color	60-300M AVG.	OK	OK	✓	OK	GOOD DIVERS.	120	yes	OK	✓		
NE PRT. & TYPOG.	50-150M NORMAL	LOTS OF WEEKLY	OK	✓	NO HARD AVLB.	✓	555	yes	FARMS CARDS		✓	
J. Higgs - local prtr.	25-250M	OK	SOME BIG BOOKS	ONE TABLOID	OK	OK	35	yes	OK	✓		
SDM PRINTERS	SHORT RUNS	MONTHLY	ALL SMALL	✓	NO CONTACT	✓	375	NO	FARMS COVERS			COLOR +FARM
Fairchild Press, Inc.	100M-300M	GOOD MIX	OK	✓	OK	OK	190	yes		✓		

(152)

When selecting a printer, consider making a list of features either critical for or desirable to your magazine. It's better to eliminate up front those printers who, for some reason or another, simply should not be considered for your job.

End of second stage

At this point, a list of absolute priorities has been recorded. If a printer doesn't meet these basic requirements, he won't be asked to bid the work. Remember, though, that the parameters in this stage include only the "absolutes." No relative comparison has yet been made as to who can do the better job. Rather, the list has been narrowed down only to those who can do the job at all.□

349

DRAWING YOUR SPECS

At this point in the process, you should have a feel for the type of printer that you'll be dealing with. This means that you're ready to ask for the first estimates. If you attack this problem cold, you will probably fall into the classic trap. Each printer you contact will ask you for a sample product, along with your press run figure and mailing requirements. And each printer will come back to you with his estimate. Some will price ink separately, some will give you prices for each piece of color used, and some will give you a blanket bid with press and prep included.

With luck, you could examine the bids and select the right printer for your work. It takes luck, though, because you won't have a true apples-to-apples comparison—which is why you should draw up your own comprehensive specifications sheet. Basically, this sheet will be a "fill-in-the-blanks" form that will allow you to directly compare prices from one printer to another—without wondering whether a figure was accidentally buried or omitted.

The specs that you supply will be as complex (or simple) as your job. If you produce a weekly newsmagazine with a variable page count and several regionals, you will naturally have a more complex bid than will the publisher who produces a simple, annual catalog. Just be sure that your specifications include all the significant prices and functions. Let's look at a basic approach.

The fundamentals

The first page of your specs can be very similar to page one of bids that you've probably already seen. The broad information it contains lets the printer know what type of product he'll be dealing with. If, for example, your publication is a monthly with a lot of four color, the printer will immediately consider press and bindery time for such work. If he doesn't have any four-color time available to meet your schedule, you'll get a prompt reply, and no estimate. More important, neither of you will have wasted the other's time.

Page one of your spec sheet might look something like this:

Title: John Doe Magazine

Frequency: Monthly. Mailed during first week of each month.

Quantity: 15,000. Anticipate 20,000 within three years.

No. pages: Varies: 96, 104, 112, plus cover.

Trim size: 8-1/4″ x 10-1/2″ current. Can be adjusted slightly to meet equipment requirements.

Copy: B/W: Negatives; Color: Transparencies.

Color forms: Four color normally used on three forms; 48-pages total.

Stock: Body: 40-lb. coated, supplied; Cover: 80-lb. coated, furnished by printer.

Inserts: Bind-ins, two supplied.

Labeling: 12,000. List supplied.

Binding: 3-wire saddle, trim 3 sides.

That's not too complicated, and it lets potential suppliers know what they'll be bidding on. Although such sketchy information is not used in the actual bid, it does serve as an introduction to your mechanical material.

The detailed specifications should be broken into several main areas: preparation, press forms, paper, ink, bindery, delivery, and schedule. This chapter will describe all these elements in some detail and will also illustrate a sample invoice. But before going further, consider these two points:

First, printers might disagree with this type of bid solicitation. Most bid a job according to an established format and don't like to change their method of operation. Remember, though, that you are the person who must evaluate the bids. Your sole purpose is to get accurate figures that you can compare. If necessary, you can accept bids in the printer's format, but only if it supplies enough information for you to transpose to your stock form. Better yet, ask the printer to do the transposition and sign the "alternate" form. That will help ensure that you will later have a true comparison.

Second, realize that this chapter can't cover every important point that may arise. Your needs could be entirely different from the next publisher's. One customer stresses quality, while another stresses schedules. The examples given are examples only, and might have to be greatly modified to be of use to you.

The spec sheets

The following sample specification sheets (Illustrations 153–158) demonstrate how a publisher might describe his magazine or catalog. Although each sheet is oriented toward pricing, each also provides specific information on how you intend to produce the material. Let's briefly discuss the areas presented.

•*Preparation:* You could list hundreds of variations on prep, but there's no need to go overboard at this stage. The basic costs for camera work and strips should suffice.

Note that the prep sheet (and most others) starts with a simple introduction (Illustration 153). In this case, the publisher mentions that he supplies paste-ups and four-color advertising negatives.

DRAWING YOUR SPECS

In order to compare color-separation prices, you should state your needs. "Pleasing color" is priced differently at most firms than fully corrected separations. You might also ask on your spec sheet whether the separations will be produced by the plant in-house or sent to an outside firm.

•*Press forms*: Here you're asking for the costs of plates, makeready, and running for the particular forms you use (Illustration 154). You can also leave a blank area to give the printer an option. He just may have a more economical arrangement that would interest you.

PREPARATION

Material supplied: Paste-ups. Windows used for standard B/W photos (if desired by printer). Halftones to be 133-line. Supplied 4-C ad material is right reading, emulsion-down negative. Windows supplied for square tint areas (if desired by printer) in positive or negative clear window.

Single color

Shoot supplied line material to 10″ x 12″ neg $_____

Strip single-color neg $_____

Strip supplied 4-C material $_____

Shoot B/W halftone to 5″ x 7″ neg $_____

Strip first halftone on eight-page flat $_____

Strip additional halftone on eight-page flat
   (if applicable) $_____

Add square-finish tint, 5″ x 7″ $_____

16-page, folded, two-sided simple B/W proof $_____

Pleasing process color

First separation, 5″ x 7″, including proof
   (check most economical available from you)
   [   ] Cromalin, [   ] Color Key,
   [   ] Transfer Key, [   ] Matchprint, [   ]____ $_____

Additional separation same focus with above $_____

Strip first photo on 4-C side $_____

Strip additional photo on 4-C side $_____

Eight-page 4-C flat proof (check most economical
   available from you)
   [   ] Cromalin, [   ] Color Key,
   [   ] Transfer Key, [   ] Matchprint, [   ]____ $_____

(153)

352

Press work and the other activities that follow prep are bid on a per-thousand basis. This example uses 50M as the base quantity but also asks for additional thousands. It's obviously quite important to ask for the price of additionals: Because you will certainly pay for an occasional batch of extra copies, you will want to know the price in advance. This is basic common sense.

•*Paper*: This shouldn't be too complicated. If you supply the stock, you need only a consumption projection. If the printer is to furnish it, give him a trade name (if you have one) on which to base the bid. Later, you will be comparing one firm's projection and pricing to another's. By looking at the poundage on your bid, you'll know who's using less stock (but not why). You will also be able to

PRESS FORMS

Includes plates, makeready, running. Exclude paper and ink. Bid specified signatures if available; include any other signature configurations you feel are beneficial.

Pages	Printed	Delivered	50 M	Add'l M
8	1/1	1-8	$_____	$_____
8	4/1	1-8	$_____	$_____
8	4/4	1-8	$_____	$_____
16	1/1	1-16	$_____	$_____
16	2/1, 2/2	2-8s	$_____	$_____
16	4/4	1-16	$_____	$_____
32	1/1, 1/1	1-32	$_____	$_____
32	4/4, 1/1	1-32	$_____	$_____
32	4/4, 2/2	2-16s	$_____	$_____
_____	_____	_____	$_____	$_____
_____	_____	_____	$_____	$_____
_____	_____	_____	$_____	$_____
_____	_____	_____	$_____	$_____

Cover printing

Include plates, makeready, running. Stock will be 100 lbs., 25″ x 38″ basis 100 lb. Exclude paper and ink. Printed 4/4.

$_____ $_____

(154)

determine which printers make a large profit by purchasing stock for you (Illustration 155).

•*Ink*: You will probably want to pay for ink separately, especially if you have a moderate-to-high press run. It's just too expensive to ignore, and you will probably be ahead by paying an actual consumption price (which could be the printer's cost plus 10 percent or so). If you don't pay for ink in relation to how much you consume, the printer will be forced to pad the press costs or raise prices later. And, if you can arrange to pay for actual ink used, you may want to try to pay by the pound. Most printers can give you a reasonably accurate idea of how much ink is used on your job. This payment method is fairer than the "per page/per color" method. The reason: At times you will use a light tint on a page, rather than "painting it" with several near solids. Paying by the pound covers both uses, while paying by the color (or page) would be an average figure. More on ink later in this chapter.

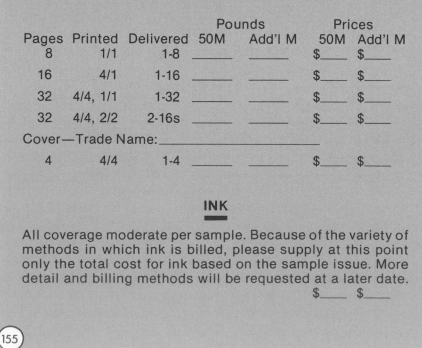

PAPER

At this time, printer supplies all paper. Publisher reserves option to supply all stock in future. Prices should include any applicable markups and/or storage or handling charges. Include sample stock if available.

Text: 25″ x 38″ basis 45-pound, coated groundwood or #5 magazine grade stock or similar.

Trade Name:_____

			Pounds		Prices	
Pages	Printed	Delivered	50M	Add'l M	50M	Add'l M
8	1/1	1-8	_____	_____	$____	$____
16	4/1	1-16	_____	_____	$____	$____
32	4/4, 1/1	1-32	_____	_____	$____	$____
32	4/4, 2/2	2-16s	_____	_____	$____	$____

Cover—Trade Name:_____

4	4/4	1-4	_____	_____	$____	$____

INK

All coverage moderate per sample. Because of the variety of methods in which ink is billed, please supply at this point only the total cost for ink based on the sample issue. More detail and billing methods will be requested at a later date.

$____ $____

(155)

Bindery: You're dealing with several printers at this point and don't know how they bid their bindery equipment. One might have a separate price for each number of pockets used, while another might bid in range form (three to five pockets at the same price, for example).

Your requirements will dictate what other information to request, such as availability of card feeders, blow-in devices, and flat wrappers, and so on. (Illustration 156).

It isn't likely that your mailing list would be incompatible with a printer's system, but it is possible. Go ahead and spell out the type of list that you're using to be safe.

Schedule: This information can be very useful both to you and the printer. It could be that your work is ideal for a specific press slot—if that slot is acceptable to you. Many estimates, made on the

---

BINDERY

Three-wire, saddle-stitched, trimmed three sides, maximum page count 128, plus cover and four four-page insert cards (partial page). Makeready, stitch, trim. Mailing prices solicited separately. If you mail in line, please break prices out and list separately from bindery.

	50M	Add'l M
Up to 6 pockets	$____	$_____
7 pockets	$____	$_____
8 pockets	$____	$_____
9 pockets	$____	$_____
10 pockets	$____	$_____
11 pockets	$____	$_____
12 pockets	$____	$_____
____ (max) pockets	$____	$_____
1 card feeder (if available)	$____	$_____
____ (max) card feeders (if available)	$____	$_____

MAILING

We supply Cheshire, four-across east-west, Zip Code sequence, fully marked for manual sorting (machine code marks available). Label, bag, bundle, deliver to USPS. Mailed second class. Assume 128-page issue, plus cover.

$____	$_____

(156)

presumption that schedules aren't rigid, are simply wasted efforts (Illustration 157).

•*Sample Invoice*: Finally, you can prepare a standard sample invoice (Illustration 158). Based on previous jobs, you can estimate a typical number of strips, separations, and bindery pockets, etc., and use the appropriate figures in summary form.

The beauty of this form is that it provides—on a single page—an accurate cost for your product, which you can compare directly to other bids. No razzle-dazzle. No fancy proposals. Just a dollars-and-cents approach to what the printer can do at a flat price.

Price or quality

Keep in mind that the spec sheet provides useful information, but it won't tell you enough. Accurate prices are essential in a comparison, but they must be evaluated in conjunction with other information and relative to your scale of values. The subject will be covered more fully in "The Evaluation" at the end of this section.

Paying for ink

It is no secret that ink contains petroleum products. No secret either that petroleum products are outrageously expensive and getting more expensive. So it should be no surprise that printers are mighty cautious about billing customers for the amount of ink used on a job.

Couple the above with today's increased amount of four-color

SCHEDULE

Based on 128-page magazine plus cover, publisher to close issue per printing form as requested by printer. Details to be worked out later. This is for overall planning purposes only. Indicate "Day" from the first activity, counting working days only, ending with the total number of working days to produce and mail the magazine.

	Working Day #
Color separations due at printer	1
Paste-ups (or partial paste-ups based on printer/publisher mutual schedule) due at printer	_____
Proofs (or partial proofs) to customer	_____
On press	_____
In bindery	_____
Complete (total working days)	_____

(157)

printing, which demands far more ink than black-and-white reproduction, and the stage is set: Customers are getting nailed with ink bills—bills that can easily constitute over 5 percent of a magazine invoice.

So it's quite logical that printers have begun to warm up to the idea of billing ink separately from other materials and labor. Over the past few years, several different billing methods have been devel-

CHAPTER 66

SAMPLE INVOICE

Preparation

Shoot 64 pages (line negatives)	$_____
Strip 64 pages (listed above)	$_____
Shoot 24 halftones	$_____
Strip 24 halftones (listed above)	$_____
Strip 32 pages supplied B/W ads (no folios)	$_____
Strip 32 pages supplied 4-C ads (no folios)	$_____
4 eight-page flat proofs	$_____
128-page simple book-dummy proof plus cover	$_____

Press

	50M	Add'l M
1 32-pager as 32, 4/4, 1/1	$____	$_____
1 32-pager as 16's, 4/4, 1/1	$____	$_____
2 32-pagers as 32's, 1/1, 1/1	$____	$_____
1 Cover 4/4	$____	$_____

Ink

	50M	Add'l M
Estimate, for above printing	$____	$_____

Paper

	Pounds		Cost	
	50M	Add'l M	50M	Add'l M
Body paper	_____	_____	$____	$____
Cover paper	_____	_____	$____	$____

Bind and mail

	50M	Add'l M
Six pockets	$____	$_____
Mailing	$____	$_____
Total sample invoice	$____	$_____

158

357

oped. Some are better than others, which means that in the long run some will cost you less.

Per color/per page

One such billing method is the per color/per page system. Basically, it works like this: If you use black ink on a coated page, price "X" will cover the cost of ink for 1,000 impressions. If you use black plus a standard process color, price "Y" will cover the same number of copies.

•*Advantages*: The chief advantage of these flat-rated prices is that you, the buyer, can anticipate ink costs in advance. True, the price of this petroleum-derived goo rises on a regular schedule, but at least you have fair warning of the hikes.

•*Disadvantages*: The main problem with this particular system is that it is, at best, an "averaging" technique. The averaged factor is obvious: You might run a headline in process yellow and process magenta, using two colors in a small area. But your cost would be the same as if you had run a full-bleed, four-color photo on the same page. And one headline hardly chews up the amount of ink consumed by a full-bleed photograph.

Also, the per color/per page technique does not show the cost of the ink itself. It shows only that the printer is charging a certain amount, which in fact may have no relation to what the printer actually pays for the stuff.

•*When to use it*: The per color/per page system isn't totally useless, however. It is the fastest, simplest method of passing ink costs directly to the customer. For those magazines that use a limited amount of process color, this billing technique would not be terribly informative, but adequate.

Per square inch

A slightly more sophisticated method of billing ink would take into account the approximate area covered by the ink itself. For example, the total coverage of the headline just mentioned might be two square inches in two colors, while the full-bleed photo would occupy 93 square inches in four colors.

The resulting figures would be billed to the customer and would theoretically cover the actual amount of ink used.

•*Advantages*: The advantage of square-inch billing over per-page billing is obvious. It takes into account that each page uses a different amount of ink. It simply is a better system.

•*Disadvantages*: But it's far from perfect. The main problem is that only one or two printers in the country are equipped to accurately estimate total density of ink coverage. A good estimate could be computed by a scanning densitometer, which records the values of each piece of film. However, the usual method of estimating total coverage is by eye, and one opinion is as good as another.

Furthermore, one customer may "paint" the page, whereas another likes light, airy, almost weak process color. The conclusion: The square-inch system is, at best, an honest guess.

•*When to use it*: Still, it is not a useless system either. On the contrary, if a printer is willing to spend the time doing reasonably close estimates of total coverage, in the end the customer will benefit from the effort. The system is closer to being accurate than per color/per page billing. It just isn't perfect.

Actual poundage

There are two other ways to measure the amount of ink used on a job. One is a rather clumsy method of weighing the ink itself; the other is by installing flow meters on the press. In either case, the advantage of measuring actual consumption is obvious: You pay only for what you use on your job. If you run light coverage, the press eats less ink; if you paint each page, you gobble up the petrols.

1. *Weighing the buckets*: This system involves a little planning by the printer, but very little equipment. Basically, the printer starts your job with the ink fountains full. The barrels (or buckets) from which the ink is taken are weighed before your job begins. Ink is removed from the barrels and added to the fountains as necessary. When the job is wrapped up, the fountains are again topped, the barrels weighed, and then you find out exactly how much ink you ate.

2. *Flow meters*: This alternative can be slightly expensive for the printer. Flow meters, which are installed above each ink fountain, record the actual volume of ink passing into the press. It isn't exactly inexpensive to retrofit a press with such equipment (although most new web presses have flow meters installed as a matter of routine), but it is a very accurate system once the setup is running.

•Advantages of actual-poundage billing: It is the ultimate tool for invoicing ink. Both customer and printer benefit because neither is guessing at bottom lines. Although the bucket/barrel weighing system is a bit cumbersome, it does provide access to true poundage used. Ink-flow measurements will surely become more popular as buyers demand accurate ink charges—charges that we will all be paying as costs continue to escalate.

•Disadvantages of actual-poundage billing: There are not obvious disadvantages to paying for what you get. When compared to any of the other methods of paying for ink, this system shines.

So, assuming that you are currently paying for ink via one of the above methods, and assuming also that flow meters will become more popular, what do you actually pay for the ink?

Most reasonable printers offer "cost plus" when the monitoring systems are accurate enough to provide a reliable consumption figure. Cost plus 10 percent is a fairly common number. Which

DRAWING YOUR SPECS

sounds fine—until your ink bill goes into the $30,000 range, not uncommon for a hefty magazine.

But what is the printer's cost?

There are two ways to look at it, and each will result in significant differences on your invoice. One printer might say, "Cost includes the time it takes to order the ink by my agent, the paperwork to track it, the floor space to store it, and the labor to haul it to press." Another might say, "Cost is what's on the invoice I receive from the manufacturer."

Whose version is correct? Both. You can say ink costs include or exclude overhead, interest charges, late payment penalties, or any other variable common to business. The critical point is that you—the ultimate purchaser of ink—know which figures your printer is using.

Your printer will probably be willing to share this information with you, even to the point of showing you actual invoices from the ink manufacturer. After all, it is your money that is being spent.

If a printer really wants to take advantage of you, no amount of detective work will prove it. For good or bad, trust is a key factor with ink, and with virtually all other items on your invoice. Just one more case for a good buyer/seller relationship bonded by optimism and faith.□

GETTING THE BIDS

Now we come to actually soliciting bids. You've already established the goals, outlined some of the basic parameters, and drawn a set of comprehensive specifications for your work. How do you go about getting the numbers?

Before suggesting "our" way, let's review the normal method of talking to a new printer: A salesman calls you on the phone (or writes you a letter) and explains that you could be saving a lot of money (and getting better quality) if you simply put your work at his plant. He rattles off a list of satisfied customers and asks you when he can stop by for a visit.

There's nothing wrong with that standard approach, but it can waste a good deal of time for both you and your potential suppliers. Here's why:

Equipment, price, geography

Selecting a new printer involves a rather complex evaluation, but one that deals in three main areas: equipment (or capabilities), price, and geography. In drawing up your original goals and specifications, you established your needs. And, no matter how badly a salesman wants to meet you, at this stage of the game the parameters are quite black and white. There's actually not much to be gained by spending several hours giving tours of your company, introducing a salesman to your layout and editorial staff, and drinking yourself into a stupor at a three-martini lunch—unless that is a goal in itself.

This is not to say that you should never invite a printing salesman into your office. If you actually believe that you must personally discuss an aspect of the job, by all means request a visit. But don't let every job-hungry printer send a rep to your door. If you were hospitable to every new sales contact, you wouldn't have enough time to evaluate the bids.

What I suggest is that you carefully screen each printer before you get into each other's offices. And if you have carefully assembled your specs—and explained why you work the way you do—most printers and salesmen will understand why you're putting the social aspects at the end of your solicitation.

The initial contact

If you rule out visits, you'll need to use some other method of contacting printers. One simple, effective way to do that is to write a letter. That way you won't spend a great deal of time on the phone while a secretary tries to determine which sales area you belong to.

Don't simply create a form letter, though. You've already established goals, and you know why you're dealing with certain printers. So go ahead and include some of that logic in your invitation to bid. A typical letter might read something like this:

362

(title, address, and so on.)

Dear Mr. Smith:

XYZ Publications is currently soliciting estimates for the production of our monthly magazine, *Homebody*.

As the enclosed spec sheet/estimate form shows, this magazine has a current press run of 75,000. We expect the run to level off at 120,000 within two years. Our current printer is doing an excellent job, but is not geared up to a run of this length.

Your firm appears to have more than enough capacity for a run such as ours, and, in addition, your geographic location would be ideal for us.

Please examine the enclosed specs and sample copy. If you are interested in preparing a bid, I'd appreciate it if you would give me a call (or drop me a note).

We are contacting only eight printers for bids, and we don't expect to ask for any other estimates.

Please don't be offended by our "fill-in-the-blanks" spec sheet. It is quite important for us to obtain valid, apples-to-apples comparisons since we will be living with our decision for a minimum of two years.

If you have any questions, please call me. And if (after you review the specs) you feel that a bid would not be practical, I'd appreciate it if you would briefly explain why.

We'd like to begin evaluating bids within 60 days, Mr. Smith, so that we can make a decision in time for our December issue—to be produced by the printer we select. Thank you for your interest.

Sincerely,

John Q. Smith
Production Manager
XYZ Publications Company

There you have it. Simple, to the point, short, sweet, and all that good stuff. There are several items in the letter, though, that are very important to a new supplier.

Why you want the estimate

First of all, the letter immediately explains why you want a bid. In this case, it's not because you're putting out a new publication or paying too much or getting marginal printing. Rather, the reason is capacity: Your current supplier can't handle your anticipated growth.

But what if the reason is quality? Should you then say something like: "Because of the substandard quality of work at our current printer...''? The answer is no. Why? First, word would quickly get back to your current supplier, who is in control of much of your material and responsible for meeting your deadlines while you search for a new printer. Second, you would cause new printers to wonder if it is, in fact, your printer who is responsible for the subquality work, or whether your company is a nit picker.

So, if you actually are moving the job for quality reasons, try to play that fact down. Think positive: "We'd like to move the printing closer to home," or "Our objective is to shift the printing to a multiplant organization," or any of a hundred other possible valid, although minor, reasons for you to abandon your printing house. Remember, if the shop truly does produce marginal work, the competition already knows it. You don't need to reinforce the information by complaining about it.

Reason for the bid request

Second, this letter explains why the firm is being invited to bid. Don't get too elaborate here or the printer will assume that he's already got the job wrapped up.

Reasons for picking a printer might include geography, reputation of quality, experience on a similar product, buying power (paper, for example), diversity, total in-house capacity, and so on.

The letter goes on to explain what you're doing and why. As already mentioned, you might run into resistance when you first use a "fill-in-the-blanks" estimate solicitation. So go ahead and explain your logic in the initial contact—but if you still can't win the printer over, just tell him that you must be able to transpose his information to your specification sheet later on. And that if you can't complete the sheet, you won't be able to compare prices; and that if you can't compare prices, your boss will ignore the bid because you told him that you'd get everyone to use the form. The fact is, if you use this type of system, you may find yourself automatically throwing away bids that don't (or won't) conform to it. Anyway, bids that don't lend themselves to comparison are often not to be trusted.

Give a deadline

Finally, the initial correspondence specifies some approximate date. Either the termination of your current contract (if any) or the cutoff date for submission of estimates would be fine. If you can, go ahead and include your ideal "decision" date (as suggested).

The supplied dates can be quite important to the printer. For example, he might be in the process of losing an account and looking for a job to fill the press hole, which could affect his price schedule. Or maybe new equipment, which would be perfect for your work, is coming in at the end of the year.

364

Ideally, you should give the printer at least a month to assemble figures. Then, try to pack your final decision-making activity into no more than a 30-day period following the bid cutoff date. That way, you won't keep the printer hanging for too long.

Depending on market conditions, you'll run into any number of "pitches" from various printers. One might tell you that he needs a decision within three weeks because he's got to sell that press slot if you don't want it. While that just might be very true, you'd be wise to stick to your original dates.

Another printer might explain that he simply can't assemble prices as you've requested them. Instead, he'd like to give you a "flat bid," and if it's in the ballpark you can work from there. Avoid that printer: There's no way he can construct a total estimate without going through, in some way or another, the very items on your list. The "flat bid" routine may get your attention, but again ask yourself: "What is the value of a bid that can't be compared?"

Up to this point, we've discussed getting the bids in proper order. Unfortunately, that's the easy part. Now let's move to the evaluation stage.□

THE EVALUATION

With the specs now sent to a handful of printers, you are patiently waiting for replies. The next problem, then, is what to do with the bids when you get them back. As you already know, the decision would be easy to make if you could use a single factor (such as price) to place the job. But it's rarely that simple. Instead, you will find yourself trying to weigh price against quality, location against facilities, speed against price, over and over and again and again.

What you might end up with is a jumbled collection of numbers, notes, and suggestions. Making a decision from such a mess is difficult. Defending your decision is even tougher. That's why you may want to rely on an orderly, maybe even a clinical, method of comparing one bid against another. How do you do that? Read on.

Knowing your needs

In the earlier chapters of this solicitation section, methods of establishing your goals and relating them to printing firms were discussed. The evaluation process is no different: Again, you should record what you are looking for in specific areas. Then, once you've recorded your evaluation criteria, you can indicate just how important each factor is. This "relative value" can later be applied to the "scores" that you give the printers.

In the sample evaluation that follows, some important details are assumed: 1) that each of the printers in the running has already met the list of parameters (meaning that you have already determined that certain printers can do the job, while others have already been scratched) and 2) that while the bids are being worked up, the production manager is busy talking to clients of each potential printer, obtaining samples and getting answers to his (her) questions about equipment and financial stability, and so on. This information is required to complete your printer comparisons.

How it works

This evaluation system is based on some elementary mathematics. All it requires is that you first establish your priorities and then give each factor a rating of importance (on a one-to-10 scale). For example, let's say "quality" is critical to your operation. You would give it a rating of 10. Then you would rate a potential supplier, giving him a score based on your investigations. Now you multiply your factor by his score: A printer who scores "eight" in quality would get a total of 80 points in the quality category. On the other hand, a printer who scored a two would have only 20 points, while a score of zero would produce no points.

With this system, then, you can use any number of variables—10 or 1,000—and still come up with a final composite rating for each printer. This rating will include each printer's strengths and weaknesses and will make it relatively easy for you to explain your final selection. If later there is any doubt as to how or why you selected a printer, your records will defend (or incriminate) you.

The big advantage, though, is that this system gets you up and out of the "gut feeling" level of printer selection, and it provides you with a method of summarizing all your thoughts, reactions, and facts in a form that can be quickly explained to others in your company. And, if there is any doubt about your technique, it's a simple matter to change your ratings (at the request of your boss, for example) and tabulate the scores.

Keep in mind that nobody can tell you what is important to *your* company. You must make these decisions based on your knowledge of the product and the people involved. Therefore, the following sample "logic list" is a "sample" only. What is important in the sample could be insignificant to you. Remember, it is possible that your own "critical" components could be completely missing from this demonstration.

Sample criteria sheet

Here, then, is the logic used at the fictitious XYZ Publications Company to determine which of several printers is best for them. Each printer has completed and returned a spec sheet, and XYZ has investigated (by phone, letter, and rumor) the finalists in relation to the following nine factors:

1. *Location*: All the printers are within a reasonable distance from our offices, and the postal zone analysis does not give any one a significant advantage. Since travel time to and from the printer is a consideration, our publisher-value rating here is five.

2. *Quality*: We seek above-average printing, but nothing extreme. Our rating of importance is eight.

3. *Paper availability*: Our weak position in the paper market means we must rely on our future printer to supply all stock. In addition, our special stock is very hard to come by. Therefore, our rating is 10.

4. *Prepwork*: XYZ does not require elaborate prepwork, and most printers will have more than adequate facilities. However, a color scanner and an in-house correction ability would be very advantageous. Our rating: five.

5. *Press capacity and redundancy*: Since our press forms are rather complex, we would prefer in-house backup. Printers who can't supply in-house backup will be forced to send work out, which would affect quality. Our rating for press redundancy is seven.

6. *Bindery*: We do not have any special bindery needs or problems. Our stitching is simple. Rating: three.

7. *Schedule*: As demonstrated in the past, our schedule is not too rigid and can be adjusted to take advantage of press time. Rating: four.

THE EVALUATION

8. *Price*: Because we are definitely trying to lower production costs, this is another high priority. Rating: 10.

9. *Other*: Although we feel our needs and plans are fully anticipated, this category—with a rating of one—will be used to provide credit for services that could be of additional benefit to us.

The above logic explains the large evaluation sheet shown in Illustration 159. Each factor is listed, along with the publisher's value rating of importance. Space has also been provided for comments that briefly explain the printer's "score."

This rather cold, digital method of evaluating printers can be quite helpful when the competition is tight. The importance of an attribute is given a rating by the publisher. Then the printer's strengths are given a rating. By multiplying the two and adding all "scores," you can demonstrate exactly why you chose one printer over another.

EVALUATION SUMMARY: ESTIMATE DATED: _AUG_, 197_8_

JOHN SMITH PRESS, INC.

MILWAUKEE, WISCONSIN

	PUBLISHER VALUE	× PRINTER'S "SCORE"	= TOTAL POINTS
1. Location WOULD PUT US IN GOOD POSTAL ZONE, BUT REQUIRE EXTENSIVE TRAVEL	5	5	25
2. Quality SAMPLES + TYPE OF CUSTOMERS INDICATE BELOW-AVERAGE QUALITY CONTROL	8	3	24
3. Paper Availability APPEARS TO NEED CUSTOMER TO FILL COATED ALLOCATION	10	10	100
4. Prepwork A BIT ARCHAIC, TO SAY THE LEAST. NO COLOR SEP, NO 4·C PROOFS, ETC.	5	1	5
5. Press Capacity and Redundancy COULD FARM OUT; NO REAL BACK-UP IN HOUSE	7	3	21
6. Bindery RECENT ADDITION. NICE EQUIP. BLOW-IN, CARD-FEEDER, FLAT-WRAPPER.	3	9	27
7. Schedule WE'D FIT IN FINE WITH THEIR CURRENT PROD. SITUATION	4	10	40
8. Price LOWEST OF THE EIGHT PRINTERS BEING EVALUATED	10	10	100
9. Other SMALL, IN-HOUSE FORMS PRESS. HAS POTENTIAL	1	4	4
TOTAL			346

Notes: _This is a small but capable shop, and should be considered on basis of price + ambition._

As you can see, those scores are then multiplied by the "Publisher Value." The result is a total point score for that aspect of the job. And, when all those point scores are added, you have a single, easy-to-compare, final total number.

For practice, you can change the "Publisher's Value" numbers or the "Printer's Score" and see what happens to the total. For example, if this printer could not supply paper, his score of 346 would drop by 100 points.

Chances are that when you compare several printers to one another, many scores will be fairly close. That's when this system comes in handy: It can collect dozens of subtle advantages and convert them into an obvious (although small) lead. And not a gut-feeling lead, but one that is the direct result of your honest, critical evaluation of each printer's strengths and weaknesses.

Final decision

No system is perfect, though. This rating system merely helps you keep track of your observations and summarize them in a mathematical fashion. It will not make you a good observer, but it will help you to record and present your case.

But if you are honest and accurate in recording your research, you'll find yourself ready to make a final decision. Two or three printers will have an obvious lead over the others, and your chance of making a gross error should be almost nil.□

MAKING A DECISION

There's something to be said for any system (such as this one) that allows you to compare an unlimited number of variables and come up with a number of composite ratings. But, of course, no system is flawless. And although this one reduces the amount of "gut-feeling" work, it doesn't make the decisions for you. The final step is to consider the human factors (fudge factors, if you will), the probabilities and the "impossibilities" that can't (but will) occur. The following "case histories" are examples of what you might look out for.

Corporate changes

A large publisher had narrowed his printing search down to a handful of potential suppliers. One of them, naturally, had the lowest price, which was substantially lower than the competition. The decision could have been made to go with the low-priced firm, but according to the publisher, "Something wasn't right." And even though the price was mighty attractive, the decision was made to go with a higher-priced competitor.

As it happened, the low price was merely a gimmick—although it couldn't be detected at the time. The printer was preparing to sell the company, and the contract with this publisher would have gone with the sale (unless arrangements would have been made later to exclude assignment, which is a legal topic beyond the scope of this discussion). The printer was, in fact, trying to lure the publisher into his plant because his presence would have made the company more marketable.

It's quite hard to prove that such a concept is at work. The printer will deny it before, during, and after the fact. But, in this case, the clue was an unrealistically low price.

Sales approach

In our second example, the publisher's representatives were completely "turned off" by the printer's sales force. The production manager and a few cohorts arranged to fly to the printer's city, review some last-minute figures, tour the plant, and head home. All went well during the first evening: wine, lobster, music, and fun. Nothing wrong with that.

The next day during a plant tour, visitors asked questions about equipment, but the salesmen either had wrong answers or no answers. Things were starting to slide.

Finally, they sat down to review the final figures, which—for some unexplained reason—were never prepared. A short speech was delivered instead. It went something like this: "All printers make the same profit. Paper costs the same nearly everywhere. We can do it for whatever they do it for, so tell us how much you want to pay."

We're not attacking salesmen in general, but in any profession, there are always a few who make it look bad for the rest. In this case, the salesmen were simply unprepared, and their business style was radically at odds with that of their potential clients.

Methods of operation

Another case involved a large printer who was trying to land a fairly hefty account. The specs were right and the price was good, but throughout the negotiations, the buyer noticed that he never spoke with a person who had the authority to give him an answer.

As a test, he placed a small commercial job with the printer to see how they'd operate under the gun. He deliberately (and, I think, cleverly) introduced a few minor "emergencies" and noted how they were handled. In this case, his suspicions were proven realistic: Even the most minor problem was not handled directly by his plant contact, and, to his dismay, most questions seemed to require the assistance of a vice president of one kind or another.

That type of activity isn't necessarily bad. It's just that this buyer was accustomed to dealing direct, to getting instant answers to minor questions, and to talking with the people who actually did the job. So for him, the only solution was another printer.

Touring the plant

You will probably decide to tour the plants of any printers under serious consideration. The tour itself will give you an impression of how the printer operates. Many buyers are impressed by clean walkways, organized storage areas, and uniformed employees. Just as many are turned off by haphazard stacks of printed material, scraps of paper scattered about, and casual clothes on the employees.

Again, you are dealing with impressions, but they do mean something: The general feeling you get as you view the plant (orderliness, haphazard inventories, attention to detail or lack thereof) will probably reflect the manner in which your job will be handled. If the storage area looks sloppy, plan on losing a few skids in there. If the bindery is stuck in a corner and poorly lighted, you might expect that the entire finishing operation is low priority at the plant.

Personality clashes

It's also not uncommon for a real personality clash to develop between buyer and seller. Witness this true case:

A production manager, who wasn't particularly sharp but had happened into the position because a close relative owned the publishing company, was given a lot of authority and enjoyed using it.

In the pressroom, he routinely antagonized the pressmen and the plant manager, who always stood by when the customer came in for an okay. Well, one day in the pressroom, the old "straw and

371

camel's back'' threshold was crossed. Result? Almost a barroom brawl, with the production manager finally being literally thrown out the front door. Of course, the job was moved to another company.

Conclusion

In summary, then, the systematic approach can be a great aid: It will help you get an apples-to-apples comparison, prevent you from overlooking small details, and provide you with a convenient way to summarize your views.

But that's all the system can do. From that point on, your own experience, gut feeling, suspicions, and hunches take over. If you don't think you'll get along with the printer's representatives, admit it. If you think the plant is too disorganized, say so. After all, you'll have to live with your decision for several months or years. And, in many ways, your job depends on the selection you make, so your personal observations are important.

What will you do in those rare cases when you don't have any reactions strong enough to "swing" a decision? Then, you'll be able to go by the numbers and give the job to the printer who rated highest on your scorecard.□

SECTION XI: REPORTING PRODUCTION COSTS

INTRODUCTION: GETTING STARTED

The person who purchases printing is inevitably involved in the economics of publishing. He or she attempts to get the most out every dollar spent by selecting, for each job, the right printer, paper, ink, machinery, location, and so forth.

Whether you purchase printing for yourself or for your employer, you'll want the satisfaction of knowing that reproduction dollars are well spent. So, you will need to consider three main areas when evaluating work that you have placed.

Quality: The definition of quality is very elusive. As you examine the jobs that you purchased last year, it's up to you to decide whether the quality was generally acceptable.

The relation of quality to economy is usually strong. By shopping around, you can almost always pay just a little more (or less), and the finished piece will look just a little nicer (or poorer). Taken to an extreme, a run of five million could be produced on a sheetfed press every month. The quality would be superb, but it would be completely outweighed by excessive cost factors.

Delivery: Was your work delivered according to your expectations? Did you consistently miss mailing dates? Were you constantly getting bumped off your schedule because of your printer's overloaded shop? Did equipment malfunctions force you into emergencies on a regular basis? The answers to these questions are critical.

Price: Finally, you can consider looking at your overall printing/paper costs, but with this viewpoint: If either quality or delivery is not satisfactory, your cost breakdowns may be inaccurate. The reason is that you'll probably be shopping for a new printer (or spending more where you're at). Something will have to give in order for the print quality to improve. That something might be better paper, more expensive color separations, or simply more ''lead time'' for the work.

The point here is that when you have a problem in any major area—quality, delivery, or price—the remedy will probably affect all three categories.

If all three categories are looking good, your evaluation can then break off into realistic CPM (cost per thousand) and CPUs (cost per unit) that will show not only where money was spent, but also where it will be going, and why. In any case, thorough cost breakdowns are worth the effort, and they're fun to do, too.

But before you dive in, you have several decisions to make. In addition to answering the questions about quality and time, you will need to determine which costs to include.

Four main cost areas

If you are associated with a large company, chances are you spend a good deal of time with your financial officer evaluating costs. You may work within a strict system and budget. If that's the case, your company probably has some sort of cost reporting/charge-back system. That system could include everything from the utilities to the bathroom tissue, with a percentage of each being allocated to each department.

CHAPTER 70

Or, you may be with a small company or on your own. In that case, you probably don't complicate things as much as the larger firms do, but you still would want to know where the print and paper money is going.

The following list shows the four main areas of printing costs. Larger firms normally incorporate many or all of the items in this list, while smaller firms often use only those that relate directly to printing and paper.

I. Direct costs, external
   A. Prep work
      1. Color separations
      2. Camera, stripping, proofs
      3. Proofs and alterations
   B. Paper (including freight charges)
   C. Printing and binding (labeling)
   D. Delivery (excluding postage)

II. Indirect costs, external
   A. Travel to printer
   B. Miscellaneous
      1. Copy changes
      2. Reruns
      3. Late changes

III. Direct costs, internal
   A. Materials and equipment (depreciation)
   B. Salaries
   C. Recruitment/relocation

IV. Indirect supportive costs, internal
   A. Utilities
   B. Staff (financial, maintenance, etc.)
   C. Building (rent or depreciation)

It's obvious that by using all of the above, the result will be a very specialized reflection of your cost to print a magazine, brochure, catalog, or whatever. True, it might be very accurate. But what would it mean? Not much. For that reason, it's always a good idea to run your breakdowns separately and to group them by categories. That way, you can customize reports for a variety of uses. The company president, for example, might want to know only how the external costs have changed during the past year, while the financial officer would be more interested in your department's salaries versus production costs.□

REPORTING DIRECT EXTERNAL COSTS

will begin with the most notorious of cost affectors: direct external costs. These include prep work, paper, printing and binding (labeling), and delivery. Each area has its own sub-areas of concern. Prep work, for example, is broken into three main areas.

Direct external costs: Prep work

1. *Color separations:* Unless you have reason to do otherwise, it should be adequate to break color-separation costs into "cost per subject." Those costs should include the actual separation charges, costs of color proofs, cost to strip for proofs (if any), charges for alterations of color, and any stripping charges for process photos or art. That last point is extremely important. Here's why:

First, you may be sending your separation work to a color lab rather than to your printer. You may be getting material duped and mounted (charges that should be included in the color separation category), which would *reduce* stripping costs at the printer. Or, you may have each photo separated individually, which would *increase* the stripping charges.

Second, your color-stripping costs may be "buried." That occurs when your prep billing is not broken into units of work, but simply billed as time. In that case, you must either refer to your printer's estimate to determine the cost per color strip, or have him supply you with a breakout on the invoice. Either method will work. The point is to include dupes, mounts, and strips in the proper color-separation category.

Then you can determine your cost per separation. Simply divide the dollars spent by the number of photos or pieces of art printed. You can do this over any period of time, either by the "job printed" (per monthly publication, for example), or annually.

The cost per subject will come in very handy when you make a procedural change. You'll see exactly what the net effect will be when you dupe subjects rather than separate them individually, or what the dollar difference of any change will be.

The cost-per-subject method has strong advantages over a simple "color-sep per-issue/book" method. The reason? Because you may use 50 color photos in one job and 10 in the next. Without appropriate back-up information, it could look as if color costs are going up and down. The cost-per-subject technique shows more stability while also indicating the fine points: Job A color was less expensive than Job B color because of excessive color corrections.

2. *Camera, stripping, proofs:* For this breakdown, your own experience will dictate just how complicated you must get. If you print a weekly in two-color and each issue has the same page count, you might do well to lump all charges in this category annually and divide the total by the number of "issues printed."

However, if your work has a great deal of variety, you have other options as well. You could 1) report this cost on a per-page (or

CHAPTER 71

per-thousand-pages) basis or 2) report the cost on a per-job basis. The first would show stability except during price increases, while the second would show price fluctuation in relation to the size of each job. If you have any doubt about which method is best, simply use them both. (It makes more interesting reading, anyhow.)

You may also want to add additional categories to prep work. For instance, if you do considerable halftone work, a separate breakout might be helpful. Or you may do repetitive work and decide to spread color/prep/camera work over several different products.

Finally, you may be one of the publishers who has a complete litho camera department. If so, you must decide whether darkroom salaries, materials, and equipment will be included in prep costs (which are grouped with external costs) or internal costs.

3. *Proofs and alterations:* Finally, you'd include the costs of proofs and alterations. In determining these costs, you would use whatever system you chose for camera, stripping, and proofs—*i.e.,* either per-page or per-job. It is a good idea to keep proof prices separate from alteration charges. You may find the breakout useful when an editor gets carried away with reading proofs for spelling errors or when an art director or editor makes a dramatic change. The ''running tab'' of alteration charges even makes a nice wall decoration for production-type people.

A prep breakdown example

After breaking out your prices in a method of your own design (or the one described here), you'll have a base from which to operate. It's good ammunition for agreement (or disagreement) with printers, artists, publishers, and so on.

Illustration 160 is a three-month summary showing that color-separation charges are fluctuating on a relative scale. If the chart maker has adequate back-up information, he could probably assemble a sister chart that would plot those fluctuations according to the number and type of separations made, and then be able to show the most economical number and grouping of color work.

This breakout of preparation charges is part of a larger, integrated cost reporting system. The point is to understand not just what was paid, but to keep a record of why.

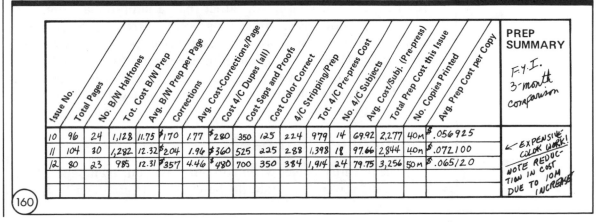

Issue No.	Total Pages	No. B/W Halftones	Tot. Cost B/W Prep	Avg. B/W Prep per Page	Corrections	Avg. Cost-Corrections/Page	Cost 4/C Dupes (all)	Cost Seps and Proofs	Cost Color Correct	4/C Stripping/Prep	Tot. 4/C Pre-press Cost	No. 4/C Subjects	Avg. Cost/Subj. (Pre-press)	Total Prep Cost this Issue	No. Copies Printed	Avg. Prep Cost per Copy	PREP SUMMARY
10	96	24	1,128	11.75	$170	1.77	$280	350	125	224	979	14	69.92	2,277	40m	$.056925	F.Y.I. 3-month comparison
11	104	30	1,282	12.32	$204	1.96	$360	525	225	288	1,398	18	97.66	2,844	40m	$.072100	← EXPENSIVE COLOR WORK!
12	80	23	985	12.31	$357	4.46	$480	700	350	384	1,914	24	79.75	3,256	50m	$.065120	NOTE REDUCTION IN COST DUE TO 10M INCREASE

(160)

379

Direct external costs: Paper

The primary goal of paper-cost reporting is obvious: to establish the amount spent on paper for a particular job. Although that goal is simple, achieving it can sometimes seem an impossible task. The difficulty will be in direct proportion to your own activity (if any) in the paper-buying market and the complexity of your work.

Printer-supplied paper

If you do not purchase paper, you probably see it broken out on your printer's invoice. Nothing could be easier than to divide the number of delivered products by the amount of paper used (in dollars). And it works. But it is realistic only if you received an accurate bid. You would come up with a cost per unit (CPU) or cost per thousand (CPM). But are your final figures accurate? It's not likely.

What your results will show is that the printer charges you "x" amount of dollars for paper. The figures won't be accurate if they include any excess charges—for example, a "cushion" to protect the printer in case of overconsumption, a profit margin, storage charges, handling charges, excess usage because of an oversized roll or sheet, rush charges, or shipping charges.

Consequently, the figures may be inaccurate in this respect: Although they will show you what you paid the printer for paper, they won't necessarily indicate what the paper was worth or how much of your "paper dollar" was actually spent on paper itself.

That gray area could matter very little to you or your financial officer because it's just as tax deductible as the more accurate version. These factors, though, often explain the "unexplainable" rise or fall in prices between similar jobs, and can be the deciding factor in placing print orders.

Getting the paper estimate early is important for this reason: The printer determines the poundage of paper that he expects to use and gives you a price. That price may not be firm (because of fluctuations in the paper market), but the poundage should not vary. Therefore, you should ask that the estimates show the poundage and the price of paper to be consumed, rather than a lump-dollar sum.

If paper does rise in price (and you've agreed to pay current prices), you'll simply substitute the new price (per hundredweight, most likely) and multiply it by the poundage in the estimate. Also ask for written notice of paper increases, specifying that it must be in your hands before a job goes on press. Then there will be little room for argument later on.

Publisher-supplied paper

The picture changes when you purchase your own paper. You will, of course, want to establish the CPU/CPM just described, but you'll also have other goals. You'll want to work closely with your financial department not only to establish those goals, but also to work toward achieving them in two additional areas:

1. *Actual cost of paper used:* This won't be a problem on a one-time job, but if you stock paper for a periodical, you will have to deal with paper prices that will constantly fluctuate. For example, you could get a shipment each month, yet consume only 90 percent of each delivery. If there is a price increase each month, your actual cost cannot be determined unless you rely on a reporting system: First-in first-out does the trick nicely.

2. *Value of paper owned:* Because of price increases, the value of your paper can rise. That figure, however, is not used for tax purposes. Its real benefit to you (and your financial people) is to keep everyone aware of the insurance and replacement costs of the stock. The replacement cost comes in handy in the event that your printer borrows or overconsumes paper: He or she would probably be expected to pay the same price that you would later pay to put more stock in inventory.

Each of these areas can be applied to a given job. "Actual-CPU/paper" will tell you what the most recent job cost; "value-CPU/paper" will tell you what it would cost the next time around.

Getting accurate usage estimates

If you purchase your paper, you'll want to have the printing job estimated in poundage—just as if the printer were supplying it. Naturally, you won't need a paper price. The job will be either one-time (such as a test run on a catalog) or repetitive (as in the case of magazines).

The one-time (or commercial) job will be no problem: If the printer overconsumes, he will credit you according to your agreement —at your purchase price of the stock. But for magazines, the situation becomes more complex.

Printers who use their customers' stock generally supply consumption standards. These figures will show whether your printer did better or worse with your paper than his estimate said he would. For example, let's assume that the printer expects to use 50,000 pounds of paper per issue. The job is a 12-times-per-year magazine and the printing contract goes for two years.

From the printer's viewpoint, the paper consumption estimate must allow for comfortable production of good-quality products. Naturally, the higher his estimated paper consumption, the easier it is to work without risk of overconsuming the customer's stock, which would entail some sort of expense for the printer.

The buyer, though, for his own economy, wants low consumption standards, yet high enough to ensure that the printer has an adequate cushion to provide quality. It is possible that a "too-low" estimate will eventually produce bindery material that belongs in the waste heap.

Using the above example, suppose the magazine happens to run exactly 50,000 copies each month for two years and, at the end of the two years, the estimate and the actual consumption of paper agreed. Result? Perfection. But what if the printer used 5 percent more paper per issue than allowed? The printer then owes the publisher 60,000 pounds of paper. At $35/hundredweight, that is $21,000.

Or what if the printer used 5 percent less paper than estimated in the original consumption standard? Would the publisher owe the printer $21,000 in paper? Oddly enough, that's the way the government places its print orders. It allows printers to retain underconsumed paper stock. But publishers generally strive to keep that stock as their own by generating special clauses in the contract to provide for it. These are part of the "War on Waste" agreements (described in Section VIII) and offer mutual benefits when quality remains the same (or increases) and paper consumption falls.

Period of resolution

The example just given used an entire period of a two-year contract to determine whether the printer exceeded his total allowable usage of customer stock. In practice, shorter intervals are used. So if your immediate task is to report the actual costs of a given month's magazine, how are you going to generate your numbers? You don't want to wait six months or 12 months or 24 to find out what an issue cost to print. You want to know right now.

Unfortunately, there is no stock answer to this problem. Here are the reasons:

If you report what the printer actually used and allow a period of one year for him to "average out" the consumption, you could see an artificial rise and fall in your paper prices. One issue could appear to cost more than another identical issue. Why? Because although the printer might consume 5 percent more in January, he also might consume 5 percent less in February. And the final tally for those two months would be "even." But if you kept records based on those individual two months, January's cost would apparently be high and February's low—with no logic. Explaining that to your financial officer or publisher could cause headaches.

Two reporting standards

It all leads to this: If you supply paper, you and your printer will first agree how much will be consumed per press form and quantity. Your resolution of this consumption (whether the printer consumed more or less) will probably be done annually. The printer, then, has a year to even out his average consumption of paper per magazine, press form, quantity, and so forth.

Then, in attempting to find out what last month's issue cost, you have two figures to work with.

1. *Estimated consumption:* In the long run, you know that the printer cannot use more paper than allowed in the original estimate. You also know what the paper cost you. Therefore, you could report that the cost of paper should directly relate to the printer's estimate, and you could use that figure for planning purposes.

2. *Actual consumption:* What if the printer makes headway against wasted paper and consistently uses *less* than anticipated? In this case, reporting the cost of a magazine based on the estimated consumption would lead you to overstate what the actual issue cost. Therefore, you might want to monitor actual consumption and—if the printer consistently uses less than allowed—pass those figures on as actual production costs. They would be lower than the estimated production costs you used when the contract began.

If you refer to Illustration 161, you will note that it is possible

Actual or standard cost? Buying paper can be confusing, especially when it is tied to consumption standards expressed in the printing contract. Much to the dismay of the accountant types, you just might not know how much your paper costs (to the penny) for months after you use it.

PAPER: ACTUAL COST REPORT (SAMPLE)

ISSUE NUMBER	PRESS RUN	NO. OF BODY PAGES	TOTAL BODY PAPER LBS. CONSUMED	PERCENT INCREASE (DECREASE)	COST PER HUNDREDWEIGHT	TOTAL BODY PAPER COST THIS ISSUE	AVERAGE COST PER 1,000 PAGES	PERCENT INCREASE (DECREASE)
8	50,000	96	28,580	—	26.50	7,573.70	1.58	—
9	50,000	96	28,424	−.5	26.50	7,532.36	1.57	−.5
10	50,800	112	35,522	+20	27.10	9,626.46	1.69	+7.1
11	52,550	128	35,882	+1	27.10	9,724.02	1.45	−16
12	58,100	112	34,726	−3.3	28.30	9827.46	1.51	+3.9

PAPER: STANDARD COST REPORT (SAMPLE)

ISSUE NO.	PRESS RUN	NO. OF BODY PAGES	STANDARD POUNDAGE	PAPER COST/ HUNDREDWEIGHT	PERCENT INCREASE (DECREASE)	TOTAL STANDARD PAPER COST	COST PER COPY	COST PER 1,000 PAGES	PERCENT INCREASE (DECREASE)	ACTUAL USAGE: OVER (UNDER) THIS ISSUE	CUMULATIVE OVER (UNDER) BALANCE
8	50,000	96	26,844	26.50		7,113.66	.14227	1.48	—	+1736	1,736
9	50,000	96	26,844	26.50	—	7,113.66	.14227	1.48	—	+1580	3,316
10	50,800	112	32,272	27.10	+2.2	8,745.71	.17216	1.54	+3.9	+250	3,566
11	52,550	128	37,412	27.10	—	10,138.65	.19293	1.51	−1.2	−1,530	2,036
12	58,100	112	36,332	28.30	+4.2	10,281.97	.17697	1.58	+4.4	−1,806	(430)

161

to report consumption both ways. The actual cost report shows what the publisher paid for the paper and how much of it was used to produce a given issue. The standard-cost report uses standard consumption figures and compares them directly to the actual figures.

The top half of the illustration shows that the printer fluctuates a lot in the amount of paper used compared to the original estimate. The last column shows an initial issue-to-issue decrease (in thousands of pages produced) of a half percent. This figure then jumps to an increase of 7.1 percent over the estimate, then down to 16 percent under the allowable paper to be used, and finally back to almost 4 percent above the standard.

The bottom half of Illustration 161 shows those figures converted into actual pounds of paper either underconsumed or overconsumed (actual usage over/under this issue). Then it accumulates the over- or underusage, meaning it takes into account all previous issues in the contract or resolution period. The result in the bottom-right entry shows that the printer actually consumed 430 pounds of paper less than he could have (meaning he is right on the button).

Based, then, on five issues, the paper costs are exactly what the printer estimated in pounds. Because the publisher is buying it direct, the dollar amount varies, depending on what the mills charge the publisher.

If the publisher used only the first chart, he would be seeing the artificial rises and falls of paper usage. If he used the second, it would become apparent that consumption averages itself out over the five-issue period.

What is the real cost of paper per average issue? The second chart provides the information, not the first. At the end of this five-issue sample, the true cost for paper is virtually exactly what the estimate predicted.

Direct external costs: Printing and binding

In the section describing various methods of breaking down the cost of paper for your internal calculations and projections, printing was kept totally separate—for good reason: Paper is a material that is subject to rises and falls in prices; printing is a competitive service in a small world of its own. Lumping printing with paper would make your records less efficient.

Printing costs include all labor, union agreements, and so forth. Cost increases in this particular area, if not kept separate from paper, could contribute to what might look like an overall, more-expensive product. If labor goes up at one plant, it is possible to move the job to another plant and keep all the prices down. But without accurate breakdowns of printing versus paper, cost increases would be difficult to track down, and solutions more difficult to implement.

Here's an example of a typical problem:

You receive notification of a paper price increase that will go

384

into effect with your February printing. At the same time, though, you decide to add 16 pages to your product—and to print it on a different press.

Since your final costs would be affected by several variables, a thorough breakdown is necessary to obtain a realistic interpretation. A "lump sum" cost increase wouldn't tell you exactly what (if anything) costs more. Obviously, then, it makes sense to break manufacturing into several divisions.

Manufacturing variables

In the example given, work was moved from one press to another. If those presses delivered different products (16's versus 32's, 32's versus 48's, etc.), they would probably be subject to completely different price schedules.

And, if those price schedules were significant enough, either of the following would be possibilities: 1) Money saved by the change in manufacturing could be more than the paper increase mentioned earlier, or 2) additional costs resulting from such a switch would be added to the paper increase, creating a double dose of price jumps.

Now try to factor in the effects of an additional 16-page signature, and your true costs can become very elusive numbers.

So, in order to get the most accurate picture of your printing costs, you will need to break your expenses into as many fragments as practical and then compile them in an understandable manner. It's much easier to do than it may seem at first.

Selecting a method

Before you begin to set up a suitable cost system for your printing and manufacturing expenses, you must select a method that will fit your individual needs.

Depending on your situation, you could decide to report 1) cost per page, 2) cost per unit, 3) cost per job (or printing cycle), or 4) a combination.

In addition, each of these methods can be broken down. Your "cost-per" figures might include breakdowns of tabloid/digest-size pages, four-color/black and white, and commercial/contract work. Here's how the three methods are applied:

1. *Cost-per-thousand pages:* The production manager of a single magazine (rather than a family) might logically decide to report costs on a per-thousand-page basis. This technique allows for an increase or decrease in the product's size, while showing otherwise stabilized expenses.

Cost-per-thousand pages can be used for any publication (or group of publications) that regularly prints on the same press, uses the same approximate amount of color per printing, and trims to the same dimensions. Fluctuation in page count doesn't alter the validity of the final tabulations either. Thus, a publisher of several magazines or catalogs could use this method if all products were similar.

2. *Cost per unit:* This method—per unit, or per copy—is subject to limitations that make it useful in fewer situations than cost-per-page reports. In that "cost per copy" must be used in price comparisons, all jobs must be virtually the same. If there are significant differences among them, the results will show in "phantom" price fluctuations.

However, reporting cost per unit does have some important applications. One is in reporting the cost of catalogs and promotional pieces. Most direct mail catalogs are measured on their total cost per thousand in the mail versus revenue produced. That measuring device doesn't "care" how many pages were in the catalog or whether it was all full-color printing. Therefore, the cost per copy is the required component. Reporting it on a per-thousand-copy basis is a matter of preference.

However, you may want to report cost per copy along with another method (such as per page). The more complete the picture, the easier it will be for you to place the next order (and evaluate total performance of the current job).

Another situation that is ideal for per-copy reporting occurs when you are producing identical work at different printing plants or running the same job several times at the same plant. If you decide to have a long press run split between two firms in different locations, the per-copy breakdown would give you some pretty solid information regarding the benefits of location or equipment.

3. *Cost per job:* This is the most limited method of the three. A cost-per-printing job doesn't take much into account. Variations in the quantity delivered, in the number of pages and/or color, and in the type of press have no effect. The only figure used for comparison is the total spent on manufacturing the job.

But again, there are situations in which reporting the cost per job is valuable. If, for example, you print 15,000 association magazines per month and each has the same number of pages, same color usage, and same paper stock, and your order hasn't changed in five years—why get complicated? The deciding factor will be the bottom line of the monthly invoice, regardless of how you slice the pie.

Putting a system to work

There's no trick to using any of these methods. Once you select your system, it's only a matter of mathematical division to achieve the final figures. But there are several cost areas that you will want to break into separate components. Your own experience will tell you which of the following points (and others that you may add) should be included.

•*Plates, makeready, running:* This cost is normally broken out on estimates and invoices. If you don't receive it that way, ask your printer (or those estimating your future work) to break it out.

The importance of these three components being grouped together (and away from other cost factors) is that each is affected by your job's complexity. For example: Five-color process on two sides of a sheet (or web) will require more plates, longer makeready, and slower running time than four-color work of the same dimensions.

•*Ink:* This is one of the expenses that at one time was tossed into the plate/makeready/run category. Because of the prices of petrochemical products, ink is beginning to show up as a separate part of the printing estimate and invoice. Having your ink costs listed separately is sometimes an education. It often amounts to 5 percent of the total print/paper cost, and could even be 10 percent of your printer's invoice. Rising oil prices won't lower these percentages, either. Ink is normally listed as "actual" or "per-color per-page."

•*Bindery costs:* If you use a variable number of signatures (or print a variety of sizes), your bindery costs are probably billed on a "per station" basis of some sort. Nine pockets, for example, would cost less to run than a dozen. It is important to break these costs out and examine them if you also incorporate inserts of blow-ins, or deliver signatures of fluctuating page counts.

Example: A 96-page catalog might be printed either as 16's or 32's, but the only printing variation could feasibly be the press delivery. That is, 32's could cost approximately the same as 16's on press because the total output is the same. (On a web press, one more person might be needed to "jog" or stack the delivery, while on a sheet-fed press, there might be no labor difference at all.) But when that catalog gets to the bindery, twice as many pockets will be required to stitch or perfect-bind the 16 than the 32, which will raise the price considerably.

Just how much the price rises will depend on how it was estimated. One printer might specify a price for each additional pocket, while another will give you a "pocket range." If "three" and "six" fall in the same range, there would be a substantial increase at another range.

These estimating techniques are not arbitrary. The "range" bid is based on the point at which another person is required to operate the binding machine. The "per additional pocket" system is convenient in averaging and smoothing out actual costs.

In practice, you will use simple division to determine what it costs to bind each copy (or thousand copies, or the job as a whole). But you'll also want to examine the job as a total entity: Would a different delivery have lowered the binding cost? Would the lower cost have been enhanced or offset by different paper consumption for the alternate delivery? Did an unexpected insert card mess up your plans at the last minute?

Also, different bindery techniques may be called for when you look the whole job over: Some printers offer their customers card feeders, which operate less expensively than an additional pocket.

Going back to the "pocket range" estimate, another question is, could usage of a card feeder rather than a pocket have saved money?

It's apparent that cost reporting has more than one application. It not only tells you just where you have spent press, ink, and bindery money, but also gives you the tools required to spend less in the future on the same product.

A press/bindery example

The sample report (Illustration 162, next page) shows how a typical job-to-job cost breakdown might look. This example assumes that a per-thousand-page report is adequate for this job.

The report shows certain obvious cost variations: Press and bindery between the two catalogs are substantially different, while ink is about the same. But there's more information available on the summary to explain exactly why prices jumped.

The main technical difference between the two catalogs is that the February version had three bind-in or card-fed inserts, while the one in March had four. The additional insert created the demand for the printing of 16's instead of 32's (because with 32's, all possible insert positions were already in use). That added 8.6 percent to the cost of presswork for virtually the same product.

In the bindery, the additional pocket was an extra cost, too, and those prices went up by 11 percent. The net result is that the need for an additional pocket in the bindery cost about $850, a significant (7 percent) hike on a $10,000 run. And these costs don't include the actual expenses of printing the insert card. If the cards were "house," the total difference would be even greater.

Figures like these help you to plan successive jobs. For example, the next time your catalog goes to press, the true costs of "just one more insert" would be available. Those expenses could be weighed against the possible revenues the card would produce, and the decision to include or scratch it would be based on more than just a rough "guesstimate."

Direct external costs: Delivery

Before you get into reporting delivery and/or postage costs, you must first answer two key questions: 1) How much control do you actually have over delivery expenses? and 2) Do you want to report those costs that are completely out of your control?

Delivery is basically a matter of weight and geography. Your job is to get a specific poundage of material from one place to another—on time and for a reasonable amount of money. With that simple definition in mind, let's examine these two questions.

• *To report or not to report:* The location of a printing plant is of obvious importance to the buyer. You wouldn't normally get company letterhead stationery printed thousands of miles from your office because it wouldn't be convenient. On the other hand, it's not uncommon to place an expensive printing job hundreds or thousands of miles from your home office. Naturally, the decision to print that far away isn't arbitrary and, in the long run, should be cost effective.

If you as production director make the decisions about printing sites, then delivery expenses might well be a factor in your print-

CHAPTER 71

As described in the text, subtle differences can have major consequences. This comparison demonstrates how the addition of an insert card dramatically increased the cost of a catalog.

SPRING CATALOG COSTS	CAT: FEBRUARY '78		CAT: MARCH '78	
NUMBER OF COPIES PRINTED:	53,214		55,156	
BODY PAGES PER COPY:	96		96	
TOTAL PGS. PRINTED (1,000's):	5,108.5		5,294.9	

PRESS:			Notes			Notes
No. 4-C 32's: Cost:	2	6,826.62		2	6,911.53	
No. B/W 32's: Cost:	1	1,442.46		–	–	
No. 4-C 16's: Cost:	–	–			–	NOTE 942.89 DIFF.
No. B/W 16's: Cost:	–	–		2	2,385.35	
Total Press:	3	8,269.08		4	9,296.88	
Press per 1,000 pages:		1.62			1.76	UP 8.6%

INK:			Notes			Notes
No. 4-C pages: Cost:	45	661.52		49	746.61	UP 13%
No. 3-C pages: Cost:	11	111.95		7	73.84	DOWN 33%
No. 2-C pages: Cost:	2	11.67	9% OF TOTAL BILL	3	18.14	–
No. 1-C pages: Cost:	38	134.06		37	135.30	–
Total Ink:		919.20			973.89	
Ink per 1,000 pages:		.18			.18	

BINDERY:			Notes			Notes
Total No. Pockets: Cost:	5	851.47		7	1016.97	UP 19%
No. Card-feeders: Cost:	1	63.83		1	66.81	
Other Inserts (included in total pockets):	2	–	POCKET RANGE NOT AFFECTED	3	–	CREATED NEED FOR 16's + POCKET
Total Bindery:	7/1	915.30		10/1	1,083.78	
Bindery per 1,000 pages:		.18			.20	UP 11%

TOTAL PRESS/INK/BINDERY:	10,103.58		11,354.55	UP 12%
PRESS/INK/BINDERY PER 1,000 PAGES:	1.98		2.14	UP 8.3%

(162)

cost reports. The same is true for the "weight" aspect of the printing: If you can and do control the weight of the finished product (by selecting appropriate paper stock), then the cost effects of delivering lighter products should be integrated into your final cost breakdown.

But what if you don't have control? For example, you might be limited to using a specific type (weight) of paper or have a permanent relationship with a printer (and thus no choice in considering a new location). Then why get complicated? Incorporation of delivery expenses would do little but cloud your final figures: An increase in freight expense would seem to raise your printing costs, but if you can't make the decision to reduce volume or weight, you just don't have enough control to change the general picture.

So, regarding the first question: If you cannot control the weight or printing location of your product, why bother to report delivery expenses (such as freight or postage) in your final reports? List them separately, as incidental expenses, but not as part of the printing cost. If you do have control over location and weight, you will want to incorporate cost increases or decreases into the picture.

• *The "no control" situation:* Other factors seem to be out of the hands of mortal men. Postal increases of 400 percent in 10 years is history, and history tends to repeat itself.

If you pay a rate-per-piece-mailed and incorporate postage into your production costs, you'll naturally see the bottom line rise constantly, regardless of similar product weights. So, given a product of the same size and weight—printing every week or so—you may decide to keep postage from fuzzing up your picture.

On the other hand, maybe your company has ways to deal with postage hikes: a variable number of pages in a publication, paper weight, size, and quantity of advertising (which mails at a cost higher than "editorial" material does), and so on. If that's the case, a reduction in weight and pages might produce a significant postal savings. That savings should be coupled with reduced or increased printing expenses for the final picture.

So, in answering the second question—whether or not to report out-of-control costs—you need to consider whether your company has any counterattacks available, such as weight reductions. If not, then you may not want to clutter your printing-cost reports with postal costs.

Delivery and postage reports

With that lengthy introduction out of the way, we can discuss the rather simple procedures involved in reporting delivery expenses.

The chart shown here (Illustration 163) is based on a sample magazine that can control page count, paper weight, and so forth. By presenting the figures in this format, the production manager of this publication could begin to make accurate conclusions.

Most obvious is the fact that a reduction in the weight of the product had significant effects on the total bill. This would not be apparent if the chart did not show postage/delivery on a thousand-page (or per-page, if you prefer) basis. For example, note that the "Average Per Copy" total delivery expense is nearly the same for issues 33 and 34. That just happens to be a coincidence and is the result of the variations in total number of pages, quantity mailed, and so forth.

Another bit of information the chart reveals is that the 64-page issue does not mail as cost effectively as the 96-page issue. That difference, too, shows up in the per-thousand breakdown ("Postage/M pages").

Naturally, a chart like this must be customized to your own needs. You may not have material trucked or your freight expenses may be so small as to be insignificant. Whatever your breakdown looks like, it will be even more valuable when coupled to other cost factors. A reduction in paper weight might save postage, but what does it do to material costs and press billings? When all the numbers are compiled, you can ask whether a paper stock change, or almost any other change, is really worth it—in dollars and cents.

I don't advocate the misuse or abuse of numbers, but there are a few tricks that you can play with them. The chart ("% INCREASE/DECR."), for instance, shows that true delivery costs (based on the amount of material shipped or mailed) dropped 21 percent between issues 33 and 34. That's a good chunk. Yet by simply looking at the total amount spent on delivering the two issues ($2,706 vs. $2,694), you could say that delivery expenses are rising—a far cry from a 21 percent reduction!

Although it's not nice to juggle numbers around to suit your audience, you should be aware of the techniques. They may one day explain some of the confusing figures you might see your competition using.□

Delivery and postage expenses aren't too controllable, but must be watched. This comparison shows how the switch to a lighter weight stock coupled to page count affects postal and trucking expenses.

DELIVERY & POSTAGE EXPENSES

Issue	32	33	34		
No. pages	96	64	80		
Weight/M pages	4.8828	4.8828	3.9062 *		
Copies mailed	48,269	49,193	50,052		
Postage/copy (Avg)	.06067	.048402	.0477321		
Postage/M pages	.6319	.7562	.5966		
Advertising %	23%	28%	25%		
Copies trucked	23,800	24,300	24,600		
Trucking cost	$ 460	$ 313	$ 317		
Trucking/copy	.0193	.0129	.0129		
Trucking/M pages	.2014	.2012	.1610		
TOTAL DELIVERY EXPENSES	$3388.38	$2694.04	$2706.07		
AVERAGE PER COPY	.0470105	.036657	.0362491		
AVERAGE/M PAGES	.48960	.57270	.45310		
% INCREASE/DECR.	—	+16%	−21%		

* SWITCH TO LIGHTER STOCK

163

REPORTING INDIRECT EXTERNAL COSTS

Previously discussed have been costs that were directly related to labor or materials. Those charges included prep work, paper, printing and binding, and delivery. There are other expenses, though, that are even harder to categorize. These charges, indirect external costs, deserve a category of their own.

Indirect external costs: Travel to printer

Certain travel expenses would not be included as printing expenditures. Travel to conventions, for example, should be a departmental expense, not a printing cost. Other travel costs, such as airfare for press checks, troubleshooting trips, and so on, are part of getting the job done and should be handled as an indirect printing cost. Travel costs should be evaluated annually, using the following criteria:

1. *Was the travel necessary?* For example, did you consistently send a staff member to deliver jobs that could have been delivered by air freight? Did you use a private or chartered airplane when a commercial airliner would have done the trick?

2. *Is the location right?* You may be printing 1,000 miles from home, while a competent printer, right in your backyard, could do the job at a savings if travel costs were considered. This should weigh on a future decision.

3. *Was travel a significant expense?* Spending $5,000 on annual travel may be reasonable if your job costs $500,000. But if the job costs only $50,000 annually, then 10 percent of your total printing cost (direct and indirect) is the result of travel.

Indirect external costs: Miscellaneous

1. *Copy changes:* Another area that should be broken out of normal printing charges is the cost of a copy change, when that change is made at the wrong time. It is quite common for a customer to do a press check with the intent of getting the color "just right" —only to find a gross error in copy. This could be a missing photo caption, wrong issue date, or any number of things. Your problem, though, is where to "charge it off."

Let's say that you have the sole responsibility of doing a press check. In the process of so doing, you notice that, because of a typo, a headline accidentally includes an obscene word. You didn't make the error yourself (it's an editorial problem), but you have it corrected when you see it—to the tune of $2,000. You certainly don't want the money charged to production: It would affect your budget, printing estimate, and so on. So although the actual cost of the correction may be for plates and a makeready, it should not be recorded as a production expense. Rather, it should be recorded in a separate category, which you can call whatever name you choose: editorial blunders, cost of late corrections, or something even more appropriate and insulting to the guilty party.

The point is that you don't want the "optional" printing expenses to reflect badly on either yourself or your printer because neither of you is to blame. And depending on the flexibility of your accounting department, you might even arrange to have the above mistake officially recorded as an editorial expense.

2. *Reruns:* Here's another situation that you might encounter. You get your estimates, get a last-minute check on the ideal delivery quantity, place the order—and everything is just fine. Then suddenly you're told that the figures were wrong and that you'll need to order an additional 10 percent—no ifs about it. Your job is already off press and in the bindery, so you pay for another makeready—a significant cost.

Is it a production expense? Again, the accounting department should get into the act. If you were not responsible either for estimating the required quantity or for the error, you shouldn't have to carry the additional expense in the production department. But if it was your error—well, don't make it too often or you'll be job hunting pretty quick. In any case, the cost of going back on press should not be lumped into the total expense picture. That would reflect badly on the printer who, in this case, is not to blame.

3. *Late charges:* Still another oddity can pop up when you fail to meet a deadline. Let's say that you agree to deliver negatives to your printer by a certain day and he agrees to meet your very critical mailing date. Then, when you don't make it on time, the printer says that he'll still mail on schedule if you pay overtime.

So back to the question: Who caused the late delivery? Certainly not the printer, so he should be "clean" when the cost evaluations begin. The guilty party should carry the expense. If the late delivery to the printer was caused by a set of late advertising negatives, the advertising department should be advised of the overtime costs and be charged internally for it.

Although the "indirect" external printing costs of copy changes, reruns, and late charges should be relatively low, it's technically possible for them to exceed your total, regular printing and paper expenses. Therefore, it's a good idea to evaluate them on at least an annual basis.□

CHAPTER 72

REPORTING DIRECT AND INDIRECT INTERNAL COSTS

So far we've covered "outside" costs of prep work, paper, printing and bindery, and delivery procedures. Each of these areas can be objectively and accurately evaluated because they involve fixed quantities. If "x" amount of material is printed for "y" amount of dollars, simple mathematics will eventually tell you whether the purchase was cost effective or not.

For the most part, controlling and evaluating these outside charges are the main economic functions of a production manager. But when internal and external expenses overlap, the same objective standards must be used to judge in-house performance. Let's look at just two direct internal costs, and then at some indirect (supportive) internal costs.

Materials and equipment

For example, you do your paste-up in-house, which requires certain machinery, tables and chairs, and materials. Those items cost money, and that expense is actually part of getting the job produced and printed. If the printer performed all paste-up functions, there would be no question about how much was spent, and why. Yet the in-house costs are often blurred, or sometimes even ignored.

The importance of examining in-house costs is even more obvious if you produce your own negatives. That is a function nearly any printer could perform. However, some publishers prefer to do it themselves—which means they're spending less at the printer, but more on materials and equipment. Is the cost of film, maintenance and depreciation, and so forth, accurately reflected in the total expense of the product? Possibly an additional person is necessary to run the darkroom—and that expense, too, must be included in the bottom-line figures.

Salaries

That brings us to "other" salaries. If you're running an art or paste-up department, is your money being spent wisely? Or could you get the work done cheaper, faster, and better by simply shutting down your department and relying on a professional prep shop?

That same question can also be applied to typesetting departments. Is it actually costing you substantially more to set your own type than it would to have it done outside? There's no way to even begin to find out unless you consider the total departmental expenses as they relate to your total annual production.

Indirect internal costs

The picture can get even more complicated. Your organization may use a charge-back system that reminds you that your department uses a percentage of the building's floor space, electricity, and maintenance services for a specific annual dollar amount. That particular cost is probably something that you can't control at all. For example, if the rental percentage is quite high, can you move your department out of the parent building to save money? Not likely. Nor could you do much to lower the electric bill.

One way to deal with charge-back memos (memos that can affect your department's budget and make you look like a loser) is to consider this question: If the department weren't there at all, how much would actually be saved? Let's say your art department uses 20 percent of the building's floor space and is memo-billed for 20 percent of the rent. If you shut the department down, would any rent be saved? If not, you may be wasting time on the whole charge-back concept. And if you can't talk your financial people out of using it, you may simply want to ignore it.

On the other hand, let's say that you rent adjoining offices and that shutting down the art department would mean you'd stop paying rent on a square footage of office area. In that case, you'd want to keep close track of your rent charge-back since it is a controllable expense that affects your general cost effectiveness.□

CHAPTER 73

COST REPORTS, BUDGETS, AND SUMMARIES

Reporting the internal costs outlined in this section can be quite educational. Your department might be operating well in excess of budget, which can look bad. Yet an accurate production-oriented, cost-reporting system could prove that you're actually producing material at a less-than-anticipated cost—but you're just producing a lot more of it. In any event, before you set up a grand, internal, cost-reporting system, you must decide which costs should be included. As before, the basic qualifying question is, "Can the cost be controlled?" If it can't, there's little need to complicate things by reporting it as a printing expense.

Then, you must decide upon some sort of reference. You might choose to reference production to the total number of annual pages published, or to the total number of catalogs produced, or to whatever specifically meets your requirements.

Finally, you might want to consider what options you have in the event you find a cost-ineffective area. Could you feasibly shut down the darkroom, or is it sacred to the company president's son? Could you abandon the typesetting department, or would that mean you'd never meet another deadline? Depending on what the bottom line finally looks like, you just might find that a long-held belief in the need for a certain in-house service could quickly change.

Setting up and using a report

Our sample report (Illustration 164) shows how a publisher might evaluate in-house functions that relate to getting a job printed. For example, let's assume the publisher has a complete paste-up department and is considering building a darkroom.

We'll also assume that the building is publisher-owned, so rent is not a controllable or a necessary cost consideration. This publisher is quite ruthless about getting the most for every dollar spent, and if any department looks like a loser, it will be dumped.

Often, publishers install complete departments without giving thought to the cost to staff, equip and run them. This brutal look at doing paste-up in-house tells the publisher to forget it, unless money is no object.

PASTE-UP DEPT.	1976	1977	1978
Materials/supplies	$6,545	$7,812	$8,980
Equipment (5-year dep.)	1,800	2,200	2,400
No. employees (reference)	(2)	(2)	(3)
Salaries, fringes	24,500	27,800	42,600
Total	32,845	37,812	53,980
Appx. annual paste-ups:	2,200	2,750	3,430
Average cost/paste-up:	14.93	13.74	15.74
Vs. outside estimate:	11.00	11.00	12.00

DARKROOM INVESTIGATION SUMMARY:	1978
Materials, supplies	$4,300
Salary, fringes (1 person)	15,000
Equipment (5-year dep.)	2,500
Total	21,800
Appx. negs shot per year:	3,430
Average cost/neg:	6.35
Vs. outside estimate:	5.00

(164)

The paste-up department summary as shown in Illustration 164 provides the following information:

•When the in-house costs for three years are compared to estimates on getting work done outside, the department operates at a net loss. That loss amounts to $8,645 for 1976, $7,562 for 1977, and $12,820 for 1978. (These figures are the result of multiplying the outside estimate by the total paste-ups produced and then subtracting that number from the department's actual cost of operation.)

•The department operated most efficiently during 1977 when the increased workload (number of paste-ups) was handled by the same number of employees.

•The department suffered a 24 percent slump in efficiency when it added an employee in 1978. That could have happened because there was too much work for two persons, but not enough for three.

•If efficiency and cost are the deciding factors, the department would be shut down. (And remember, the boss is ruthless.)

The decision usually isn't so cut-and-dried, though. If the department were closed, would the paste-ups have the same quality? Would they be finished on time? Those questions are often more important than the potential savings of closing a department (or simply not creating a new one). But even if you are committed to doing paste-ups in-house, a thorough cost evaluation will tell you just how efficiently you're running the shop and where you can improve the department's cost effectiveness.

The importance of wages

As you probably realize, the most expensive creatures in the typical darkroom or typesetting department are the people who run the machinery. For example, you might be considering a $70,000 equipment expansion. If that equipment requires two operators, you'd be spending, say, $22,000 annually for the staff, or $154,000 over a seven-year period. Total equipment depreciation over that period of time is the equipment cost itself, which is a mere $70,000—or less than half the wages that you pay to run it.

Consider the effects of miscalculating: Instead of needing two persons, what if you later found out that you needed three? You'd have missed your seven-year operating estimate by $77,000, or by more than the cost of the equipment.

Our darkroom operating cost chart (Illustration 164) demonstrates that point. While it is apparently not practical to build and operate a darkroom (because of the higher actual cost of producing each negative), the main reason it's impractical is the full-time salary of an employee.

Based on the quantity of material produced, it might be feasible to hire a part-time (rather than a full-time) camera operator. If that change saved $5,000 yearly, then the average cost per negative would drop to $4.90—which is a slight savings over the current outside charge. That savings, coupled with the convenience and control of having an in-house darkroom, might make a decision to build a darkroom quite valid.

Naturally, any cost-reporting system that you establish must be used over a considerable period of time before it can be of real benefit. Expenses for a single issue or publication won't tell you much more than, "Yes, money was spent here and there."

At the end of a year, though, you'll have what amounts to a small encyclopedia on company expenditures. Then, the object will be to present a summary of expenses in a way that will make your records understandable to others in your firm.

Before you try explaining your esoteric compilations to others, you'll need to fully understand them yourself. One way to keep your fingers on the continual ups-and-downs of prices is to create a master chart of all expenses and to update it regularly.

In order to include all the variables mentioned above, you might elect to construct one large, detailed, grand summary of all activity—both internal and external. Doing so will give you the answer-at-a-glance to almost any cost question you could ask. Depending on the number of variables, though, such a "grand chart" might be just too large to have in your office. If that's the case, you can simply create a series of charts broken into several main variables such as "pre-press," "manufacture," and "post-press."

Remember, though, that a cost report must elaborate not only on the number of copies of a given publication, but also on the total pages within each copy. A "master chart" can show the results of additional pages and the pattern of total cost per copy—regardless of page considerations.

The super summary

Illustration 165 shows a portion of a master chart. The headings across the top of the chart should be specific and detailed enough to include all the costs that you have decided are pertinent. Each factor allows you to see costs in two ways:

1. *Total expenditures per category:* This might be the total printing costs, or total color separation charges per issue. It will show

It's a simple math job to do a comprehensive cost accounting for an entire magazine or catalog. Better yet, put the information on an electronic spreadsheet.

ISSUE	1. Total Copies	2. Cost/ Manufacture	3. Cost/Mfg. per Copy	4. Tot. Cost Body paper	5. No. of Body Pages	6. Body paper Cost/Copy	7. Body paper Cost/Page	8. Tot. Cost Cover Paper

(165)

the general pattern of increased or decreased spending per area and is particularly important if you work within a tight budget.

2. *Average cost per unit:* Although "total expenditures" may show that you're spending more in a particular category, you're not necessarily paying more for products or services. For example, your printing expenses may have doubled in the past year. But if the total number of copies has more than doubled, your unit costs have actually fallen.

This general approach applies to more than printing and binding. It can be used to determine patterns in prep work, paper, bindery, delivery, and so on.

What should you include in the chart? Certainly not all the information you have on hand. Rather, you'd include summaries of other, more detailed breakdowns. Presswork, for example, needn't be broken into all aspects—such as the number of plates burned, makeready per form, and so forth. To include all available information would simply waste time because you'd only be creating duplicate information.

Rather, you'd do better to include summarized costs that —when combined with other costs—will produce new information, something that the invoices don't tell you. If, later on, you need to know more about a given factor, you can always dig up the invoice and investigate more thoroughly.

A sample categorization

What's important to one publisher may be insignificant to another. Not all the cost-reporting options can be presented here, but it is possible to give a sample of what one production manager thought was important enough to record on a continuing basis. These areas were designed to provide a base for cost evaluations of a consumer magazine with the following variables: issue size, quantity of advertising, number of color separations, type of paper, total copies printed, total shipped, and total mailed.

1. *Total copies:* This is a standard reference figure used throughout the report to determine average costs per copy.

2. *Total cost to manufacture:* This amount includes only the cost of plates, makeready, running, and binding of the "issue proper." That means it does not include the cost of paper, bind-ins, blow-ins, prep and separations, and so forth.

3. *Cost/manufacture per copy:* You get this number by dividing No. 2 (total cost of manufacturing) by No. 1 (total copies delivered). Because the manufacturing costs include makereadies and other fairly stable charges, the cost to manufacture one copy normally falls as the total number of copies rises. Naturally, a significant change in the manufacturing process can negate that reduction.

4. *Total cost of body paper:* Either standard or actual cost, depending on your preference.

5. *Number of body pages in issue:* This figure includes only the issue's body; it excludes cover and insert stock, which are handled separately.

6. *Body paper cost per copy:* The result of dividing No. 4 by the standard reference, No. 1.

7. *Body paper cost per page:* Using a reference of "1,000 pages" makes this figure a bit easier to digest (66.8 cents rather than $.00668, for example). This average cost of paper per page is the most accurate representation of whether paper costs are rising, holding, or falling.

8. *Total cost of cover stock.*

9. *Cost of cover stock per copy:* Divide No 8. by No. 1.

10. *Total cost of inserts:* In this example, this figure includes printing, paper, perforations and folding, etc. If necessary, it could be broken into more variables (as cover and body paper have been).

11. *Number of inserts in issue.*

12. *Average cost per insert:* No. 10 divided by No. 11.

13. *Average cost of inserts per copy:* No. 10 divided by No. 1.

14. *Total B/W pre-press costs:* This includes the charges for halftones, proofs, stripping, and so forth.

15. *Total B/W pages.*

16. *Average pre-press cost per page:* Although you've probably gotten the hang of this already, it's No. 14 divided by No. 15.

17. & 18. *Total four-color pre-press* and *Four-color pre-press per copy:* These would be handled the same as the B/W breakdown above. You could choose either per-color separation or per-four-color page, depending on your particular situation.

19. & 20. *Total postage* and *Average postage per copy:* Both can be determined by examining the report filed by the mailer at the time the issue goes to the post office.

21. & 22. *Total other shipping costs* and *Shipping costs per copy:* These figures would include shipping charges for the newsstand (if those charges aren't recovered later) and magazines sent to you for inventory (if you receive a substantial quantity).

Summarizing the summary

Now that you've gotten the preparation work out of the way, you can begin to summarize the above points into larger areas.

•*Total cost per copy "on the printer's floor":* This figure will represent what was spent per copy, up to but not including any shipment or mailing. Thus, it doesn't show the effects of increased postage (because of weight or rate variations).

It is achieved by adding together all the "per copy" figures determined in the 22 steps. (From the example above, you would add Nos. 3, 6, 9, 13, 16, and 18.)

•*Average cost per page "on printer's floor":* The only trick in determining and using this figure is deciding what constitutes a page.

For this example, we'll count each insert page as a whole page (because of the higher relative cost of producing inserts) and the covers as four pages. These two sums would be added to No. 5. The result would be an "average page count per copy."

If you now divide the average cost per copy "on the printer's floor" by the total "average page count per copy," you'll get a new figure: the total average cost of materials and manufacturing per page before mailing. (As we mentioned earlier, it's easier to use "per thousand pages" and avoid a lot of post-decimal zeroes.)

•*Average cost per mailed page:* Now that you know what a page costs, you need only add postage to determine what a mailed page costs. By dividing No. 20 (average cost to mail a copy) by the average number of pages in an issue, you'll have "postage per page." Add that to the above cost per page, and you've got your answer.

•*Average cost per shipped page:* The same procedure just described is now applied to No. 22. The shipping average per page is added to the cost per page to get the average cost per shipped page.

These four general categories can now be examined in terms of percentages—from one issue to the next, or from one year to the next, or on any other basis. For that matter, each of the specific areas on the "big chart" could be examined the same way.

This interpretation seems to be the easiest to digest. For example, if you wanted to present a one-year summary at a meeting, you'd be asking an awful lot by bringing the whole chart with you, but summarizing the summary provides for quick comparisons.

Conclusion

Naturally, I'm not suggesting that the cost system shown here will work equally well for all publishers. I'm only demonstrating how the production manager (or other person responsible for cost control) might store and interpret material that will affect his decisions.

And I haven't, by any means, demonstrated all the variables that can be extracted from a thorough cost report. Your own needs will dictate how creatively you'll have to use your calculator.□

The ethics of print purchasing

Because much of this book concentrates on the purchasing of printing, it would be an oversight not to include a discussion of the ethical considerations that one must inevitably deal with in such a transaction. This is not meant as an attempt to preach or moralize, but rather to look at the causes and effects of different ethical approaches that a person with the powerful position of print buyer may take.

Let's start with an example: The customer, a publisher of several small trade magazines, was getting competitive bids for a contract with a price range of $4,000 to $6,000 for printing and paper. When the final bids were in, one printer had a bottom line of $5,200, while another came in at $4,800.

The publisher contacted the low bidder and explained that he would certainly like to give him the work, but that $4,800 was too high. He told the printer the job would be his if he could cut the bid by $500. The printer subsequently cut the price, and the publisher gave him the work.

Now, the story might have ended there, but it so happened that the competitive bidders were not total enemies. At a cocktail party, the $5,200 bidder made the comment that something was wrong with his own pricing because he had cut everything to the bone to get that job and still didn't get it. Suddenly, the printer producing the work for $4,300 (he'd knocked $500 off his bid) realized that he'd been had, and a very sour relationship was born.

Is it ethical?

Obviously, that situation was triggered by the publisher who created an artificial price in order to get his work done less expensively. But is it fair? Is it productive?

First, let's look at the publisher's side. Suppose he suspected that the two bidders were in some sort of conspiracy. In that case, he might have tried to lower the price in order to get a fair deal. If that kind of thinking is necessary, however, we're all in trouble. It would mean that there is virtually no way to get an honest bid in the printing industry.

Let's be a bit more realistic. Could it be that all printing prices are padded because all buyers try to squeeze a few pennies out before signing on the dotted line? And, if that is the case, are we in a situation where we must all grind printing prices down because printers expect it?

How many of us haven't asked a printer to cut this price off that, only to learn that it is a routine practice? Lower this printing price, lower that press price, shave something off the bindery, and "you'll get the job." For good or bad, it does seem that there is always a tiny bit of fat in the original quotation. The quantity of fat may depend on how attractive the work is to the printer at that time. So, it appears that the question of artificial prices can't be called fair or unfair based on the above facts. The printing industry can play games; prices can be manipulated. Printers can undercut a competitor for spite, or simply because they have more economical machinery for a particular job—which puts the question of ethics right back in the buyer's lap.

The net effects

In order to get closer to a position, let's look at the results of creating artificial bids.

If the printer finds out, the situation is not only embarrassing (as it was in our example) but can also trigger economic revenge. The printer's normal reaction would be to get that money back somehow. He will take pains to make sure that particular buyer gets nailed next time. Maybe he'll pad a loose area of the bill, such as prep work. Or maybe he'll be painted into a corner and take his lumps.

In addition, he will tag the buyer as a con artist. And if the buyer pulls it too often on too many printers, he will be quietly and unofficially blacklisted. In the end, the buyer will get burned.

If the printer doesn't find out, he will have to recover the loss from all his customers (assuming that the price was lowered to something less than a reasonable profit level). If the printer never realizes what happened, all his customers—you and me, for example— will get burned a little. The culprit, if he's good at creating phony bids, can then continue to have other buyers pay for a percentage of his printing. Not a fair situation, of course.

There are some subtle, cumulative effects as well: If printers get the idea that buyers are manipulating prices and creating phony competition, they will learn to protect themselves by getting their initial bids up higher. As the bids creep up, the buyers react with more aggressive price chopping, and the cycle begins to perpetuate itself. In the long run, printers as a group will still compete and buyers will still get the printing, but they all will be doing it under the umbrella of complicated low-balling, high-balling, and revenge.

Counterproductivity

In my opinion, in the long run there is nothing to be gained by knocking down a bid with an artificial price. Sure, the individual might win in an isolated situation, but eventually someone will pay the tab. When it's not the guilty party, then it's all buyers in general. If printers were consistently losing money to fast-talking customers, they'd have been out of business long ago.

So, if it's unethical to mold prices as described, how can the practice be stopped? We know it goes on, and we logically fear that prices may be padded at the time—yet the big picture says that we shouldn't play the game. The simplest solution would be for printers to bid properly from the start and to hardline buyers. If someone asks for a quote, a printer should simply assemble the initial prices in the most economical fashion, put in the profit margin, draw the bottom line, and that's that!

Take our opening example. What if the low-priced printer had said, "If Acme has us beat, more power to you. I hope they do a good job for you. Bye-bye." What would the buyer, who didn't have a lower bid in sight, have done? Either he could have gone to the higher-priced printer and paid the premium, or he could have made up some flimsy excuse ("They forgot the paper") and returned to the original low bidder.

In our example, the buyer was obviously going for the proverbial financial throat, so chances are he would have eaten humble pie and placed the job. At the same time, he probably would have given himself away. Chalk one up for the printer (who, in theory, makes a normal profit), another for the other customers who don't pay the tab on the underbid, and chalk up a lesson for the artificial bidder.

It would be nice, although optimistic, to assume that printers will spontaneously begin to provide clean, tight, rock-bottom unpadded prices. Is there anything that buyers could do to promote such practices?

Moving from optimism to idealism, here's a possibility.

Suppose you, the buyer, put specs together for an upcoming job and send bid requests to three printers. Suppose you explain to each of them, in a letter or on the phone, that you will make the specs as complete as possible in order to get the most accurate bids.

Keep supposing: You explain to each printer that only those companies that are fully capable of doing a decent quality job are being invited to submit a competitive price. (It's not at all uncommon for a buyer to mention just who else is bidding the work.) And finally, you tell them you will examine the final prices and select a printer, simple as that. No second tries.

Making suppositions is a fine mental exercise, but the acid test will be putting these ideals into practice. Will they work right off the bat? Probably not. But if all of us begin to follow through on such techniques, several things would happen.

First, you'd begin to get a reputation as a dollar-conscious square shooter. Novices in the print-purchasing field often have no idea of just how important a reputation can be.

Second, you would eventually see a trend toward consistent, competitive, bottom-line bids on the first go-around. No games, no fat to trim, and smoother sailing in picking a printer for your jobs.

In "proving" that you are dealing on the level, it doesn't hurt to release nonvolatile information to those who didn't get the job. If a losing bidder calls and asks where the job was placed, why not tell him where and why? In my view, it doesn't hurt to give a general idea of what part (or parts) of a bid prompted you to go elsewhere.

By cleaning up this area of the purchasing act, you can't

405

lose—nobody can lose. As the situation is now, far too many buyers either use artificial prices or—almost as bad—go to their favorite printer and say, "You were 4 percent high. If you can lower your price, you get the job." In those situations, for practical purposes you must keep in mind that the buyer is allowing the printer's competitor to create the selling price. That's just plain unhealthy.

Kickbacks, bribes, and other unmentionables

The subject of kickbacks isn't given much attention in the printing industry. There are several reasons for this, the most obvious being that people who give or receive kickbacks don't want to talk about it.

But using the term "kickback" may be a bit too broad since there are many different ways for a buyer to pick up some sort of freebie, be it money, material, or a favor. Therefore, this discussion will encompass "anything that doesn't show on the invoice."

Free lunch

Starting on a fairly innocent level, how about lunch? Certainly, the most common way to get something for nothing is to accept the countless invitations to lunch that most salesmen are inclined to offer. There are many valid reasons for accepting these invitations: Lunch is a good way to meet a salesperson, get a feel for his style, learn about his company, and, what the heck, eat. Although I don't know how many martinis you should drink (remember the three-martini-lunch legislation?), I do think that lunch can be a productive part of the work day.

But even something as innocent as a free lunch can be taken to excess. Those excesses often occur at dinnertime. If a salesman must constantly wheel his clients to the most expensive dinner shows in the city, and the customer expects this kind of treatment routinely, it can become a form of kickback.

As an example, I was once given a "sales pitch" from a fairly large printer in a major city. The pitch was a $300 dinner, show, and—pardon the blush—a strong insinuation that we perhaps satisfy our every desire. All within that beautiful city, and available every time we went to press. (We were never offered a complete estimate, by the way!)

The problem here is that the buyer could begin to pay more attention to the night life than to the matter at hand. On top of that, keep in mind that the salesperson isn't "giving" anything to the customer. Eventually, it all gets tacked onto the bill—but, of course, without a description.

In summary, "free lunch" isn't too dangerous as long as there is some reasonable purpose to the event. When taken to excess, it's the same as a bribe.

Cash payments

Freebies can be more blatant. It is not unheard of for a buyer to accept a cash bribe as a reward for placing a job with a particular printer. The highest offer I've personally seen was a clean, laundered $12,000—but then, I haven't seen too many. The upper limit for cash kickbacks is certainly much higher than that.

We needn't spend much time or discussion on this particular freebie: It is patently unethical. For a buyer to consider taking such a payment is dangerous and counterproductive. It is really stealing from one's own company because whatever the payment is, it will show up on the invoice over a period of time.

In addition, if someone accepts a bribe, the fact will surely get around the industry—and there goes a reputation. Finally, the person who accepts a bribe can be blackmailed into accepting technically inferior work.

Other forms of bribes

Less blatant than the above, but in the same ballpark, is the "finder's fee." This is a sum that a printer might be willing to pay the person responsible for placing an order or signing a contract. Mind you, there is nothing wrong with a finder's fee when it's used properly. For example, if an independent, freelance salesperson places your job at a printer—with whom he has no direct ties—he may be paid a straight commission over the long haul, or he may be bought off with a lump payment—a finder's fee.

We bring up the finder's fee only to point out the obvious: The finder's fee should never weave its way into the hands of the buyer. There is no ethical reason for this to happen, even if a salesperson says it is commonplace.

So much for the up front, here's-the-money routines. However, the direct cash payment to the buyer is not the most common form of kickback. The real action occurs when there is a third party in the picture.

Consider brokers versus consultants. A person can be one or the other or both—but not at the same time on the same job.

A broker is an independent salesperson who gets bids from various printers on, let's say, your printing requirements. If he places the work for you, he may bill you directly for the printing or he may have the printer bill you. In either case, there will be a commission paid to the broker.

This is routine and there's nothing wrong with it. A broker can save you the time and expense of getting a series of bids. He may be more knowledgeable than you, too, in which case he could possibly do a better job.

The consultant, on the other hand, may have the same knowledge as the broker, but instead of getting a percentage of the total

THE ETHICS
OF PRINT
PURCHASING

payment, he is paid by you, the client, to examine the job at hand, find the right production situation, and give advice. Again, there are many valid reasons to use a consultant, and it's a normal practice.

But here's the hitch: The most routine method of double-dipping in this business is for the consultant to bill the client for his advice while at the same time accepting a finder's fee (or commission or monthly percentage of the bill) from the printer. In this case, somebody gets taken for a ride. That somebody is you: the customer.

This practice is more than simply unfair. If you are paying the consultant/broker to handle your job with a printer and the printer is paying him too, what happens when something goes wrong with the job? Both paying parties will say, "Straighten this out. That's what we're paying you for." The middleman, of course, has his hands tied. Damned if he does and damned if he doesn't.

I think the "brokers/buyers" topic was aptly demonstrated in a recent mailing I received. The pitch was from a firm that offered its consultation and print-purchasing expertise at "no charge whatsoever." You may have heard similar pitches. The firm will come to your office, examine your printing requirements, and advise you that "Printer x" will save you $10,000 per year. That may well be the case, but remember that the consultation is 1) not free and 2) in need of careful scrutiny.

Is the consulting firm truly independent or is it in cahoots with a particular printer? If all is on the level, fine, but if the firm will then make its money from the printer who gets the work, then they will have been acting as print brokers. And the come-on of free consultation has merely been an advertising trick. Any broker worth his salt offers free consultation and spends time and money to secure new business. In comparison, any respectable consultant charges nicely for his services.

Unfortunately, the question of ethics for buyers isn't limited to the buyers themselves. When brokers and consultants enter the picture, the buyers run the risk of participating—sometimes unknowingly—in an unethical triangle. And the buyer, of course, is the only one who stands to lose money.

The only way for you to ease your mind is to get to know the people you deal with. A consultant should have many references; a broker should have a reputation. Any third party will probably have a history of dealing with printers. If you are entirely up-front when you are checking out a broker or a consultant, you can get honest answers (like one I received: He's a petty thief!).

In the long run, buyers can collectively work to reduce the skimming perpetrated by unethical brokers and consultants by paying attention, asking questions, and making accusations when necessary. (I should mention that I do not have low esteem for either brokers or consultants because I have acted as both.)

There's another common inducement, usually made to the novice buyer, that's not uncommon at all: a couple of airline tickets

408

to the printer's home base so you can see the plant and meet the people. I see nothing wrong in using the printer's tickets to see his plant —as long as it is with your company's approval and as long as you are somewhat interested in working with him.

The complete invoice

If you eventually pay for all these little details, it might be productive to see an invoice that's more explicit than most.

The sample (Illustration 166) that I have produced assumes that some print user, somewhere, is paying for every down-and-dirty trick, in addition to the innocent, routine expenses. My point is that your payment to the printer does include everything. Just because you don't normally see certain items doesn't mean that you're not paying for them.□

```
Total    Opera                              0.00

Total Manufacturing, fro                   8,206.55

Total Paper, from page 7                   6,362.00

          SUBTOTAL                       $16,132.55

Additionals:

Four free lunches,
     your production manager                152.24

Free trip to our plant,
     including airfare                       660.95

Free dinner and show,
     after dinner drinks, etc.               144.00

Finder's fee to your consultant           1,613.26

Bottle Scotch, your Christmas gift             9.80

Bottle good Scotch,
     Consultant Christmas gift                22.50

          TOTAL                          $18,735.30
```

(166)

Don't take this too seriously. No printer will actually invoice you for those freebies. Right? The fact is, all of those freebies are part of sales and service expenses. They are *on the invoice. They're buried in general overhead expenses.*

409

ACETATE. Clear plastic used for overlays on paste-ups, etc.

AIRBRUSHING. Painting with a hand-held, highly accurate sprayer to retouch or change photographic appearances, enhance photos, or create cutaway views.

ALIGN. Used as a proofreading mark, it means "line these elements up," such as the baselines of letters.

ALTERATION. Any change made by the customer that is in contrast to the original instructions. Usually, the customer pays for all alterations.

ASCENDER. The portions of letters that extend above the body of type. The letters "t", "f", "l", and "h" have ascenders while "m" and "e" do not. Opposite of descender.

BACKBONE. In a perfect-bound product, the square edge created through assembly.

BASELINE. The imaginary line created by the bottoms of capital letters in a line of type.

BASIS WEIGHT. Paper industry standard for comparing thickness and weight of paper. A sheet called 50-pound, basis 25" x 38" means that 500 sheets of paper cut to 25" x 38" would weigh 50 pounds.

BIND. To staple or glue a printed product and trim it to its intended size. See perfect binding, saddle stitching.

BLACK. One of the four process colors.

BLACKSPOT. Sheets of red, orange, or black paper positioned on a paste-up to indicate where a photo will print. The paper photographs as black, creating a "window" on the film negative, into which a halftone negative might later be stripped.

BLANKET. The thick rubber sheet that wraps around a cylinder on the press. The plate prints onto the blanket, and the blanket prints onto the paper.

BLEED. Printing that appears to run off the page. In fact, it is printed on excess paper, which is then trimmed off.

BLIND. In litho printing, a plate that has lost its ability to print has "gone blind."

BLOCKOUT. The effect achieved when the background of a photo is not allowed to print.

BLOW-IN. In a magazine, a loosely inserted element, such as an order card.

BLOW UP. To enlarge.

BLUELINE. A simple proof that shows the pages either blue on white or blue on yellow.

BP. Abbreviation for blueprint, brownprint and other simple one-color proofs.

BRISTOL. Generic name for a stiff paper that compares to postcard weight or heavier.

BROWNPRINT. A simple proofing system, similar to blueprint, blueline, and BP, etc. Brownprints favor ammonia-type developers and do not offer very good resolution.

BULLET. A round dot.

BUMP. An exposure used when making a halftone to control highlights.

GLOSSARY

BURN. An exposure to a printing plate.

BURNISH. To apply pressure to elements that have been waxed and placed in position on a paste-up. Normally done with a slippery piece of paper and a burnisher, which is a piece of plastic created for the purpose.

CARD FEEDER. A special unit on a binder that allows the insertion of a card without using a standard bindery pocket.

CHOKE. To make an image slightly smaller to facilitate registration on press. Example: to choke a light blue background into dark green lettering. Also called skinny. See *spread*.

CHOP FOLD. A fold made in which a folding blade "chops" the paper in half.

CIC. Abbreviation for common impression cylinder, which is found on a rather odd type of press that features four blankets running in pressure with a single cylinder.

CLOSED HEAD. Folding technique in which the tops of pages are attached to other pages before trimming. See *open head*.

COATED STOCK. Any paper which, after manufacture, is treated with a surface coating of clay and other materials. Provides for a better printing surface. When newsprint is coated, it takes on the characteristics of typical coated magazine paper.

COLD TYPE. Another term for phototypesetting (as opposed to hot metal type, which is nearly antiquated). See *hot metal*.

COLOR CORRECTION. To modify the tonal qualities of a color-separated set of negatives. Normally done by skilled artists, but also done by rescanning (reseparating) the photo or artwork with filters.

COLOR KEY. A four-color proofing system that uses the layered-acetate method of generating full color.

COLOR SEPARATION. Activity performed on a litho camera or scanner that breaks a photo into the four primary colors by exposing them onto four different pieces of film.

COMBINATION FOLDER. A folder that uses three different types of folds during each pass of a signature. The folds used are jaw, former, and, chop. See *jaw fold, former fold,* and *chop fold*.

COMMON FOCUS. When shooting halftones or making color separations, more than one element can be shot at one time if they are of common focus, such as both 78 percent or both 100 percent, etc.

COMPOSITION. Term describing either phototypesetting or phototypesetting plus any other assembly required to get a page ready for printing.

CONDENSED. Typesetting faces that have a tall, narrow appearance.

CONTACT. As a noun, material created through contact exposure rather than shot on camera. As a verb, to place elements in contact with one another (original and film) and make a print.

CONTINUOUS TONE. Any item (a photograph, for example) that has densities that change from dark to light in infinite steps (as opposed to a halftone, which breaks the photo into large and small dots).

CORNERMARKS. Lines on a paste-up that indicate where the page will be trimmed.

CPM. Abbreviation for cost per thousand.

412

CREEP. Effect seen on a saddle-stitched product in which the inner pages are smaller (shorter) than the outer pages because of the thickness at the fold.

CROMALIN. High-quality process-color proof designed to closely simulate what the job will look like on press. Registered trademark of DuPont.

CRT. Abbreviation for cathode ray tube, which is similar to a TV tube.

CWT. Abbreviation for hundredweight, which is used in pricing paper. $40/CWT means $40-per-hundred pounds.

CUTOFF. The fixed dimension of a web press that dictates the maximum height or width of a page (depending on the direction and travel of printing).

CYAN. One of the four process colors. Cyan has a blue appearance.

DECKLE. In describing paper, the untrimmed edge of a sheet having a ragged appearance. Often seen on wedding invitations.

DESCENDER. Portions of letters that extend below the body of the type. See ascender.

DENSITOMETER. Machine that measures the intensity of a color, or black.

DIECUT. Technique of using a specially made die to punch out a portion of a page or to create oddly shaped perforations.

DIGITAL or DIGITIZED TYPESETTING. Any typesetting system that stores the shapes of letters electronically rather than photographically.

D-MAX. Abbreviation for maximum density, *i.e.*, of a film or an exposure system. Thus, a machine or a paper with a high D-Max can produce an exceptionally dense exposure, which then will both photograph and/or contact better.

DOUBLE BURN. To make more than one exposure onto a printing plate with more than one piece of film.

DOUBLE FORMER. Folder on a web press that delivers two signatures folded the same way, using only a former fold and a jaw fold.

DOUBLING. Inadvertent press effect that prints two dots where halftone film only had one. Indicated by a very dark looking printed halftone.

DROPOUT or DROPOUT HALFTONE. When shooting a halftone, an exposure that tends to overexpose or "blast" away the background, which is either gray or white.

DUOTONE. Printing a photograph in two colors, such as black and orange. When the inks mix, the printed piece takes on the appearance of a third color (in this case, brown).

DUPE or DUPLICATE TRANSPARENCY. An enlarged or reduced copy of an original resulting in a transparent color film similar to a color slide, but of any size.

DYLUX. Registered trademark of DuPont. A common, blue-on-yellow proofing system.

ELLIPTICAL DOT. In a halftone or screen, the elongated dot created by the screen itself (as opposed to round and square dots).

EMBOSSING. Printing activity that presses an image onto a sheet of paper and that usually requires a special die to be made beforehand. Usually done on a letterpress.

413

GLOSSARY

EMULSION. The side of a sheet of film sensitive to light.

ENAMEL. Finish on a sheet of paper that shows a highly glossy surface. An enameled sheet has better printing characteristics and is more expensive than a simple coated sheet. The paper is usually manufactured "free of groundwood pulp," which adds to the expense.

ETCHING or DOT ETCHING. Method used to make color corrections in which chemicals eat away at the dots to make them smaller.

FACE. Abbreviation for typeface.

FAKE COLOR. Generation of color using tints of process colors rather than using matched inks. Simple example: Yellow and blue printing together will make green, a fake color. Green ink on the press is a "real" color.

FATTY. See *spread*.

FELT SIDE. The side of a sheet of paper that was not in contact with the wire former. The felt side has a slightly rougher texture than the wire side.

FLASH. An exposure which, when making a halftone, enhances detail and shadow areas of the photo.

FLAT. Describes stripped pages that will all print on the same side of a sheet of paper.

FLOP. To turn a photo's image over so that what was on the left will now be on the right, and vice versa.

FLYING PASTER. Machine on a web press that splices one roll of paper to another while the press is running and the paper moving.

FOLIO. Page number.

FONT. A complete alphabet of characters. For example, a typesetter operator might call for "Font 1" on a machine, into which position might then be loaded Century Roman.

FOOT. The bottom of a page.

FORMER FOLD. Fold in which paper is drawn over a triangular-shaped metal device, thus folding it in half.

FREE SHEET. Paper made without the use of groundwood pulp. Uses rags and other high-quality scrap for its base material. Thus, the term means "free of groundwood pulp."

GALLEY. The "first proof" of typesetting as it comes off the typesetting machine. At this stage, type is not pasted-up nor is it in page form. Thus, a galley is a long narrow strip of typesetting that has not yet been assembled on a paste-up.

GANG. To group several items for printing, photography, or color separation, etc.

GHOST. A printing condition in which an image becomes fainter than intended because of its position relative to another image, which has conflicting ink demands. Typically occurs when one page prints above another on a large press.

GOLDENROD. Gold-colored paper used in the stripping process to prevent light from reaching where it shouldn't.

GRAIN. In paper, the general orientation of the tiny paper fibers from which the sheet is made. If a sheet is folded against the grain, it means that many fibers are broken during the folding process, giving a ragged and weak fold.

GUSSETTING. What happens when many sheets of paper are folded more than once: The paper wrinkles at the point where folds intersect.

GUTTER. The portion of a page nearest the fold.

HALF WEB. (1) Running a roll of half-normal width on any web. (2) A web press that can run a roll half the width normally run on a full-sized web.

HALFTONE. In lithography, describes a photograph that has been broken into a pattern of small dots. When printed, the halftone closely simulates the appearance of the original photograph.

HEAD. The top of a page.

HICKEY. A small spot of "missing ink" on a printed page that occurs because of impurities or contaminants on the blanket, plate, or inking rollers.

HIGHLIGHT. Exposure which, when shooting a halftone, controls the light areas of the photo being shot.

HOT METAL TYPE. An out-of-date typesetting technique in which lead and tin were melted to form characters that were then put on the printing press. See *cold type*.

IMPOSITION. Term that describes where a given page will be printed in relation to other pages printed on the same side of the sheet of paper at the same time.

IN LINE. Two or more pages running one above the other on a printed sheet.

INTERFACING. Connecting two or more computerized machines, such as word processors and typesetters, via telephone lines or computer disk.

INTERLEAVED. The mixing or folding together of different types of paper or paper printed in different colors (four-color, two-color, etc.).

ITALIC. Typesetting that has a diagonal appearance. Today, often confused with artificially slanted type. Italic typefaces have been specifically designed and often have a cursive appearance.

JAW FOLD. One of three common folds on a web press in which the sheet to be folded is pressed into an indentation in a cylinder.

JUSTIFIED. Typeset copy that has flush left and flush right margins. See ragged.

KERNING. In typesetting, the removal of (white) space between pairs of letters that would otherwise appear to have too much space between them, such as AV, Ty, etc.

KEYLINE. (1) A paste-up. (2) A thin rule that should print, such as a rule around a photo. The notation would be "print keyline."

KISS. To butt one printed element up against another.

KISS BLEED. To trim a printed image exactly where the image ends because of a "short" film.

LAMINATE. To apply a thin application of plastic or other coating to a printed piece.

LAP. Same as lip.

LATERAL REVERSE. Another term for flop.

GLOSSARY

LAYOUT. Any sketch or other indication that specifies the appearance of a printed page.

LEAD, LEADING. Space between lines of typeset copy. Derived from hot-metal days when thin strips of lead were placed between lines to add (white) space. Also called body leading or linespace.

LEADER. As in dot leader, to fill out a line with a character, most often a period.

LETTERPRESS. Type of printing (or diecutting or perforating) that requires a raised image of the original, which—when inked—will be pressed into contact with the paper.

LETTERSPACE. To add or subtract from the otherwise standard amount of (white) space between letters.

LIGATURE. A pair of characters that fit together so poorly that a new design is implemented to make it look better. Typical ligatures are fi, fl and ff.

LINE. Outside of its obvious definition, "line" indicates material that can be reproduced without tints or halftones. The words you are now reading were shot as line.

LINESPACE. To add leading between lines of typeset copy. See leading.

LIP. The edge of a sheet of paper that sticks out if the paper is folded off center. In saddle stitching, the bindery machine grabs each item by its lip.

LOFTING. Tendency of a saddle-stitched product to seem thicker at the fold than at the margins.

LWC. Abbreviation for lightweight coated, a thin paper stock used for magazines and catalogs.

M. Abbreviation for 1,000. 15M is 15 thousand.

MAGENTA. One of the four process colors, magenta has a red/pink appearance.

MAKE GOOD. To print a product over at no cost or to run an ad again at no cost because of quality problems the first time around.

MAKEREADY. All activity required at the press prior to the time a good copy is printed.

MARGIN. The portion of a page that is toward the "outside" edge. Opposite of "gutter."

MASK. Sheet of film or paper that prevents unwanted exposure onto the plate or other film.

MATCHPRINT. Process-color proofing system that laminates colors onto any suitable paper, such as the grade the magazine will actually be printed on.

MATTE. A dull, unglossy finish to the surface of paper.

MEASURE. The width of a typeset column, usually measured in picas.

MECHANICAL. Synonym for paste-up.

MIDDLETONES. In a printed halftone, the portions that are as dark as they are light, or about 50 percent of maximum intensity.

MINI-WEB. Slang for half web.

MOIRE. The unwanted visual effect created when screen angles are not properly controlled in multi-color printing.

416

MYLAR. Stable, clear film often used because it has superior qualities to acetate.

NEGATIVE. Usually describes a sheet of photographic film that after exposure and processing is dark where the original was light and clear where the original was dark.

OFFSET LITHOGRAPHY. Only common form of lithography in which the printing plate deposits ink on a rubber-coated roller, which then prints on the paper. "Offset" means the plate does not come into contact with the paper.

OFFSETTING. What happens when a sheet of freshly printed paper is stacked with others and material transfers to the backs of the sheets above.

ON-LINE. In typesetting, describes a computer system that can connect to other computer systems or typesetters, including word processors.

OPACITY. The ability of paper to prevent see-through from one side to another.

OPAQUE. To eliminate (by painting out) tiny pinholes and other imperfections in a film negative that would otherwise print when the negative is exposed to the plate.

OPEN HEAD. Folding method in which pages are loose or unattached to one another at the tops (in contrast to closed head). See *closed head*.

ORIGINAL. Any artwork, photo, or paste-up that is the first generation or the "original" from which the printer will create film.

ORPHAN. Word or short line at the top of a column of a page. See *widow*.

OVERLAY. A sheet of acetate or Mylar upon which certain elements are placed, rather than placing them directly on the paste-up or mechanical.

PANTONE MATCHING SYSTEM. A standardized system for matching colors from PMS swatchbooks to the ink formulas required on press. PMS colors are "true" colors, in contrast to the four process colors (magenta, cyan, yellow and black), which can simulate a wide range of colors. PMS colors are more pure than process matches.

PASTE-UP. As a noun, a page ready to be shot on camera. Paste-ups are always shot as line. As a verb, to assemble the elements of a page and affix them (with glue or wax) into their intended positions.

PERFECT BINDING. Binding method that glues the cover to the body pages and creates a square backbone. See *bind*.

PERFECTING PRESS. A press that prints on both sides of a sheet at the same time, or in one pass through the press.

PERFORATION or PERF. Punched, dotted lines.

PHOTOCOMPOSITION. Term used to describe phototypesetting and/or complete page makeup.

PHOTOSTAT. A line shot made on photographic paper.

PHOTOTYPESETTING. To set type via the photographic method (as opposed to hot-metal typesetting).

PICA (WIDTH). Typesetting term of measure, approximately one-sixth of an inch.

PICKING. In printing, the unwanted pulling on surface paper fibers. When enough are "picked" off the sheet, press problems occur.

GLOSSARY

PLATE. As a noun, the metal upon which has been exposed the image to be printed, wrapped around a cylinder. As a verb, to make a printing plate.

PLUGGING. Press condition that makes a printed photo appear dirty or filled in. Can be because of a bad halftone or ink/water problems on the press.

PMS. See Pantone Matching System.

PMT. Photo Mechanical Transfer, an inexpensive, fast way to make a photostat. Registered trademark of Eastman Kodak.

POCKET. A designated section of a binder that accepts one signature of the printed product.

POINT. About 1/72nd of an inch. A unit of measure in typesetting used to designate the heights of letters or the thickness of rules.

POSITIVE. Any positive-reading image. Also used to describe positive film, rather than the more conventional negative film.

PRECOLLATION. Partial assembly of a magazine because of a limited number of bindery pockets.

PRE-PRESS, PREP. Any and all activity that occurs before printing plates are made.

PRESS PROOF. A proof which, rather than being created with chemicals and dyes, is actually printed on a special proofing press.

PRESTRIP. To strip a page or multiple pages with the intention of duplicating the film to one-piece per process color before making plates. Often a necessity for complex stripping jobs.

PRIMARIES. The four colors used in litho printing that create a close simulation of a full-color original. The primaries are yellow, magenta, cyan, and black.

PROCESS COLOR. Describes four-color printing, the purpose of which is to simulate full-color photos. Printing uses the four process primaries: yellow, magenta, cyan, and black.

PROOF. Any representation shown to the customer for approval before printing.

QUAD. A typesetting adjective. Quad left means flush left; quad right, flush right.

RAGGED. Ragged right, ragged left, means the material will have unjustified (uneven borders) on one side, the other, or both. See *justified*.

RAIL. On a saddle binder, the part upon which the signatures, once opened, ride.

RAPID ACCESS. Film and chemistry system in which development temperatures and times are not very critical. Permanent, high-quality system (as opposed to stabilization processing).

REGISTRATION. Quality of printing in which all colors print exactly where they should, preventing fuzzy or blurred photos in process-color printing.

RESCREEN. To shoot as a halftone something that already has a screen (or has been shot as a halftone, in other words). Generally a bad idea because it will lose density and possibly acquire a moire.

REVERSE. To change blacks to whites, whites to blacks.

418

REVERSE LEAD. Ability that a typesetting machine has to back up the phototypesetting paper and make more exposures on it, such as the second of two columns of type.

ROLL STAND. Part of a web press that holds the rolls of paper prior to and during printing.

ROMAN. Standard or upright type (as opposed to italic).

ROP. Abbreviation for run of publication or run of press. Meaning: Use whatever colored inks are available, or place the ad wherever it happens to fit.

ROSETTE. The dot pattern desired when four-color printing is being done correctly. Opposite of moire.

ROTATION. The sequence in which colors are applied in process-color printing. A standard rotation is yellow, magenta, cyan, and black.

RUBBER CEMENT. A glue commonly used for affixing paper to other paper, film, or acetate.

SADDLE STITCHING. Binding method that folds all pages and staples them at the fold. See *bind*.

SCALE. To figure out the enlargement or reduction required to make a photo or artwork fit a designated area.

SCANNER. An electronic camera that does color separations.

SCORE. To press a straight line into paper. Facilitates folding so the paper won't crack at the foldline.

SCREEN. An even pattern of small dots that when printed will appear to reduce the intensity of ink, such as making black ink appear gray.

SCREEN ANGLE. Specific angles that in four-color printing will prevent a moire from occurring. Screen angles are generally about 15 degrees apart.

SEPARATION. See color separation.

SERIF. The "feet" of certain typestyles. "Gothic" typestyles are straight or curved lines, whereas serif typestyles have fine "crossbars." For example, at the top and bottom of the letter I.

SET SOLID. To set type with no additional leading between lines.

SETOFF. See offsetting.

SHEETFED. A press that prints on precut sheets of paper, as opposed to a web press, which prints from a continuous roll.

SHRINK WRAP. To wrap an item (or stack of magazines) in heat-sensitive plastic and then heat it so the plastic shrinks around the bundle for shipping.

SIGNATURE. A folded section of a printed product. A 16-page signature is 16 of x number of pages, folded and ready for bindery.

SKINNY. See choke.

SLUG. Archaic for a line of typeset copy.

SPLIT FOUNTAIN. To run more than one color of ink from a printing unit which would otherwise run a single color.

SPREAD. (1) Two magazine pages next to each other in the finished product. (2) To slightly expand type or artwork so that it prints into a background color. Example: Light blue type printing against a dark red background would be spread. See choke.

STABILIZATION PROCESSING/PAPER. Development system that uses only one or two chemicals in a simple processor to develop typesetting paper or photostats. Generally, stabilization development is not as durable as rapid-access development, but it is much less expensive.

STAT. See photostat.

STEP and REPEAT. Plate exposure technique used to conserve film. Exposes same film on various portions of plate as required.

STET. Proofreading notation that means "leave it as it was." Often used to say, "I marked this to be changed, but I changed my mind, so ignore all of this."

STITCH. Stapling. To saddle stitch is to staple a product at its fold. To side stitch is to staple or sew a product near the gutter.

STRIP, STRIPPING. To position film into its proper position for printing. Stripping is often done with red lithographer's tape because red tape can be used to prevent unwanted light from reaching the printing plate.

TACK. As in ink tack, the property that makes ink stick to either the paper or to other wet ink.

TIPPING. The gluing of a page to a signature or cover. Often used for supplied inserts.

TRANSFER KEY. Lamination-type proofing system that uses a polyester base sheet.

TRAP or TRAPPING. Ability of wet ink to accept another layer of wet ink on top of it. Required for web printing, which is a wet-on-wet process.

TYPEFACE. Specific name of the design of a full alphabet of characters, such as Helvetica, Century, etc.

TYPO, TYPOGRAPHICAL ERROR. Mistake made by a typesetter, usually corrected by typesetter at no charge.

UNCOATED. Paper that has a slightly rough, unshiny finish upon which no coatings were applied after manufacture.

UNDERCOLOR. Describes the ink tones that are not needed to print a photo, but which would otherwise have been on the film produced by the camera or scanner. Undercolor removal is the process by which film is corrected so that only the amount of ink absolutely needed to reproduce the photo will be on the final film and plates.

UNIT. On a press, a group of rollers and related equipment that can print one color on one side of a sheet of paper.

UNJUSTIFIED. Typesetting with a flush-left border and a ragged-right border.

UPPER and LOWER. Capitals and lowercase letters.

VARNISHING. Application of a clear, shiny coating to a printed piece.

VIGNETTE. To make the background of a photo fade away.

WAXER. Machine that applies a thin coating of wax to elements to be pasted up.

WEB. A moving sheet of paper. A web press is fed from a roll of paper and cuts and folds it after printing.

WIDE WEB. Slang for a press that prints 16 pages on one side of a moving web.

WIDOW. A short line or single word at the end of a paragraph or column of type. Some think this is unattractive, while others aren't bothered by it. See *orphan*.

WINDOW. Same as blackspot.

WIRE SIDE. The side of a sheet of paper which, during manufacture, was in contact with the wire formers. Tends to be smoother than the felt side.

WORK and TURN. To design a printed piece so that it can be printed on a sheetfed press, then turned over and printed on the backside with the same printing plate, thereby reducing plate costs.

X-HEIGHT. The height of the lowercase x used for aesthetic comparisons of typefaces.

YELLOW. One of the four process colors.

Jeffery Parnau is an independent printing consultant, president of Parnau Graphics, and publisher of several printing-related journals. He has been active in printing and production management for all his business life.

In 1978 he founded Parnau Graphics and began speaking extensively in both the United States and Europe on production-related topics. He has been a monthly columnist writing on production for FOLIO: THE MAGAZINE FOR MAGAZINE MANAGEMENT since 1978. In 1979 he founded *Print Buyer*, a newsletter for production directors of magazines and catalogs.

Book Specifications: Body type—11-point English Times
                     Captions—10-point English Times Italic
                     Chapter Headings—18- and 14-point
                                       English Times
                     Section Headings—36-point English Times

Graphic Design by Carla B Jaffe